Critical Essays on
MARGUERITE DURAS

CRITICAL ESSAYS
ON
WORLD LITERATURE

Robert Lecker, General Editor
McGill University

◆

Critical Essays on
MARGUERITE DURAS

◆

edited by
BETTINA L. KNAPP

G. K. Hall & Co.
An Imprint of Simon & Schuster Macmillan
New York

Prentice Hall International
London   Mexico City   New Delhi   Singapore   Sydney   Toronto

G. K. Hall & Co.
An Imprint of Simon & Schuster Macmillan
1633 Broadway
New York, NY 10019

Library of Congress Cataloging-in-Publication Data

Critical essays on Marguerite Duras / edited by Bettina L. Knapp.
    p.   cm. — (Critical essays on world literature)
    Includes bibliographical references and index.
    ISBN 0-7838-0058-4
    1. Duras, Marguerite—Criticism and interpretation. I. Knapp,
Bettina Liebowitz, 1926– .
    PQ2607.U8245Z6335   1998
    843'.912—dc21   97-36439
                                            CIP

The paper meets the requirements of ANSI/NISO Z3948-1992 (Permanence of Paper).

10 9 8 7 6 5 4 3 2 1

Printed in the United States of America

Contents

◆

Publisher's Note

◆

Producing a volume that contains both newly commissioned and reprinted material presents the publisher with the challenge of balancing the desire to achieve stylistic consistency with the need to preserve the integrity of works first published elsewhere. In the Critical Essays series, essays commissioned especially for a particular volume are edited to be consistent with G. K. Hall's house style; reprinted essays appear in the style in which they were first published, with only typographical errors corrected and French citations in the original frequently deleted. Consequently, shifts in style from one essay to another are the result of our efforts to be faithful to each text as it was originally published.

Introduction

BETTINA L. KNAPP

Marguerite Duras (1914–1996) was intrigued by the plethora of divergent reactions and analyses appended to her novels, plays, and film scripts. Although she was deeply grateful for a positive press and understandably hurt by a negative one, no sooner did a work of hers enter the public domain than she distanced herself from its fate, focusing her energies on the volume to come. Unlike other authors, who hang on to their writings or possess them, treating them like personal property, Duras was convinced that books, like human beings, must be allowed a modicum of independence. Whether in the literary, musical, or pictorial domain, creations, like children, must be awarded the freedom to enjoy a life of their own—to flow with or against the current.[1]

Duras never ceased to be beguiled, if not amused, by the generosity with which critics—particularly lay psychologists and psychiatrists—affixed their varied and pithy medical diagnoses to her protagonists. The list of mental aberrations ascribed to her characters is quite staggering: narcissism, fetishism, voyeurism, nymphomania, sadism, masochism, sexism, bodyism, hetaerism, androgyny, and more. The scientific jargon the critics used to depict the symptoms of those diseases could lead one to believe that, far from writing fiction, Duras had authored a series of clinical reports. Nonetheless, the critics writing on the mental problems afflicting the creatures of Duras's fantasy indicated their direct involvement with her true-to-life characters—or, depending on the literary schools of the day, her noncharacters—who were embossed on distant and frequently mystifying dreamscapes.

Marguerite Duras, who catapulted to fame in the 1950s and 1960s, earned international recognition in the seventies and was made a legend in the eighties. Despite her renown for *Hiroshima mon amour,* which won the International Critics Prize at the Cannes Film Festival in 1959 and the New York Film Critics Award the following year, she was not awarded the highly coveted Goncourt Prize until 1984—and this for *The Lover.* Was her name passed over for personal or political reasons? Were the reviews—ranging from dithyrambic to detractive—responsible for such neglect?

Although Duras's first and second novels—*The Impudents* (1943) and *The Tranquil Life* (1944)—won the admiration of a close circle of friends, public accolades were directed her way only with the appearance of *The Sea Wall* (1950). Critics were virtually unanimous in labeling it the work of a "talented young writer," comparable in style, they suggested independently, to Steinbeck, Faulkner, and Hemingway.[2] In Gérard D'Houville's review of Duras's *The Sailor from Gibraltar* (1952), he alluded to *The Sea Wall* as revelatory of her talent, "so original, so daring, so new."[3] G. Gaëtan Picon was impressed by "the complexity and the eclecticism of means."[4] More than anyone else, however, Raymond Queneau—philosopher, mathematician, and founder of Oulipo ("Ouvroir de Littérature Potentielle")—sensed the nature of Duras's gifts: her innovative style, her imagination, and her profound sensitivity. Queneau responded not only to her unique way with words but to the broad emotional, spiritual, and social sweep of their subtexts as well. That *The Sea Wall,* by the unknown Duras, sold 5,000 copies in its first week of publication validated for society Queneau's assessment of her talent.

Timing was also a factor in the launching of Duras's writings. Young authors such as Sarraute, Robbe-Grillet, Butor, and Pinget were astir with new—perhaps even revolutionary—literary ideas. Although each had a personal credo vis-à-vis the art of writing, they did share certain general principles, and they were loosely grouped under the rubric of New Novelists or New Realists. Most important, they sought to do away with the well-worn and outdated characteristics of traditional novels that had peaked in the nineteenth century under such luminaries as Stendhal, Balzac, and Flaubert. They also sought to extract the novel from its conventionally systematized and meaningless depiction of characters, to do away with its old-fashioned and predictable plots, and to transcend linear time schemes.

Duras's agenda nevertheless differed notably from that of the New Novelists. Whereas they functioned cerebrally and rationally, planning, plotting, outlining, even diagramming the course their works were to take, Duras's highly emotional writings seemed just to sweep into being—rapidly, instinctively, introjectively. Like an ejection—or an expulsion—each work appeared to release, at least momentarily, a powerful substance encapsulated within her being. Nonetheless, her works had affinities with those of the New Novelists. Like them, she distilled her thoughts and formulated her insights in compact plotless sequences revolving around noncharacters. Unlike the New Novelists, however, she endowed her polymorphous and polysemous prose with her own set of stylistic effects: a special vocabulary, a system of punctuation, lilting or abrasive rhythms, and strident or mellifluous musicalities.

The desperate and mysterious inner urgency that haunted Duras's being *drove* her to writing—just as alcohol, with different results, would in time become her ruling principle. Whereas the catharsis she experienced with every new publication allowed her to peel away whatever emotional detritus had fastened itself onto her flesh and psyche and thus enabled her to glimpse her own *history,* alcohol had the opposite effect. It dulled her vision and feelings to the point of veiling, even momentarily obliterating, the course of her pain and anguish. Although her volumes—one and all—may be looked upon as heroic attempts to affirm *her* identity by restoring *her* past (paradoxically living as well as dead), the pernicious effects of alcohol corroded these efforts. Nevertheless, writing held Duras viscerally and spiritually in thrall.

Novels, short stories, film scenarios, plays, articles, essays, and interviews propelled themselves into existence at an incredibly rapid rate: *The Sailor from Gibraltar* (1952), *The Little Horses of Tarquinia* (1953), *Whole Days in the Trees* (1954), *Le Square* (1955), *Moderato cantabile* (1958), *The Viaducts of Seine-et-Oise* (1959), *10:30 on a Summer Night* (1960), *Hiroshima mon amour* (1960), *Une Aussi longue absence* (1961), *The Afternoon of Mr. Andesmas* (1962), *The Ravishing of Lol V. Stein* (1964), *The Vice-Consul* (1965), *La Musica* (1966), *L'Amante anglaise* (1967), *Suzanne Andler, Yes, peut-être, Le Shaga* (1968), *Destroy, She Said* (1969), *Nathalie Granger* (1972), *India Song, La Femme du Gange* (1973), and so it went. The new voice that had impacted and would continue to impact on the French—and international—scene drew encomiums from the intelligentsia. Christine Garnier expressed her reactions to *Whole Days in the Trees:*

> Our heart is seized, we are fascinated, we know that the magic will last. . . . We had liked the tone of her famous novel, *The Sea Wall,* and the unusual dialogue she wrote for Resnais' film, *Hiroshima mon amour,* but perhaps nowhere better than in these *Whole Days in the Trees* did she know how to unveil the chiaroscuros, the moving sands [of human relationships], and to impress us with [mere] somnambulists.[5]

Jacques Lacan, the Freudian psychoanalyst, had nothing but praise for Duras's *Ravishing of Lol V. Stein,* referring to it as "clinically perfect delirium."[6] Garnishing the list of eminent critics, scholars, and writers who verbalized their panegyrics were Maurice Nadeau, Claude Mauriac, and Gaëtan Picon. The latter drew smiles from his readers when he suggested that Duras had not only written a second "*Madame Bovary* [but had also] revised Béla Bartok." Maurice Blanchot, Claude Roy, and Nathalie Sarraute were also fully aware of her multidimensional talents. Although Jacques Lemarchand of the *Figaro littéraire,* one of the finest drama critics of the time, underscored Duras's successful rejection of conventional theatrical forms, he wrote at length of the new elements she introduced to the stage. Her fantasy figures, for example, borne from her own flesh and blood, spoke words—in halftones and asides—that no one before Duras had had the courage to utter onstage. He also commented on the sensitivity of her dialogues, "the alternating song, the song with two voices trying to harmonize." Gustave Joly of *L'Aurore* noted that Duras's "fleeting harshness" was reminiscent of Genet's *The Maids.* Claude Olivier of

Les Lettres françaises noted that *The Square* was "real theater" (Vircondelet, 166). Is it any wonder that such stars as Madeleine Renaud, Jeanne Moreau, Delphine Seyrig, Miou-Miou, Bulle Ogier, Sami Frey, Gérard Depardieu, Michael Lonsdale, and Emmanuèle Riva were attracted to Duras's orbit?

Whatever genre Duras adopted, the voices and images inhabiting her poetic prose assumed moments of intense but controlled anguish. As single or dual voices, they reached dramatic highs and lows that operated powerfully on both listeners and viewers. What could have been simply a banal discussion, Katharine Jensen noted, always turned into a hypnotic unfolding.

> The two [participants] together create a "bi-film": two stories—one in words, one in pictures—[in] which each tells something different. The voices and images, moving separately, at their own pace, break the expected unity between sound and sight, between speech and act. The listener-viewer is split, pulled in various directions by competing stimuli, by contradictory and superposable meanings. In the contradictions, multiplicity, and gap within sound, within vision, and between them, the listener-viewer, faced with the unexpected, has the choice of taking meaning from the bi-film or of making meaning in it. This choice, whether conscious or unconscious, of taking or making meaning holds within it the promise and the threat of self-loss and self-recognition.[7]

Not surprisingly for a writer whose popularity grew with each passing year, detractors were also plentiful—and on the rise. Some critics took umbrage at the "virility," "violence," "fury," and "madness" Duras invested in her creatures. Nor was she spared acidulous attacks by critics for her politics, depending, to be sure, on their persuasion. There was good cause to question her association during World War II with both the Vichy government and the German Occupation forces, her tardiness in joining the Resistance, and her later membership in the Communist Party.

Staunch upholders of tradition, namely such well-known and respected critics as Luc Estang of *La Croix* and Kléber Haedens of *Paris-Presse,* in no way withheld their judgmental litanies concerning what they viewed as Duras's stylistic defects. They castigated her ungrammatical syntax, her repetitions, her peculiar use of parataxis, personal-pronoun subjects, proper nouns, half-words, silences and/or dead spots. Her dilation of time, nonplots, subplots, and identityless characters with meaningless gestures also aroused their ire. These bothersome literary tics or mannerisms were devices, they maintained, that served to add to the already ambiguously dismal nature of her works.[8] When writing about *The Vice-Consul,* Haedens conveyed little or no understanding of Duras's artistry or sensitivity:

> The obvious purpose of these chapters about the wretched girl is to remind us that Marguerite Duras keeps her attention firmly fixed on the black side of the world's misery. There is, however, something far too mechanical about this

compulsory compassion for us to be greatly affected by it; all the more so in that the story of the unhappy Cambodian girl is not, so to speak true [it is part of the novel by Peter Morgan]. . . . Consequently the most realistic parts of the book end up by losing their realism.[9]

Others, such as André Thérive, blamed her and the other antinovelist writers for the "suicide" of fine literary works.[10] The previously mentioned critics and others of their ilk not only failed to understand Duras's intentions but, even more important, never *felt* her poetry.

J.-J. Gautier of the *Figaro* labeled her "a poor man's Maeterlinck," a "soporific Beckett," whose language was "pidgin." So trite and dull was Duras's "horror" theater, declared Caviglioli of the *Canard enchaîné,* that he concocted the term "Durasoir" to characterize her work. The conventional critic Gilbert Guilleminault claimed that the audience at a Duras play never knew what was happening to the disembodied voices parading about onstage.[11]

Even the sensitive Robert Poulet found *Moderato cantabile* disconcerting: "The reader must expend so much thought to understand where the scene is taking place, who is present, what is happening, that no amount of romanesque enchantment could possibly take hold."[12] Yet the very ambiguity of Duras's protagonists, their displacements, blanks, blackouts, omissions, and intentionally confused recountings of incidents, in large measure accounted for her innovative approach as well as for her success in disturbing and provoking the reader.

The voids existing in Duras's writing style, as noted by so many critics, paralleled a gaping abyss in her own life. She herself made mention of alcohol's corrosive effect on her writing style. During her periods of detoxification she actually experienced the blanks or blackouts her protagonists know. She explained:

> Yes, it really began with *The Ravishing of Lol V. Stein.* At that time I was coming out of treatment for alcoholism, so I don't know whether this fright—I've thought about it a lot and I've never managed to figure it out—whether this fright that I knew while writing . . . wasn't also [triggered] by the fear of being without alcohol; whether it wasn't the aftereffect of detoxication. I can't tell.[13]

Duras's works, it must be conceded, were bewildering to some audiences and readers, particularly those accustomed to easily accessible flesh-and-blood characters, concrete events, and linear time schemes. Duras remarked,

> Nothing advances. Nothing goes anywhere, but things move. . . .
> On the inside there's an extraordinary surveillance so that nothing escapes. . . . But what it's about is simply noticing . . . the accidents: that is, a displacement, a voice. . . .

They're public voices that don't address each other. Just as they don't move, they don't address one another.[14]

Critics such as Dominique Noguez, however, not only understood but empathized with Duras's stylistic transformations. Her reduction of pace, considered stultifyingly dull by some readers, added for Noguez a whole new and timeless quality to the narrative. Her slackening rhythms, for example, invested a sense of duration and of eternalness—even of the cosmic—both in the events and in the nonprotagonists who were continuously slipping in and out of her field of vision. Duras did not deal with temporal reality; she tapped atemporal spheres.[15]

Feminists, believing that the women constellating Duras's works were catalysts and represented power principles, rallied to her banner. Some gynocritics, taking their lead from Elaine Showalter, appended the adjective *subversive,* used as a compliment, to Duras's works. That her writings with regard to sexual politics were considered "incendiary" and "seditious" indicated a step toward freeing women from oppression. Such subjugation was defined as "the muting, silencing, or crushing of our true nature and our true language, in the denial of our specificity and difference in a world dominated by men, to whose alien ways we are forced to conform."[16]

Hélène Cixous, Luce Irigaray, and Michèle Montrelay were convinced that "feminine" language was "rooted in female anatomy, a necessary consequence of the presence of a vagina and the absence of a penis, but that this type of language has been suppressed by the masculine form in the male-dominated culture in which we live." By eluding "the constraints of the masculine," in *Moderato cantabile* and in the works that followed, Duras seemed to convince feminists in general that she was using "language in a more 'feminine' way".[17]

Sylvie Venet maintained that because Duras was "on the edge of madness," her "dislocated" and "disruptive" syntax "cannot be read according to preestablished codes" and for this reason is to be considered "feminine." Moreover, because Duras's style is disjointed, writes Marcelle Marini, it "attacks the organisation of discourse; suppressing links, breaking up its linear unfolding with repetitions, making way for suspensions, spacing, breaks, and multiple distortions; prioritizing the word over the sentence."[18]

According to Karen Kaivola's laudatory remarks, Duras *is* the personification of ambivalence, disruption, and contradiction: "she produces nonpolemical forms with which to shape essentially polemical subjects, focusing on complex relationships among gender, sexuality, desire, the body, loss, power, vulnerability, and violence—and, especially, on the implications of such relationships for female subjects."[19] Feminists agree *grosso modo* that the dismemberment of traditional codes that Duras's writing style accomplished enabled females to see more clearly into the meaning of *the woman's experience* and thus into the ramifications of living in a world dominated by men's language.

Although Duras was grateful to those who brought her work to the attention of the public at large, she nevertheless belonged to no school, sect, or group. She perhaps feared that in some insidious way such identification might subvert her freedom of thought or feeling. Indeed, Duras the artist, the creative spirit, refused to be classified with any one group, no matter its pedigree. Independent in every sense of the word, she remained devoted to her work: "When I write . . . I let something take over inside me that probably flows from femininity. . . . Perhaps, . . . before being Duras, I am—simply—a woman."[20]

Why, we may ask, although she shared ideological and stylistic formulas with some of her contemporaries, did Duras produce works that differed so markedly from theirs? What encouraged some exegetes to consider her a marginal figure and the quality of her oeuvre "strange" and "hallucinatory"?

To shed some light on the multileveled, exciting, but also perplexing nature of her work, let us briefly review the background of Marguerite Donnadieu (later changed to Duras). She was born in Gia-Dinh, near Saigon, of French parents who had gone to Indochina to carve out a future for themselves. Both were teachers in France's colonial service: her mother, Marie Legrand, taught native children; her father, Henri, taught mathematics to French students. After being appointed to a post in Phnom Penh in 1918, he developed amoebic dysentery, returned to France on his doctor's advice, and died shortly thereafter. Mme. Donnadieu remained in Indochina with Marguerite and her two older brothers, Pierre and Paulo, the latter referred to lovingly by his sister as her "little brother." The family returned to the Lot-et-Garonne region of France in 1919, remaining there only long enough to sell the Donnadieu property. Two years later they were back in Cambodia, Mme. Donnadieu teaching first at Sadec, then at Vinh-Long, on the Mékong River. The image of this large body of water that flowed into Cambodia, Siam, and Laos, along with the ever-alluring black sampans bobbing up and down in the distance, the colorful jonquils dotting the land masses and blowing their memorable perfumes her way, was to inspire Duras over and over in her writings.

By 1926 Duras was sent to Saigon, to live at the Pension Lyautey and to study at the Lycée Chasseloup-Laubat. Four years later, she met her Chinese lover.

Whenever Duras the writer reflected on her childhood and youth, her sorrow was mitigated by intense joy and nostalgia.

> It's difficult for me to talk about that period [Indochina] in my life. My father died when I was very young [four years old]. My mother was extremely poor. She was a teacher in a native Vietnamese school. After my father's death she

used up her meager savings to buy a large government concession—a kind of land development scheme [in Prey-Nop, the Kampot province of Cambodia near the Siamese border]. When it came time to plant the rice we realized only too late that nothing would grow in this area. Each year, during high tides (which come with the equinox), the sea floods the entire land mass in this region. The rice we had planted died. My mother bought a kind of lagoon with her life savings. We had nothing left.

What my mother did not realize was that large sums of money had to be given to the white civil servants in order to be able to purchase fertile land. She was ruined. I was twelve years old then. Because of my mother's extreme poverty she became a kind of Vietnamese. She was closer to the Vietnamese than she was to the whites. We were never received by the whites, socially that is, since we were members of the last rung on the social ladder.

And this fantastic, fabulous injustice which had been done to my mother was probably the most traumatic experience in my life. To have seen my mother weep, go mad with grief; to be disdained by everyone, hounded by creditors—to have to sell every last thing. In fact, during our rest hour, my mother used to send me to the local Chinese jewelers to sell whatever baubles we had left. With that money we bought a little meat for our evening meal. It was the first time I knew the meaning of injustice—and equality at the same time. . . . We lived with the Vietnamese, completely, I spoke Vietnamese almost better than I did French. These are my *childhood riches*. . . .

As far as my writing is concerned, I am still haunted or mesmerized by the type of **mono-landscape** in Vietnam. The flatness and dullness of the plains which I used to see as a child all over **Indochina** still live within me. Perhaps this is why I do not like mountains even today. . . . **Indochina** offers a kind of hallucinatory landscape; long stretches of rice fields, swamps.[21]

In 1932 the Donnadieu family sailed back to France, their ship first skirting the Indian coastline, then going north to the Suez Canal and on to the Mediterranean. Marguerite and Pierre remained in France, but Mme. Donnadieu and Paulo later returned to Indochina.[22]

Although Duras spent much of her time studying law and political science in Paris, earning a degree in these disciplines, her real interests lay in writing, theater, music, and the other arts. That she found it difficult to integrate into the French intellectual landscape was understandable given her highly emotional and impulsive makeup. Its structured regimen, spoon-fed as it was on Cartesian methodology and logic, left her feeling displaced, dispossessed, and disconnected. Unlike such *thinking* types as Sarraute, Butor, Robbe-Grillet, Pinget, and Beckett, Duras was a *feeling* type. Nor, like them, was she a theorist. Her carefully spun tales harbored irrational beings—who were, as some critics maintained, truly "out of this world."

What distinguished Duras most incisively from the New Novelists and from such writers as Sartre and Beauvoir, as well as from Camus, Malraux, and most others of the period, was her excoriating but unconscious sense of bereavement. She forever mourned something that had been irretrievably lost: her child-hood. Despite the insecurities, hardships, and feelings of degradation she had suffered as a youngster—including her poverty and her family's exclusion by the class-conscious French colonial establishment—she felt spiritually and psycho-logically anchored to that period in her life as a *puella aeterna*. In retrospect Viet-nam and Cambodia seemed wonderfully beautiful, wild, thrilling—and idyllic. Judging from the multiple and varied recreations of her childhood and youth in her writings, interviews, and filmic sequences, the past never ceased to impact on her psyche. That each of her written or verbal references to her young years dif-fered ever so slightly may suggest that she had both an inability and an unwill-ingness to deal with her exit from Vietnam and Cambodia. Could her so-called textual and verbal inaccuracies be blamed, as has been claimed, on her faulty (or, as it is alluded to today, her repressed) memory? Or were the vision-memories that floated in and out of her consciousness intrinsic to her art? The discrepancies concerning her past, implicit in both her texts and statements, might also explain her refusal to return to the dream-paradise of her youth. Might a return to Vietnam and Cambodia have compelled her to reassess her childhood and youth, to face facts, thus wrenching her fantasy world from her—and setting her even further adrift? Ironically, France, the country of her ancestors, became on an unconscious level her land of exile. "I don't feel French," she said to Elia Kazan.[23] For Duras, then, writing may be referred to as a kind of mediation, a filtration process: a transfiguration of her memories by the wizardry of her imagination.

Her society of "strange," "hallucinatory," and semisilent phantasms, for-ever wandering, wavering, and waiting, became manifest in half-words, in barely audible feeling tones, eye movements, and gestures. They moved about their shadowy realms like so many intense echoes, fleeting essences, fluid presences—as if they had stepped out full-blown from ancient Viet-namese and Cambodian shadow plays.

Duras, the seeker, the subversive provoker, always in search of the inaccessi-ble—her past—remained, no matter her age, the archetypal *puella*, the eter-nal young girl who never grew up. Having run freely and expansively as a child in the real forests of Vietnam and Cambodia, she transposed them into the figurations of such works as *Jaune le soleil, Nathalie Granger, Destroy, She Said,* and *L'Amour;* the forest remained her elected habitat. Its wildness, dan-gers, secrets, and mysteries haunted, mesmerized, and enriched her fantasy world. Whenever departing from Mother Nature's primitive and nutritive environment, Duras, the *puella,* always looked back and within—toward an *unknown.* Wistfully and contemplatively, she confessed,

> Others look at the forest, look at it from a distance, but do not enter it. The forest is the forest of my childhood. I know it. As a small child, I lived on land bordering the virgin forest, in Indochina, and the forest was forbidden, because it was dangerous, for its serpents, insects, tigers, and all of that. And we, we

went anyway, we children, we weren't frightened. We who were born there, we weren't afraid of the forest.[24]

Moving from Duras's early childhood to a day near the close of her life, we read the last entry in *That's All,* a slim volume of 55 pages in diarylike form, in which nearly each entry bears a date. On the afternoon of 1 August 1995, she wrote,

I believe it is all over. That my life is finished. I am no longer anything.[25]

But Duras was and is *something.* Her remarkable works—*The Ravishing of Lol V. Stein, The Vice-Consul, L'Amour, India Song,* and many more—attest to her eternal earthly and supernal presence.

We begin our assessment of Duras's writings with insights offered by the psychiatrist Jacques Lacan and the philosopher-author Maurice Blanchot. Jacques Lacan's "Homage to Marguerite Duras, on *The Ravishing of Lol V. Stein*"[26] is fascinating for the psychoanalytical and linguistic ramifications he appends to the word *ravishing* in the novel's title. Also revealing are his probings of some of the work's motifs, the ball scenes in particular, and why they, above all else, remain indelibly engraved in the protagonist's and readers' memories. Lacan explains as well his ideas concerning the role of the artist vis-à-vis that of the psychoanalyst, and he makes what could be termed a characteristically modest assertion: that "Marguerite Duras knows, without me, what I teach."

Maurice Blanchot's philosophical and linguistic decortications revolve around Duras's *Destroy, She Said.* By questioning its genre—is it a " 'book'? a 'film'? the interval between the two?"—he sets the stage for toppling notions that attempt to delimit the creative instinct. In his inquiry, he ponders the type of language that would not only befit a definition of the genres just mentioned but would also serve to explain the meaning of the words *Destroy, She Said.* Could the word *destroy* suggest love? music? How could the notion of emptiness be interpreted, arising as it does, paradoxically, as an aftermath of the destructive act? What of its "movement" through space, and "toward death"? And what of the sense of "mystery" embedded in the notions of "reality" and of "an alien truth" that also figure in the events of the novel?

The function of the cry and the howl, as they live out their course on Duras's literary stage, is eloquently dealt with in "Territories of the Cry" by Viviane Forrester. At what juncture in Duras's works do these abstract manifestations of anguish become voice? What are their implications, and those of other, inaudible motifs—memory, time, distance, death, and categories that transcend language?

In Marilyn Schuster's salient analysis of *The Sea Wall,* Duras's first successful novel, and of her short story "The Boa," those works fall under the rubric of a young girl's "Coming of Age in Indochina." Schuster underscores questions revolving around colonialism and the resulting conflicts: the narrator, although "privileged by race and nationality," is nevertheless "marginalized because of sex and class." The imagistic representation of a woman's attempt to understand and deal with "her awakening sexuality" is highlighted in precise and poignant, although detached, terms in "The Boa." This cautionary tale, revolving around two voyeuristic incidents, sheds light on certain thematics that figure in Duras's future works.

Micheline Tison-Braun's study of *The Tranquil Life*—its title is an example of Durassian irony, since the events depicted are marked by "savage violence"—highlights the protagonist's remarkable introspective meditations set against the solitude of a seascape. An exorcistic purification ritual of sorts, these meditations may be viewed as an example of indwelling, in keeping in many ways with an Oriental philosophical sensibility. It encourages the protagonist to withdraw or to detach herself from the workaday world and to rove within her own self—there to experience the *void*.

Trista Selous's essay "The Blanks," the title itself pointing up an important aspect of Duras's literary technique, shows that authentic meaning may emerge into being, paradoxically, through "inferences" and "resonances"—nothingness. Selous's clear and succinct explorations of a difficult subject subsume the "crucial" but "ill-defined" notion of what has been alluded to so frequently as Duras's feminine writing. Selous's cogent arguments are based on excerpted passages from *The Sea Wall, Moderato cantabile, The Ravishing of Lol V. Stein, The Vice-Consul,* and *Destroy, She Said.* Because Duras's leitmotifs altered during the course of years, Selous chose works that emphasize "different stages" in her literary development. The novels under scrutiny, therefore, range from Duras's early works, identified by critics as "psychological realism," to the abstract and "more experimental forms" that attracted her later.

In his article "Elective Empathies and Musical Affinities," John W. Kneller studies the manner in which Duras uses the musical thematics of Anton Diabelli's sonatina in *Moderato cantabile.* Although enhancing past and present time schemes, she also heightened and conflated the dramatic involvement of two sets of lovers. Once Kneller defines the term *moderato cantabile* and its implications in Duras's novel, he compares her use of music as a literary device with that of Flaubert and Proust. His sensitive and cogent reading of *Moderato cantabile* as a literary score emphasizes the manner in which music arrests the attention of the protagonists, for example by blocking out the noises of the harbor activities, by identifying certain events with specific motifs, and by developing "two contrasting themes in the mind of the heroine," all of which are "analogous to the sonata form."

Karen Kaivola's essay "The Subversion of Power" scrutinizes the thematics in *The Ravishing of Lol V. Stein, L'Amour,* and *The Vice-Consul.* Her expertise in psychoanalysis, feminism, deconstructionism, and postmodernism, as well as in traditional literary analyses, gives her multifaceted explorations of those novels increased cachet. Never dogmatic, never one-sided in her judgments, she presents her case as meticulously and as objectively as possible and, we may add, most graciously, inviting the reader to draw her or his own conclusions.

Sharon Willis's seminal exploration "*Le Vice-Consul* and *L'Amour:* A World in Default" addresses multiple motifs, among them "the connection between the mother-screen-sign and the cry, in a process which resembles the repetition and delay of mourning, that process by which the subject relinquishes a loved object by draining or displacing the object-cathexis." Discussed in depth are such concepts as mourning, hysteria, deficiency, and divestiture; images and phantasms revolving around the mirror, the sea, and the mother (*mer/mére*); biological rhythms, including the cyclical sequence of starvation/nourishment/vomiting; pregnancy/expulsion; tonal, vocal, and dialogic exchanges of narrative voices; mental processes associated with substitute- and repressed-memory syndrome; figures of speech identified with repetition, doubling, omission, retroaction, and disruption.

Leslie Hill's "Writing Sexual Relations" researches Duras's later works, those published during the 1980s and 1990s. Virtual restatements or reworkings of earlier novels, plays, and films, they bring the author's increasingly painful fixations to the limelight. No longer do traditional couples, for example, play center stage, either psychologically or philosophically. Instead, themes of incest between brother and sister are emphasized, as in such plays as *Agatha* (1981), which was filmed the same year as *Agatha and Unlimited Readings.* In *Agatha* "sexual desire, hovering perpetually on the brink of ecstatic consummation, albeit only by proxy or in retrospect, prepares to enact that which, in normal circumstances, and in most known human societies, lies far beyond the pale of exclusion." *Savanah Bay* (1983), dramatizing a love story of mythical dimension, is "mediated and refracted through the words of two women." The male and female protagonists' suicide at the drama's conclusion is Duras's way of commemorating the couple's powerful desire for one another. Melodramatic as well is *La Musica deuxième* (1985): Although divorced and aware that they have outgrown each other, the couple nevertheless not only articulate their recollections of the years they lived together but also reveal their yearnings for a past that no longer exists. *The Malady of Death* (1982) and *Blue Eyes, Black Hair* (1986) plumb themes revolving around sickness, death, and sexual relationships between a homosexual male and a heterosexual female. The impossibility of knowing happiness leaves the protagonists and the reader with a *Racinian* sense of failure, loss, solitude, rage, and despair.

Michael Bishop's study "The Poetry of Marguerite Duras" is unique in its depth and sensitivity and most of all in the light he sheds on the mysteries implicit in Durassian poetics. Bishop's approach is twofold. With great understanding of the until-now-unaccessed elements of Duras's aesthetics, Bishop probes "questions of incomprehensibility and unknowing, paradox and simplicity/complexity," as well as "matters of atemporality, structure and rhythm." The last section of Bishop's study consists of a fascinating reading of Duras's poem-film *Caesarea*. Among the many exciting aspects of his analysis, he points to the manner in which Duras fleshed out the name Caesarea and "litanized, musicalized, emblematized" its sonorities. Because she did so, the polis lost "its absolute temporal, historical attachment in a blurring of time, an eternalization and pluralization of the meaning of what Caesarea once witnessed and still" did for Duras and for all those drawn to meditation.

"Sacred Theater: A Religious Pagan," by Liliane Papin and translated by John W. Kneller, details unique elements in such Duras stage plays as *Whole Days in the Trees,* directed by Jean-Louis Barrault and performed by Madeleine Renaud (who also acted in *L'Amante anglaise* and in *Savanah Bay*). Unlike other dramatists, Duras did not set firm dividing lines between film, theater, and the novel. On the contrary, she divested herself of traditional categories imposed on genres, preferring to maintain a fluid relationship between a variety of undifferentiated art forms. *India Song,* labeled "text-theater-film," is a case in point. In "Sacred Theater," Papin also highlights Duras's affinities with Antonin Artaud's concept of theater as "ritual" and "ceremony" as well as Duras's differences with this very principle, as attested to by her creation of a "paradoxical language of silence."

"What Alissa Knows. . . . Mutants Mutating: *Destroy, She Said* Terrorizes Psychology" by Sharon Spencer is both innovative and riveting. Although as text and film *Destroy, She Said* is enigmatic to the point of being virtually inexplicable, Spencer's reading is clear and psychologically spellbinding, dealing as it does with questions of jealousy, hypocrisy, aggressiveness, mental and emotional confusion, blurring and crossing over of identities, inescapable sexual allurement with multiple and shifting partners, powerful murderous tendencies, and lives lived within a paradoxical framework of utter emptiness.

Deborah N. Glassman's *"Le Vice-Consul* and *India Song:* Dolores Mundi" examines two of Duras's films. Her detailed analysis of the narrative frames, the mirrored spaces, the spatial signposts, the multiplication and dislocation of the images, underscore the innovative qualities of "the most visually arresting of [Duras's] Indian Cycle films." It is no wonder, as Glassman so aptly states, that "no other shibboleth is so often used to describe the effect of Duras's works on readers and filmgoers as the term *fascination.* Fascination is a theme and an effect with a performative dimension in Duras's texts."

Jeanine Parisier Plottel's extremely well researched study of "The Politics of Marguerite Duras" focuses on the writer's comportment during World War II. Although such a subject is thematically existential, the ambiguities and contradictions confronting a scholar broaching it are at least as complex as probings of Duras's fiction. Let us briefly glance at the problems involved. In *L'Empire Français* (1940), for example, which Duras coauthored with Philippe Roques, both writers advocated maintaining a French empire for reasons of security in a time of national danger. They therefore were convinced that the

French colonies in North Africa should launch their military might against the Nazis. Understandably, *L'Empire Français* was assailed by such collaborators as Lucien Rebatet, in his *Les décombres,* and by others of that ilk. In 1942, however, we find most surprisingly that Duras was employed by Le Cercle de la Librairie, a Vichy publishing house. Although scholars have been denied access to its archives, some believe, as Plottell notes, that "there was [on Duras's part] much cooperation with the enemy." By 1943 Duras again seemed to have turned a corner when she joined François Mitterand and other friends in the Resistance. Nevertheless, questions again arise as to Duras's friendship with Charles Delval, a collaborator who was employed by Gestapo headquarters in Paris and executed after the war. Ambiguous as well is the fact that her entourage included, among others, such well-known collaborators as Ramon and Betty Fernandez. We may also wonder what motivated Duras after the war to point up the unfairness of Robert Brasillach's execution while, as Plottel writes, "she herself was whitewashed." But then, how exact is our knowledge concerning the subject?

As Duras herself notes at the conclusion of her volume *The War,*

> Today, beyond the windows, there was the forest, and the wind had started to blow.
> The roses have died in that other, northern country, one rose after another, carried off by winter.
> It's dark. I can't see the words I've written any more. I can't see anything except my motionless hand which has stopped writing to you.[27]

Notes

1. Xavière Gauthier and Marguerite Duras, *Les Parleuses* (Paris: Editions de Minuit, 1974), 195.
2. Alfred Cismaru, *Marguerite Duras* (New York: Twayne, 1972), 31, 35.
3. Cismaru, 39; qtd. in Gérard D'Houville, "Lectures romanesques," *La Revue des deux mondes* (15 December 1952): 728–29.
4. Gaetan Picon, *Panorama de la nouvelle littérature* (Paris: Grasset, 1960), 252.
5. Cismaru, 67; qtd. in Christine Garnier, "Revue dramatique," *La Revue des deux mondes* (February 1966): 455–56.
6. Jacques Lacan, "Homage to Marguerite Duras, on *The Ravishing of Lol V. Stein,*" trans. Peter Connor, in *Marguerite Duras* (San Francisco: City Lights Books, 1987), 122.
7. Gauthier and Duras, *From Woman to Woman,* afterword by K. Jensen (Lincoln: University of Nebraska Press, 1987), 181.
8. Alain Vircondelet, *Duras: A Biography,* trans. Thomas Buckley (Normal, Ill.: Dalkey Archive Press, 1994), 149.
9. Cismaru, 113; qtd. in Kléber Haedens, "A Sleep Walker," *Atlas* (April 1966): 254–55.
10. Cismaru, 114; qtd. in André Thérive, "Marguerite Duras: *Le Vice-Consul,*" *La Revue des deux mondes* (1 July 1966): 116.
11. Vircondelet, 166, 236 ff.).

12. Robert Poulet, "Le Régle du jeu transgressé," *Moderato Cantabile* (Paris: October 18, 1962): 153.
13. Gautier and Duras, *From Woman to Woman,* 3.
14. *Ibid.,* 4–5.
15. Dominique Noguez, "La Gloire des mots," *L'Arc 98* (Paris: Editions Le JAS, 1985), 24–40; "Les India Song de Marguerite Duras," *Cahiers du 20e siecle 9: cinéma et literature* (Paris: Klincksieck, 1978).
16. Trista Selous, *The Other Woman: Feminism and Femininity in the Work of Marguerite Duras* (New Haven: Yale University Press, 1988), 3.
17. *Ibid.,* 4.
18. Selous, 12; Sylvie Venet, *Femme dans l'écriture: Marguerite Duras,* 4; Marcelle Marini, *Territoires du féminin,* 51. All from Selous *Ibid.* 12.
19. K. Kaivola, *All Contraries Confounded: The Lyrical Fiction of Virginia Woolf, Djuna Barnes, and Marguerite Duras* (Iowa City: University of Iowa Press, 1991), 102.
20. Susan Husserl-Kapit, "An Interview with Marguerite Duras," *Signs 1* (Winter 1975): 428.
21. Bettina L. Knapp, *Off-Stage Voices* (Troy, N.Y.: The Whitston Press, 1975), 131 ff.
22. Paulo died in 1942 in Indochina of bronchial pneumonia due to lack of medicines during the Japanese occupation.
23. Marguerite Duras, "Les Yeux verts", *Cahiers du cinéma* 312–13 (June, 1980): 200.
24. Michelle Porte, *Les Lieux de Marguerite Duras* (Paris: Minuit, 1977). See also *The Places of Marguerite Duras,* trans. Edith Cohen, *Enclitic 7.1* (1984): 54–61, and (1984): 55–62.
25. Marguerite Duras, *That's All.* Paris: P.O.L. 1995.
26. *Marguerite Duras by Marguerite Duras,* 122.
27. Marguerite Duras, *The War.* Trans. Barbara Bray. New York: Pantheon, 1986, 182.

Works Cited

Blanchot, Maurice. *"Destroy."* *Marguerite Duras.* San Francisco: City Lights Books, 1987.
Coward, David. *Duras: Moderato Cantabile.* London: Grant and Cutler Ltd., 1981.
Forrestier, Viviane. "Territories of the Cry." In *Marguerite Duras.* San Francisco: City Lights Books, 1987.
Hill, Leslie. *Marguerite Duras: Apocalyptic Desires.* London: Routledge, 1993.
Noguez, Dominique. "La Gloire des mots." In *L'Arc 98.* Paris: Editions Le JAS, 1985, 24–40.
Papin, Liliane. *L'Autre scène: Le Théâtre de Marguerite Duras.* Saratoga, Cal.: Anma Libri and Co., 1988.
Pautrot, Jean-Louis. *La Musique oubliée.* Genève: Droz, 1994.
Schuster, Marilyn R. *Marguerite Duras Revisited.* New York: Twayne, 1993.
Tison-Braun, Micheline. *Marguerite Duras.* Amsterdam: Rodopi, 1985.
Willis, Sharon. *Marguerite Duras: Writing on the Body.* Urbana: University of Illinois Press, 1987.

Homage to Marguerite Duras, on *Le ravissement de Lol V. Stein*

Jacques Lacan

Le ravissement—this word is enigmatic. Does it have an objective or a subjective dimension—is it a ravishing or a being ravished—as determined by Lol V. Stein?

Ravished. We think of the soul, and of the effect wrought by beauty. But we shall free ourselves, as best we can, from this readily available meaning, by means of a symbol.

A woman who ravishes is also the image imposed on us by this wounded figure, exiled from things, whom you dare not touch, but who makes you her prey.

The two movements, however, are knotted together in a cipher that is revealed in a name skillfully crafted in the contour of writing: Lol V. Stein.

Lol V. Stein: paper wings, V, scissors, Stein, stone, in love's guessing game you lose yourself.

One replies: O, open mouth, why do I take three leaps on the water, out of the game of love, where do I plunge?

Such artistry suggests that the ravisher is Marguerite Duras, and we are the ravished. But if, to quicken our steps behind Lol's steps, which resonate through the novel, we were to hear them behind us without having run into anyone, is it then that her creature moves within a space which is doubled; or is it rather that one of us has passed through the other, and which of us, in that case, has let himself be traversed?

Or do we now realize that the cipher is to be calculated in some other way: for to figure it out, one must count *oneself* three.

But let's read.

The scene of which the entire novel is but a recollection describes the enrapturing of two in a dance that fuses them together before the entire ball

Le ravissement de Lol V. Stein was published in America under the title *The Ravishing of Lol Stein,* Grove Press, 1966. Reprinted from *Marguerite Duras by Marguerite Duras* (San Francisco: City Lights Books, 1987), 122–29. Reprinted by permission. Translated by Peter Connor.

and under the eyes of Lol, the third, who endures the abduction of her fiancé by a woman who had only suddenly to appear.

And to get at what Lol is seeking from this moment on, must we not have her say, *"Je me deux,"* to conjugate, with Apollinaire, *"douloir?"*[1]

But, precisely, she cannot say that she suffers.

Thinking along the lines of some cliché, we might say she is repeating the event. But we should look more closely than this.

This is roughly what we discern in this scene, to which Lol will return many times, where she watches a pair of lovers in whom she has found, as if by chance, a friend who was close to her before the drama, and who helped her even as it unfolded: Tatiana.

This is not the event, but a knot retying itself there. And it is what this knot ties up that actually ravishes—but then again, whom?

The least we can say is that at this point the story puts one character in balance, and not only because Marguerite Duras has invested this character with the narrative voice: the other partner of the couple. His name, Jacques Hold.

Nor is he what he appears to be when I say: the narrative voice. He is, rather, its anguish. Once again the ambiguity returns: is it his anguish, or that of the narrative? He does not, in any case, simply display the machinery, but is in fact one of its mainsprings, and he does not know just how taken up in it he is.

This allows me to introduce Marguerite Duras here, having moreover her consent to do so, as the third ternary, of which one of the terms remains the ravishment of Lol V. Stein caught as an object in her own knot, and in which I myself am the third to propose a ravishment, in my case, a decidedly subjective one.

What I have just described is not a madrigal, but a limit of method, one whose positive and negative value I hope to affirm here. A subject is a scientific *term,* something perfectly calculable, and this reminder of its status should terminate what can only be called by its name, boorishness: let us say the pedantry of a certain kind of psychoanalysis. This frivolous aspect of psychoanalysis, to remain sensitive, one hopes, to those who immerse themselves in it, ought to indicate to them that they are sliding towards stupidity; for example, by attributing an author's avowed technique to some neurosis: boorishness. Or again, by showing it to be an explicit adoption of certain mechanisms which would thereby make an unconscious edifice of it: stupidity.

I think that even if I were to hear it from Marguerite Duras herself that, in her entire *oeuvre,* she doesn't know where Lol has come from, and even if I could glean this from the next sentence she says to me, the only advantage that the psychoanalyst has the right to draw from his position, were this then to be recognized as such, is to recall with Freud that in his work the artist always precedes him, and that he does not have to play the psychologist where the artist paves the way for him.

This is precisely what I acknowledge to be the case in the ravishing of Lol V. Stein, where it turns out that Marguerite Duras knows, without me, what I teach.

In this respect, I do not wrong her genius in bringing my critique to bear on the virtue of her talents.

In paying homage to her, all that I shall show is that the practice of the letter converges with the workings of the unconscious.

Let me assure whoever might read these lines by the dimming or rising footlights—indeed, from those future shores where Jean-Louis Barrault, through his *Cahiers,*[2] would harbor the unique conjunction of the theatrical act—that the thread I will be unraveling takes its bearings at every moment, and to the letter, from the ravishing of Lol V. Stein; and furthermore, that work going on today at my school certainly crosses paths with it. Moreover, I do not so much address myself to this reader as I draw upon his inmost being in order to practice the knot I unravel.

This thread is to be picked up in the first scene, where Lol is robbed of her lover; that is to say, it is to be traced in the motif of the dress which sustains the phantasm (to which Lol is soon to become fixed) of a beyond that she cannot find the word for, this word which, as it closes the doors on the three of them, might have espoused her at the moment her lover was to raise up the woman's black dress to unveil her nakedness. Will this go further? Yes, to this unspeakable nakedness that insinuates itself into the place of her own body. There everything stops.

Is this not enough to reveal to us what has happened to Lol, and what it says about love; that is, about this image, an image of the self in which the other dresses you and in which you are dressed, and which, when you are robbed of it, lets you be just what underneath? What is left to be said about that evening, Lol, in all your passion of nineteen years, so taken with your dress which wore your nakedness, giving it its brilliance?

What you are left with, then, is what they said about you when you were a child, that you were never all there.

But what exactly is this vacuity? It begins to take on a meaning: you were, yes, for one night until dawn, when something in that place gave way, the center of attention.

What lies concealed in this locution? A center is not the same on all surfaces. Singular on a flat surface, everywhere on a sphere, on a more complex surface it can produce an odd knot. This last knot is ours.

Because you sense that all this has to do with an envelope having neither an inside nor an outside, and in the seam of its center every gaze turns back into your own, that these gazes are your own, which your own saturates and which, Lol, you will forever crave from every passerby. Let us follow Lol as she passes from one to the other, seizing from them this talisman which everyone is so eager to cast off: the gaze.

Every gaze will be yours, Lol, as the fascinated Jacques Hold will say to himself, for himself, ready to love "all of Lol."

There is in fact a grammar of the subject which has taken note of this stroke of genius. It will return under the pen which pointed it out to me.

You can verify it, this gaze is everywhere in the novel. And the woman of the event is easy to recognize, since Marguerite Duras has depicted her as non-gaze.

I teach that vision splits itself between the image and the gaze, that the first model for the gaze is the stain,[3] from which is derived the radar that the splitting of the eye offers up to the scopic field.

The gaze spreads itself as a stroke on the canvas, making you lower your own gaze before the work of the painter.

Of that which requires your attention one says, "*ça vous regarde*": this looks at you.

But rather, it is the attention of that which is regarding you that has to be obtained. For you do not know the anguish of what gazes at you without, however, regarding you.

It is this anguish that takes hold of Jacques Hold when, from the window of the cheap hotel where he awaits Tatiana, he discovers, stretched out at the edge of the rye field before him, Lol.

Do you read on a comic level his panicky agitation, be it violent or only dreamed, before, significantly, he gets a grip on himself, before he tells himself that Lol can probably see him. Just a little more calm, and then the next phase, when she knows that he can see her.

Still, he must show her Tatiana, propitiatory at the window, no longer moved by the fact that Tatiana hasn't noticed anything, cynical at having already sacrificed her to the law of Lol, since it is in the certainty of obeying Lol's desire that he will go through the motions with his lover, upsetting her with those words of love whose floodgates, he knows, can only be opened by the other, but these same cowardly words tell him that this is not what he wants, not for her.

Above all, do not be deceived about the locus of the gaze here. It is not Lol who looks, if only because she sees nothing. She is not the voyeur. She is realized only in what happens.

Only when Lol, with the appropriate words, elevates the gaze to the status of a pure object for the still innocent Jacques Hold is its place revealed.

"Naked, naked under her black hair," these words from the lips of Lol mark the passage of Tatiana's beauty into a function of the intolerable stain which pertains to this object.

This function is no longer compatible with the narcissistic image in which the lovers try to contain their love, and Jacques Hold immediately feels the effects of this.

From that moment on, in their dedication to realizing Lol's phantasm, they will be less and less themselves.

What is manifest in Jacques Hold, his division of the subject, will no longer concern us here. We are interested rather in how he fits into this three-fold being, in which Lol is suspended, laying over his emptiness the "I think" of a bad dream which makes up the content of the book. But in so doing, he contents himself with giving her a consciousness of being that is sustained outside of herself, in Tatiana.

It is Lol, however, who puts together this threefold being. And it is because the "thought" of Jacques Hold comes to haunt Lol too insistently at the end of the novel, when he accompanies her on a pilgrimage to the scene of the event, that Lol goes mad.

The episode in fact contains signs of this, but I would point out that I heard this from Marguerite Duras.

The last sentence of the novel, which brings Lol back to the rye field, seems to me to bring about a much less decisive end than my remark would suggest. One suspects from it a caution against the pathos of understanding. Lol is not to be understood, she is not to be saved from ravishment.

Even more superfluous is my own commentary on what Marguerite Duras has done in giving a discursive existence to her creature.

For the very thought, by means of which I would restore to her a knowledge which was always hers, could never encumber her with the consciousness of being an object, since she has already recuperated this object through her art.

This is the meaning of sublimation, something that still confounds psychoanalysts because, in handing down the term to them, Freud's mouth remained sewn shut.

His only warning was that the satisfaction it brings should not be considered illusory.

But clearly he didn't speak out loudly enough since, thanks to them, the public remains persuaded to the contrary. And the public will remain so if the psychoanalysts don't come around to acknowledging that sublimation is to be measured by the number of copies sold for the author.

This leads us to the ethics of psychoanalysis, a topic which, in my seminar, produced a schism within the unsteady ranks of the audience.

In front of everyone, however, I confessed one day that throughout the entire year my hand had been held in some invisible place by another Marguerite, Marguerite of the *Heptameron*.[4] It is not without consequence that I find here this coincidence of names.

It seems quite natural to me to find in Marguerite Duras that severe and militant charity that animates the stories of Marguerite d'Angoulême, when they can be read free from those prejudices which are intended solely to screen us off from their locus of truth.

This is the idea of the "gallant" story. In a masterful work, Lucien Febvre has tried to expose the trap it sets.

I would draw attention to the fact that Marguerite Duras has received from her readers a striking and unanimous affirmation of this strange way of loving: of that particular way of loving which the character—whom I placed not in the role of narrator but of subject—brings as an offering to Lol, the third person indeed, but far from being the excluded third.

I am delighted to see this proof that the serious still have some rights after four centuries in which the novel feigned sentimentality, firstly to pervert the techniques of the convention of courtly love into a mere fictional account, and then to cover up the losses incurred—losses parried by the convention of courtly love—as it developed into the novel of marital promiscuity.

And the style which you adopt, Marguerite Duras, throughout your Heptameron, might well have paved the way for the great historian I mentioned earlier to attempt to understand some of these stories for what they really are: true stories.

But sociological reflections on the many changing moods of life's pain are but little when compared to the relationship that the structure of desire, which is always of the Other, has with the object that causes it.

Take the exemplary tale in Book X of Amador, who is not a choir boy. Devoted even unto death to a love which, for all its impossibility, is in no way Platonic, he sees his own enigma all the more clearly by not viewing it in terms of the ideal of the Victorian happy ending.

For the point at which the gaze turns back into beauty, as I have described it, is the threshold between-two-deaths, a place I have defined, and which is not merely what those who are far removed from it might think: it is the place of misery.

It seems to me, Marguerite Duras, from what I know of your work, that your characters are to be found gravitating around this place, and you have situated them in a world familiar to us in order to show that the noble women and gentlemen of ancient pageantry are everywhere, and they are just as valiant in their quests; and should they be caught in the thorns of an uncontrollable love, towards that stain, celestial nocturne, of a being offered up to the mercy of all . . ., at half past ten on a summer's evening.

You probably couldn't come to the aid of your creations, new Marguerite, bearing a myth of the personal soul. But does not the rather hopeless charity with which you animate them proceed from the faith which you have in such abundance, as you celebrate the taciturn wedding of an empty life with an indescribable object.

Notes

1. *Je me deux* is the first person reflexive form of the now archaic French infinitive, meaning to feel sorrow. It means, therefore, "I feel sorrow," but also, read in another way, it can

mean literally, "I two myself." No English verb captures the ambiguity of the French; the closest approximation might be, "I am rent," which suggests the splitting of the subject of which Lacan will be speaking. (TN)

2.   This article first appeared in the *Cahiers Renault-Barrault,* December 1965. (TN)

3.   For an understanding of the function of the stain in Lacan's theory of the gaze, see his "The Split between the Eye and the Gaze" in *The Four Fundamental Concepts of Psychoanalysis,* trans. Alan Sheridan, New York: Norton, 1977, pp. 67–78. (TN)

4.   Marguerite d'Angoulême (1492–1549), author of the *Heptameron,* published posthumously in 1558–59. The seventy-two tales of the *Heptameron,* told by a group of travelers delayed by a flood on their return from a Pyrenean spa, illustrate the triumph of virtue and honor. (TN)

Destroy

MAURICE BLANCHOT

Destroy: it fell to a book (is it a "book"? a "film"? the interval between the two?) to give us this word like an unknown word, offered by a completely different language of which it is the promise, a language that perhaps has only this one word to say.[1] But to hear it is difficult for us who are still part of the old world. And, hearing it, we still hear ourselves, our need for security, our assumed self-possession, our petty dislikes, our lasting resentments. Destroy is then, at best, the consolation of despair, a *watchword* which merely appeases the menace of time in us.

How can we hear it without using vocabularies that knowledge, and moreover a legitimate knowledge, puts at our disposal? Let us say calmly, one must love in order to destroy, and one who could destroy by a pure movement of love would not wound, would not destroy, but only give, bestowing an infinite emptiness where the word destroy becomes a non-privative, non-positive, neutral word which bears neutral desire. *Destroy.*

It is only a murmur. Not a unique term glorified by its unity, but a word that is multiplied in a rarefied space and by someone who pronounces it anonymously, the figure of a young woman who comes from a place without horizons, from ageless youth, from a youth that makes her very old or too young to appear as only young. Thus the Greeks hailed in each adolescent the expectation of an oracular word.

To *destroy:* how it echoes—softly, tenderly, absolutely. A word—an infinitive marked by the infinite—without a subject; a work—destruction—which is accomplished by the word itself. Nothing but our knowledge can recapture it, especially if it awaits the possibilities of action. It is like a brightness in the heart, an unexpected secret. It is confided to us so that finally, destroying itself, it destroys us for a future forever separated from all that is present.

Characters? Yes, they assume the position of characters, of men, women, and shadows, and yet they are immobile *points of singularity,* although a course of movement through a rarefied space—in the sense that almost nothing can happen there—is traced from one to another, a multilinear course along

Reprinted from *Marguerite Duras by Marguerite Duras* (San Francisco: City Lights Books, 1987), 130–33. Reprinted by permission. Excerpted from *L'Amitié* (Gallimard).

which these immobile points never cease to change places and, finding themselves identical, to change. A rarefied space rendered infinite by the effect of
rarity, up to the limit which nonetheless doesn't limit it.

Assuredly, what is happening there happens in a place we can name: a
hotel, a park and, beyond, the forest. Let's not interpret. It is a place in the
world, our world; we have all lived there. Still, while open on all sides by
nature, it is strictly delimited and even closed: sacred in the ancient sense,
separate. There, it seems, before the action of the book or the film's interrogation begins, that death—a certain way of dying—has done its work, has
introduced a mortal inertia. Everything there is empty, missing, in relation to
the things of our society: missing, in regard to the events that seem to occur
there—meals, games, feelings, language, books that are not written, are not
read, and even nights which belong, in their intensity, to an already defunct
passion. Nothing is comfortable because nothing in this place can be completely real or unreal, as if writing staged, against a fascinating background of
absence, only the semblance of phrases, residues of language, imitations of
thought, simulations of being. Presence unsustained by any presence, be it
yet-to-come or in the past—a forgetting that supposes nothing forgotten,
and which is detached from all memory, without certainties. Ever. A word, a
single word, last or first, intervenes there with all the discrete brilliance of an
utterance borne by the gods: *destroy.* And here we recapture the second
requirement of this new word, because if one must love in order to destroy,
one must also, before destroying, be liberated from everything—from ourselves, from living possibilities, and also from dead and mortal things—by
death itself. To die, to love: only then will we be able to approach that fundamental destruction, one that an alien truth destines for us (as neutral as it is
desirable, as violent as it is distant from all aggressive powers).

Where do they come from? Who are they? Certainly beings like ourselves; there are no others in this world. But, in fact, beings already radically
destroyed (hence, the allusion to Judaism); yet, in such a way that far from
leaving unhappy scars, this erosion, this devastation or infinite movement
toward death, which lives in them as their only memory of themselves (in
one, as the flash of lightning which finally reveals an absence; in another, as a
slow, unfinished progression of time; and, in the girl, through her youth,
because she is fully destroyed by her absolute relationship to youth), these
things liberated them through gentleness, for attention to others, for a nonpossessive, unspecified, unlimited love, liberated them for all this and for the
singular word that they each carry, having received it from the youngest, the
young woman of the night, the one who, alone, can "say" it with perfect
truth: *destroy, she said.*

Sometimes, they evoke mysteriously what the gods have been for the
ancient Greeks—always on an equal footing with them, as familiar as they
are alien, as close as they are far away. New gods, free from all divinity, still
and always to come, although descended from the most ancient past; men

then, but relieved of human weight, of human truth, but not of desire nor of madness, which are not human traits. Gods, perhaps, in their multiple singularity, in their imperceptible duality, that rapport of themselves with the name of night, oblivion, and the shared simplicity of eros and thanatos—death and desire finally within our reach. Yes, gods, but, according to the unsolved enigma of Dionysus, mad gods; and it is a kind of divine exchange that, before the last laugh, in the absolute innocence to which we must accede, leads them to designate their youthful companion as the one who is mad in essence, mad beyond all knowledge of madness (the same figure perhaps that Nietzsche, from the depths of his own insanity, called Ariadne).

Leucate, Leucade, the brightness of the word "destroy," this word that shines but doesn't enlighten, even under the empty sky, always ravaged by the absence of the gods. And do not think that such a word, now that it has been pronounced for us, can belong to or be assimilated by us. If the "forest" without mystery or symbolism is nothing other than a limit impossible to transgress, yet always surpassed in its impassability, it is from there—the place without a place, the outside—in the tumult of silence (such was Dionysus, the most tumultuous, the most silent), apart from all possible signification, that the truth of this alien word emerges. It comes to us, from the farthest point, across the great clamor of destroyed music, coming, perhaps deceptively, like the very beginning of all music. Something, sovereignty itself, disappears here, appears here, without our being able to distinguish between appearance and disappearance, nor between fear and hope, desire and death, the end and beginning of time, between the truth of the return and the madness of the return. It's not only music (beauty) that is announced as destroyed and nevertheless renascent; it is, more mysteriously, that we witness and take part in *destruction as music*. More mysteriously and more dangerously. The danger is immense; the pain will be immense. What will become of this word that destroys? We don't know. We know only that each of us must bear it, with ever after at our side the young, innocent companion, the one who gives and receives death as though eternally.

Note

1.   I refer to the book *Détruire, dit-elle* (*Destroy, She Said*) by Marguerite Duras.

Territories of the Cry

VIVIANE FORRESTER

Forget memory. So slow, this world where flowers fade, and the stones. *India Song* destroys the distance where time insinuates itself. Anne-Marie Stretter— "she is in the past," Marguerite Duras told me one day, "she has this grace." A reign without bounds, without hope of boundaries (death itself doesn't make the least difference any more) in this place, the space of the screen where the worst things live undefined, uncategorized, outside language. Here is life in its simplicity, where incurable beauty and love refer back, like hunger, to pure unendurable presence, where mirrors do nothing but replicate. Sun, mirrors, lamps in the shadows, and flowers—like the original apple is anodyne and like these roses in whose recesses a vegetal, exhausted Delphine Seyrig is shipwrecked, in an instant—reveal more about this ultimate story where nothing can end because it has already ended. We haven't left paradise. That was it— eternity, the horror. The Vice-Consul knows it. The sublime beauty in Marguerite Duras reveals it, and the terrible sweetness that engulfed Anne-Marie Stretter, surrounded by her lovers. Nothing touches her. Michael Richardson's hand, so tender, at night, on her hair, is useless. Useless, his embrace, their embraces. They are resigned to it, to love and ecstasy that lead to nothing else, transgress nothing. All those things that Duras's books touched, that they challenged and demonstrated through the most translucent indications suddenly appeared naked, erasing what made a palimpsest: the identity between the signifier and the signified. It seems that here the signifier, splintered into diverse media, each of them autonomous (image, sound, space, continuity, direction), cancels itself out, and that being springs forth, at last.

Now, what always underlies Duras's work, and life, what History has tried from its beginning to suppress, what cannot be said *or* proposed *or* heard (but which film permits, we find, in its flexibility, its clarity, its dynamic simultaneities) can break out: the cry. Something forbidden, a major interdiction.

The Vice-Consul's cry. Forever and ever heard by Anne-Marie Stretter, by Marguerite Duras, and held back by the man from Lahore. This howling is the language that truly belongs to the earth and its inhabitants. A response.

Reprinted from *Marguerite Duras by Marguerite Duras.* (San Francisco: City Lights Books, 1987), 161–63. Reprinted by permission.

There is no other. Discourse, even speech and music itself exist to distract us from it. This time we hear it. It spreads, opens out. We see the distance it covers. And by seeing it, we hear it.

The Vice-Consul and Anne-Marie Stretter are the same, always separated, fused in this separation. They speak as they dance at the French Embassy. So as to say nothing, to say that there is nothing. Nothing to say. That they know. And he (Michaël Lonsdale) whose unforgettable gaze at the lovers by the Ganges at the beginning of the film held the most unbearable knowledge, he—the subject of scandal, locus of love, the one they are going to send away—announces that he is going to cry out. He is going to display his brute suffering, the demented knowledge he has of it, the state he incarnates: understanding. And it is here that the cry reaches its source. The primal source. The man who was all gaze is going to become voice, a sound that was inaudible until now, the only sound in the world.

And we hear a cry. We hear it said, proclaimed, that someone loves. We hear what has never ceased. Anne-Marie Stretter—erect, calm, innocent—dances, frozen in this cry that she has never stopped crying out in silence. Over which the music that she loves and fears sometimes makes a screen (or a passageway?). Motionless, next to the equally motionless man, she accepts, submits, acknowledges. The cry comes like falling rain. It is everywhere, outside the screen. It absorbs dimensions, space; it surrounds, disperses, meanders. Lonsdale's voice becomes geographic. An opera. Everything is stripped to the most obscene purity. A territory without shame. The name of Anna-Maria Guardi is scattered, linked to the music that Anne-Marie Stretter, under her maiden name, had played earlier in Venice, far from any embassies. The cry of a name. Name of the cry. Rocked by the swelling of a paroxysm that could conceivably create love. But no one is shouting. Scarcely a sound. Nevertheless, the cry is there, inextinguishable. And so we think of Marguerite Duras who must hear it all the time and know that she hears it, who seeks and flees from it. Here the screen becomes the concrete space of what she calls the crisis of writing.

The man, the woman are still standing, forever motionless, navigating, navigated. Then a gesture, a man's hand moves slowly toward the bare skin of a shoulder. That's all. That still exists. Nothing else is possible. In the late hours, the Vice-Consul moves away. It's on the morning lane that the vibrations of the cry still reverberate. The world of dawn, pale echo of the terrible expanse on which the Vice-Consul's silhouette, seen from the back, disappears from view once again. He walks in rags, the same ones he's been wearing since Lahore (where he shot at lepers and dogs in the Shalimar gardens, and at himself, in the mirror, at home). Slowly the silence settles in again, identical with the shouting from now on.

Still echoing intermittently in the embassy drawing rooms is the name Anna-Maria Guardi, now once more Anne-Marie Stretter, who regains her body and the body of the other—desire—with a wounded smile. The cry is extinguished as the beggar woman's song is reborn, a natural sound like the song of a bird, poignant in its ignorance, rejoining in its utter misery the Vice-Consul's impassioned act. Cries of fishermen, of workers, raucous cries of birds, the world creates itself anew, covers over the scandalous uproar. The rest will follow; the story and the impossible ending of the story are inscribed there. Some signs, roses, the effigy of a life and that map of the Indies at the end, flesh of the world, inscribed in a certain silence that the cry will sign.

The Tranquil Life

MICHELINE TISON-BRAUN

All Marguerite Duras' writing bears the stamp of a childhood spent in Vietnam: in particular her very first novel. *La Vie tranquille (The Tranquil Life),* in which the action is far removed from the East. Indeed right in the middle, like a dramatic peak in the narrative, we find fifty or so pages that show in a form that is both modern and French the explicit influence of Oriental psychology—Buddhist psychology—on the author's thinking and sensitivity.

Many themes are common to *Barrage (The Sea Wall)* and *The Tranquil Life:* ill luck, misery, solitude, boredom and the rebellion against it; as well there is the attachment to her brother, and the attraction to violence. But the atmosphere in the two works is quite different. *The Tranquil Life*—much closer to Mauriac than to the American (or allegedly American) novel that was in vogue after the war—is set in the framework of a French country landscape, the charm of which draws from the writer some fine descriptive touches; the technique she uses is psychological analysis, and even introspection in the French style. The pellucid style, unpretentious and often poetic, excludes the familiarities and coarseness found in *The Sea Wall.* But above all there are fifty or so pages perhaps unequalled in post-war literature, relating the heroine's examination of her conscience in the solitude of a sojourn by the sea, which represent the peak and the novelistic turning point of this work.

A savage violence characterizes this novel with the paradoxical title. It opens with a murder at the end of a long and bloody fight—and continues through a particularly horrible suicide of passion (the victim lay down under a train): finally, a drowning puts an end to the central meditation like a recall to reality. All these dramas, provoked or tolerated by the heroine-narrator in a somnambulant state, were indications of a real unconscious vocation as a domestic sorceress, interrupted abruptly by the examination of her conscience down by the sea. Throughout these pages we are watching a veritable purification by light, an exorcism. The demons flee before the great Durassian archetypes—the same ones that were to reappear in the Lol V. Stein cycle: the sea, the sun, the sand unfolding its inhuman expanses to infinity. Unlike the

From *Marguerite Duras* (Amsterdam: Rodopi, 1985), 19–25. Reprinted by permission. Translated by Barbara McGilvray.

rest of the novel, this meditation excludes any voluntary, ordered thought. The narrator simply allows herself to be, and observes herself with surprise. The manner of liberation offered here, which is simply the abandoning of the mirages of desire, is in some ways reminiscent of oriental philosophies, except that with Marguerite Duras this is never explicitly mentioned. Rather, it is as though even without her pondering the question, her Indochinese childhood predisposed her to a certain type of sensibility—a sensibility she never bothered to develop on a philosophical level, and one moreover which leads from an oriental detachment to an utterly pagan sensuality. Just as the recluses of old sought grace in places that were known in Christian times as "deserts," the heroine has withdrawn from the world for a time. Weary of dramas, the one she herself has caused and the one she was unable to prevent or even foresee, she searches in her innermost self for the foundations of this "tranquil life," which in a sense is invoked by her own desires. ("The tranquil life will be ours.") It is not the routine of tedium lived by her family before the dramas, in which the parents continue to vegetate, no longer even rising from their beds; nor is it the animal stupor of the disliked servant; nor the bottled-up passion of her brother the murderer. It is indicated perhaps by the strange light emanating from Tiène, the stranger, her lover, whose inexplicable stay with the family seems to mask some secret wisdom. We shall never know. We understand only that one cannot emerge from the bleakness of tedium through passion. It killed the brother ("This was no longer the same brother. A dangerous joy inhabited him") (Duras, *The Tranquil Life,* 57). The infinity of desire is irremediable. "Beyond Luce, he is searching for something he cannot attain by means of madness or reason" (*TL,* 67). The lovestruck heroine for her part knows that all desire is fleeting, beginning with her own: "One day I shall no longer love Tiène" (*TL,* 161).

The seaside purification is followed by an initiation. This experience begins with her distancing herself from the world, feeling a repugnance for human contact which she is unable to conquer. Alone, and searching for her essential being, the narrator discards the superficial layers of her Self one by one, like old garments. First she dissociates herself from her physical appearance. She sees herself—sees *it*—with some amazement in the wardrobe mirror which is open at an unusual angle, moving about, opening her suitcase, arranging things . . . That image was not me, she thinks, but "I know not what fraternal individual filled with hate, silently challenging my identity" (*TL,* 122). Soon the room is filled with these false Selves, the creations of others which one finally believes are oneself. Thus, *I* is another (in an opposite sense to Rimbaud), in fact a multitude of others whom the narrator is unable to assemble and recognise in her memory. It is another who has lived in her place (*TL,* 123), attached to her Self "by a thread that could have broken at any moment," and so "I was on the verge of plunging into madness" (*TL,* 123). The experience of the Self cut up in small pieces is not alienated, but instead dominates this part of the meditation. "A throng of shapes were to appear and attempt to be me, then at once disappear as if the fact that they did not suit me reduced them to nothing" (*TL,* 123).

Everything changes when, instead of looking at her body, she takes it into her head to feel it in the throbbing of her blood, and in the thousand indistinct impressions forgotten by her consciousness for twenty-five years. If only she had "lived with greater care!" (*TL,* 126). Her life's time has been stolen from her, or she has allowed it to escape through inattention. The mystery of incarnation, felt from within her body, is not be to be shaken by logical thought. At times endowed with a monstrous autonomy, at times a haven of unrecognized intimacy, utter certainty and an identity unto itself, the incarnate being cannot know itself through rational exploration of causes and intentions, but only by allowing itself to exist with the passing of its impressions, backing up its reverie with a watchful lucidity.

Again and again in the course of the long meditation the external world is glimpsed: our attention is compelled by the sound of the waves or the cries of sea-birds. Then the thoughts adjust themselves to the feelings, stretching and winding about them in a succession of unsubstantial metamorphoses. A few obstinate memories linger on—her lover, her dead brother; these too are subjected to slow gyrations that cause them to disintegrate. The boredom has vanished: it was product of the intellect, born in the empty space that lies between the existent Self and the Self of reflection. The feeling of this space is what dominates from now on. The narrator, as a woman, feels like a "thoroughfare" for the generations of the future, a refuge and shelter, but also original emptiness, "visceral insufficiency," "an empty cry" (*TL,* 129). Here, with thoughts of Tiène, astonishment creeps in at the essentially unfaithful nature of passion. Long before his death her brother had been forgotten for Tiène, just as Tiène will be forgotten sooner or later. A constant of the Durassian experience is already emerging: the permanence of desire and the incidental nature of its object.

Yet these scraps of the fragmented Self floating "on the same level . . . like pieces of flotsam in the sea" (TL, 136), bereft of sense, retain their shape "in a way that is at once absurd and unforgettable" (TL, 136). For the narrator, detached from her biography as she was from her body, henceforth feels that the thing she called her personality is external to her, something purely incidental. "I am a certain form into which someone has poured a certain history which is not mine." "The thoughts of my person . . . are somewhere outside of me, quiet and numbed like one among all the things that are under the sun" (*TL,* 136). She could have been someone else, or not have been at all: she feels herself "indefinitely replaceable" (*TL,* 178). An eloquent symbol is offered by a small box which the sea washes up and then reclaims: "These four wood panels contained a real history, a real lack of history, which proclaimed itself to the heavens" (*TL,* 137). And yet the paradox remains, that the mind creating this fragmented Self is itself a center, beginning from which another identity can be reconstructed.

In the acknowledged contingency and the perfect emptiness of the old Self, a few prime truths linger on—truths of sensation: once upon a time the impressions of August, scents of the woods and the plain, rides on the sweaty-flanked mare; now, the play of light on the icy sparkling sea, the warmth of the sand. Sensation is richer and more varied than sentiment and thought; it communicates to those who can penetrate it the secret of life intensely lived. It was the tyranny of the intellect that generated boredom: "I have lived with reason and wisdom," the narrator reflects, ". . . a virgin to the age of twenty-five . . . sparing of my body, of my life . . . I should have stayed awake with the wind crying out to be heard . . . been receptive . . ." (*TL,* 131). In this perfect availability we detect an echo of what *Les Nourritures terrestres* taught after Nietzsche and, after Gide, *L'Etranger* and *Sisyphe.* It is not a question of becoming one with creation or with creatures: this kind of identification appears to be condemned as illusory (in a paragraph that is admittedly obscure) (*TL,* 128–9). Indeed, far from denying the incarnate being in its solitude, one must go deeply into it until the life force in each sensation offered is felt within.

In this condition, time is in no way abolished; it is only time as a one-way street from past to future that has disappeared. The feeling of continuity remains, in a still time where the ambivalence of forgetfulness is evident. This is salutary, for life is fixed in the memory of events: "Everything decays into memory and nothing more can be invented" (*TL,* 126). "Once the ability to forget is lost, a certain life is permanently missing" (*TL,* 131). Yet from another point of view, "there is no forgetting" (*TL,* 140) since the essential survives outside the memory of events, "crouched at the very bottom of forgetfulness" (*TL,* 135). Certainly, the smooth time of the deep does not eliminate the time of incarnation, avariciously meted out: "My flesh . . . devours the days one after the other, always with the same avidity" (*TL,* 139). Yet our death is part of us, and no matter in what guise it presents itself, it will be recognised and perhaps accepted in the tragic intensity of reality. Similarly, the metamorphosis of both beings and feelings loses its sting—the "never again" of unidirectional time.

Thus, beyond the specters of the Self and desire, we divine *la vie tranquille,* the true peaceful life where boredom is unknown. No doubt it would be better to speak of a *vie légère* (as long as the word is not used pejoratively), since this life, in full consciousness of solitude and unhappiness, joyously unfolds down by "the sea that is dancing, dancing" (*TL,* 139, 160) like Zarathustra, in an interval of lucidity which is not intellectual analysis, but self-renewal preceding all reflection. A new kind of lucidity thus replaces the classic introspective knowledge. This lucidity is at the core of an inner life which is not thought, but felt and, if we may say so, actively dreamed (the active, observed dream being the opposite of passive reverie). It originates in a new extraordinary Self, a consciousness distinct from any content—be it emotion or idea—and from any description ("The idea, wandering about like someone intoxicated . . .") (*TL,* 177).

Nowhere in all Marguerite Duras' writing is there a clearer statement of her existential experience and the implicit act of faith that underpins it. In the soul swept clear the fullness of life is divined, and it is rhythm and cycles in the continuity of a present that has no contours. Temporality is reabsorbed into absolute Being, with no past or future, but constantly shifting. In this way a kind of atemporal and impersonal eternity can be created. In a consciousness washed clean of all events there remains this memory of Being which preceded and surrounds the incarnation. Previously, the narrator perceived herself as a creature of passage; henceforth she sees herself as a transitory incarnation of universal life, a stage in the universal being taking the Self as its temporary metaphor. This intuition is described in a lyrical passage:

> On the sea, everywhere at once, flowers burst forth. I think I hear them sprouting . . . a thousand metres deep. The ocean spits its sap into these bursting foam blossoms. I have spent time in the hot muddy halls of the earth which spat me up from its depths, and now I am here . . . I am flower. Every part of my body has burst beneath the force of the day. I feel the proud weariness of being born, of reaching the end of this birth process. (*TL,* 143–4)

Perhaps thought, left to its own devices, will consider us superfluous—but only thought. In the context of life there is merely tragic awareness, happy to exist. Thus, restored to its place, thought can reappear ("I who am looking at them") (*TL,* 143). It will surrender unashamedly to the dazzlement of the miracle: "Before me, there was nothing in my place. Now, there is Me in place of nothing" (*TL,* 144).

The narrator has already been emboldened to experience death: she enters the sea and becomes identified with the wave which she allows to roll her over (*TL,* 145–6). This is apparently an actual rite of baptism as still practised in certain religions. The body's reaction is harmonious, giving in and protecting itself as appropriate (in contrast, we may suppose, to the reactions of the drowned swimmer who made the mistake of struggling and begging for just a little more air). The contact of the wave represents the decisive test, the peak of the meditation: "I was a little girl. Just now I have become adult" (*TL,* 146).

For several days the soul remains in still waters. Then little by little, as the end of the retreat approaches, the pragmatic Self reappears, while the deep Self in its return to the surface repeats the initiatic journey in reverse: it rediscovers time (the leitmotif of the early meditations is repeated: already thirty days since Jerome's death, seventeen days since Nicolas' death, for twenty-five years, . . . how many days to reach . . .). With memories and plans comes the return of an increasingly profound solitude, and the whole procession of thoughts (*TL,* 161). Finally, boredom, which is identification with stagnant time (as the time of the depths was communion with total life).

The letter from Tiène stirs up all her thoughts and concerns, and her contradictory desires. The narrator alternately wants to "leave an exemplary trail" or, discouraged, to "die wretchedly, the death of a little dog" (*TL,* 167).

In this reascending movement she breaks the communion with the sea. "In an order of things which has no feeling, one is this disordered nothing which feels" (*TL,* 168). This indeed is to be superfluous; however she recalls another vision. She accepts that henceforth she will enter into solitude as into a religious order. She will find herself back in her "lapping" marshes of tedium (*TL,* 171) and of hope (false hope) which was the "white beacon of her death" (*TL,* 172), not forgetting however the lesson learned in her solitude: the reality of her deep being.

We cannot say whether the attempt at detachment has miscarried, whether the narrator, merely grown more lucid, will be imprisoned again in "her head over-filled with blood and brains" and given over to "all the bellowing of [her] desires" (*TL,* 179). The story's ending is hurried and unclear: return, sickness, jealousy, then a conclusion that is on the whole optimistic, but unsatisfactory. Once more in a state of flux after her fleeting contact with Being, we do not know if the narrator will abandon the "madness of the search for happiness," or if she has already found it.

The striking thing in this still imperfect novel is the gift demonstrated by the author (too perfect to be completely intentional) for maintaining a detachment from the characters and the reader, for creating distances. Certainly it succeeds in aesthetic terms, but one suspects a failure on the philosophical and human level. The restrained tone of the meditation was announced from the start by the narrator's indifference. The brutal murder of her uncle, which she had provoked without hatred in order to put an end to the stupor that was engulfing her family, was something she enjoyed, to be sure, but without sadism; fascinated by "the force of her brother" but more inconvenienced than horrified by the suffering of the victim, whom she dehumanises by reducing him to mere external behavior. Later, her indifference to the cries of the injured man who is left waiting hours for morphine seems to stem not so much from callousness, which would be monstrous, as from a break in contact with reality. Similarly her impressions at the time of the funeral: we could be reading *L'Etranger* when we learn that the coffin "smelt of waxed wood; its shape was splayed, narrowing down towards the feet" (*TL,* 40–41). This somnambulant detachment, so oddly combined here with the meditation on Being, will characterize most of Duras' characters, from Suzanne in *The Sea Wall* to Anne Desbarèdes and Anne-Marie Stretter taking the first steps towards the supreme detachment of madness. It is to the ambiguity of the "peaceful" novel that we must return for an understanding of so many absent characters, people taking refuge in absence.

The (slightly suspect) detachment of the peaceful work and the romanti-cism of *The Sea Wall,* both of which extend into her later writing, are like the two separate poles of the same imaginary world, or two legacies of childhood not yet fully assimilated. It is not without significance that the first novel is dedicated "to my mother," as if to soothe this troubled soul by recalling the rustic inheritance of the past; though after this source work the author appears to have experienced a need for turbulent writing to rid herself of her Indochinese memories, as of a blood clot, before embarking on her definitive course.

Coming of Age in Indochina:
The Sea Wall and "The Boa"

MARILYN R. SCHUSTER

Most American readers know Marguerite Duras primarily through *The Lover* (1984) and, therefore, as a French woman who grew up in Indochina. Very few of Duras's works, however, represent the landscapes of her childhood directly. Colonialism and the colonial mentality permeate most of her work, but are displaced onto an imaginary Indian landscape or small provincial cities in France. *The Sea Wall* (1950), the first of her novels to win a substantial popular and critical success, *Eden-Cinema* (1977), a play based on *The Sea Wall,* and "The Boa" (1954), a short story, are the only texts before *The Lover* that Duras situates in Indochina. *The Lover* itself is, in many ways, a retelling of *The Sea Wall.*

The Sea Wall: Colonial Fictions. *The Sea Wall* can be read as a countertext to colonial fictions, a story told to unmask the lies invented by colonial authorities to lure unwitting victims and to maintain control. Narrated in the third person, it is told from the point of view of Suzanne, privileged by race and nationality but marginalized because of sex and class.

Briefly, *The Sea Wall* tells the story of a mother (never named) and her children: Joseph, who is twenty, and Suzanne, seventeen. Widowed when the children were very young, the mother supports them by playing the piano to accompany silent films at the Eden Cinema. She saves her money and, after ten years, buys rights to a concession—land to be farmed and, ultimately, owned by French settlers—from colonial authorities. She learns too late that good concessions go only to those willing to bribe the authorities. Her land is inundated yearly by the Pacific Ocean, making it impossible to cultivate.

She devises a scheme to build sea walls to hold back the tides and enlists the help of the peasants who also inhabit this remote land—500 kilometers from the city. Tiny crabs eat away at the structures and the sea walls give way with the first tide. The mother refuses to let go of the mad hope that she can overcome both the authorities and the elements. She becomes increasingly sick and mad until she dies at the end of the novel. Resistance, in the

From *Marguerite Duras Revisited* (New York: Twayne Publishers, 1993), 14–27. Reprinted by permission.

mother's story, is shown to be pointless, so the children dream of escape: from the mother, whom they love, and from the poverty of the concession, which they hate. Each imagines a lover who would take them away: Joseph would rescue a stranded (rich) woman, Suzanne would be rescued by a rich man. Eventually the son of a wealthy planter, Monsieur Jo, takes an interest in Suzanne. As his race is never specified, the reader is supposed to understand that he is white. In many ways, however, he resembles the Chinese lover in *The Lover* and, like him, is seen as repulsive and unacceptable by the girl's brother. A legitimate union between them is deemed impossible by Monsieur Jo's father because of class, just as in *The Lover,* marriage is rejected by the Chinese lover's father because of race.

Joseph is ultimately taken in by a rich woman and escapes to the city. At the end of the novel he returns for the mother's burial, incites the peasants to insurrection against the colonial agents, and goes back to the city. Suzanne also leaves, but her fate is less clear. Jean Agosti, another settler slightly better off than the mother, has taken her as a lover, but she chooses to leave him in order to escape the sterility and poverty of that remote land. There is no closure at the end of the book, only stories in suspension and the vague promise of revolt.

Like so many of Duras's novels, *The Sea Wall* is about fictions and desire. It was a fiction that lured the mother to the colonies in the first place. As young schoolteachers in northern France, the mother and her husband saw colonial recruitment posters inviting them to make their fortune in exotic lands like those they had read about in the romantic works of Pierre Loti: " 'Enlist in the Colonial Army!' said some. And others: 'Young People, a Fortune awaits you in the Colonies!' The picture usually showed a Colonial couple, dressed in white, sitting in rocking-chairs under banana trees while natives busied themselves around them." As teachers in schools for the Indochinese, rather than for white children of the ruling class, however, they do not belong to the class represented by the poster. Further marginalized and impoverished by widowhood, the mother has deeper connections to the "natives" than she has to the leisured class of white colonials.

The posters and popular literature that promote romantic exoticism represent fictions of leisure and privilege that disguise the truth of exploitation underlying colonial dominance. The mother is a naive reader of these fictions, unable to discern the fiction as a fabrication, mistaking it for a transparent representation of the truth. Finally, it drives her mad. Suzanne and Joseph, more canny readers of the fictions that entrapped their mother, create a fiction of escape. They are both readers and creators of stories that can be read, literally, as escape fiction. Though their fictions, like the recruitment poster, are nourished by conventional clichés, Joseph and Suzanne retain a certain degree of narrative control. They are both readers and narrators of stories that combine cultural expectations and personal dreams. The differences between Joseph's stories and Suzanne's reveal the differences between what it means to be a man and what it means to be a woman in their social circumstances, particularly the differences in how each experiences sexuality and desire.

The first example of Joseph as a storyteller occurs in the second chapter when the mother, Joseph, and Suzanne go to the canteen in Ram, the village nearest their concession. It is the evening of their first encounter with Monsieur Jo. For Joseph, the conditions of life on the concession have become intolerable. Everything they touch seems to fall to ruin: his ancient car, an old horse that has just died, the sea walls the mother has tried to build. Joseph turns the pain and poverty of their existence into a series of jokes by inventing a hyperbolic narrative that progresses from bad to worse, along the lines of "if you thought that was bad, wait until you hear this." He gains control of the room through his stories, creating a huge joke ("la grande rigolade"). It is through his narrative that we first learn the story of the sea walls, either a tragedy or a joke depending on the day, adds the narrator. To tell a story confers power—over the meaning of events and over those who listen or read.

Joseph's central story in the book is the story of his escape from the mother and the concession. At first it is a gap in the narrative because, as readers, we are limited to Suzanne's consciousness, and she can only note his absence for over a week during a trip to the big city the children make with their mother. Later, he tells Suzanne the story in terms that are self-consciously narrative. After a prologue that begins "I went to the movies" (*SW*, 203; *B*, 221), he leads into the heart of the story: "Here begins the most extraordinary night of my life."

In many ways, the cinema is to the children what romantic literature and the recruitment poster were to their parents: idealized images that shape their dreams, perhaps trapping them in an illusion that is always beyond reach. But the cinema, as represented in this book, is a zone one can move in and out of, a darkened space in which desire circulates freely. Like music, alcohol, drugs, and madness, the cinema creates a zone of semiconsciousness that acts as a buffer against harsh realities while nourishing desire. Both Joseph and Suzanne go to the movies hoping to lose themselves, hoping to be washed over by the screen images, but also hoping to find dream lovers. They grew up beneath the flickering screen as their mother played the piano at the Eden Cinema. But the mother was denied the escape provided by cinema: She could not see the screen from where she sat.

The story of desire and escape that Joseph tells begins, significantly, at the movies, the privileged scene of fantasy, where he had gone to pick up a new woman. His familiar lover, Carmen, a sometime prostitute who helps run the hotel where they always stay in the city, is too familiar, unable to stimulate fantasy and desire. He says he had "grown sick and tired of Carmen, it was almost like sleeping with a sister when I slept with her" (*SW*, 203; *B*, 221). The story Joseph tells to Suzanne is punctuated by remarks to the effect that she must tell this to "Ma," she must remember this story so that she will remember him. He wants the story, in other words, to remain behind, to stand in for him when he is gone.

The story he tells centers on a beautiful and wealthy woman, Lina, who sits next to him at the movies, with her husband, asleep, on the other side. She flirts with Joseph and their exchange becomes more fascinating than the story on the screen. After the movie, she and her husband take Joseph drinking. Joseph's desire is intensified by alcohol, music, and dance. At one point, Joseph dances with another woman. When he returns to Lina, she says: "When I saw you dancing with that girl, I called out to you, but you didn't hear" (*SW,* 213; *B,* 233). This triangle of desire (a woman observing her lover transfer his desire to another woman, watching her own exclusion, speaking and yet unheard) prefigures in important ways the central obsession of the Lol V. Stein cycle written fifteen years later. The husband eventually passes out and Lina and Joseph make love in her expensive car. They then spend eight uninterrupted days and nights at a hotel.

Joseph tells Suzanne his story just before Lina comes to the concession to take him back to the city with her. As she listens to Joseph, Suzanne becomes his apprentice in storytelling and in life: "Suzanne did not get the full significance of Joseph's words, but she listened to them religiously, as to a hymn of virility and truth. Thinking them over she perceived with emotion that she herself felt able to conduct her life as Joseph said she must. She saw, then, that what she admired in Joseph was also in herself" (*SW,* 224–25; *B,* 246). To Suzanne, Joseph speaks in "the Master's voice," the slogan on the side of his favorite victrola, another instrument of escape and dreams.

Once she listens to his stories, her own story incorporates his terms, revealing the effect of her apprenticeship to his authority. Suzanne's story follows a trajectory that is almost the inverse of Joseph's. He sleeps with Carmen, among others, a woman of his class, and tires of her because she seems like "a sister." He then realizes a fantasy love, discovering Lina in the movies and finding a way out of misery through her attention. Suzanne first meets Monsieur Jo, who appears to be the dream lover she had imagined would take her away. But Joseph does not like him, and she realizes that he will never marry her so she loses interest in him. After Joseph's departure, she agrees to sleep with Agosti. She is attracted to him to the degree that he begins to resemble her brother.

Suzanne learns from Monsieur Jo the power of her body as an object of desire and exchange. He offers her a gift if she will let him watch her in the shower. Later he offers her a diamond if she will spend several days in the city with him. She refuses, but he gives her a diamond ring anyway. When the mother, Joseph, and Suzanne go to the city to sell the ring, Joseph meets Lina. Indirectly, Suzanne's body has brought Joseph to his dream lover.

The topography of the city reproduces the class and race hierarchies of the colony. The *baut quartier,* or upper district, is the protected quarter belonging to rich whites who circulate in luxurious cars. Throughout the novel, cars inspire envy and desire or frustration. For example, Monsieur Jo's limousine, a Léon Bollée, is an emblem of wealth and power, a car belonging to dreams or the cinema, promising escape. Joseph's Citroen is ridiculous, part of his "great joke." Other districts belong to the indigenous people who travel by tram. The mother and her children stay at a hotel in a transient district where salesmen and sailors circulate. Suzanne, dressed and tutored by Carmen in how to use her femininity, goes to the upper district but feels the unpitying looks of the rich whites. She cannot have access to this district on her own as Joseph can. The only place in which she can escape the judgment of their gaze is the cinema, where she rediscovers the free circulation of desire, sharing touches with anonymous men, experiencing the cinema as a "palpitating gloom" ("obscurité féconde") (*SW,* 178; *B,* 192).

By chance, Monsieur Jo finds Suzanne one day in the city and his car supplants the cinema as a scene of fantasy and desire. In the protection of the Léon Bollée, she rediscovers the power of her body and sees the upper district differently: Moving through the streets and the bright lights, she experiences the city as if it were a film. Monsieur Jo touches her breasts and tells her they are beautiful: "The thing had been said very softly. But it had been said. For the first time . . . above the terrifying city, Suzanne saw her breasts, saw the erection of her breasts higher than anything that stood up in the city: Her breasts, then, would be justified. She smiled" (*SW,* 180; *B,* 195). Only through a man's gaze—even an unacceptable man—does Suzanne feel the power of her body.

After Joseph tells her the story of his extraordinary affair, Suzanne agrees to sleep with a man. Agosti, who begins to remind Suzanne of Joseph by his laugh and gestures, comes to get her, not in a Léon Bollée but in a modest Renault; he takes her to a clearing in a forest on his plantation and makes love to her. She would have preferred his hotel room at Ram with the shutters closed, she thinks: "it would have been a little like the violent darkness of the cinema." Like Joseph and Lina, they then spend eight days and nights at the hotel room, but this time the mother has her last crisis. Suzanne returns to watch her die. Suzanne's love story imitates Joseph's in certain respects: It enables separation from the mother and a way out of the concession and all it represents. The ending of her story is far less certain, however. She says she is leaving, but to what is left unresolved. Agosti is not a way out, as Lina is, because he belongs to the same remote community as Suzanne.

Suzanne, then, borrows Joseph's story to try to create her own. But the transfer to a woman's story is not entirely satisfactory and the differences between them are striking. Joseph, for example, loses erotic interest when a woman begins to remind him of "a sister." For Suzanne a man becomes desirable when he begins to resemble her brother. Joseph circulates freely in the city; Suzanne is constrained unless she is with a man. Joseph gets his fantasy lover and leaves more ordinary lovers behind; Suzanne rejects her fantasy lover and gets Agosti, then no one, in his place. The contrasts between the two stories confirm stereotypes about gender and the asymmetrical experience of gender for men and women in their particular cultural context.

The novel also presents a series of women's stories that further compel Suzanne to listen to Joseph and try to "conduct her life as Joseph said she must" (*SW,* 225; *B,* 246). The models of womanhood available to Suzanne include the mad mother (isolated, angry, and powerless), the peasants (reduced to reproductive machines), and Lina (unavailable to Suzanne as a model because of class). Suzanne expresses deep ambivalence, both desire and distrust, toward Carmen, who is valued because Joseph sleeps with her and who tries to be a mentor to Suzanne in the ways of femininity. Even as Carmen teaches her how to use her body, Suzanne imagines herself in Joseph's place, watching her. In this gesture she learns the desire of the female body through the male gaze and then represses her appropriation of the male gaze, fearful, perhaps, of being in that position as desire circulates:

> Suzanne knew that it was in this room that Joseph had slept with Carmen. When Carmen undressed in front of her, she thought of it every time. And every time that made one more difference—not with Carmen, but with Joseph. . . . Suzanne itemized her every evening, and every evening her difference from Joseph was accentuated. Suzanne had undressed in front of Carmen only once. Then, Carmen had taken her into her arms. . . . It was that same evening that Carmen asked her to bring her the first man she picked up. Suzanne promised. But never again did she undress in front of Carmen. (*SW,* 162; *B,* 174)

At the end of the novel, though, Suzanne's story is unfinished.

In a note to the play *Eden Cinema,* based on *The Sea Wall* and written more than twenty years later, Duras makes it very clear that she does not want closure at the end of this novel. In 1957, René Clément made a film based on *The Sea Wall* in which he rewrote the ending. Rather than have the children leave the concession after the mother's death, Clément has them stay on, as Duras says in her note, "like American pioneers in the Middle West, 'to continue their parents' work.' " In Duras's view, this was an "irremediable betrayal" of the meaning of the novel. The children should leave the colony and the story should end with the violence and potential rebellion unresolved; the parents' work, in the context of the corruption and exploitation represented by the colony, was a travesty. In the play, Duras has the mother rather than Joseph incite violence. Her "work" is not to settle the colony but to unsettle it.

Suzanne derives her sense of the terms and power of femininity and fiction from Joseph and, to a degree, from Monsieur Jo. The pleasure she experiences with Agosti is possible once she sees Joseph's features projected on his body. Suzanne and Joseph both seek escape in the zone of semiconsciousness produced by alcohol, drugs, music, and the cinema. The threshold between reality and the zone of semiconsciousness is permeable in *The Sea Wall,* but clearly marked. Desire discovered in the fantasies of semiconsciousness maintains the erotic in everyday reality. "The Boa" and *The Sailor from Gibraltar* offer further explorations of female sexuality and the meanings of fiction.

"The Boa": A Cautionary Tale. In 1954, Duras published four short stories under the title *Des Journées entières dans les arbres (Whole Days in the Trees).* Just as *The Tranquil Life* tells a story of female subjectivity, one of the stories in this volume, "The Boa," presents a story of female sexuality. Although the story is told in the first person, both temporal and geographic distance between the adult narrator and her younger self is carefully established at the beginning: "This happened in a large city in a French colony, around 1928" (*WD,* 71; *J,* 99). The use of an impersonal, reflexive construction ("cela se passait") reinforces the distancing of the narrator and is the first mark of split female subjectivity in this text, in which the woman tries to read her own adolescence. In the story, the adult narrator situates her thirteen-year-old self between two spectacles that provided the only terms available to her to understand her awakening sexuality.

The narrator describes her younger self as a poor student at Mademoiselle Barbet's boarding school for girls. The other girls have friends in town, and every Sunday their developing minds and bodies are nourished by endless adventures: cinema, teas, drives in the country, afternoons at the pool or tennis courts. The narrator, however, has no such social life and spends all her time with the seventy-five-year-old spinster, Mlle Barbet. Mlle Barbet provides the girl with the two spectacles that mark her coming of age. Every Sunday she takes her to the zoo, where, with other fascinated onlookers, they watch a boa constrictor consume a live chicken. If they arrive too late, they contemplate the boa napping on "a bed of chicken feathers" (*WD,* 72; *J,* 100). They remain transfixed because "there was nothing more to see, but we knew what had happened a moment before, and each of us stood before the boa, deep in thought" (*WD,* 72; *J,* 100–101).

The other spectacle is provided by Mlle Barbet herself, with the girl as an unwilling witness. In a routine as certain as the boa's, Mlle Barbet calls the girl into her room. Under the pretext of showing the girl her fine lingerie, Mlle Barbet exhibits her seminude body. The old woman had never shown her body to anyone before and would never show it to anyone else because of her advanced age. She instructs the girl that beautiful lingerie is important in life, a lesson she learned too late.

The narrator adds that Mlle Barbet's body exudes a terrible odor that permeates the entire boarding school; she had noticed the odor before, but could not locate it before seeing the woman's exposed body. The old woman sighs during their secret sessions, saying "I have wasted my life. . . . He never came" (*WD,* 74; *J,* 105). The girl is induced by her own impoverished circumstances to tell the woman that she has a full life, that she is rich and has beautiful lingerie: The rest is unimportant.

This Sunday double feature, repeated weekly for two years, is developed in great detail by the narrator, who spends most of the story linking, contrasting, and interpreting the two spectacles because they illuminate the only two avenues through which the young girl could imagine her future. The narrator insists that one weekly event without the other would have led to other effects. If, for example, she had witnessed only the boa's devouring of the chicken, she might have seen in the boa the force of evil and in his victim, goodness and innocence; she might have understood the world as an eternal struggle between these two forces revealing the presence of God. Or, she could have been led to rebel (*WD*, 73; *J*, 102). She could have internalized the weekly lesson at the zoo, that is, as a morality tale, a story of good and evil leading to conformity or rebellion.

The spectacle of Mlle Barbet alone might have led the girl to understand social inequities and the "multiple forms of oppression" that result. Coupled with the zoo experience, the second spectacle shifts the meanings of both because of the terrifying glimpse of aging female flesh, undiscovered by the male gaze and imprisoned in its own virginity. Together, the two events become not a morality tale of good and evil, of inequity and injustice, but a cautionary tale of female sexuality. The terms the narrator uses to reconstruct each event and the conclusions she draws articulate a specific construction of the female body and heterosexuality. Within the terms of the story—shown especially in the contrast between the young narrator and her school friends—she seems to suggest that this is an anomalous construction. At the same time, fatalistic language and implications of social determinism suggest that this is a distilled experience of female sexuality rather than an anomalous one. In any case, the highly individualized definition of female sexuality elaborated in this text will be generalized in other texts by Duras, passing imperceptibly from one woman's story to the story of "woman." For that reason, as well as the fact that this is one of the few texts with explicit autobiographical references situated in Indochina and written before *The Lover*, "The Boa" merits close consideration.

From the start, the narrator insists that she is an involuntary, yet complicit, solitary voyeur of Mlle Barbet. The girl undergoes this weekly drama and keeps Mlle Barbet's secret in exchange for Mlle Barbet's silence about her mother's poverty. The girl is in the school because her mother thinks that it is the only way she will meet a husband and thus find a way out of poverty and marginalization in the strictly ordered society of the colony.

The girl shares her mother's belief that Mlle Barbet is better suited to help her find a husband, even though the old woman's "secular virginity" exudes the odor of death that permeates the school (*WD*, 74; *J*, 105). The narrator specifies that Mlle Barbet is consumed by lack, by "the lack of the man who never came" (*WD*, 74; *J*, 105). Each week, after leaving the old woman, the girl returns to her room, looks at her own body in the mirror, and admires her white breasts. In a gesture that superimposes the boa and female sexuality, she says that her breasts provide the only source of pleasure for her in the entire house: "Outside the house there was the boa, here there were my breasts" (WD, 76; J, 107). Feeling trapped in the school, the girl goes out on the balcony to attract the attention of passing soldiers.

The spectacles of the old woman and of the snake involve consumption and violence valued in opposite ways. Mlle Barbet is consumed by lack, and the private viewing of her enclosed, undiscovered sexuality inspires disgust and dread. The boa consumes his prey, and his public act is characterized as a sacred crime inspiring horror and respect. The boa itself is described in hyperbolic, highly sexualized terms: "Curled into himself, black . . . in admirable form—a plump roundness, tender, muscular, a column of black marble . . . with shudders of contained power, the boa devoured this chicken in the course of a single process of digestion . . . transubstantiation accomplished with the sacred calm of ritual. In this formidable, inner silence, chicken became serpent" (WD, 72; J, 101). This spectacle in the open daylight attracts spectators who are fascinated, entranced by the vital beauty and violence of the beast. In sharp contrast, the narrator calls Mlle Barbet's secret "hidden" and "nocturnal."

The narrator does not read the formative stories of her youth as a simple contrast between powerful male and sterile female sexuality, two stories of devouring desire—one the passionate devouring of an innocent, the other the passionless devouring of the self by a hypocritical innocence. In her work on reader theory, Jean Kennard talks about the shaping role of both gender and sexuality in the recognition and interpretation of literary conventions. She shows how new meanings can be assigned to conventions to subvert their apparent or traditional sense. The narrator of "The Boa" can be read as a woman thinking back on the cultural texts available to her to understand and revalue her sexuality through a complex negotiation between her needs and the stories available. Duras accomplishes this negotiation by mapping a story of female sexuality onto the spectacle of the boa constrictor so that *both* stories recount possibilities for female sexuality. Female sexuality is redeemed by the power of the phallus in the first story, condemned by its own inadequacy in the second.

To map a story of female sexuality onto the story of the boa, the narrator must negotiate a complex series of substitutions and displacements. Her narrative sleights of hand recall the convoluted associations and displacements of a Freudian map of female sexuality—one that privileges the penis and defines woman by lack. The slippage that results from this imperfect, if ingenious, mapping compounds the division within the woman/girl's experience of the female body marked thematically by the two spectacles.

In an increasingly intense meditation on the links between the spectacle of the boa and of Mlle Barbet, the narrator expresses the despair she felt as a girl: unable to flee the closed world of Mlle Barbet, "nocturnal monster," unable to join the fertile world revealed by the boa, "monster of the day." In a passage presented as a waking fantasy, she imagines the world represented by the boa. She fantasizes a green paradise, a scene where "innumerable carnal exchanges were achieved by one organism devouring, assimilating, coupling with another in processes that were at once orgiastic and calm" (*WD*, 78; *J*, 110). The contrast of this paradise with the prison of Mlle Barbet leads her to define two types of horror. One horror—hidden vices, shameful secrets, hypocrisy, concealed disease—inspires a deep aversion. The other—the horror of assassins, crime, the outlaw—inspires admiration. The boa is the "perfect image" of this second kind of horror that elicits respect. In a series of substitutions she expresses contempt for those who would condemn certain species such as "cold, silent snakes . . . cruel, hypocritical cats." She establishes one category of human being that could be considered among these privileged outlaws: the prostitute. She parenthetically links assassins and prostitutes, imagining both in "the jungle of great capital cities, hunting their prey which they then consumed with the impudence and imperiousness of fatalistic temperaments" (*WD*, 79; *J*, 112). She thus establishes a train of associations that shifts the story from the masculine figure of the snake to the male assassin/outlaw to the feminine figure of the prostitute, from the jungle to the city.

The transfer of value from the snake to the prostitute also takes place at a deeper, linguistic level. The boa consumes a chicken, put in the masculine in the French: "un poulet." A common word for prostitute in French, which is implied though not invoked in the story, is the feminine form of chicken: "une poule." The prostitute figure in the story, like the chicken that is ingested by the boa and becomes one with his flesh, is absorbed into the values of the phallic figure of the snake. Another substitution and transfer of values is hinted at more explicitly in the story. The same soldiers who walk under her balcony are also spectators at the zoo. She would attract their gaze, fascinate them, in the same way as the boa, substituting herself for the great serpent in her fantasy.

At the moment that she transfers values from the male figures to the female, the image of Mlle Barbet erupts into her fantasy as a reminder of the body she is fleeing. She tells herself that if she does not marry, at least the brothel would provide an escape for her. This leads her to a fantasy of the brothel: "a sort of temple of defloration where, in all purity . . . young girls in my state, to whom marriage was not accorded, would go to have their bodies discovered by unknown men, men who belonged to the selfsame species" (*WD*, 79; *J*, 112). The brothel, painted green, recalls the zoo garden as well as the tamarind trees that shade her balcony, where she tries to attract the gaze of passing soldiers. She imagines this as a silent place, marked by a sacred anonymity; girls would wear masks in order to enter. Anonymity pays homage to "the absolute lack of 'personality' of the boa, ideal bearer that he was of the naked, virginal mask" (*WD*, 79; *J*, 113). The ritual initiation and anonymity shift this from the story of one girl to the story of woman, from a specific sexual awakening to a model of female sexuality. She imagines cabins in which one could "cleanse oneself of one's virginity, to have the solitude removed from one's body" (*WD,* 80; *J,* 113).

The oscillation between the brothel fantasy and the memory of her despair on the balcony, between the snake and the prostitute, situates her as both spectator and participant in an initiation where phallic sexuality is worshiped and woman is freed of the isolation and lack of her body. She invokes another, earlier childhood memory as "corroboration" of this way of seeing the world. One day her brother asked her to show him her sex. When she refused, he said "girls could die from not using it, and that hiding it suffocated you and made you seriously ill" (*WD,* 80; *J,* 113). The spectacle of Mlle Barbet's body seems to confirm her brother's dire prediction. Her brother's voice, like the "fraternal image" that Francine sees in the mirror in *The Tranquil Life* and the voice of "virility and truth" that Suzanne hears in Joseph's stories, is the voice of male authority. In an image that recalls Suzanne's pleasure in Monsieur Jo's gaze, the narrator generalizes the power of male authority by saying, as she remembers Mlle Barbet's decaying body: "From the moment a breast had served a man, even by merely allowing him to see it, to take note of its shape, its roundness, its firmness—from the moment a breast was able to nourish the seed of a man's desire, it was saved from withering from disuse" (*WD,* 80; *J,* 114).

While admitting the terror of being consumed that the boa inspired, the narrator appropriates that story to imagine the female body and female sexuality redeemed by the male gaze and desire. In "The Boa," female heterosexuality defined by the phallus is intrinsically linked to a loathing of the female body. The key transition in her fantasy chain of images that allows the narrator to transform the story of the boa into the story of the prostitute and, hence, into a model for female sexuality, is the glorification of crime and the figure of the outlaw. And yet, I would argue, Duras has not written a story of outlaw female sexuality. Her representation of female sexuality is outlaw only in its flamboyant display and excess, without the pretense of monogamy. Far from being deviant, the construction of desire and the deployment of erotic power in this representation remains conventional. Rather than disrupt sexual and social order in this narrative, she imagines a way for woman to fit into the dominant construction of heterosexuality that privileges the phallus and demeans the woman's body.

The early works of Duras are often characterized as realist fiction. *The Sea Wall* and "The Boa" seem to fit that assessment, particularly in narrative structure and the descriptive details of the Indochinese landscape and colonial milieu. The center of interest in these texts, however, is the source and power of stories themselves, the shaping force of fiction. In *The Sea Wall,* the zone of semiconsciousness induced by drugs, alcohol, music, and movies, and sustained in madness, provides escape from the unbearable "real." Fantasy and fiction are cultivated in the zone of semiconsciousness and allow for the free circulation of desire. Fictions confer power. Joseph's stories give him the power to redefine the catastrophes of their life and to capture an audience. His stories also provide a means for Suzanne to understand and define herself.

In "The Boa," the narrator looks to formative stories to understand her sexuality. Most of the narrative is focused on fantasy, on imagination and interpretation, rather than on realist representations. There is a potential tension in these works between the conventions of realism and Duras's explicit attention to fiction and its power to shape meaning. The illusion of an unmediated representation of reality that realist fiction tries to maintain is undermined when the artifice of fiction and the power of interpretation become important thematic concerns.

The Blanks

TRISTA SELOUS

I want to start my investigation of Duras's work by looking at the "blanks," which Gauthier calls "the place of the woman," and which are so crucial, if ill-defined to the view that Duras's writing is "feminine." I shall try to analyse how they are produced and to establish in what ways, if any, they relate to ideas of "femininity." Duras's writing practice has changed considerably over the years, so I shall analyse passages from several texts which mark what I see as different stages. I start with a passage from one of her early novels, *Un barrage contre le pacifique,* which is written in a more conventional style of psychological realism than most of her later work, so to that extent, this passage can serve as a "control," with which the later, more experimental forms can be compared. The passage follows the account of M. Jo's first meeting with Suzanne, Joseph and their mother, and informs the reader as to who M. Jo is, before the story of his pursuit of Suzanne gets under way.

So this was whom they had met.

M. Jo was the only son of a very rich speculator, whose fortune was a paragon of colonial fortunes. He had begun by speculating on plots of land on the outskirts of the largest town in the colony. The growth of the town had been so rapid that in five years he had made sufficient profits to reinvest his gains. Instead of speculating on new plots, he built on them. He built houses to be let at low rents, called "native compartments," which were the first of this type in the colony. These compartments were terraced, they all had little adjoining yards at the back and gave on to the street at the front. They were cheap to build and at that time they answered the needs of a whole class of native shopkeepers. They were very popular. After ten years, compartments of this type were springing up all over the colony. Experience proved, moreover, that they lent themselves very well to the propagation of bubonic plague and cholera. But as only the owners had been informed of the results of the studies that had been commissioned by the colony's governors, the number of compartment tenants continued to grow.

Next M. Jo's father became interested in the rubber planters in the North. The rubber boom was such that many had quickly set themselves up as

From *The Other Woman: Feminism and Femininity in the Works of Marguerite Duras* (New Haven: Yale University Press, 1988), 88–137. Reprinted by permission.

planters, from one day to the next, without knowing anything about it. Their plantations failed. M. Jo's father kept an eye on them. He bought them up. As they were in a bad state, he payed very little for them. Then he appointed managers, got them back in business. Rubber made a lot of money, but too little for his liking. One or two years later, he sold them off at astronomical prices to newcomers chosen preferably from among the least experienced. In most cases, he was able to buy them back within two years.

M. Jo was the pathetically inept child of this inventive man. His very large fortune had only one heir, and that heir had not a flicker of imagination. There lay the weak point of this life, the only definitive one: you cannot speculate on your child. You think you are hatching a little eagle, and what crawls out from under your desk is a cuckoo. And what can you do about it? What steps can you take against this injustice of fate?

He had sent him to Europe to pursue studies for which he was not destined. Stupidity has its own clairvoyance: he took care not to pursue them. When he learned of this, his father brought him back and tried to interest him in a few of his businesses. M. Jo tried in all decency to make up for the injustice to which his father had fallen victim. But it can happen that one is not destined for anything definite, not even for that form of thinly disguised idleness. Nevertheless, he made a decent effort. For, decent, he was; willing, he was. But the problem lay elsewhere. And perhaps he would not have become as stupid as even his father resigned himself to believing he was, if he had not been brought up against the grain. Alone, without a father, without the handicap of that stifling fortune, perhaps he would have been able to amend his nature with more success. But it had never occurred to his father that M. Jo might be the victim of an injustice. He had never seen any injustice other than the one by which he had been struck himself, in his son. And as that fate was organic, irremediable, he could only be saddened by it. He had never discovered the cause of that other injustice to which his son was victim. And yet it was nevertheless one for which he could no doubt have found a remedy. It would perhaps have been enough for him to disinherit M. Jo; M. Jo would then have escaped the too heavy legacy that his inheritance had proved to be. But he had not thought of it. He was intelligent enough. But intelligence has habits of thinking, which prevent it from perceiving the conditions of its own existence.

This was the admirer who fell to the lot of Suzanne, one evening in Ram. It could be said that he fell just as much to the lot of Joseph and their mother.[1]

This passage is written in a style which could be called "commonsense" or "naïve" realism, where the narration purports unproblematically to construct a fictional world in imitation of extratextual "reality." A separate section at the end of its chapter, it forms a break in the unravelling of the story, during which the character and background of M. Jo are established. It sets up M. Jo as a referent in the fantasy of the "real world" which the reader is invited to build up around *Un barrage contre le Pacifique*. The relation of realist fiction to reality is ambiguous; the reader knows that the events and characters described are not "real" in the sense that they do not exist other than as a product of the text, or at least not exactly in the form in which they appear there. Napoleon Bonaparte is a real historical figure and the battle of Borodino actually took place in 1812 but the reader of Leo Tolstoy's *War and Peace,* which describes them both, reads it as a work of fiction set at a particular historical period, whose portrayal of people and events that could be described as "real" may or may not be "accurate." The ambiguity arises out of the way in which the fiction produces a "real world." The discourses it uses and the form of a narrative in the third person are not confined to fiction. They are similar to, or the same as, discourses used in biography or history, for example, where the text is assumed to be "accurately" describing "real" persons and events. This overlapping of discourses allows both "real" and fictional worlds to be rendered intelligible in similar terms, so that the fictional is produced as "real," and constructs a narratee who accepts it as real. The reader is invited to take the place of the narratee whilst reading, although at the same time of course s/he knows that what is recounted is not "real."[2]

In order for realist writing to portray a coherent "reality" purporting to correspond to Reality, the language it uses must not in itself be problematic. So contradictions between or within discourses are avoided, allowing the language to become "transparent" and appear referential or expressive. The above passage is an example of this type of writing. The first part takes the form of a biography, recounting, in chronological order, the stages of the process by which M. Jo's father made his money. The main tense in French is the past historic, which is almost exclusively a written form, used to describe a completed action in the past. It is the tense of History, Biography and Literature, which Roland Barthes describes, in *Le Degré zéro de l'écriture,* as "the ideal tool for all building of universes."[3] The sentences in this part of the passage are simple in structure and relate the events in sequence and without embellishment. The passing of time is marked at appropriate intervals, with notations such as "in five years," "after ten years" and "next." The sequence of events described resembles accounts of the accumulation of wealth by colonialists to be found in both fictional and non-fictional works concerning colonialism, and it is possible to "situate" them both historically, in the first half of the twentieth century, and geographically in what was then Indochina, although the country is not specified other than as "the colony."

The second part of the passage is concerned with M. Jo's character. It describes him in terms of the convention according to which the individual has fixed psychological traits. The narration defines M. Jo in terms of the interaction between his personal "nature" and the context into which he is born and in which he grows up, following the view that human psychology is produced in the action of the individual's environment on certain innate and genetically determined dispositions. M. Jo is the innately stupid son of a very shrewd and wealthy man, rendered even more foolish than he might otherwise have been by the wealth with which he is surrounded. The result is a man who is "decent," "willing," but who is at the same time "pathetically inept." It is in the light of this established character that the reader is invited to understand M. Jo's actions on reading this passage.

The passage then tells the reader/narratee "what happened" and "who M. Jo is" in an uncomplicated way, leaving little room for uncertainty in either case. However, it would be misleading to describe the language as purely "expressive" in effect. It also produces a personalised "point of view," a specific attitude to events and persons on the part of the narrator. The use of third person narration in the past historic has for effect the production of an omniscient narrator, who is outside the story, knows the meaning of each event in relation to [the] whole, and gradually reveals it all to the narratee. The conventions of realist fiction permit such a narrator's intrusion in a more personal capacity into the narration, and examples of "intervention" in the narrative by the narrator are legion. The forms it takes may differ. In *War and Peace,* for example, the narrator launches into long discussions of philosophical questions relating to cause, effect and the individual. In the passage under discussion here, the narrator's presence is undoubtedly felt but this occurs more indirectly, in the ironic tone of the writing.

The ironic tone of the passage is produced at the points of conflict in its discourse. The coherence of the discourse is not seriously threatened, but it is not without cracks. It is the presence of these cracks which creates an implicit criticism of M. Jo's wealthy father and of the whole colonial system within the description of the former's rise to riches.

M. Jo's father's accumulation of wealth is described as "a paragon of colonial fortunes." A "paragon" in its usual sense is something which provides a pattern for other examples of the same type of thing. Then follows the account of how he made his money building houses for the native (colonised) population, houses called "compartments," rather than "apartments," "flats," or "houses," these being words more usually employed to describe the dwelling-places of human beings—those of the colonisers, for example. The exploitative nature of the enterprise is confirmed when we are told that these "compartments" lent themselves very well to the propagation of bubonic plague and cholera. But as only the owners had been informed of the results of the studies that had been commissioned by the colony's governors, the number of compartment tenants continued to grow. The ironic effect is produced here first by the use of "very well" to qualify the way in which the plague and cholera spread in the "compartments," since the usual connotations of the names of these diseases are in direct opposition to anything being "very well." There is further irony in the use of "as," which gives a logical link to the two halves of the sentence. The reader is thus led to infer that it is logical that, if only the owners know that the "compartments" are dangerous, they will not tell the people who might rent them, since such a step would prejudice their chances of making money, even though it might also prevent the deaths of their prospective tenants. The implication is, of course, that to the coloniser, money is more important than the lives of the colonised people.

The story of M. Jo's father's rise continues with the description of how he played on the inexperience and ineptitude of would-be rubber plantation owners, fellow colonialists, encouraging or at least facilitating their failure for his own profit. The whole story is one of exploitation as the source of M. Jo's father's money. And this is the "paragon of colonial fortunes," which others should take note of and follow. The irony then springs from the use of *modèle,* which connotes something good, worthy of imitation, to refer to a story of greed and exploitation.

Our Western capitalist culture carries the idea that wealth accumulated is not to be frittered away by the person who accumulates it, but should instead be reinvested, increased and passed on to the son (*sic*) and heir. This assumption is firmly entrenched in dominant ideology and as there is nothing in the story of M. Jo's father's rise which contradicts it, it will be shared by the narratee—the reader who is constructed by the text. This means there is a certain irony in the description of the wily speculator's "pathetically inept child" for the father is obliged to confer the money he used such ingenuity to acquire on an imbecile who would have been better off without it. Given the teleological nature of the process of accumulating wealth, that is, that its final aim is the foundation of a wealthy dynasty, M. Jo's imbecility and general unworthiness render all the efforts of his father vain as he is obviously incapable of taking over the business. There is irony in the contrast between the narratee's expectations concerning the bestowal of wealth, expectations arising from the context of capitalism, and the impossibility of those expectations being fulfilled, due to a quirk of fate beyond the control even of M. Jo's father: "you cannot speculate on your child." Further ironic effect is produced by the use of "injustice" and "handicap," since these words are usually used to refer to the effects of grinding poverty, such as that of Suzanne's family, rather than to that of a "stifling fortune." Since it is the acquisition of wealth which is usually considered beneficial to the individual, the idea that M. Jo's father could best have ended the injustice by disinheriting his son reverses the convention and disturbs the smoothness of the discourse. Moreover, after the story of M. Jo's father, it is impossible to regard him simply as the victim of injustice, when he also perpetrates it; so there is an ironic disturbance here too.

It is this disturbance of the discourse which sets up the point of view of the narrator. According to Tzvetan Todorov's "principle of pertinence" (*principe de pertinence*), "following which, if an utterance exists, there has to be a reason for it,"[4] unexpected incongruities in a discourse must be interpreted: a "receiver"—hearer or reader—must assume an intention to mean on the part of the utterer. To put this in Lacanian terms, the receiver assumes that the utterance represents a desire on the part of another subject, which has meaning and can be interpreted. In a text, it is what Wayne C. Booth calls the "implied author" who is constructed as occupying the place of the ultimate source of meaning, but this author "speaks" through the narrator. In the case of a third person narration where the narrator's attitude is implied rather than specified, as is the case in *Un barrage contre le Pacifique,* the reader/narratee can easily assume that the author named on the cover and the narrator are the same, so that the narrator and implied author merge. In this passage, then, the reader makes sense of the (albeit slight) contradictions in the discourse by assuming a narrator (who may be Duras), who controls that discourse and is using it to mean, whose desire shapes its form and is present in the conflicts in the discourse of the text.

The production of the narrator is reinforced by the ironic asides of the narration, the generalisations about the nature of things, such as "you cannot speculate on your child," or "intelligence has its habits of thinking, which prevent it from perceiving the conditions of its own existence." Such comments imply a superior knowledge and produce the omniscient narrator as something Lacan terms a *sujet supposé savoir* or subject supposed to know. The narrator is the locus of authority and guarantor of the truth—the "accuracy" in relation to the "real world" both inside and outside the text—of what is being recounted. In Booth's terms, s/he is a reliable narrator.

The narrator is constructed as relating events with a purpose in mind and from a point of view. In this passage, the point of view would seem to be that colonialism fosters the enrichment of the cunning coloniser at the expense of the weak colonised and the foolish in general, plus the view that wealth is not the answer to every problem. The narrator is produced as separate from the characters, M. Jo and his father, and this has the effect of distancing the narratee from them as well. The reader is invited to take the position of the narratee and to look at the characters in the light of the narrator's insights. So the narrator tells the reader what to think, whether or not the latter accepts the offered viewpoint.

The only ambiguity lies in those parts of the passage which are ironic. There is one example of free indirect style, where the narrator's voice and that of M. Jo's father merge: "you think you're hatching a little eagle and what crawls out from under your desk but a cuckoo? And what can you do about it? What defence have you got against this unjust fate?" The narrator is generalising here ("you" is my translation of *on*) from the point of view of those, such as M. Jo's father, who have been smitten by "injustice" in the form of children who are not worthy of them. However, this invitation to see it from M. Jo's father's point of view has an ironic ring to it, as the "unjust fate" follows an account of the injustice perpetrated by him. As with other ironic parts of the passage, the disturbance of the overall point of view of the narration serves to produce an ironic narrator, rather than simply a shift of the point of view of the text to that of M. Jo's father. The shift occurs in only three lines of the whole passage, and is done in free indirect style, which produces both narrator and character at the same time, thus keeping the narrator as an entity separable from the character.

This strengthens the narrator's position as the place from which the text is to be understood. The desire to mean something on the part of the individual narrator, as inferred by the reader/narratee, is both produced by and guarantees the possibility of the latter's interpretation of the text. The reader assumes that events related mean something in relation to each other, that questions will be answered and that s/he will be able to follow the movement of the narrator's desire from the beginning of the text to the end, where the "point" or "meaning" of the text will be graspable.

Un barrage contre le Pacifique ends with the answer to the question "will Suzanne leave the plain and, if so, who with?" Suzanne's desire to leave the plain and how she conceives of doing it are established early in the text: "One day a man would stop, perhaps, why not? because he had caught a glimpse of her by the bridge. Maybe he would be attracted to her and he would ask her to go to the town with him."[5] There follows M. Jo's arrival on the scene and the growing inevitability of his not being the man with whom Suzanne will leave the plain. After the final rejection of M. Jo comes the story of the selling of the diamond, which proves difficult and effects no great change in the lives of the characters. Then, with their mother's death, comes the final solution: Suzanne leaves the plain not with a lover, but with her brother.[6] Her life is irredeemably altered and the question "will she escape from the plain?" has been answered. The ending of the text coming as it does with the answer that she will leave with Joseph makes that question appear to have been the motive force behind the text, giving a retrospective coherence to the whole although many other questions are generated, or potentially generated, by the novel.

The sequence of events provides a structure which assures the reader that s/he is following a progression to an ultimate end. The most immediately obvious reading of works of realist fiction is one which privileges the unfolding of the plot. The reader is invited to read to find out "what happened next" until s/he reaches the end. In *Un barrage contre le Pacifique,* the story is fairly slow-moving and there is a large number of passages which are to a greater or lesser extent extraneous to the progression of the plot, which is itself quite loose. There is the description of "old Bart,"[7] for example, who is a very minor character, or the story of the rise of M. Jo's father cited above, or the description of Suzanne's visit to the cinema.[8] The basic structure of a progression of events ties these diverse passages together. It provides a coherence for the text. However, the reader reflecting on the text, or the critic, who differs from the latter in that s/he writes her/his reflections down, might also extrapolate certain "themes" from the diversity of these passages, inferring a coherent desire motivating the presence of different aspects of the text and seeing them as related to each other in terms of "what they are trying to say." For example, one could link Suzanne's experience of the cinema and the film she sees of lovers kissing to the story of the mother's attempts to build dams against the Pacific, in terms of a theme of the interplay of fantasy and reality. "Old Bart" and M. Jo's father are both examples of corrupt colonialists, and can both be read as part of a general indictment of colonialism, which I would see as one of the themes of the novel.

To sum up then, *Un barrage contre le Pacifique* is a realist novel, which lends itself to being read in a relatively unproblematic way as the coherent manifestation of the desire(s) of a narrator, who can be easily conflated with the implied author. The reader attributes to the author/narrator both knowledge of the psychology of the characters, of the significance of the events described, etc., and a reason for relating them to others. The desire of the author/narrator sometimes appears to be moving in different directions at once, allowing the text to be read in terms of themes as well as plot. The narrator and implied author might sometimes become separate, or, as when free indirect style is used, the narrator might become partially merged with a character. However, overall the text appears coherent and authoritative. It tells the reader what there is to know, that is the plot, the psychology of the characters, and "what the author meant," or "was trying to say" in the text, through its themes, or the point of view of the narration.

In some types of realist fiction, the plot appears as the most important aspect of the narration. In many thrillers, for example, the reader reads for the pleasure of suspense, waiting for the questions posed by the text to be answered by the progression of events. In other texts, the themes will seem more important. This is arguably the case in *Un barrage contre le Pacifique*, where the story in itself is simple and there is little sense of suspense. The plot here seems to be the vehicle which allows certain problems to be explored as diverse in nature as those of relations within the family and the effects of colonialism. The reader or critic can extrapolate such themes from the accounts of events and characters, although it is possible just to read for the plot, which unfolds bit by bit in chronological sequence, from the point of view of an interested, and not entirely detached, observer.

I now want to look at *Moderato cantabile,* which is a very different piece of writing. As opposed to *Un barrage contre le Pacifique*, which recounts events and gives insights, usually through free indirect style, into the psychology of the characters, "in *Moderato cantabile,* not only does it not say what happened, but it may be that nothing happens at all"[9] and, even supposing something is happening, "who can give a name to what happens between strangers, to what is happening now between Anne Desbaresdes and Chauvin?"[10] In this text, according to one critic, Duras refuses "to name, to recount, to entertain, to fill the blanks."[11] It is possible, however, to give a brief reconstruction of the events described, as Jean Mistler does:

> Anne Desbaresdes was a chance witness to a crime of passion in a quayside café, whilst her little boy was having his piano lesson. She goes back to this café several times and questions a man whom she meets there each time. We have the impression that the man knows no more about it than Anne and moreover

that she scarcely listens to what he tells her. After five or six meetings, there has been no action, but we have a vague feeling that the psychological positions have been transformed.[12]

Mistler, as his article clearly shows, is not impressed. But those who are praise Duras's ability to produce silence and "blanks" in her writing. So what is happening in this text, and how does Duras do it?

Perhaps the first point to make is that a large part of *Moderato cantabile* is taken up with a reconstruction of events which culminate in the shooting at the end of the first chapter. This reconstruction is undertaken by two figures, Anne Desbaresdes and Chauvin, neither of whom "know what really happened" and will never be able to know, since one of the protagonists is dead and the other mad. Because of the way in which the text is narrated, this story is always out of reach of the authoritative narration and is equally out of reach of Anne and Chauvin. It has already happened before the chronological point where the text begins and is thus produced as an unattainable object of knowledge a "blank."

However, even in the events actually narrated by the text, there are gaps and silences. I have taken two passages for analysis in order to see how Duras produces effects of silence; the first is representative of the dialogue which makes up much of the text and the second is taken from the section recounting the dinner party, which contains little dialogue, but where a similar process is at work as in the first passage. The first passage is taken from the end of Anne Desbaresdes's first conversation with Chauvin:

The first men came in. The child pushed his way through them, curious, and reached his mother, who pulled him against her in an automatic clasping movement.

"You are Madame Desbaresdes. The wife of the head of Import Export and of Coastal Foundries. You live on Sea Boulevard."

Another siren sounded, quieter than the first, from the other end of the quay. A tugboat came in. The child freed himself, quite roughly, ran off.

"He's learning the piano," she said. "He's got ability, but I must admit, he's very unwilling."

Again to make space for the men entering the café at regular intervals and in very large numbers, he drew a little closer to her. The first clients left. Still more came in. Between them, in the play of their comings and goings, one could see the sun setting in the sea, the sky which was aflame and the child who, on the other side of the quay, was playing all alone at games whose secret was indiscernible at that distance. He was jumping over imaginary obstacles, must have been singing.

"I want so many things at once for that child that I don't know how to go about it, where to begin. And I go about it very badly. I must go home because it is late."

"I have often seen you. I never imagined that one day you would come up here with your child."

The café owner turned up the volume of the radio a little for those of the later clients who had just come in. Anne Desbaresdes turned towards the counter, made a face, accepted the noise, forgot it.

"If you knew all the happiness that one wants for them, as if it were possible. Perhaps it might be better sometimes if they took them away from us. I can't seem to be reasonable about this child."

"You have a beautiful house at the end of Sea Boulevard. A large walled garden."

She looked at him, perplexed, brought back to the present.

"But these piano lessons give me great pleasure," she stated.

The child, harried by the dusk, came back towards them once more. He stayed there contemplating all the people, the clients. The man gestured to Anne Desbaresdes to look outside. He smiled at her.

"Look," he said, "the days are getting longer, longer . . ."

Anne Desbaresdes looked, rearranged her coat carefully, slowly.

"Do you work in this town, Monsieur?"

"In this town, yes. If you come back, I'll try to find out something more and I'll tell it to you."

She lowered her eyes, remembered and grew pale.

"Blood on her mouth," she said, "and he was kissing her, kissing her."

She pulled herself together: "what you said, you were just supposing it?"

"I said nothing."

The sun had sunk so low now that it touched the man's face. His body, standing, leaning slightly on the counter, had already been catching it for some time.

"Having seen it, one can't stop oneself, don't you think, it's almost inevitable?"

"I said nothing," the man repeated. "But I think he aimed for her heart, as she asked him to do."

Anne Desbaresdes groaned. A soft, almost licentious moan came from the woman.

"It's odd, I don't want to go home," she said.

He took up his glass abruptly, finished it at one go, did not answer, turned his eyes away from her.

"I must have drunk too much," she went on, "you see, that's it."

"That's it, yes," said the man.

The café had almost emptied. People came in more rarely. As she washed her glasses, the owner watched them out of the corner of her eye, intrigued, no doubt, at seeing them stay on so long. The child, who had gone back to the door, was contemplating the now silent quayside. Standing in front of the man, turning her back on the harbour, Anne Desbaresdes stayed silent for a long time more. He did not seem to notice her presence.

"It would have been impossible for me not to come back," she said at last.

"I also came back for the same reason as you."[13]

This passage, like the rest of *Moderato cantabile,* is written in the past historic, constructor of universes and of the observer who records them. However, unlike the passage from *Un barrage contre le Pacifique* which I have discussed above, it does not produce a narrator with a point of view in the sense of an attitude, such as irony, with regard to what is narrated. The discourse is not disturbed in the way that it was in the previous passage by conflicting meanings. This makes the style appear almost hyper-realist, like the transcription of a photograph. It appears to be a simple description of the events, a recording, as if by a kind of verbal camera, with no comment on the part of the narrator. This allows the language to appear "transparent," with none of the colouring or "distortion" which can be read into a text where the reader infers a narrator with a "personality" who is directing the former's perception of events.

So the "impersonal narrator" is reduced almost to transparency, disappearing into the language, only seeming to encroach on the recording of events at points of uncertainty ("whose secret was indiscernible at that distance," "must have been singing"). This encroachment does set up a point of view, but in a spatial sense. The passage is written in such a way as to make it possible for the reader to construct a fantasised image of the café by the quay, with workers coming and going, and where two people, Anne Desbaresdes and Chauvin, are talking by the bar. This is all put forward with little or no apparent mediation or interpretation on the part of the narrator. An unthreatened illusion of reference is maintained throughout.

Anne and Chauvin are produced as "real people," seen as if by a camera. But "real people" are more than surfaces; Anne and Chauvin have names, a vaguely defined social status, and by realist implication, psychology and desires. The main thread running through the passage is the dialogue between them. Nevertheless, their conversation does not proceed unproblematically. In the first half of the passage they do not appear to be talking about the same thing. Anne is talking about her child, whilst Chauvin is talking about Anne. Furthermore, the dialogue is punctuated by descriptions of the child's actions, the café owner turning up the radio, or Anne's own actions. These actions are, for the most part, written in the past historic, the tense used to mark the speech of Anne and Chauvin, the tense of definite, completed action. The effect of this is that the utterances of Anne and Chauvin and the actions or descriptions which punctuate them are given equal importance and appear to follow each other chronologically. The difference this makes to the flow of the narration can be seen when the above passage is compared to the following exchange between Suzanne and M. Jo in *Un barrage contre le Pacifique,* when M. Jo is trying to get Suzanne to open the door and let him see her washing.

> —"To think that you're completely naked, to think that you're completely naked," he repeated in a toneless voice.
> "Some bargain," said Suzanne. "If we swapped places, I wouldn't want to see you."

When she pictured M. Jo, without his diamond, his hat, or his limousine, walking along in a swimming costume, for example, on the beach at Ram, Suzanne's anger grew all the greater.

"Why don't you go bathing at Ram?"

M. Jo recovered his cool a little and pushed (against the door) less hard.

"I am not allowed to bathe in the sea," he said, as firmly as he could.

Suzanne was soaping herself, happily. He had bought her some lavender scented soap and ever since she had been bathing two or three times a day so that she could cover herself in perfume. The scent of the lavender floated out to M. Jo and, by allowing him to follow the stages of Suzanne's bathing more easily, rendered his torture all the more subtle.

"Why aren't you allowed to bathe?"

"Because I have a weak constitution and bathing in the sea tires me. Open up, my sweet little Suzanne . . . just one second . . ."

"That's not true, it's because you're ugly."

She could imagine him, pressed up against the door, swallowing everything she said to him because he knew he would win.

"One second, just one second . . ."[14]

In this exchange the dialogue is interrupted by two fairly long passages, the one beginning "When she pictured . . ." and the other beginning "Suzanne was soaping herself, happily." However, both these passages have their main verbs in the imperfect tense, the tense of indefinite time. This means that the actions described in the imperfect do not interrupt the actions described in the past historic, but can be read as happening at the same time, providing a background for the words. In the *Moderato cantabile* passage this is not the case. The result is that the reader/narratee assumes a gap between two parts of the dialogue in which, for example, the café-owner turns up the radio, Anne turns towards the bar, makes a face, resigns herself to the noise and forgets it, before speaking. This produces a gap in the dialogue, when neither speaks while these actions are performed. Thus a dialogue full of silences can be produced without the narration having to make this explicit; the silences arise in the spaces between the utterances of the figures, made by the intercalation of narration in the past historic between instances of direct speech.

The passage also produces effects of silence in what the speakers actually do say, by creating the impression that there is something they are not saying, or are avoiding saying. In the first part of the passage it would appear that what Anne and Chauvin each say bears no relation to the words of the other. Alone, this section of the dialogue would appear absurd(ist). The speeches of Anne and Chauvin would appear to be lacking in "pertinence"; the reason for their existence would at best be obscure in terms of accepted conventions of dialogue, which uphold the view that when two people talk together their utterances have some relevance to each other. For here, whilst each independently appears to be capable of coherent thought, they seem unable to follow each other's drift. However, after Anne asks Chauvin if he works in the town, the conversation picks up and each speech appears to be connected in some way to the previous one. Although the connexions may not be immediately obvious, the reader can assume that when Chauvin says, "I'll try to find out something more," he is referring to the shooting, that the memory of the latter event makes Anne turn pale and that it is the man's kissing of the dead woman to which she refers when she says "Having seen it." "One can't stop oneself" can be referred back to a previous speech of Anne's: "I've thought about it more and more since yesterday evening . . . since my child's piano lesson. I couldn't have stopped myself from coming today, you see."[15] "It" here refers to the shooting. After Chauvin has said he will try to find out more, both figures appear to be talking about the incident, after the disconnected conversation they had been having before. The reader can then reasonably infer that that shooting is of interest to both of them, following the idea that these are "real people," whose utterances are not completely random. Continuing in this vein, the reader can also assume that Chauvin's words about the shooting have the effect of making Anne groan in a way which was "almost licentious," since the groan immediately follows them. The proximity of the two suggests cause and effect. The reader might then assume that Anne's loss of desire to go home is also something to do with what has just been said and the "almost licentious" sound that she has just made. Because, with a little effort, the reader can find or invent a "pertinence" in this part of the dialogue, s/he can continue to read Anne and Chauvin as "real people," and assume that there is something which Anne is trying to justify when she says, "I must have drunk too much . . . That's it," even if it is totally unstated what "it" might be. Such an assumption is also possible in relation to Chauvin's words: "I also came back for the same reason as you." No reason has been given but "real people" have reasons for doing things, or say they do, or even say they have not when they really have. So runs the convention. From the vantage point of the all-seeing, but not necessarily all-comprehending eye of the narrator, the reader may not know exactly what the reason that Chauvin refers to is; but since the latter apparently does, s/he assumes it exists.

It is then by compelling the reader to make the associations necessary to find the "pertinence" of the utterances attributed to Anne and Chauvin that the text produces an effect of things left unsaid. The reader supplies the associative links, but notices they are missing. With the hindsight of Anne and Chauvin's exchange on the subject of the shooting, the reader can also infer a suppression of this topic during the disconnected part of the conversation, since their willingness to talk about it has apparently carried over from an earlier exchange. Perhaps, the reader might think, it was that suppression which made their conversation so fragmented and disconnected. Perhaps not. We cannot know for sure.

The second passage from *Moderato cantabile* that I want to discuss also relies on the reader's desire to find the "pertinence" of the words s/he reads.

However, here it is not the utterances of the figures in the text which require interpretation, it is the narration.

> The magnolia petal is smooth, with a naked grain. The fingers crush it, tearing it, then, forbidden, stop, lie on the table once more, wait, adopt an attitude of composure, which is illusory. For one has noticed. Anne Desbaresdes tries a smile of apology for having been unable to do otherwise, but she is drunk and her face takes on the shameless appearance of confession. The look grows heavier, impassive, but it has already painfully recovered from all astonishment. One has always expected this.
>
> Anne Desbaresdes drinks another glass of wine all at once her eyes half closed. She has already reached the point of being unable to do otherwise. She discovers, in drinking, the confirmation of what had been until then an obscure desire and a shameful consolation in this discovery.
>
> Other women drink in their turn, they likewise raise arms which are naked, delectable, irreproachable, but are those of wives. On the beach, the man whistles a song heard in the afternoon in a quayside café.
>
> The moon has risen and with it here is the beginning of the cold, late-coming night. It is not impossible that the man is cold.[16]

Here the first link to be made is between the magnolia flower worn by Anne as a corsage at the dinner-party and the one Chauvin has described her as wearing when he saw her before:

> "You are resting your elbows on the grand piano. Between your breasts, which are naked beneath your dress, is that magnolia flower."
>
> Anne Desbaresdes, very attentively, listened to this story.
>
> "Yes."
>
> "When you lean over, the flower brushes against the outline of your breasts. You have pinned it carelessly, too high. It is an enormous flower, you chose it at random, too large for you. Its petals are still hard, in fact it reached its full flowering just the night before."[17]

In Chauvin's description, the magnolia is associated with Anne's breasts. The reader is encouraged to infer Chauvin's sexual interest in Anne from his clear memory of how the flower touched her breasts. The magnolia flower worn by Anne during the dinner-party scene carries the weight of this earlier magnolia with it. The very use of the word "magnolia," followed by "naked grain," echoing the earlier "naked breasts," is almost bound to recall for the reader the sexual connotations of the earlier conversation, whether or not it reminds her/him of the actual words previously used. The magnolia has become the symbol for something sexual, for Chauvin's desire, which has never been explicitly articulated. Chauvin's sexual desire is a fantasy of the reader's, an inference, unstated. The magnolia refers to it as something which has been kept silent, whose articulation is absent, left "blank." The same process is at work with the wine, which can be read as a symbol for Anne's (sexual) desire, having potentially acquired this meaning (to add to the ancient bacchanalian symbolism that it carries amongst others) in the preceding chapters. And in this case, the symbolic value of the wine is confirmed. Reinforcing the impression of the presence of Anne's desire, the reader is then told that other women besides Anne "likewise raise arms which are naked, delectable, irreproachable, but are those of wives." The "but" marks them out as different from, even inferior to, Anne. Anne is also a wife, the reader might remember, but straight after these words comes a reference to the man on the beach and the "quayside café." Although this sentence brings a complete break with the last in terms of the place and person it refers to, because it is in the same paragraph it appears to be linked to what precedes it and the reader assumes the connexion.

At this point the reader, if s/he is going to be able to "make sense" out of what is being recounted, must almost inevitably infer that the man is Chauvin, that Anne's desire has something to do with him and their meetings in the café, that that desire is sexual in some way and that it makes her different from the other women, because it is for a man who is not her husband. None of this is stated; instead it is left "blank," to be more or less unconsciously assumed by the reader.

The other notable "blank" to be found in this passage is around the use of *on* ("one"). In the preceding part of the chapter, *on* recurs, excusing Anne for lateness.[18] In the passage cited above, *on* has noticed Anne fingering the magnolia and becomes the source of a look and an opinion. *On* has become some-one specific. This is, of course, inference on the part of myself as reader, but it is an inference which nothing contradicts and which everything suggests. Later, at the end of the chapter, *on* will look into the child's room and see Anne lying on the floor. *On* here takes the form of *une ombre* ("a shadow").[19] It would be almost perverse not to assume that *on* is Anne's husband but he is never mentioned by name. He is without any explicit existence in the text other than as *on* (and when Chauvin refers to him) but because the reader can infer him as the referent of *on,* he is constructed as a man to whom reference has been avoided, evaded, or perhaps suppressed. He has become a "blank."

In *Moderato cantabile,* "blanks" may be produced by means of the juxtaposition of sentences which then seem to be connected, as above and, as I have indicated earlier, in dialogue. Alternatively, they may be produced by the use of symbolism, as in the case of the magnolia or the wine, where the signifiers *magnolia* and *vin* both become loaded with resonances, so that their significance seems to the reader to exceed the possibility of its articulation and so becomes constructed as inarticulable. The "blanks" are thus those elements of the reader's fantasy which the text produces by means other than explicit articulation. They are created through the operations of the reader's desire to "make sense" of the text. The reader can only embark upon such an enterprise if s/he assumes that there is a sense to make, that is, if s/he assumes the presence of an effort of coherent representation, a desire on the part of the author to mean something by the text,[20] in terms of which the elements s/he is given do "go together."

Of course, most, if not all works of fiction require some work of inference on the part of the reader. For example, in the passage from *Un barrage contre le Pacifique,* the reader's inference is required to produce the irony of the narrator; and other authors besides Duras have used similar techniques to create an effect of "blanks." A notable example of such an effect can be seen in Alain Robbe-Grillet's *Le Voyeur,* in which the reader is invited to understand that the central character, Mathias, has committed a murder which is not actually recounted. Like *Moderato cantabile,* this is a third person narration. However, it is entirely in free indirect style, which gives the reader/narratee insight into Mathias's thought processes throughout. This allows the reader to explain the "blank" in terms of Mathias's psychology: he has suppressed the murder and the text can be read as an attempt to render his confused, disavowing thought processes.

In *Moderato cantabile,* the reader might be able to understand the "blanks" in dialogue in psychological terms but the narration itself is too impersonal and detached to make its "blanks" appear effects of a personalised narrator's suppression of things s/he does not want to describe, or think about. However, the reader's confidence that the elements of the narrative do "make sense" is aided by apparently transparent reference to the "real world." And the story is clearly not out of control; on the contrary, it is fixed and finished in the past historic, seen through the eyes of this impartial narrator, told in the most apparently impersonal of language. Because of the apparent impartiality of the narration, and thus its authority as source of objective knowledge, the reader is not led to infer that the "blanks" are the result of any deliberate omission of information. The narration appears simply to record what there is to tell, rather than having been "edited down" from some fuller original version. The result is that where things are left unsaid, it seems that they are in some sense unsayable.

Le Ravissement de Lol V. Stein is a first person narration, narrated by someone who turns out, on page 74, to be Jacques Hold, lover of Tatiana Karl and eventually of Lol. Here, the most obvious "blank" is Lol herself, and this is explicitly stated: "To know nothing about Lol was already to know her. One could, it seemed to me, know still less, less and less about Lol V. Stein."[21] And this is the narrator's aim:

> Like one parched, I long to drink the misty and insipid milk of the words that come from Lol V. Stein's mouth, to be part of the thing lied by her. Let her carry me off, let the affair at last turn out differently from now on, let her grind me up with the rest, I shall be servile, let hope lie in being ground up with the rest, being servile.[22]

The story the narrator tells is of his desire for Lol and his attempt, doomed ultimately to failure, to achieve the end described above. Lol is constructed as the focal point of the text because the questions the text asks are: who is Lol? and what does she want? These questions, as is clear from the beginning, are unanswerable. The narrator makes constant reference to the unknowable nature of Lol V. Stein, "her burnt up being . . . her ravaged nature."[23] She herself is largely silent. In areas where she might be expected to manifest personality, or desires, such as in the organisation of her house and garden, the only evidence of individuality is in her extreme desire to conform:

A strict order reigned in Lol's house at U. Bridge [. . .] The arrangement of the bedrooms, of the sitting-room, was a faithful reproduction of that seen in shop windows; the layout of the garden, which Lol took care of, reproduced that of the other gardens in U. Bridge. Lol was copying, but whom? the others, all the others, the greatest possible number of other people.[24]

Jacques Hold begins her story with a "false version that Tatiana Karl tells and that which I have invented about the night of the Casino at T. Beach. Starting from these, I shall tell my story of Lol V. Stein."[25] The authority of a large part of the text is then in doubt. Those parts that appear authoritative are those which recount things that happen in the presence of the narrator. These are written in the present tense, which gives them a certain immediacy and presence, and thus authority. The narrator is not lying or inventing, he is describing. However, his knowledge is limited to what he can see; the rest is supposition. For example, when he and Lol are talking about Tatiana in the tea rooms in Green Town:

I can see that a dream has almost been reached. Flesh is tearing, bleeding, awakening. She is trying to listen to an inner tumult, she does not succeed, she is overcome by the realization, albeit incomplete, of her desire. She blinks rapidly under the effects of light which is too strong. I stop looking at her for the time that the very long ending of this moment lasts.[26]

What is "happening," what is of interest to the narrator, is invisible, as it is to the reader, whose desire for knowledge, at least when s/he adopts the place of the narratee in an unselfconscious reading, is hooked into that of the narrator as it is constructed by the text. It is Lol's "inner tumult," which remains always beyond the narrator's grasp because he cannot see it.

A kind of voyeurism pervades *Le Ravissement de Lol V. Stein,* and the voyeur can never see all, is never participant in the action, does not even want to be. Jacques Hold watches Lol but she is unknowable, even her appearance is "bland," somehow indefinite. Lol in her turn watches Michael Richardson and Anne-Marie Stretter, or Jacques Hold and Tatiana Karl but she loses sight of the first couple when they leave the casino at T. Beach, and all she sees of the second is what is visible from the field behind the hotel. Even then, what she wants to see is herself being forgotten, herself as an absence, a "blank."

Like Anne and Chauvin, Lol is trying to reconstruct a lost event, that of the ball at T. Beach. But when she and Jacques Hold visit the T. Beach casino, nothing happens. For the reader/narratee, the moment is constructed as lost forever yet its effects are still present in Lol. It is present and not, produced as an absence, an unattainable knowledge, because it is present only as a memory.

Whereas, in *Moderato cantabile,* the writing itself seems to leave gaps where the reader must infer connexions, the narration of *Le Ravissement de Lol V. Stein* makes the necessary connexions in the sequence of events and provides a certain amount of "psychology." Jean Bedford is "easy to reassure,"[27] Jacques Hold interprets the thoughts and feelings of Lol and Tatiana during a conversation between the three of them:

> "You frighten me Lol."
> Lol is surprised. Her surprise strikes exactly the fear that Tatiana is not admitting to. She has uncovered the lie. It's done. She asks gravely:
> "What are you frightened of Tatiana?"
> Suddenly Tatiana is no longer hiding anything. But without admitting the real meaning of her fear.
> "I don't know."
> Lol looks around the sitting-room once more and explains to Tatiana a different thing from the one Tatiana would have liked to know. She returns, Tatiana is caught in her own trap, to the happiness of Lol V. Stein.
> "But I didn't want anything, you understand, Tatiana, I didn't want any of what there is, of what happens. Nothing stays."
> "And if you had wanted it, wouldn't it be the same now?"
> Lol considers and her air of reflection, her forgetful pretence has the perfection of artistry. I know she is saying the first thing that comes into her head:
> "It's the same. On the first day it was the same as it is now. For me."[28]

Jacques Hold tells the reader what he knows, but because he is a figure in the text, his knowledge is constructed as limited and lacking the automatic authority of the third person narration. Even before he introduces himself, the first person narration is full of uncertainty although, because the identity of the narrator is in doubt (it could even be the implied author), the limits of the narrator's knowledge and authority are less clearly defined. Jacques Hold interprets, but he is fallible. With Tatiana Karl, Pierre Beugner, or Jean Bedford, he seems to be able to fill in the psychological details, interpreting their words and giving the reader insights into their hidden meanings. With Lol, on the other hand, his insights are always into the limitations of the possibility of insight. For example:

She snuggles against me again, shuts her eyes, keeps silent, attentively. Her contentment breathes deeply at my side. No sign of her difference under my hand, in my sight. And yet, and yet. Who is there at this moment, so near and so far, what prowling ideas keep coming to visit her, by night, by day, in all lights? at this very moment? At this moment when I might believe her to be in this train, next to me, as other women would be?[29]

Lol is different from "other women," "Tatiana Karl, for example."[30] For her difference to be felt, for her to be produced as a "blank," the rest of the text must be comparatively "full." And so it is. Some details the reader might wish to speculate on are absent, such as the names of Lol's children, for example, but, like the number of Lady Macbeth's children, such information is not constructed as missing. The reader does not need to know such things and is in no way encouraged to ponder on them. In *Moderato cantabile* the psychology and the connections between descriptions implicitly produced by the realist narrative are perceived as "missing" or "suppressed," because otherwise the narration seems so authoritative and unproblematically transparent. Here, however, the psychology and connexions are present, just as might be expected in a realist text, narrated in the first person by a narrator closely involved with the other figures. Jacques Hold even has insights into Lol's psyche, and describes it as having a certain coherence. That coherence, however, is the coherence of absence, for the reader is told that what is absent in Lol is suffering and the meaningfulness of "personality." It is the absence which is Lol which is the object of the narrator's interest and the answer to the questions posed by the text, which thus appears to be constructed around a "blank."

Le Vice-consul, like *Le Ravissement de Lol V. Stein,* is apparently constructed around absence personified. This time it is in three different figures: the beggar-woman, Anne-Marie Stretter and the eponymous hero. The interplay of points of view from which this novel is narrated is more complex than that of those texts I have discussed so far for although the narration is primarily in the third person, the narrator of the story of the beggar-woman is Peter Morgan, who is writing his version of her life. This novel also resembles *Moderato cantabile* and *Le Ravissement de Lol V. Stein* in the great importance it gives to events which occur before the chronological point where the narration begins, these events being the actions of the vice-consul at Lahore and the journey of the beggar-woman from Battambang to Calcutta. As in the other two novels, much of the text is taken up by the attempts of figures such as Peter Morgan and Charles Rossett to reconstruct what happened.

The narration progresses to a large extent through dialogue, particularly during the reception at the French embassy, where there is much discussion of and interest in the vice-consul and/or Anne-Marie Stretter, often on the part of those simply designated as *on.* As in *Le Ravissement de Lol V. Stein,* the effect of "blanks" is produced through the interest shown by some figures in the text in others about whom nothing can ultimately be known. Nothing can be known about the beggar-woman because she is mad; her memory is "obliterated," she does not speak any recognisable language, but merely sings in what may or may not be the language of Savannakhet, Laos, and repeats the vocable "Battambang." She cannot be questioned, she can only be invented and this is Peter Morgan's project.

The vice-consul can and does speak, but he cannot explain himself. This is made clear fairly early on in the text, when Charles Rossett reads the vice-consul's letter to the ambassador, in which he says:

> I cannot explain myself, either concerning what I did at Lahore, or as to the why of this refusal. No outside authority, nor those of our administration, could really be interested, I think, in what I would say. The administration should not see in this refusal either mistrust or disdain with regard to anybody. But I shall simply limit myself here to stating that I find it impossible to give a comprehensible account of what happened at Lahore.[31]

The mystery is established, never to be resolved, at least, not explicitly. Moreover, the vice-consul's actions, his random shooting of lepers in the gardens of Shalimar, are often referred to simply by the name of the place where he perpetrated the act, Lahore. In this way, the name Lahore comes to act both as a symbol for the vice-consul's inexplicable psychological state—"One thinks: He had to see Lahore to be sure of Lahore? Ah! In this town he used a cruel language"[32]—and also as a euphemism for his actions, which are thus constructed as too awful, or impossible, to name, as in the following dialogue between Charles Rossett and the vice-consul:

> "What do people say? That the worst is what?"
> "Lahore."
> "It's so repellent, Lahore, that nothing else can be found to compare it with?"
> "People can't help themselves . . . I'm sorry to say this to you, but one cannot understand Lahore, however hard one tries."
> "That's true," said the vice-consul.[33]

The vice-consul himself, like those of his actions which are designated by the name Lahore, is constructed as repellent and incomprehensible. When he walks in the gardens in front of the ambassador's office, "Other people come out and walk through the gardens. It is midday. No one comes up to him."[34] The ambassador tells Charles Rossett: "We have staying with us at the moment a charming young English friend who cannot stand the sight of the vice-consul of Lahore . . . It's not fear exactly, it's a sort of uneasiness . . . People avoid him, yes, I admit it . . . I avoid him a little."[35] The vice-consul makes a hole in the social scene wherever he goes. At the reception at the embassy he talks to Charles Rossett, the ambassador and the Spanish vice-consul's wife, but all with apparently little enthusiasm and with total incomprehension on the part of his interlocutors. The sole exception to this lack of interest and understanding comes in his conversation with Anne-Marie Stretter. He has already declared to Charles Rossett that he loves her and waits all evening to dance with her. When finally he does so, she seems to understand him as no one else has; but what she understands is unclear:

> "I would like you to say that you see the inevitable side of Lahore. Answer me."
> She does not reply.
> "It is very important that you should see it, even for a very short moment."
> She backs away slightly, startled. She thinks she ought to smile. He does not smile. She is also trembling now.
> "I don't know how to say . . . On your file there is the word impossible. Is that the word this time?"
> He remains silent. She asks again:
> "Is that the word? Answer me . . ."
> "I don't know myself, I'm trying to find it with you."
> "Perhaps there is another word?"
> "That is no longer the problem."
> "I can see the inevitable side of Lahore," she says. "I could already see it yesterday, but I didn't know it."
> "That is all."[36]

Because Anne-Marie Stretter seems able to see what the vice-consul means, the reader can assume that he does in fact mean something. However, that something is "blank," inexpressible in words, but understandable in other ways, at least by certain people such as Anne-Marie Stretter. In order to "make sense" of what is going on, the reader will try to understand the inexpressible also, following the clues that s/he is given in the text such as the vice-consul's interest in leprosy, the *bonheur gai* ("joyful happiness") he experienced at Montfort, or any of the other details to be gleaned about the vice-consul, either from the latter's speeches or from the suppositions of others.

At the same time, Anne-Marie Stretter becomes constructed as being in touch with this inexpressible. Like the vice-consul, she has already been the object of a certain amount of speculation. At the beginning of the account of the reception at the embassy, we are told:

> The woman from Calcutta intrigues people. No one really knows how she occupies her time, she mainly receives people here, very little at home, in her residence which dates from the days of the first trading-posts, on the banks of the Ganges. Nevertheless, she occupies herself somehow. Is it by eliminating the other possible occupations that one decides that she reads? Yes. After the time spent playing tennis, and the time for walking, what else would she do, shut up at home?[37]

What indeed? The reader's speculation is invited and the missing answer is thus constructed as a "blank." Later, when they are dancing together, Anne-Marie Stretter affirms her understanding of and allegiance to the vice-consul:

> "I know who you are," she says. "We do not need to know each other any better. Do not be mistaken."
> "I am not mistaken."
> "I take life lightly," her hand tries to withdraw itself, "that's what I do, everyone is right, for me, everyone is completely, profoundly right."
> "Don't try to go back on what you have said, there's no longer any point."
> "That's true."
> "You are with me."
> "Yes."
> "At this moment," he pleads, "be with me. What did you say?"
> "Nothing important."
> "We are going to part."
> "I am with you."
> "Yes."
> "I am with you here completely, as with no one else, here this evening, in India."[38]

Here are two people who seem to understand one another. Anne-Marie Stretter knows "who the vice-consul is" and does so by knowing very little about him, other than what he did at Lahore. The reader is invited to infer that her knowledge is unformulated and primarily sympathetic, a supposition made stronger when she says to him "I am with you." Later, in answer to the question, "In fact, who was the vice-consul from Lahore like?" Anne-Marie Stretter replies, "Me."[39] Her dancing with the vice-consul and her affirmation that she understands and is sympathetic to him, sets Anne-Marie Stretter apart from the other figures, who do not understand him at all and mostly avoid him when possible. She is in the same category as he, different from the rest, linked by a bond of tacit, "blank" understanding. She is also singled out by all the male figures, except for the director of the European Circle, as an object of sexual interest. But the reader is given little direct insight into her psyche. She does not speak much and when she does, other than to the vice-consul, she appears distant and barely involved in the conversation. She spends a lot of time asleep. Michael Richard explains her attraction for men in the following terms: "And what if the vice-consul from Lahore was just that, one of those men who seek out this woman, in whose presence they believe oblivion will come?"[40] This is reminiscent of Lol V. Stein, whose attraction for Jacques Hold lay in her ungraspable "blandness," in which everything is "ground up." Like Lol, Anne-Marie Stretter is "bland" and distant. She is unknowable and ungraspable.

In *Moderato cantabile* and *Le Ravissement de Lol V. Stein,* the narration seemed to be "uttered" from fixed points: in the former, it was the all-seeing eye of the narrator, who could, however, only know what was visible; in the latter it was Jacques Hold, who observed or invented the story of Lol V. Stein. In *Le Vice-consul,* the point from which the text is narrated shifts and is not always easily defined. For example, in the following extract from the account of the reception at the embassy, much of the information is conveyed in free indirect style by the undefined *on,* or by one of the guests. *On dit* can be trans-lated variously into English as "they say," "people say," "it is said," "someone says," or "one says," and, as none of these will do for all the instances of *on* in this passage, I have had to translate it in two different ways, "someone" and "one," which alters the effect of the original French.

> Someone says: Look, there he is, there's Michael Richard . . . don't you know?
>
> Michael Richard is in his thirties. His elegance draws people's attention as soon as he comes in. He looks around for Anne-Marie Stretter, finds her, smiles at her.
>
> Someone says: Don't you know that for two years . . . all Calcutta knows about it.
>
> Near Charles Rossett the whistling voice: he has come from the other end of the buffet, a glass of champagne in his hand.
>
> "You look very preoccupied."
>
> Someone says: He's still here, the vice-consul, look how late he's staying.
>
> Someone thinks: So he had to see Lahore to be sure of Lahore? Ah! In this town he used a cruel language.
>
> Don't say anything to him, thinks Charles Rossett, stay on the alert. No doubt he has not yet seen Michael Richard, anyway, what does it matter? What does he see? Her, you would think, only her.
>
> "I want some champagne," says Charles Rossett, "since I've been here I've been drinking too much . . ."
>
> One thinks of him in interrogatory terms. That woman's bicycle, Anne-Marie Stretter's, how does it appear to you?
>
> One hears the reply: I have nothing to say about the reasons . . .
>
> One muses: And when he was confirmed in the belief he had held before see-ing Lahore as to what Lahore was, he called death down upon Lahore.
>
> A woman: The priest says that God provides the explanation if one prays to him. Someone laughs.
>
> "You'll see," says the vice-consul to Charles Rossett, "here drunkenness is always the same."
>
> They drink. Anne-Marie Stretter is in the salon next door with George Crawn, Michael Richard and a young Englishman who came in with him. Charles Rossett will know where she is until the end of the night.[41]

In this passage, the inferred origin of the words jumps around from *on* to Charles Rossett, to the vice-consul, to the narrator. The first three instances of *on,* where *on* speaks, could be inferred by the reader to be remarks made by unspecified guests at the reception watching the proceedings, who are not intimate friends of the Stretters. However, the reader/narratee will be drawn to the assumption that the *on* who "thinks," "hears," or "muses" is someone who has spoken with the vice-consul, who knows his story and is interested in it; someone fairly specific. S/he may well be led to speculate who it might be. Could it be Charles Rossett, who has seen the vice-consul with Anne-Marie Stretter's bicycle? Perhaps so, as the third person narration often seems privy to his thoughts, as it is to those of Peter Morgan. Too specific to be impersonal, *on* must be a person with a name; but that name is missing. It has become a "blank."

As well as the identity of *on,* the reader might speculate as to the meaning of the words attributed to "a woman." Following the "pertinence principle," s/he might well assume that they are of relevance to the previous thoughts attributed to *on,* which are about the vice-consul. However, no clues are given here. If the reader infers that there is a link, it is left unstated by the detached narration, and thus constructed as "suppressed," unsayable or "blank."

Le Vice-consul is a third person narration, but it does not hold the figures it portrays at equal distance. Like *Le Ravissement de Lol V. Stein,* it constructs certain figures such as the beggar-woman, Anne-Marie Stretter, the vice-consul, as objects of interest of others, for Peter Morgan, Charles Rossett, and *on.* The first three are all linked with each other in various ways throughout the text and also with India, to which they appear to have a special relation. The beggar-woman walks and walks until she comes to Calcutta, where suddenly, "she stays."[42] She becomes associated with the lepers: "Right next to her sleeping body are those of the lepers,"[43] and it is she whom Peter Morgan follows and writes about as part of his attempt to "grasp the suffering of Calcutta, to throw himself into it, so that it might be done and his ignorance cease with the grasping of suffering."[44]

The beggar-woman is constructed as quite different and separate from the British and French colonisers. Her story is told separately from that of the white figures, and when she does appear in the rest of the text, she is mad, her speech means nothing, she owns nothing to give her an identity the Europeans can understand. The latter react to her in different ways. Peter Morgan apparently copes with her by trying to reconstruct her story, Charles Rossett, when he meets her on the island of the Prince of Wales Hotel, is horrified and scuttles back into the enclosure where only whites are allowed. Both are affected by her strangeness and incomprehensibility, but neither can just accept it. They either flee or try to rationalise it.

Anne-Marie Stretter also seems interested in her, but differently so. It is she who identifies the language of the beggar-woman's song as perhaps that of Savannakhet, from where they both have come, down the Mekong and thence to Calcutta. Anne-Marie Stretter leaves water out for the lepers and the beggar-woman during the monsoon and the latter follows her to the islands. In Peter Morgan's book both of them will figure. They seem to coexist peacefully, to their mutual benefit.

The vice-consul is linked to India and to Anne-Marie Stretter by his actions in Lahore. In his conversation with the "Director" of the European Circle, who repeats everything he tells him, he says of his youth at Neuilly:

> The thing was, Director, I was waiting for India, I was waiting for you, I did not yet know it. Whilst waiting, at Neuilly, I was clumsy. I broke lamps. Say: the lamps broke and fell. I heard them smash in the empty corridors. You can say: already, at Neuilly, you understand?[45]

Already, in Neuilly, the vice-consul apparently felt things that were to crystallise in Lahore. His breaking of lamps is a forerunner to his smashing mirrors in Lahore; in his youth he is destined for India.

The other thing he does in Lahore is to shoot lepers. Leprosy seems to be a preoccupation amongst Calcutta's white inhabitants (we never hear about the rest). One woman has to be sent back to Europe because she is afraid she has leprosy, and lepers are discussed at the reception. For example, "Did you know that lepers burst when hit like sacks full of dust?"[46] The vice-consul describes to Anne-Marie Stretter the impossibility of explaining his actions at Lahore in terms of leprosy:

> "Why do you speak to me of leprosy?"
> "Because I have the impression that if I tried to tell you what I would like to be able to tell you, everything would dissolve into dust . . ."[47]

Later he says to the Spanish vice-consul's wife: "I want leprosy, rather than being frightened of it."[48] Through constant reference to it, leprosy acquires symbolic value as a kind of dreadful absolute, to which different relations are possible. Most of white society avoids it and fear of it is usual amongst new arrivals. However, the vice-consul desires it, Anne-Marie Stretter and the begger-woman coexist with it. Indeed, the beggar-woman has gone beyond its reach: "Nothing more can happen to her, leprosy itself . . ."[49]

Apart from the story of the beggar-woman, the heat and leprosy are the most salient features of India mentioned in the text. Like leprosy, India is beyond the grasp of the whites, who find comfort in re-creating "France in India."[50]

Since neither the beggar-woman nor Anne-Marie Stretter are afraid of leprosy in the way that most of white society is, they appear to have a different relation to India as well. Peter Morgan wants to grasp "India's suffering" by writing, whereas the beggar-woman, with her terrible life, is past all suffering; Anne-Marie Stretter accepts it and sleeps; the vice-consul has plunged himself into it. Each of these three characters is built around what is constructed as an impossibility of articulation, the "blank" of suffering India, and through them India itself becomes a vast "blank," which Europeans, in the shapes of Peter Morgan and Charles Rossett, can struggle to render intelligible and articulate, but which must always elude them: "Boredom, here, is a feeling of colossal abandonment, of a size with India itself, the country sets the tone"[51] and "You know, India is a bottomless pit of indifference, in which everything is swallowed up."[52]

So *Le Vice-consul* presents the reader with at least two different figures attempting to reconstruct what is essentially the same vast "blank" around India, and personified in different ways by the beggar-woman, the vice-consul and Anne-Marie Stretter. Third person narration is kept to a minimum. It does not describe India but through the unanswered, and apparently unanswerable questions posed in the text, makes it appear as the unknowable which has caught the beggar-woman, Anne-Marie Stretter and the vice-consul and rendered them incomprehensible as well.

The last of the texts I want to discuss in detail in relation to "blanks" is *Détruire, dit-elle*. This is in some ways the most explicit, but in others the most obscure of the five. The style is similar to that of *Le Vice-consul* inasmuch as the text is basically a third person narrative, of which most is taken up with direct speech. Those parts which are not in direct speech are composed of short, simple sentences describing the figures' actions, or aspects of their surroundings. These read like the stage directions for a play—in fact there is a *note pour les représentations* ("note for performances") at the end—and *Détruire, dit-elle* also became a film of the same name. The sparseness of the text is perhaps what led Maurice Blanchot to ask, "is it 'a book'? 'a film'? something between the two?"[53] However, I want to discuss it here in its manifestation as a novel.

The obscurity of *Détruire, dit-elle* lies in what might be described as the minimalism of the construction of the figures, Alissa, Stein, Max Thor, Elizabeth Alione, and the hotel in which they are staying. The descriptions of these figures and their hotel is in Duras's familiar style of very short sentences describing primarily what is visible. The text opens:

> Cloudy weather.
> The picture windows are closed.
> From the dining room side, where he is, the grounds cannot be seen.
> She though, yes, she can see, she is looking. Her table is touching the window-ledge.
> Because of the bright light, she is screwing up her eyes. Her eyes move one way, then the other. Other clients are also watching these tennis matches that he himself cannot see.[54]

There are no detailed descriptions of the hotel. Max Thor, the "he" watching Elizabeth Alione here, will never be described at all, although she will be. The narration gives just enough information to set a scene, and all is done in this clipped, simple style, without contradiction or complication. The language seems impersonally transparent, the information it gives perfectly clear, it is just that there is not very much of it. Blanchot reassures the anxious: "Characters? Yes, they are in the positions of characters," "Certainly, what is happening there happens in a place that we can put a name to: a hotel, the grounds, and, beyond, a forest," "Where do they come from? Who are they? Certainly they are beings like ourselves: there are no others in this world."[55] However, in *Détruire, dit-elle,* Duras eschews many of the conventions of realist fiction which she has maintained until now, stripping the figures of all "character" while their behaviour does not follow conventional rules. For example, here is the first conversation between Alissa and Stein, who have never met before:

> "Alissa," he calls at last. "It's Stein."
> "Stein."
> "Yes. I'm here."
> She does not move. Stein slips to the ground, places his head on Alissa's knees.
> "I don't know you, Alissa," says Stein.
> "He has stopped loving me in a certain way perhaps?"
> "It's here that he realised that he could no longer imagine his life without you."
> They are silent. He places his hands on Alissa's body.
> "You are part of me, Alissa. Your fragile body is part of my body. And I don't know you."[56]

This is clearly not realist dialogue in the sense that all the preliminary formalities and introductory conversations that one might expect to take place when two people first meet are absent. However, if the reader takes the place of the narratee and enters into the terms of the text, then this conversation is getting down to the "essentials" of what *Détruire, dit-elle* is about, what it stages: madness, despair and the workings of desire.

Alissa and Stein's conversation is representative of the rest of the novel in style and tone. Most of the dialogues concern the immediate events described, with the exception of those in which Elizabeth Alione talks about her pregnancy, the young doctor and her stillborn child. The action is entirely confined to the hotel and to the interaction between Max Thor, Stein, Alissa, Elizabeth Alione and, at the end, Bernard Alione. Passing references are made to the existence of other guests at the hotel, but they do not encroach in any way upon the events or conversations described. The text creates a world which seems hermetically sealed, where everything that goes to make everyday life as it is usually described is absent. Within this world, Max Thor, Stein and Alissa pursue Elizabeth Alione. But to what end? This is intimated, rather than articulated. Whilst Alissa and Elizabeth Alione are talking, Stein and Max Thor are watching: Stein says "Capital destruction will first take place at the hands of Alissa."[57] Elizabeth Alione seems to be the target for this destruction, but she avoids it by going home with her husband. Alissa, who is to bring the destruction about, is, like the beggar-woman of *Le Vice-consul,* mad. Like Lol V. Stein, who at the time of her marriage to Jean Bedford, "was looking younger. She might have been taken for a fifteen-year-old,"[58] and who "still looked unhealthily young" when Jacques Hold meets her, Alissa is very young—young enough to be her husband's daughter. Furthermore, she never grows any older:

> "How old is Alissa?"
> "Eighteen."
> "And when you met her?"
> "Eighteen."[59]

Like the Anne-Marie Stretter of India Song (and by inference, she of *Le Vice-consul*), or "the woman" of *L'Amour,* Alissa *est à celui qui la veut* ("is any man's who wants her").[60] She is a "blank" inasmuch as it seems there is nothing to know about her; she has no "personality," nor, apparently, a history, for she never gets any older. Stein and Max Thor are almost as "blank." Max Thor is a teacher, but what he teaches is "history . . . of the future." " 'There's nothing any more,' says Max Thor. 'So I don't speak. My pupils sleep.' "[61] About Stein, the reader is told nothing other than that he is Jewish. Alissa says to Elizabeth Alione, "I can't talk about Stein"[62] and this stated impossibility fuels the production of a "blank" around him.

In *Détruire, dit-elle,* an important event has once more occurred before the chronological beginning of the narration. This is Elizabeth Alione's relationship with the young doctor. What happened between them is not clear, but apparently it has made her interesting to Stein, Max Thor and Alissa:

> "I realized," says Elizabeth Alione softly, "that you were interested in me because of . . . that alone. And that perhaps you were right."
> "That what?"
> Elizabeth gestures, she does not know. Alissa takes Elizabeth Alione by the shoulders.
> Elizabeth turns. They are both caught in a mirror.
> "Who reminds you of that man?" asks Alissa in the mirror, "of that young doctor?"
> "Stein, perhaps."
> "Look," says Alissa.
> Silence. Their heads have drawn close together.
> "We are like each other," says Alissa: "we would love Stein if it were possible to love."[63]

Exactly what it is that interests the three in Elizabeth Alione is never stated, but merely designated as "that," the inexpressible. However, the reader/narratee is led to understand that she is ripe for "capital destruction"; which is perhaps what Alissa is attempting when she expresses disgust at the story of how Elizabeth Alione showed the young doctor's letter to her husband:

> Elizabeth shouts.
>   "Do you want to reduce me to despair?"
> Alissa smiles at her.
>   "Yes, stop talking."[64]

It is up to the reader to infer what might come of Elizabeth's despair but it seems possible to conclude, from this dialogue, that her experience with the young doctor has brought her closer to Alissa, Stein and Max Thor, and has begun the process of destruction. This process seems to be one she is too frightened to continue, but which would, if she let it go on, render her the same as the others, described by Blanchot as "radically ravaged beings."[65] Nothing can be known about such beings, because they lack the trappings of identity such as those that Lol V. Stein built, if unconvincingly, for herself at U. Bridge. The only things that give them individual identities are their names, the descriptions of both men as Jewish and a brief reference to the past of Max Thor and Alissa. Their names, the suggestion of race or history and the lack of any indications to the contrary lead the reader/narratee to understand that these are indeed "beings like ourselves," that is, that the text is portraying, or intending to portray, "human beings" in a world purporting to bear some relation to the extra-textual "real world." But the lack of any further information with which s/he can construct some more complex form of identity for these figures, information which more traditional works of fiction would normally provide, means that they appear "ravaged."

The text uses Duras's familiar realist technique of simple description of the visible, the hotel windows, certain actions on the part of the figures. But the information supplied is scant, and most of it concerns what cannot be known—a kind of anti-information; its chief role seems to be to indicate what cannot be told or known: a vast "blank" in life.

So, in Duras's later novels, the "blanks" appear as points where the inexpressible erupts into the narration, where linguistic meaning breaks down. It might indeed be possible to draw, as Marini and others have done, analogies between Duras's "blanks" and silences or blockings of sense in the speech of analysands. However, rather than seeing Duras's "blanks" as manifestations of a "feminine libidinal organization," expressing itself through her writing, I would suggest that they are produced by the internal workings of the texts. My survey of five of Duras's novels has revealed recurrent features which are productive of "blanks," and I have identified these as follows.

The Lost Moment

Realist novels tend to begin with or just before the occurrence of the first major event which sets the unfolding of the plot in motion: *War and Peace* begins with Pierre's coming into his inheritance, the start of the wars between Russia and France under Napoleon and Nicolay's and Sonya's vows, all of which are the conditions which make various strands of the plot possible; Albert Camus's novel *La Peste* begins with Rieux's discovery of the first dead rat; *Un barrage contre le Pacifique* begins with the death of the horse and the decision taken by Suzanne, Joseph and their mother to go into Ram, where they meet M. Jo.

In contrast to these, in the more experimental novels I have discussed, the major catalyst, the event which is constructed as setting the text in motion, occurs "beyond the scope" of the narration. In *Moderato cantabile,* the shooting occurs outside the room where the "eye" of the narration is recording Anne Desbaresdes's child's piano lesson, whilst in the others the event, the Lahore shooting, the ball at S. Thala, or Elizabeth Alione's relationship with the young doctor, occurs before the chronological beginning of the text. This is a very common feature of Duras's work, and such an event plays a part in most, if not all of her texts. Even in *Un barrage contre le Pacifique,* the dam of the title was built and destroyed before the death of the horse which opens the novel. However, the story of the dam is recounted by the narrator as a flashback. The reader is told what happened. Furthermore, the part it plays in the text is structurally different from that of, for example, the Lahore shooting. It is not set up as a problem which the text is trying (and failing) to solve in the same way.

Beginning with Duras's next published work, *Le Marin de Gibraltar,* the "lost event" is no longer simply recounted by the narration, but is reconstructed by figures in the text. The structure of a novel can be seen in terms of a movement towards the answer, revealed at the end, to a question or questions posed at the beginning. In Duras's novels, the movement towards reconstruction of the lost event provides one of the motor forces behind the structure of the text, although arguably it is more important in some (*L'Amante anglaise, Moderato cantabile*) than in others (*Dix heures et demie du soir en été, Détruire, dit-elle*). However, the figures are portrayed as unable to describe the event or its effects and, in those novels where the third person narration might, with its authoritative voice, explain to the reader exactly what happened and what s/he should understand by it, as happens, for example, in *Un barrage contre le Pacifique,* the event always occurs "off stage," beyond the scope of a highly reliable, but limited (for example, to what is visible from a particular place) narrator. In this way the reconstruction is rendered impossible, although the effects of the lost event reverberate through the text and constant reference is made to it. The reader/narratee thus feels a lack of knowledge of "what really happened" though s/he knows that something did, because its effects are still felt. The absent event, or more particularly, its meaning, the reason why it causes certain effects, thus appears as a "blank," which can never be filled in, because it is always "off limits." The answers to questions relating to this event are thus constructed as definitively absent.

THE WITHERING AWAY OF CHARACTER

Even in her earliest works, Duras does not go into very great detail in the creation of "character." The reader is not given detailed descriptions of the figures in the novels: their histories, idiosyncrasies of speech, the colour of their eyes, etc. Nevertheless, until *Moderato cantabile,* the information given appears adequate in terms of the conventions of psychological realism, which is a category into which the novels fit with relative ease. The characters are constructed as "real people," who could be assumed to exist outside the text, and, like "real people" portrayed through discourses other than those of realist fiction, such as those of biography, history or contemporary journalism, they have desires which can be, and are, articulated. They then act in accordance with those desires, like, for instance, Suzanne who wants to leave the plain, is bored by M. Jo and thinks a great deal of her mother and brother. Her actions in *Un barrage contre le Pacifique* are comprehensible in these terms.

With *Moderato cantabile* there is a change. The reader/narratee is still presented with figures whom s/he reads as being "real" in the way that other figures in texts of realist fiction might be said to be read as being "real," that is, the reader can imagine them as potentially existing beyond and being described by, rather than produced by, the text. Most of Duras's figures have names which are, with the exception of Jean-Marc de H . . ., the vice-consul, given in full and often repeated. This naming of the characters fixes them in terms of a social being and status[66] and also contributes to the reader's imagining them as "real people," designated, but not fully defined by their name. The name makes the figure present as an individual, but in doing so constructs that figure as someone about whom more could be known. This effect is heightened by Duras's use, in many cases, of the full name of a figure (Anne Desbaresdes, Lol V. Stein, Anne-Marie Stretter) where the frequent appearance of that figure might be expected to lead to a shortened form of the name being used in the text. The repeated use of the full name gives an impression of formality to the narration, as if the narrator were not intimate with the figure thus named; the latter is thus produced as more distant and unknowable, and at the same time more imposing, than if a shorter form were used.

The reader/narratee imagines the figures as being subjects of desire ("real people") and so reads their actions as manifestations of the presence of their desires and their fears. However, the nature of their desires is never articulated although its presence is strongly suggested. In *Moderato cantabile,* the meetings of Anne Desbaresdes and Chauvin make up the main body of the text but exactly *why* they meet is never stated. Their desire is constructed as both what, in one strand of the narration, the text is "about" and that which goes unexplained. In the years that follow *Moderato cantabile,* Duras produces sparser and sparser texts in the same vein, where the desire of the figures portrayed is constructed as both the *raison d'être* of the text and as that which cannot be spoken.

The figures are portrayed for the most part outside a precise social context. This may be due to a temporary escape in the form of a holiday (*Dix heures et demie du soir en été, Détruire, dit-elle*), or to the age of the figures concerned (*L'Après-midi de M. Andesmas*); it may be that one of the most important figures is mad, and thus to some extent "outside" society (*L'Amour, L'Amante anglaise, Le Vice-consul*); often one of the key figures portrayed is a woman married to a wealthy man, who therefore has time on her hands and is able to follow the dictates of her desires (Lol V. Stein, Anne Desbaresdes, Anne-Marie Stretter). In some later texts (*L'Amour, La Maladie de la mort, L'Homme assis dans le couloir*), the figures have neither names nor history; indeed, these texts appear more as fantasies which may be of relevance to "reality," but do not attempt to portray it, almost all the conventions and devices which realist fiction uses to produce an impression of imitating "reality" having been abandoned.

As the figures become less and less "filled out," and the texts become more and more confined to the manifestation of their (ill-defined) desires as opposed to portraying their "characters," so their desires become less and less clearly articulated and the importance of *oubli* ("oblivion") and of the individual figures' attaining of a state in which they are "ravaged" grows. In this way, the reader is led to concentrate on attempts to reach, and manifestations of, a state about which nothing can be said, whilst any other details about the figures are, with each successive text, pared away further and further. This trend continues into Duras's film-making, and is finally reversed with the publication of *L'Amant* (1984) and *La Douleur* (1985).

Symbolism

In many of Duras's texts, certain signifiers acquire resonances which make them appear as symbols for something which remains undefined. This is the case in *Moderato cantabile* with *la fleur de magnolia,* or *la vedette;* in *Le Vice-consul* with *la lèpre,* or *Lahore,* in *Détruire, ditelle* with *la forêt,* and there are many other instances. These signifiers appear to be elevated to the status of symbols through their repeated occurrence in certain contexts although in fact, they cannot be said to be symbols in the true sense of the term, since they do not stand in the place of something precise. I have already discussed this in relation to the *fleur de magnolia, la lèpre,* and *Lahore* in the context of the novels in which they occur. In every case the reader is invited to infer the desire, fear, or horror of the figures in the text in relation to these signifiers, but is never told exactly what the cause of these emotions is. In this way, these and other signifiers appear as symbols for something which exists but is unnamable, or else become symbols for an emotion. Their use thus produces "blanks" arising because a signifier such as *la fleur de magnolia* carries with it all the resonances of all the unstated but inferred meanings which accrue to it as the text progresses.

"Seamless" Discourse

It is at those points of the text where, in order for the reader to continue reading it as a coherent whole, with a movement carrying it from beginning to end, s/he has to infer links between things that are not explicitly connected, or assume meanings that are not given in the text itself, that the "blanks" are produced. The reader's inference takes the place of the information that the text does not provide.

The "blanks" appear as an impossibility of articulation, rather than as information which could have been included and which has simply been omitted through some whim or lack of knowledge on the part of the narrator. The reader/narratee does not "fill in" the "blanks" whilst reading, at least not consciously, although s/he might want to do so after reading. The text itself gives clues, but not answers, and the "blanks" remain "blanks" although critics and editors of annotated editions might have given their own versions of how to fill them in.

In her work after and including *Moderato cantabile,* Duras achieves this effect by reducing the "scope" of the narration. These texts do not construct an omniscient narrator, or even a narrator whose knowledge is limited but who interprets events, understands the motivations of the figures portrayed and suggests readings to the reader from a spatial and/or temporal "vantage point," as happens in *Un barrage contre le Pacifique.* Instead, the place of the narrator, and the knowledge available to her/him are restricted. In *Un barrage contre le Pacifique,* the omniscient narrator is produced as having a "point of view" at points of contradiction in the discourse of the text. The reader/narratee infers a desire on the part of a personalised narrator, which produces these contradictions and must be interpreted, in order for sense to be made of the narration. The narrator is produced in this text as having an ironic overview of what is recounted from a position "outside" the text. S/he is the mediator, through whom the reader's understanding must pass, and has opinions on what s/he narrates, which the reader is aware of, if dimly.

With *Moderato cantabile,* this type of narrator disappears. The text is in the past historic, thus narrated from a position temporally "outside" the text. However, the narrator is constructed as not having an opinion or a point of view on what s/he is narrating, but as merely recording what s/he saw. In fact, the narrator is not produced as a distinctive "voice" at all, but seems to disappear into the impersonal discourse of the text. This is the case in other third person narrations, such as *Le Vice-consul, Détruire, dit-elle* and *L'Amour,* where again, the narrator appears to be recording simply what is visible; except that in the case of these three texts, the narration is in the present tense, thus rendering more strongly the immediacy of the visible, whilst also preventing the construction of the narrator as "outside" what is happening.

The "disappearance" of the narrator is facilitated by lack of disturbance in the discourse of the text. The narration does not contradict itself, nor, for the most part, does it require much interpretative work on the part of the reader to discover—or invent—the pertinence of the words. Sentences are kept as simple as possible and apparently describe only what might be seen from a particular vantage point: for example, in the café in *Moderato cantabile,* or in the hotel in *Détruire, dit-elle,* with as little use of any rhetorical devices as possible. There are occasions where the narration seems uncertain, as, for example, in *Moderato cantabile* when it is said of the child,[67] "he appeared to be thinking, took his time, and perhaps he was lying." Yet whilst it might be said that this uncertainty temporarily breaks the "transparency" of the text and produces an uncertain narrator, the uncertainty reinforces the narrator's role as that of faithfully recording just what is visible, lacking knowledge and refusing to interpret anything else.[68]

In the case of *Le Ravissement de Lol V. Stein,* the text is not a third person narration. Jacques Hold, the first person narrator, apparently "invents" much of the story, infers motives for behaviour on the part of the other figures, and interprets their actions. However, his account of Lol is largely in terms of what he can see, even if what he sees is not what one might expect to be put into the category of the visible: "I see everything. I see love itself."[69] Such divergence from the conventions of what is and is not visible can be understood by the reader in terms of Jacques Hold's specific vision, he being the subject who "utters" the narration. Furthermore, his narration uses, for the most part, a style which is only a little less sparse than that of the third person narration of *Moderato cantabile* or *Le Vice-consul,* and where the reader infers a simple recording of events without rhetorical embellishments. Jacques Hold is not, it seems, fond of simile, metaphor, synechdoche, or any other figure of speech which might possibly trouble the apparent transparency of his language. The discourse of *Le Ravissement de Lol V. Stein* is seldom, if ever, disturbed by conflicting meanings or inconsistencies which might bring its veracity into doubt, and any peculiarities of style can be put down to momentary wanderings on the part of Jacques Hold's desire.

It is perhaps significant that the narration of Duras's texts is so often, with the exception of *L'Amante anglaise,* the narration of the visible. The scopic drive, according to Lacan, "is the one which most completely avoids the limit of castration,"[70] allowing the subject the greatest sense of identification, both in relation to, and with the object. Moreover, much of his theory of the role of the phallus rests on the importance of the sight of the penis. "Seeing is believing," as they say. The undisturbed discourse of the visible in Duras's texts gives the reader an authoritative and apparently objective account of "what happened," avoiding any disturbing eruptions of the unconscious into the process of reading. Linear time is observed throughout unless, as in *Le Ravissement de Lol V. Stein,* flashbacks are sanctioned by the presence of a first person narrator, constructed as a man with faculties of memory and imagination. Thus Duras constructs a kind of ultra-clear, hyper-realist discourse with meticulous precision.

At this point it seems apposite to look at Duras's and Gauthier's suggestions that the former's texts exhibit "a reworking of usual grammatical sense," or a "violent rejection of syntax." Both these ideas would run contrary to the view that I am putting forward, that Duras uses language in such a way as to produce an impression of almost complete expressivity, at least in the strictly narrative parts of her texts. The phrase from *L'Amour* that Gauthier quotes comes from the following passage:

Someone is walking, nearby.

The man who was watching passes between the woman with closed eyes and the other in the distance, he who is coming, going, a prisoner. The pounding of his footsteps can be heard on the wooden promenade that runs along the shore. The footsteps are irregular, uncertain.

The triangle loses shape, breaks up. It has just lost its shape: in fact, the man is passing, one can see him, one can hear him.

One can hear: the gap between the footsteps grows. The man must be looking at the woman with closed eyes who is placed in his path.

Yes. The footsteps stop. He is looking at her.

The man who is walking along by the sea, and only he, maintains his initial movement. He is still walking with the infinite step of a prisoner.

The woman is being looked at.

She has her legs stretched out. She is in dark light, embedded in the wall. Eyes shut.

Does not feel herself being seen. Does not know she is looked at.

Stays facing the sea. Face white. Hands half buried in the sand, immobile like the body. Force stopped, displaced towards absence. Stopped in her movement of flight. Not knowing this. Not knowing herself.[71]

Whilst it seems clear that this passage reveals some unusual use of language, I do not think that it really breaks any grammatical rules, except by omission of, for example the subject "she" of "does not know she is being looked at"; and the subject is not strictly speaking necessary here, since the feminine agreement of the past participle shows that the subject of the verb must be feminine, and that feminine subject could be none other than *elle, la femme* ("the woman"). Similarly, in the last paragraph, the reader/narratee can easily infer, and if necessary supply, those subjects or verbs which have been omitted: "(Her) face (is) white."

This does not appear to me to constitute either a "reworking of usual grammatical sense," or a "violent rejection of syntax." On the contrary, it relies on the reader being able to situate the words s/he reads within a syntactic structure in the context of which they can have meaning. The ability of the narration to signify depends upon the resilience of syntax to the omission of subjects and verbs, on the linguistic competence which enables the reader to "make sense" of this particular performance. I will return to the question of the effects of exactly what has been omitted, the subjects and verbs in the description of the woman, or the feminine subject of the passive verbs, when I come to discuss Duras's construction of the women figures in her novels later on. Suffice it to say here that it is precisely because the reader knows what is grammatically required that s/he not only notices that certain elements are missing (something funny has happened to the syntax), but is also able to read despite their absence.

In this passage there are no contradictions, no problems of interpretation arising from conflicts within the discourse. The narrator describes, as if s/he were present at the scene and in the present tense, what s/he hears and sees. Even those verbs which have *elle* as subject and require an insight into the psychic workings of "the woman," such as *Ne ressent pas être vue* ("Does not feel herself being seen"), or *L'ignorant, s'ignorant* ("Not knowing this, not knowing herself"), seem, to me at least, in the light of the rest of the passage, to be attributable to one who observes and infers, rather than to a narrator who "knows" what "the woman" is thinking. What does occur in this passage, and in many other places in Duras's texts, is a kind of extreme precision and fixing of what is being described. Here it can be seen in the two expressions of the man watching the woman: *il la regarde* ("he looks at her") and then, a few lines later, *la femme est regardée* ("the woman is looked at"). Here the effect is almost one of the cinematic technique of shot-reverse shot; first the reader is given the subject of the look to focus on, and then the object. Or perhaps in "he looks at her" what the reader fantasises is the look, which disappears into its object in "the woman is looked at." Either way, the vantage point offered to the reader by the narration is not disturbed.

Duras often creates an effect of hyper-precision in a temporal sense, by use of tenses. In *Moderato cantabile,* for example:

> Anne Desbaresdes waited for that minute, then she tried to get up from her chair. She succeeded, got up. Chauvin was looking away. The men still avoided resting their eyes on the adulteress. She was up.[72]

Here we have the movement from an action, "got up," to a state, "She was up." The narration gives the reader not only the process, but also its goal, the end of that process, which the verb in the past historic alone does not convey with sufficient precision.

So this hyper-realism facilitates the production of "blanks" by giving extremely precise and clear information about the visible, but about very little else, other than that which can be inferred from what is visible, as in the passage from *L'Amour* just cited. The psychological motivations for the figures' actions are not recorded and must be inferred by the reader/narratee. Furthermore, much of what is recorded is dialogue, in which the figures who, in the words of Henri Hell, "only exist, in fact, through their speech," make manifest the presence of their desires, but never state what those desires are. Jacques Hold invents, Michael Richard suggests, but their inventions and suggestions reveal the desire for silence—oblivion—whilst the voice of the third person narration is unable even to articulate as much as that. At the same time, the clarity and precision with which the texts are narrated do everything to facilitate the reader's imagined idea of "what is happening," and do not confuse by presenting more than one angle from which to view events and figures. This single position from which the "visible" is narrated gives an air of objectivity and truth to the narration. There is no interpretation here, it implies, merely a recording. Let the reader make of it what s/he will.

In the light of this insistence on the visible in her writing, it is interesting to consider how Duras uses a visual medium, that of film, to create "blanks" similar to those produced by her texts. In films such as *India Song,* or *Aurélia Steiner, dit Aurélia Melbourne,* she manages to undermine the power of the immediate presence of the visible by the relation of soundtrack to image. In both of these films, the soundtrack tells a story. In *India Song* one voice questions another about a story which is more or less that of *Le Vice-consul,* whilst on the screen, a handful of actors represent, rather than portray the protagonists in a way which is linked to the story that unfolds, but which is obviously not meant to be an accurate depiction of that story. In *Aurélia Steiner, dit Aurélia Melbourne,* the images are of Paris seen from the Seine and have no direct link to the soundtrack, which tells the story of a seduction.

The effect of disconnexion between soundtrack and image in both cases is, in a sense, one of interference. The person watching the film cannot simply imagine what is happening on the basis of the soundtrack, because the images are there, partially occupying the place of imaginary images to go with the words. At the same time, the power of the images themselves, the meaning they might have if seen in isolation, is undermined by the soundtrack, which imposes different meanings upon them in a way which is not fixed. The ultimate effect, particularly, I think, in *India Song,* where the relation of image to sound is all the more fluid because there is a link of content between them, is one of uncertainty. The person watching is offered a story which is not quite within reach, nothing is present, the images may refer to the story, but they do not tell it, the story itself is a reconstruction of something in the past, the protagonists are dead. As in the novels, there is a sense that knowledge is unattainable, because the information offered is not definite, or not enough, suggested rather than present. Instead there is an impossibility of visual representation where that knowledge might be, a "blank."

Words have an infinite capacity to produce meanings. Within the conventions of realism, they have an endless capacity to name and to describe. In her writing, Duras restricts the productive, and apparent descriptive capacity of her words to the visible. She uses words to create images—which lack the Imaginary plenitude of actual images, since they are only images evoked by words. However, as fantasies of the visible, they carry the traces of Imaginary wholeness and monolithic certainty, and this certainty in the fantasy enables Duras to create "blanks" where knowledge is understood to be missing, whilst also avoiding the potential plentitude of actual images. In her films, on the other hand, she undercuts the plenitude of the real image by using the power of words to create images which do not coincide with those on the screen, or to suggest ways of understanding the image which are not instantly apparent. In both cases, both films and writing, it is the interaction of Symbolic and Imaginary, the interplay of certainties and lack of knowledge, that Duras uses to create the "blanks."

But does this make her work feminine, or the "blanks" the place of the woman? To the extent that they are produced from inferences and resonances, it is perhaps possible to see the "blanks" as points of "non-sense," where too many different meanings cluster around a particular signifier so that it can no longer mean and becomes opaque; or as points where a doubling, or a plurality of meanings are produced, in the manner of Irigaray's "woman-speak." In this light it might be possible to view the "blank" symbolised by *la fleur de magnolia* in *Moderato cantabile,* for example, as a manifestation of Montrelay's "feminine" effects within language although, it would not be true to say that "everything is manifest, nothing is hidden" in the case of this, or any other of the blanks.

However, as I have explained in my discussion of the Lacanian analysts, I do not think such a way of using language can be called specifically "feminine" in itself; for it works in the same way as innuendo or jokes, by controlling and using the power of unconscious links between signifiers, and I do not see why or how such universally found phenomena can be gendered. Furthermore, I do not think it is possible to see them as disrupting the rules by which (masculine) language or literature work. Rather, they are dependent upon the resilience of the rules to omissions. Duras's "blanks" may require that the reader assume meanings on an unconscious, or pre-conscious level, but they do not break meaning down. The power of her writing comes from understatement and interpretation, rather than the eruption of the unconscious into the conscious process of reading with untameable excesses of meaning.

Notes

1. *Un barrage contre le Pacifique,* Paris, Gallimard, Folio series, 1950, pp 62–5.
2. A crossing over between fiction and "reality" would seem to be even more complete in the cinema, judging by the disclaimer carried by some films, to stress the fictional nature of what is being shown.
3. Roland Barthes, *Le Degré zéro de l'écriture,* Paris, Le Seuil, Points series, 1972, p 26.
4. Tzvetan Todorov, *Symbolisme et interpretation,* Paris, Le Seuil, 1978, p 26.
5. *Un barrage contre le Pacifique,* p 21.
6. For a more detailed discussion of the relationship between Suzanne and Joseph, see pp 213–16 of Selous' *The Other Woman.*
7. *Un barrage contre le Pacifique,* pp 40–1.
8. ibid., pp 188–9.
9. Gaëton Picon, "Moderato cantabile dans l'oeuvre de Marguerite Duras," in *Moderato cantabile,* Paris, Minuit, 10/18 series, 1958, p 169.
10. ibid., p 171.
11. Madeleine Alleins, "Un langage qui recuse la quiétude, du savoir," in *Moderato Cantabile,* Paris, Minuit, 10/18, 1958, p 159.
12. Jean Mistler, "Un essai non une oeuvre achevée," in *Moderato cantabile,* Paris, Minuit, 10/18, 1958, p 162.
13. Ibid., pp 30–40.
14. *Un barrage contre le Pacifique,* pp 104–5.
15. *Moderato cantabile,* p 30.
16. ibid., pp 97–8.
17. ibid., pp 79–80.
18. ibid., p 93.
19. ibid., p 103.
20. Something which Jean Mistler seems unsure about. "Critics are within their rights to ask why this second attempt; for it cannot be anything other than an attempt, with the aim of creating a finished work later on" (*Moderato cantabile,* p 162).
21. *Le Ravissement de Lol V. Stein,* Paris, Gallimard, Folio series, 1964, p 81.
22. ibid., p 106.
23. ibid., p 113.
24. ibid., pp 33–4.
25. ibid., p 14.
26. ibid., p 131.
27. ibid., p 34.
28. ibid., pp 49–50.
29. ibid., p 168.
30. ibid.
31. *Le Vice-consul,* Paris, Gallimard, 1966, p 39.
32. ibid., p 137.
33. ibid., pp 104–5.
34. ibid., p 45.

35. ibid.

36. ibid., pp 127–8.

37. ibid., pp 93–4.

38. ibid., pp 143–4.

39. ibid., p 204.

40. ibid., p 159.

41. ibid., pp 137–8.

42. ibid., p 71.

43. ibid., p 29.

44. ibid.

45. ibid., p 88.

46. ibid., p 114.

47. ibid., p 125.

48. ibid., p 131.

49. ibid., p 157.

50. ibid., p 100.

51. ibid., p 116.

52. ibid., p 117.

53. Maurice Blanchot, "Détruire," in *Marguerite Duras,* Paris, Albatros, Ça Çinéma series, 1979, p 139.

54. *Détruire, dit-elle,* Paris, Minuit, 1969, p 9.

55. Blanchot, op cit, p 140.

56. *Détruire, dit-elle,* pp 49–50.

57. ibid., p 59.

58. *Le Ravissement de Lol V. Stein,* p 29.

59. *Détruire,* dit-elle, p 134.

60. ibid., p 131.

61. ibid., p 122.

62. ibid., p 78.

63. ibid., p 99.

64. ibid., p 98.

65. Blanchot, op. cit., p 141. I have translated *détruire* and *êtres détruits* here as "to ravage" and "ravaged beings" respectively, but have rendered *destruction* as "destruction."

66. In this context, the truncation of the vice-consul's name fits into the tradition of realist fiction where characters are often designated in such a way "to protect their reputations," since the text is constructing them as "real people."

67. *Moderato cantabile,* p 66.

68. In the light of my use of the word "recording," it is interesting to note that in *L'Amante anglaise,* where there is no narrator as such, the text being composed of a series of dialogues, it is stated at the beginning, *tout ce qui est dit ici est enregistré* ("everything that is said here is a recording") (*L'Amante anglaise,* London, Heinmann, 1972, p 23). It is as if here Duras were experimenting with a different sense, with the ear of the tape-recorder, rather than the eye of the camera. Like the eye, the ear does not interpret or judge, but merely records what it hears, faithfully and impartially.

69. *Le Ravissement de Lol V. Stein,* p 105.

70. Lacan, *Les Quatre Concepts fondamentaux de la psychanalyse,* p 74.

71. *L'Amour,* Paris, Crallimard, 1971, pp 9–10.

72. *Moderato cantabile,* p 114.

Elective Empathies and Musical Affinities

John W. Kneller

The title of Marguerite Duras's novel invites us to read it in a special way. Of course there is no musical composition bearing the directions, "Moderato cantabile." Moderato, meaning "at a moderate tempo," is used either singly, or qualifying some other mark of time, as Allegro moderato, or Andante moderato, when it has the result of lessening the force of the simple direction. Cantabile, meaning "singable," is placed against a phrase when it is to be sung. But this does not mean that the novel should be sung at a moderato tempo. Moderato epitomizes the conventionality, the restraint, the routine, the longanimity imposed upon the principal character, Anne Desbaresdes, by her social position as wife of a rich industrialist in a seaport in western France. Cantabile is the invitation to freedom, to lack of restraint, to unconventionality and ultimately to intemperance, passion, and violence. *Moderato cantabile* is not the story of a twentieth century Phèdre gripped by an adulterous passion for a laborer in her husband's factory, nor is it the retelling of Emma Bovary's plight in a new setting, though both of these hypotheses have been put forth. *Moderato cantabile* is the gradual unfolding of the two contrasting themes implicit in the title. A proper interpretation of the work can best be achieved by analogy with a musical form.

The form suggests itself in the first chapter. Anne Desbaresdes is watching her son take his piano lesson in the studio of a certain Mademoiselle Giraud overlooking the harbor. The cantankerous old piano teacher asks the recalcitrant child to read what is written on the score. "Moderato cantabile," he says, but when asked what it means, he replies that he does not know. The piece he is studying is a sonatina of Diabelli. Anton Diabelli, the Austrian music publisher whose waltz provided the theme for Beethoven's thirty-three variations that bear his name, also composed a number of compositions for teaching purposes. The sonatina, a form particularly convenient for the making of instructional pieces, resembles the sonata, except that it is shorter, simpler, slenderer. The sonata-form refers specifically to the first movement of a sonata, string quartet, concerto or symphony and it may be divided into three parts: exposition, development, and recapitulation. Two contrasting themes

From *Yale French Studies*, 27 (1961), 114–20. Reprinted by permission.

unfold their potentialities through the three stages and end in a coda or clos-ing theme. Literary applications of this form may be found in Thomas Mann's *Tonio Kroger,* and in Proust's *Swann in Love.* Because it is shorter, simpler, slen-derer, and freer, the sonatina form is particularly appropriate for this short piece of Marguerite Duras.

The music lesson played over the steady obligato of harbor activity con-stitutes a statement of the novel's first theme. The routine of Anne's hum-drum existence allows her to accompany her son every Friday when he goes to the studio of Mademoiselle Giraud. The boy does not want to learn the piano and he is sitting before the instrument in mute, motionless, stubborn rebel-lion when a woman's scream is heard in the street below. This is the first statement of the contrasting theme. The music lesson goes on in spite of the clamor of voices and when it is over, Anne and the boy go downstairs to find out what has happened. Leaving him on Mademoiselle Giraud's porch, she works her way through the crowd to the front of a café and looks in one of the open windows. In the semi-darkness of a back room, she makes out a woman lying motionless on the floor. Sprawled over the outstretched figure and clutching at her shoulders, a man is repeatedly calling her, "My love, my love." While the police take a statement from the proprietress of the café, the man, oblivious to the crowd that is watching him, continues to lie on top of the woman, to press his face against hers, against her blood-smeared mouth. He is finally led out of the café and into a police wagon. During all this, Anne's boy sits quietly on the porch humming the sonatina of Diabelli.

The two themes thus presented in the first chapter will gradually develop in the seven ensuing ones. In the second chapter it is the following day, Saturday, late in the afternoon. Anne, taking a walk along the port with her child, goes into the café. The boy goes out on the sidewalk to play; Anne orders a glass of wine. Except for the proprietress, there is only one other cus-tomer in the café, a man reading a newspaper. Anne is in an extremely ner-vous state, as evidenced by a continual trembling of her hands. The man moves over to her table, she orders more wine, and the strange dialogue begins. As the dialogue progresses, Madame Desbaresdes questions the man about the scene she has witnessed the day before. She learns that the woman was shot in the heart by her lover. The victim, mother of three, has since died, and her lover has gone mad. Loving her as much as he did, how could he have killed her? Fascinated by the crime, Anne continues her questioning:

> Seeing him carry on over her, as if from that time on it made no difference whether she were dead or alive, do you believe it's possible to come to . . . that . . . other than . . . out of despair?

This is a crucial point in the novel, for we now begin to see the purpose of Anne's questioning. In the film, *Moderato cantabile,* produced by Peter Brook, the crime is simply an excuse for Anne and the man to meet and, later, to fall in love. The novel has a completely different dimension. From this point on, the heroine is not simply satisfying an idle curiosity, or seeking an excuse for a meeting with a strange man. She is seeking complete identification with the murdered woman. From this point on, the questioning will not reveal any new facts on the case, it will be part of a series of exercises she must perform to project her own consciousness into that of the victim.

The ritual questioning which goes on during the next two chapters permits the two themes to develop. The man, whose name Anne learns is Chauvin, questions her about her life; she questions him about the crime. She asks him about the motive for the murder, whether it was true that the woman was a drunkard; how and when she decided that she wanted him to shoot her in the heart. Chauvin, on the other hand, who with other workers in the employ of her husband, has been inside the Desbaresdes mansion, tells her things that she knows only too well about her home life and personal affairs: she has been married ten years; there is a long corridor leading to her bedroom on the second floor and she keeps this corridor lighted; she does not sleep well; she watches the workers as they go to the arsenal, and sometimes as she lies awake at night their faces pass before her eyes; she likes low-necked dresses, a magnolia between her breasts; she has never cried out like the dead woman. Anne says to him, "Speak to me." He says to her, "Speak to me." If he has no new facts on the crime she tells him to make them up, to invent them. Although she is learning nothing new, a gradual change is taking place within her.

This change becomes apparent in the fifth chapter, which occurs on Friday afternoon, exactly one week after the crime was committed. Once again she is in Mademoiselle Giraud's studio listening to her child as he takes his piano lesson. The sea and harbor activity continue to play an obligato to the scales that the boy is executing. The teacher finally calls for the Sonatina of Diabelli. This time, despite his unwillingness, he plays it well. The effect on Anne is marked:

> She listened to the sonatina. It came from the darkest ages, carried to her by her child. There were times, as she listened to it, that she almost fainted. . . .

> The sonatina resounded still, carried like a feather by the barbarian, whether he willed it or not and it swept down on his mother, sentenced her to the damnation of her love. The gates of hell closed again.

This passage recalls the well-known scene from *Swann in Love* that takes place in Madame de Saint-Euverte's salon. In that scene, which climaxes the novel, Swann suddenly hears the little phrase from the Vinteuil sonata. All his efforts to put the memory of Odette's love out of his mind come to nothing as the phrase inexorably brings him all the gestures, objects and places which were part of that love.

Marguerite Duras's use of the sonatina in this chapter parallels, in a modest way, Proust's use of the little phrase. Although the sonatina does not immediately precipitate the climax of the novel, it does reveal to Anne the truth of her affective state and thus gives her the courage to do what she has to do in the last three chapters.

The events of chapter six immediately follow those of chapter five. Anne goes downstairs into the café; she meets Chauvin, who has been listening to the music lesson above; they drink more wine; they talk; she asks again questions about the other couple that he cannot answer; he again changes the subject to her life as wife of a rich upper middle class industrialist; the probing again reveals nothing new. Although she is aware that there is to be a reception in her home that evening, she lingers in the café, and drinks too much wine. This dialogue, in which neither person speaks directly to the other, in which each person continually repeats the same idea, bears a close resemblance to the antiphonal response of contrasting musical themes in the first movement of a sonatina.

The seventh chapter, which contains some of the best writing in the book, takes place in the Desbaresdes mansion. Anne arrives, very late and very drunk, with a fading magnolia between her breasts. The reproving husband and guests, the saumon glacé, the canard à l'orange, and the gossiping servants in the kitchen are all perceived through the inebriated senses of the heroine. The antiphonal responses of the contrasting themes are continued in a kind of cinematographic shift of scene: "A man loiters on the Boulevard de la Mer. A woman knows it."

> Anne Desbaresdes drinks . . . this evening the Pommard wine continues to have the overwhelming taste of the unknown lips of a man in the street. This man has left the Boulevard de la Mer, he walks around the park . . .

The guests digest the salmon, the duck, the mocha ice, but Anne cannot. While the guests disperse into the drawing-room, she goes upstairs to her son's room, lies down on the floor and vomits "the foreign food that she was forced to take." The regurgitation symbolizes the end of the conventionality theme. Anne is now ready for the final test.

Two days later she returns to the café. Chauvin is waiting. The humdrum of her home life no longer exists; she dwells on her vomiting. Like the other woman, she begins to utter "a long impatient moan." She is surprised that she has reached this state so quickly. Their hands remain fixed on the table in a kind of death pose.

> "She will never speak again," says Anne.
> "But she will. One day, a fine morning, all of a sudden, she will meet someone she knows, she will be unable to do anything but say hello. Or she will hear a child sing. The weather will be fine, she will say it is a fine day. It will begin all over again."

The murdered woman is thus resurrected before our very eyes and we are not sure whether we are watching Anne and Chauvin or the other couple. Anne goes close to Chauvin. "Their lips remain touching . . . following the same death rite as their hands, a moment ago, cold and trembling." She is ready for the final words.

> "I would like you to be dead," said Chauvin.
> "It's done," said Anne Desbaresdes.

The gradual slipping of one consciousness into another appears elsewhere in Marguerite Duras's works. In the novel *Le Marin de Gibraltar* (1952), an American woman saves a criminal's life, then falls in love with him. He disappears, and she looks for him all over the world. In her mind he becomes the "Gibraltar sailor." Rich, beautiful, obsessed, she continues her search on a big white yacht; indeed her life and her quest become one and the same thing. She takes a young French clerk aboard. It is hot, they drink a lot of wine, they make love. He questions her over and over about herself and about the Gibraltar sailor until the missing lover seems to be conjured up before our eyes in the form of the French clerk. In the film *Hiroshima mon Amour,* for which Marguerite Duras wrote the scenario, a French actress making a film in the atom-bombed city looks at her sleeping Japanese lover's hand. It gradually becomes the hand of a dead Wehrmacht soldier. The Japanese must question her constantly in order to resurrect the couple they were in the city of Nevers, under the German occupation, towards the end of the war. The actress was the German soldier's mistress. He was killed at the time of the Liberation. Her head was shaven and she was thrown into a damp cellar. Now in Hiroshima, she tries through the ritual of questioning to recapture her past love, to bring to life the German soldier and the girl of Nevers.

The earlier novel and the later film have this in common that in both the heroine is trying to relive an experience she has had, to effect a kind of metempsychosis between a past and present lover. In *Moderato cantabile,* Anne Desbaresdes goes a step further. Through the same ritual of wine and questioning, she tries to live an experience she has never had: to effect a metempsychosis between the murdered woman and herself, as well as to make the mad murderer relive in the person of Chauvin.

To achieve this more ambitious goal Marguerite Duras has constructed her novel with the greatest care. She has been careful to establish her chronology. All of the action takes place at the same time of day, between late afternoon and early evening. The first chapter takes place on a Friday, the second on the following day, the third early the following week, the fourth on the day after the third. The fifth, sixth, and seventh chapters, set in the music studio, the café and the Desbaresdes mansion respectively, all take place on the second Friday. The final chapter takes place two days later.

She has, moreover, underscored the important seventh chapter by a clever shift in verb tenses. Most of the book is written in the narrative past, but the reader is aware that this tense is only an illusion, for what is taking place is really in the present and is steadily unfolding toward the future. In the banquet scene this fiction of a narrative past is abandoned and almost all of the chapter is written in the present. Then, just before the end of the scene, either through a desire to maintain a single point of view (that of Anne in the dining room) or through a new sense of the classical proprieties requiring that such action take place off the stage, the bedroom retching scene is narrated in the future. This tense shifting contributes greatly to the vague sense of continuous duration within the fixed time limits of each chapter.

Finally, the novel achieves its fullest significance if seen not as a banal love story, but as the gradual development of two contrasting themes in the mind of the heroine, analogous to the sonata form. The form is not as rigidly adhered to as in Proust's *Swann in Love,* but *Moderato cantabile* is a less ambitious novel. It is not a sonata, it is a sonatina.

Marguerite Duras and the Subversion of Power

KAREN KAIVOLA

Duras's text shows how writing is connected to power, for as we see most emphatically in *The Ravishing of Lol Stein* and *The Vice-Consul,* to write is to shape and control experience in symbolic ways. Even if language fails to represent the world "as it really is," discursive powers are more than symbolic: they have material effects because subjects constitute themselves out of existing and available discourses. But Duras, by producing textual terrains that are unstructured and uncontained by her own lyrical, associative, fragmented discourse, also shows how subjects exceed the structuring powers of language and culture. That is, she demonstrates how writing challenges normative, complacent attitudes about identity and meaning.

In Duras's texts, subjectivities are unstructured and uncontained. As productions of unstructured textual and psychological regions, these texts, especially *L'Amour* and *India Song,* employ desire to threaten the stability of the symbolic structures in language and the psychic structures of subjectivity. (I distinguish between these two productions of desire with the expressions "destructured" and "desublimated" desire, respectively.)[1] Like Woolf and Barnes, Duras writes toward the repressed of collective culture and individual subjects, but unlike them she shows that any attempt to write is threatened by the force of what exceeds representation.

In this way, and paradoxically given her own medium, Duras refuses to grant writing itself an unambivalent, noncontradictory kind of authority. She deconstructs the authority of her own writing: she dismantles her own positions in discourse and those of the speakers in her texts. With this deconstructive tendency and at a more abstract level, Duras replicates the ambivalent, contradictory positions apparent in the fiction of Woolf and Barnes. While her fiction insists on the imperative for radical social change, it undermines—to some extent, anyway—its own authority to assume a position from which experience can be represented in a meaningful way and on which action might be based. If her work cannot assert a position, its ability to intervene in

From *All Contraries Confounded: The Lyrical Fiction of Virginia Woolf, Dhuna Barnes, and Marguerite Duras* (Iowa City: University of Iowa Press, 1991), 104–42. Reprinted by permission.

sociopolitical contexts is limited. And this is, perhaps, one of the most basic contradictions in Duras's work for feminists, the feature that makes her writing seem at once subversive of and complicit with an oppressive discursive and material status quo. Feminism concerns itself with providing cultural positions for women, whereas Duras's texts take away those positions and demonstrate women's marginality in society and in discourse.

And yet, as Jane Gallop has written, feminism tends "to accept a traditional, unified, rational, puritanical self—a self supposedly free from the violence of desire" (xii). If Duras produces a kind of female subject marginalized in society and a femininity that is marginalized in discourse, she also unsettles feminism's more traditional notions of subjectivity and desire. In so doing she does not produce representations of women as they feel they ought or would like to be. Her work is in this way disturbing and provocative, for at this particular historical moment women are hungry for new and positive representations of what it means to be female.

Another disturbing feature of Duras's writing occurs because, despite the subversion of oppressive social codes and structures, the politics of her oeuvre is often rather astonishingly contradictory, at once subversive and repressive. For example, without any sense of regret or nostalgia, *Destroy, She Said* insists on the necessity to abandon conventional social and symbolic forms. From the perspective of normative cultural assumptions, its figures are frightening and perverse, even mad. This madness is, for the Duras of the 1960s, a desirable response to existing social conditions. Duras explicitly connects the text with social changes demanded by the student-worker uprisings in France in May 1968. "Capital destruction" refers, she says, to the

> destruction of someone as a person. . . . The destruction of every power. . . . The destruction of all police. Intellectual police. Religious police. Communist police. . . . The destruction of memory. . . . The destruction of judgment. . . . I am in favor of . . . closing schools and universities, of ignorance. . . . Of falling in line with the humblest coolie and starting all over again. . . . Please understand: we are all German Jews, we are all strangers. This is a slogan from the May revolution. We are all strangers to your State, to your society, to your shady deals. ("An Interview with Marguerite Duras" 108–109)

But while she here ostensibly endorses a position that, in its commitment to sweeping away so radically all past social, intellectual, and economic privilege, recalls the philosophy behind Mao's cultural revolution, Duras's lyrical prose style in her fiction is extraordinarily nostalgic and sorrowful. While insisting on textual spaces and subjects that are not contained or structured, these texts can hardly be said to celebrate unambivalently such open forms or lack of definitive, stable positions in discourse: as Winifred Woodhull notes, Duras's texts "call for a critical evaluation of non-positionality as a privileged notion in modern theory. Far from idealizing its subversiveness, her writing

explores the culturally determined association of non-positionality with femininity and the ways in which this association contributes to women's marginality" (4). As different as Woodhull's assessment is from Duras's own description of her intent, neither position is unfounded. Duras's work is profoundly
contradictory and invites a wide range of interpretations, while it resists being
entirely contained by any unified perspective or theory.

In the midst of these texts without definitive positions, without traditional character, plot, and narrative sequence or order, Duras interjects political commentary. In *The Lover,* for example, Duras shifts from a lyrical description of the speaker and her brother playing—"I forget everything, and I
forgot to say this, that we were children who laughed, my younger brother
and I, laughed to burst, fit to die" (62)—to a recollection of meeting Robert
Brasillach and Drieu la Rochelle, French fascists who collaborated with the
Gestapo, at dinner parties (where politics was *not* a subject of conversation).
Moreover, she reflects that their collaboration with the Nazis is exactly the
same as her own later involvement with the French Communist party: "The
parallel is complete and absolute. The two things are the same, the same pity,
the same call for help, the same lack of judgment, the same superstition if you
like, that consists in believing in a political solution to the personal problem"
(68). By equating all political involvements, collapsing differences not only
among various positions but among the reasons one might choose to become
politically active, Duras seems to say that any kind of political involvement is
misguided, rooted in a mistaken belief in political solutions to what she calls
"the personal problem."

Even as it makes explicit political commentary, Duras's work insists on a
distance between discourse and an inexpressible, radical exteriority in ways
that subvert both material and discursive forms of power and control. The
word or words that would guarantee meaning and produce an undeniable,
seamless link between the material and the discursive and thereby grant
authority to writing are always absent. In *L'Amante Anglaise,* the head, which
has been cut off and which would provide a solution to the mystery of Marie-
Thérèse's murder, is missing. Lol V. Stein suffers from the word that can't be
spoken because it doesn't exist: "By its absence, this word ruins all the others,
it contaminates them, it is also the dead dog on the beach at high noon, this
hole of flesh" (38). The Vice-Consul insists he can do no more than assert that
he finds it "impossible to give an account, in terms that would be understood,
of what took place in Lahore" (27) when he shot indiscriminately into a crowd
of suffering Indian lepers. Similarly, he cannot adequately express his feelings
for Anne-Marie Stretter: "For what I want to say . . . there are no words"
(98). Certainly it would be false to call what he feels "love," though his words
repeat the conventional language of romantic love as it takes shape within the
cult of romance and passion in the West. The question that no one can for-
mulate properly, the missing head, the absent word, the inability of language
to explain or to explore what matters most precisely because of its absence—

all these factors subvert fixity and normative assumptions about language and culture. They also produce nostalgia, loss, and pain.

If these words existed, the origins of actions and foundations of subjectivity might be understood. But because they do not, origins and foundations are simultaneously inaccessible and intensely powerful, haunting, and desired because eternally absent. It is what cannot be said, what cannot be articulated using intelligible structures of thought, that results in this special kind of intriguing force. It also produces subjects without definitive shape: recognizable figures circulate among discrete texts with just enough variation to deny the fixity of a coherent, intelligible identity. Boundaries are blurred or collapsed, calling into question conceptual categories and distinctions between fiction and autobiography, image and language, pleasure and pain, gender and sexuality, the body and discourse, desire and writing. Duras's texts fashion a unique form of contradiction by simultaneously insisting on the coincidence and noncoincidence of such categories and distinctions. These texts are riddled with contradictions that stem from such a system of shifting equivalences, nonequivalences, and substitutions: fiction is fiction but also autobiography; a discrete text is self-contained but also inseparable from other texts in the Durassian oeuvre that "rewrite" the same scene differently; images are portrayed in language but exceed it; pleasure is the absence of pain but also its presence; gender informs sexuality, but sexuality exceeds the cultural construction of gender; the body is represented in language but drastically out of relation to it; desire is produced in writing but exceeds it.

In *L'Amante Anglaise,* language only inadequately represents female subjectivity and desire while emphasizing the radical split between itself and experience. This text, which subverts the traditional detective plot's assumption that motives for crimes can be inferred and discovered with the appropriate evidence, insists that the mystery of Claire Lannes—and the murder of her cousin Marie-Thérèse that Claire is presumed to have committed—remains a mystery. In the process of attempting to write a definitive account of what happened, the writer's interest shifts from the crime to Claire, who remains equally inaccessible and unknowable. *L'Amante Anglaise* is structured around three interviews with a writer whose book (the text itself) is about to come into being. The text self-consciously represents its own production, calling attention to itself as a discursive construct out of relation to material practices. It ostensibly moves toward a resolution of the mystery of Marie-Thérèse's death by making each section's interviewee possess more knowledge about Claire and the crime and by moving closer to, until finally ending with, Claire herself. But because Claire cannot provide an authoritative explanation of the incident in an "appropriate" discourse, the resolution never comes. Claire cannot account for her behavior, though she teases the writer by suggesting that if he would just ask her the right question, she could provide the information he seeks. Such a question is not forthcoming. And Claire wants to defer the ending, for as long as it is postponed the detective writer takes a more intense interest in her than anyone has for years. She is seduced when his interest in the murder turns to an interest in her and wants to maintain the connection he provides.

Claire can neither experience nor symbolize her life. If she murdered her deaf-mute cousin, her action is really a symbolic suicide: her aggression is aimed inward at her own passivity and her terribly isolated, middle-class life without passion in a small rural town. If Claire did murder her cousin, we must acknowledge that she had no motive for *that* crime. Claire's action does, however, reproduce the symbolic mutilation to which she is subjected. She is, in an important sense, "headless" herself. Thus, by murdering Marie-Thérèse she expresses her own fragmented state of subjectivity. If this is, as Woodhull has stated, an attempt to "create the direct equivalence presumed to exist between representation and lived reality" (11), the attempt fails since Claire's action is murder, not suicide. It would obviously be impossible for her to both decapitate and dismember herself, a fact that stresses, in Claire's case, the impossibility of bringing language and lived experience into alignment. Similarly, the title "L'Amante Anglaise" suggests Claire's inability to use language to adequately symbolize her experience. It transposes Claire's transposition: in a letter Claire writes "l'amante en glaise" (the clay lover) when she means "la menthe anglaise" (English mint), which indicates her radical distance from symbolic forms of expression. Duras's title combines one term from each expression to produce yet another configuration with a new meaning, "l'amante anglaise" (the English lover), which has no referent in the text since there is no English lover.

Claire's mistake connects writing, desire, and the body while stressing the noncoincidence among them, which Duras underscores with the transposed title. Although each phrase sounds the same when spoken, when written they signify differently. Claire, when writing for advice on how to grow "la menthe anglaise," her favorite plant, which she also sees as a means to cut the grease Marie-Thérèse uses in cooking, mistakenly writes "l'amante en glaise." Claire intends to find a remedy for the fat which saturates her body and for the similar congealing of her mind (she spends her days watching television). Her desires are just as stifled as they would be if they were literally saturated with congealed grease. As a lover, she has atrophied in her marriage, turned to clay. Her transposition reveals the extent to which her desire, her body, and her ability to write are all similarly bottled up. She turns to fantasies of passion—personal "solutions" to a more widespread social condition. As Duras makes clear, Claire is a representative female member of the community.[2]

Like Claire Lannes, Lol V. Stein is unable to symbolize her illness, experience, or desire, suggesting again the gap between language and experience. But whereas *L'Amante Anglaise* insists on a radical split between language and experience, *The Ravishing of Lol Stein* demonstrates the extent to which, despite this split, language nevertheless contains and shapes subjectivity differently for men and women. In this text, since it is narrated by a male doctor, Jacques Hold, who is obsessed with Lol, language reflects a particular kind of masculine perspective. Yet Jacques's unreliability and projections produce a gap between language and experience, since we see Lol through his distorting lens, which is marred by his own desires. To some extent Lol escapes being completely contained by his discourse: the extent to which she is subject to it shows that subjectivities and bodies are never absolutely out of relation to discursive practices and theories; the extent to which she escapes is a measure of the radical gap between them.

The contradictory claim Duras makes in these texts, that subjects are at once effects of discourse and exceed it, is reflected in contemporary feminist theory. One branch of feminist theory, often called Anglo-American, insists on the importance of recognizing sexual difference and the ways in which biological women are subjected to oppressive social conditions. The other branch, characterized by French feminists, focuses on the idea of "femininity" as produced and repressed in discourse. In *Marguerite Duras: Writing on the Body,* Sharon Willis notes that Duras's texts "inscribe the form of this contradiction" (14), that is, the contradictory noncoincidence between an essential femininity grounded in the body and the idea of femininity that is produced in discourse as an effect of that discourse.[3] As Willis points out, Duras's comments about her work imply a belief in an essential femininity:

> Referring to her own literary production, [Duras] comments: "We don't write at all in the same place as men. And when women don't write in the place of their desire, they don't write, they are plagiarizing" [*Les Lieux de Marguerite Duras* 102]. Duras repeats this conception of feminine writing in an interview published in *Signs,* where she associates women's writing with translation: "I think 'feminine literature' is an organic, translated writing . . . translated from blackness, from darkness. . . . The writing of women is really translated from the unknown, like a new way of communicating rather than an already formed language. But to achieve that, we have to turn away from plagiarism." (15)

But Willis adds that Duras's writing suggests a very different impulse: "These texts figure the impossibility of a discursive access to the real, while simultaneously forcing, through the pattern of breaches, of empty figures, our recognition that discourse is never out-of-relation to that unrepresentable real" (24). If we have no discursive access to the "unrepresentable real," to what exceeds and threatens culture, we cannot know, in the sense of being able to accurately conceptualize, what essential femininity might be—or, for that matter, anything else either. Thus, any attempt to represent female subjectivities, bodies, and desires differently and more authentically—without plagiarizing or imitating male desire as it is produced and privileged in representation and without replicating existing productions of female desire—is not only fraught with difficulty, it is quite simply impossible. Moreover, gender is always already produced in both material and discursive practices. The body is always already written on, making it extremely difficult to conceptualize and represent it differently in hopes of effecting social change.

Along these lines, Lol's suffering is problematic, for if she lacks subjectivity, it isn't altogether clear what the basis for her suffering might be. And if she lacks subjectivity, might she not in fact represent femininity as a discursive effect rather than a female subject in culture? As Jacques Hold asks, in a curiously ambiguous passage, "Mais qu'est-ce à dire qu'une souffrance sans sujet?" (*Le Ravissement de Lol V. Stein* 23), which I translate as, "What is one to make of a suffering without a subject?" In the Grove Press edition, Richard Seaver translates this passage as, "What is one to make of a suffering which has no apparent cause?" (13). But this translation loses the essential ambiguity of Duras's use of "sujet." The French throws both the cause of suffering and Lol's subjectivity into question: the absence of a subject suggests at once the impossibility of locating causal origins and Lol's absence as a subject. Given this ambiguity, as Jacques remarks, "to know nothing about Lol Stein was already to know her. One could, it seemed to me, know even less about her, less and less about Lol Stein" (72).

Duras's language produces a radical instability and contradictory meanings. If the origin of Lol's suffering is deeply problematic, what precisely constitutes her "ravishment" is just as confusing. In French, as in English, the word has several meanings, all of which resonate with Lol's story. It can mean rape or kidnapping—each a violation of a person's subjectivity, a taking away of integrity. But it can also mean transporting joy or delight: rapture. Unbothered by the resulting contradiction, Duras uses the term in both senses:

> M.D. Maybe that's what life is: to enter within, to let oneself be carried along by this story—this story, well, the story of others—in a constant movement of . . . how do you describe it, when you're carried off from a place?
>
> X.G. . . . abduction, ravishing.
>
> M.D. Yes, that's what it is.
>
> X.G. It's this word "ravishing" that you used; one is "ravished" from oneself; one is "ravished" from others.
>
> M.D. That's what's best. That's what's most desirable in the world. (*Woman to Woman* 42)

Jacques believes that Lol is ravished the night of the T. Beach ball, that she subsequently seeks out her own ravishment in her compulsive wish to repeat the moment of trauma, the moment when she, heretofore the object of Michael Richardson's love and affection, is completely forgotten. In his terms, "ravissement" is not desirable. But the word works in ways he does not intend, over which he has no control or authority, for in another sense Jacques ravishes Lol by appropriating her story to his own psychic needs. And perhaps it is also the reader who ravishes Lol—at least to the extent that he or she imposes, as Jacques does, an external framework upon the unknowable space at the center of Lol's story.

If Lol is ravished, she also ravishes: she is both the subject and object of the title. She transports Jacques away from himself, for she takes him away from the person he was and thought he knew. Appropriated by him, distorted by his projections and fantasies, she remains inaccessible, second to his own desires, verbal pleasures, and textual erotics. While the effect Lol has on the reader is probably not so intense, the text provides an imaginary transport for the reader as well. It takes us away, as all writing does, from ourselves into an unfamiliar terrain, while at the same time our own conscious and unconscious desires shape and produce the text. Perhaps, too, Jacques Lacan is right to suggest that it is *Duras* who ultimately ravishes *us* with such a text.[4] She ravishes us with writing that is as provocative and alluring as it is violent and disturbing.

Indeterminacy produces a seductive effect that is at once diffuse, alluring, and strange. It not only isn't clear when the story begins or ends, it isn't even clear what the story is. In one sense, Lol's story begins when she is abandoned by Michael Richardson at the ball. But others believe the story really starts long before that. Tatiana always believed Lol was different, not quite there, for she didn't ever seem to suffer like other people. For Tatiana, the original moment or event, the one that structures all that follows, does not exist. And in yet another sense, possibly the most persuasive, Lol's story begins ten years later, when she meets Jacques Hold, since the story we have doesn't exist apart from his production of it. Actually, it is his story—that is, about him—quite as much as it is Lol's. If this is the story of the "eternity of the ball in the cinema of Lol Stein" it is just as much the story of the eternity of Lol V. Stein in the cinema of Jacques Hold.

Along these lines, the text suggests that psychoanalysis is a male story—about men and male desires—with questionable and harmful effects on biological women. But it also resonates with certain aspects of psychoanalytic theory. In particular, Duras's work tends to be read frequently in the context of Lacanian psychoanalytic theory. Lacan's remark in response to *The Ravishing of Lol Stein,* that "Marguerite Duras knows, without me, what I teach" ("Homage to Marguerite Duras" 124), implies that the text illustrates his own theory and principles. His comment appropriates her work. And, given Lol's inability to symbolize her subjectivity or experience, it perhaps isn't all that astonishing a claim. As Lacan asserts, "There is woman only as excluded by the nature of things which is the nature of words, and it has to be said that if there is one thing they themselves are complaining about enough at the moment, it is well and truly that—only they don't know what they are saying, which is all the difference between them and me" (*Feminine Sexuality*

144). Yet, as the passage illustrates, Lacan's own discourse is often masterful and privileges the phallus, professing to be convinced of its own authority and veracity—and this kind of mastery is very much at issue in, and very much at odds with, Duras's texts.[5]

However, to claim that Lacan's discourse is masterful, phallocratic, and offensive is not to tell the whole story about Lacan. Lacan also insists upon the failure of the phallic order, a failure related to its inability to account for the feminine, for what is "other" to it. As Jane Gallop so cleverly puts it:

> Not simply a philosopher, but, artfully, a performer, [Lacan] is no mere father figure out to purvey the truth of his authority; he also comes out seeking his pleasure in a relation that the phallocentric universe does not circumscribe. To designate Lacan at his most stimulating and forceful is to call him something more than just phallocentric. He is also phallo-eccentric. Or, in more pointed language, he is a prick. . . . the prick is both resented by and attractive to women. . . . this epithet astoundingly often describes someone whom women . . . despite themselves, find irresistible. . . . The prick does not play by the rules; he (she) is a narcissistic tease who persuades by means of attraction and resistance, not by orderly systematic discourse. (36–37)

Lacan's discourse, by exposing its own position and desire, undermines its own assertions of mastery and authority in a tantalizing double gesture. Because Lacan dismantles his own position in this way, refusing to allow his difficult and elusive discourse to become fixed and seeking a pleasure beyond the boundaries of the paternal order, he is, as Gallop acknowledges, both disturbing and attractive to many women. His lectures were certainly well attended. Still, however ironic Lacan's discourse or performance may be, the double response women have to "the prick" is perhaps not all that different from many women's ambivalent response to the more traditional father figure. This ambivalence is one of the ways that, having been born into a society in which male authority dominates, women enact their internalization of oppression and participate in the reproduction of patriarchal values and institutions.

Lacan rewrites Freud in the context of linguistic theory and maintains that since it is within language that the "I" must be postulated, and since it is within language that women are inscribed as other, as negative difference, women's relationship to language and thus culture is problematic.[6] If for male children the entry into culture entails an acknowledgment of loss and deprivation, for female children this entry involves lacking this experience of loss, since feminine positions in discourse are not subject positions. Therefore, if language displaces the male subject it doubly displaces the female subject, and the essential experience of culture is different for male and female children. Identity within culture is always alienating, but Lacan's framework suggests it is even more alienating for female subjects. Language precedes the subject and determines differences, equivalences, and instabilities. It "speaks" the individual subjects born into it, while these subjects must use language to negotiate their relationship to society and culture. To rediscover the laws that govern this "other scene" is to discover the unstable elements of language and thus of subjectivity. Lacan's subject is not split in the sense that in a different society it could be made whole: it is created in a split, which produces the conditions whereby it can begin to conceptualize itself at all. Thus, as Lacan puts it in a discussion of the phallus as transcendental signifier, that is, as "the signifier intended to designate as a whole the effects of the signified, in that the signifier [the phallus] conditions them by its presence as a signifier" (*Ecrits* 285), "man cannot aim at being whole (the 'total personality' is another of the deviant premises of modern psychotherapy), while ever the play of displacement and condensation to which he is doomed in the exercise of his functions marks his relation as a subject to the signifier" (*Ecrits* 287). The phallus does not guarantee power and privilege in any essential way: to identify with the phallus is to acknowledge the radical instability of the "authority" and position of mastery it offers.

Lacan's subject conceptualizes itself in a radical split, in what Lacan calls the mirror stage. This representation of the subject to itself is an identification, a "transformation that takes place in the subject when he assumes an image" (*Ecrits* 2). The image the subject assumes is a fiction: it is not the subject itself but an identification with what it perceives others perceive it to be. Thus, as Lacan says, "the important point is that this form situates the agency of the ego, before its social determination, in a fictional direction, which will always remain irreducible for the individual alone" (*Ecrits* 2). The unconscious is shaped by this early splitting.

If the notion of a whole self or identity is a fantasy or fiction, so too is the idea of a stable sexual identity. If the unconscious is structured like a language, as Lacan claims, it is subject to the same instabilities: signification is the result of negative difference, where meaning is constructed according to what something is *not* rather than to what it is in itself. The man can be—and is—privileged because he is not woman, but he is not privileged because the phallus has any intrinsic value. The slippage that results because meaning and value cannot be fixed with any certainty undermines sexual identity. Sexuality is ordered in the symbolic but unstable in the unconscious. As Jacqueline Rose points out in her introduction to *Feminine Sexuality,* for Lacan sexuality belongs to the realm of masquerade.

Although Lacan's radical undermining of identity and essential sexuality seems to have much in common with Duras's representations, for Alice Jardine it is "nothing less than astonishing as an event" that Lacan has written about Marguerite Duras (172). Jardine notes that Duras is the only contemporary writer about whom Lacan has written. In addition, her novels are "the only writings by a woman consistently invoked by Lacanian analysts" (172).[7] Critical of Jacques Lacan's identification with the Jacques of the text and his remark that Duras was able to understand his theory without him, Jardine states that "for the feminist reader, this book written by a feminist has only one subject: Lol V. Stein" (175). Jardine's suggestion that feminist readers identify not with Jacques Hold but with Lol is supported by Duras's comment (itself rather surprising, I think) that many women have written to her of their powerful identification with Lol (*Woman to Woman* 117). Still, because Jacques's perspective almost entirely governs our relationship to Lol, any identification with Lol on the part of female readers is mediated through his masculine biases and desires. Jardine, along with other critics, glosses the apparent contradiction (that women are identifying not with a feminine potential for a new kind of subjectivity but with a woman who, to the extent that she is *known* at all, is produced by and is a response to male desire) by insisting that women readers are interested most in Lol (as if she existed purely or apart from Jacques's use of her), a move that resists the recognition that the text is essentially contradictory. After criticizing Jacques Lacan for identifying exclusively with Jacques Hold, Jardine suggests uncritically that feminist readings replicate what she has just faulted Lacan for.[8] She notes, however, that disparate readings are not simply the result of strict sexual identification. In Jardine's analysis of the criticism, it is nonanalysts who see in Lol the potential for a new kind of subject in the world and analysts (Lacan and Montrelay are representative here) who see Lol as a trope dissolved by the real. While the body of criticism on Duras does not bear out this distinction between analysts and nonanalysts, what finally interests Jardine is the disagreement she believes is produced by two "machines of interpretation (feminist and psychoanalytic)" (176).

Because the text is Jacques Hold's unsuccessful attempt to control language and discourse—to produce a narrative that shapes Lol, tells her story, and provides an intelligible, truthful account of her madness—it is impossible to disentangle his projections from any "essential" Lol. The validity of Jacques's discourse is precisely what's at issue. Because he interprets Lol's madness as the result of her abandonment by Michael Richardson, her fiancé, Jacques glosses over clues Lol provides to the contrary that would necessitate a story different from the one he tells. For example, Lol insists that from the moment Anne-Marie Stretter walked into the room, she "ceased to love" Michael Richardson. Lol suggests that by the time of the supposed origin of her illness or madness, the early morning hours when the ball came to an end, she was no longer in a position to be abandoned—at least not by Michael Richardson. If Lol's desire shifts with the arrival of Anne-Marie Stretter, who in many of these texts evokes desire in all the figures who surround her, the implication is that Lol's desire has been redirected toward her. It is from a conventional perspective that Lol's desire seems directed exclusively heterosexually, toward Michael. But in the triangular configurations, which echo the original triangle among Lol, Jacques, and Anne-Marie Stretter, Tatiana Karl is as important to Lol as Jacques is: Lol's desire encompasses them both.

It is not in this way directed or structured according to social codes, values, or conventions.

In one sense, Jacques's narrative strategy, as Martha Noel Evans argues in *Masks of Tradition,* evinces his reliability as a narrator. For Evans, Jacques's commentary on his own discourse produces credibility. But whether he professes to lie, invent, imagine, or report what he knows, his authority is also undermined by his inability to master or structure the story. The text subverts any credibility with its convoluted, fractured syntax, repetitions of whole sections of text almost verbatim (as if Jacques forgets what he's already reported),[9] comments revealing Jacques's own obsessive interest in Lol as illustrated by such remarks as, "On three occasions, Lol and I were the only ones laughing" (81), and admissions that entire blocks of text have been lies. This is the case in the following passage, when, from the window of the hotel room where he waits for Tatiana, Jacques spots a woman "about whose grayish blondness there could be no doubt whatsoever":

> I had a violent reaction, although I had been prepared for any eventuality, a very violent reaction I could not immediately define, something between terror and disbelief, horror and pleasure, and I was tempted by turn to cry out some warning, offer help, thrust her away forever, or involve myself forever with Lol Stein in all her complexities, fall in love with her. I stifled a cry, prayed to God for help, I ran out of the room, retraced my steps, paced the floor like a caged animal, too much alone to love or not to love, sick, sick of my frightful inability to admit what was happening. . . .
>
> I'm lying. I did not move from the window, my worst fears confirmed, fighting back the tears. (109–110)

The rhythmic intensity in the passage steadily increases, approaching melodrama, equating writing with desire, but loses its momentum when Jacques admits that he lies. It is as if the possibilities inherent in language to construct meaning, rather than the truthful representation of events, govern his discourse. These "facts" put a blunt end to his verbal erotics.

If Jacques Hold takes a more active position in culture and the production of meaning than Lol does, a more active involvement in what Lacan calls the symbolic as part of his function as narrator and shaper, it must still be said that his own subjectivity is none too stable. As Jacques wonders when he meets Lol, "What is there about me I am so completely unaware of and which she summons me to know? Who will be there, at that moment, beside her?" (96). Lol is to Jacques what Anne-Marie Stretter is to Michael Richardson: a figure to whom he is drawn for no reason he can account for rationally. After seeing Anne-Marie Stretter, Michael Richardson simply changes: "It was obvious to everyone. Obvious that he was no longer the same person they had thought he was" (7). Similarly, when Jacques becomes aware of his attraction to Lol, he becomes unknown to himself and others.

It isn't as if Lol recognizes something about Jacques that is nascent or hidden. When she picks Jacques from all the other men she could have chosen, her choice "implies no preference"; he is merely the "man from [S.] Tahla she has decided to follow" (103). The attraction is completely impersonal, having nothing to do with personality. It does not originate in a self capable of meaningful choice and action. But it triggers something important in Jacques and changes his relationship to the world by putting into play repressed structures in his own psychic life:

> Just as my hands touch Lol, the memory of an unknown man, now dead, comes back to me: he will serve as the eternal Richardson, the man from [T.] Beach, we will be mingled with him, willy-nilly, all together, we shall no longer be able to recognize one from the other, neither before, nor after, nor during, we shall lose sight of one another, forget our names, in this way we shall die for having forgotten—piece by piece, moment by moment, name by name—death. (103)

This unknown man who will function as the eternal Richardson isn't Michael Richardson. Instead, he serves as the "eternal Richardson," that third figure in the triangle that is an essential to Jacques's desire. It isn't the memory of Tatiana, who from Lol's perspective is the most apparent third party in this triangle, that comes to Jacques at this moment. It is instead the memory of another man, a man desired by the woman Jacques desires. The Jacques who narrates this story does not represent the Jacques in the story as being significantly involved with Lol because her relationship with Michael Richard reminds him of an unknown man who is now dead. Yet this unknown man is here remembered or produced by the resemblance. It isn't clear that he has a basis in Jacques's material past; it isn't clear whether he ever existed. He becomes a linguistic possibility, however, who can be brought into existence given Jacques's new involvement with Lol, an involvement that produces change and thus leads to death.

Duras's writing explodes signification by showing how language both represents and is exceeded by its own representations of subjectivity. Such explosions interrupt narrative and threaten to overwhelm the subject, as in the following passage where Jacques first learns that Lol has watched the window of the hotel room where he and Tatiana meet. Her words destroy his ordinary ability to make the world seem somewhat coherent. What happens in language separates language from experience:

> She has just said that Tatiana is naked beneath her dark hair. That sentence is the last to have been uttered. I hear: "naked beneath her dark hair, naked, naked, dark hair." The last two words especially strike with a strange and equal intensity. It's true that Tatiana was as Lol has just described her, naked beneath her dark hair. She was that way in the locked room, for her lover. The intensity of the sentence suddenly increases, the air around it has been rent, the sentence

explodes, it blows the meaning apart. I hear it with a deafening roar, and I fail to understand it, I no longer even understand that it means nothing. . . .

The nudity of Tatiana, already naked, intensifies into an overexposed image which makes it increasingly impossible to make any sense whatsoever out of it.

The void is statue. The pedestal is there: the sentence. The void is Tatiana naked beneath her dark hair, the fact. It is transformed, poured out lavishly, the fact no longer contains the fact, Tatiana emerges from herself, spills through the open windows out over the town, the roads, mire, liquid, tide of nudity. Here she is, Tatiana Karl, suddenly naked beneath her hair, between Lol [V.] Stein and me. The sentence has just faded away, I can no longer hear any sound, only silence, the sentence is dead at Lol's feet, Tatiana is back in her place. I reach out and touch, like a blind man I touch and fail to recognize anything I have already touched. (105–106)

In this remarkable passage, Lol's words produce Tatiana as immediately present and effect a change in Jacques's relationship to the world by propelling him into a space quite unknown to him. It is so disorienting that he is temporarily unable to connect with the world: his discourse disintegrates while suggesting a radical exteriority that language can merely begin to approach but never entirely contain. The sense of this radical exteriority is produced by splitting language and experience. But at the same time the passage collapses language and experience. Tatiana, at once merely a word, a collection of sounds, a void that means nothing, is also imbued with a material force. She spills out not only over and within language but over the material objects that surround Jacques—the town and the roads. Language acquires a material force comparable to the body. In the same way, the absent word becomes for Lol a "bole of flesh" as material as the dead dog on the beach. And when Lol cannot stop talking Jacques produces an image of her literally vomiting words, expelling them as if they were rejected food or nourishment, which, of course, in a sense they are, since the "right" word, the one that could make Lol well, does not exist.

Although at such moments language produces and collapses into material effects, the body nevertheless exceeds discourse and its symbolic constructions. There is a radical distance between language and material exteriority. This is made especially apparent during Lol and Jacques's trip to T. Beach, when, in several instances, Lol emphatically denies his version of things, suggesting that she is not merely a discursive effect or idea of femininity. For example, Jacques asks: "Why don't you kill yourself? Why haven't you already killed yourself?" Lol responds, "No, you're wrong, that's not it at all" (159). Her refusals mark the extent to which she is not equivalent to his production of her. It is perhaps here, in Lol's refusal to conform to Jacques's construction of her, that Duras holds out some hope for a female subjectivity that could be represented as being beyond the confines of male imaginings and desires—and perhaps even beyond the laws governing the linguistic scene.

In the final pages of the text, Lol seems increasingly distant from and indifferent to Jacques, more and more beyond the containing powers of his discourse. This distance is enhanced by her apparent ability to insert herself into the symbolic, to symbolize for the first time her own split subjectivity. She isn't a unified subject but one who is radically split, as she emphasizes when she gives herself two names: Tatiana Karl and Lol V. Stein. That Lol names herself, however, is significant and introduces a shift. No longer entirely excluded from representational practices and the production of meaning, Lol inserts herself into two positions: she becomes the woman who is desired and the woman who is excluded. By occupying two positions in the triangle herself, Lol finds a way to repeat the drama of the night of the T. Beach ball without having to be abandoned. Whereas Tatiana was the desired other in a couple, she is now, because of Lol, the third term in the triangle.

Lol's ability to represent herself in this divided way does not, however, solve the problem of the noncoincidence between language and experience. This gap still exists, even if she bridges it somewhat. To bring the two into alignment is, Duras insists, an impossible enterprise. And finally the text does not attempt to resolve the difficult questions it raises about whether an essential female difference exists or whether femininity is more appropriately understood as an effect of discourse. Asleep in the field of rye, Lol becomes an image of indifference. But given the unreliability of Jacques's discourse and his stake in containing Lol, one has to wonder whether she's really there at all.

In *L'Amour,* Duras "rewrites" *The Ravishing of Lol Stein* to insist even more emphatically on the noncoincidence between writing and experience. Abandoning a male narrator who is himself a figure in the text, Duras moves away from equating writing with culturally legitimate forms of power. Instead, she uses writing to subvert such power and in so doing approaches both a more radically destructured textual space and a more radically desublimated subject. Paradoxically, the effect is writing that seems contrary to its own representational status, for in a strange way it acquires a material force while it underscores its difference from materiality. This effect is produced because the writing so radically departs from conventional assumptions about fiction and representation.

L'Amour is so destructured it is virtually unrecognizable as part of the Lol V. Stein cycle. And yet the shifting triangular structures suggest the profusion of triangles in *The Ravishing of Lol Stein;* the wandering movements of the figures, motions without discernible directions or goals, recall Lol's wandering through S. Thala. Place, though barely distinguishable because so minimal in *L'Amour,* seems vaguely similar, and the images such as the dead dog on the beach even more so. Except for the return to the scene of the ball, the circulation of images and figures is implicit, minimal, and undeveloped. No one is named. The text promises to "name this man, the traveller—if by chance the thing is necessary—on account of the slowness of his steps, the straying of his look" (13–14).[10] It never does become necessary, though what might constitute necessity and why it would involve the way he walks or the way his look strays also isn't clear. But because the man's look strays, he recalls Jacques Hold and Michael Richardson, both of whom are described in such terms in other contexts.[11] The three central figures, though unnamed, are sexed bodies—two male, one female—in a textual terrain bordered by the sea, the sky, the sea wall, the river, and the town. The terrain lacks as much definition as the bodies lack identity or character. Within the textual space and in no particular order, the quality of light shifts, the sea rises and roars, a child cries, alarms sound, and the bodies move about, sleep, and occasionally make contact with one another. And what the figures say to one another seems simultaneously void of meaning and highly charged with a significance the reader can't begin to understand.

There is little sense to be made, and this is the point. To enter this space one must leave behind conventional habits of reading and ways of constructing meaning. Here there are no plot, characters, and narrative. Even if we're encouraged to see the parallels with Lol's story, these substitutions never quite work. When the traveler mentions the ball to the woman in connection with her first illness, she knows exactly what he's talking about. She remembers having married a musician after her illness (Lol too marries a musician) and having two children (Lol has three, all daughters). She tells the traveler that she fell ill a second time and that a man (her husband? another lover? Jacques Hold? Michael Richardson?) has died. She sleeps on the beach while he revisits the scene of the ball alone (in *The Ravishing of Lol Stein* both Lol and Jacques return to the casino). Like Lol and Jacques, the traveler encounters an attendant who shows him the room where the ball was held. From within, the two men can see the beach and the woman sleeping. In the exchange that follows, the traveler, who admits that he doesn't know the woman's name, asks the attendant if he recognizes the woman sleeping on the beach. The attendant "dit un nom" (131), but we don't know what name he says. In any case, it is a name he invents.

L'Amour isn't a text that invites what film theorists call suture. That is, it provides little if any means by which the reader might momentarily forget that the text is a fictional construct. This text never seems like life; it offers no construction of how one might actually live; with no characters and no plot, it represents nothing. Because it is so radically other to cultural conventions and stories, it is able to produce figures who are not so much individuals as markers in an ever-changing textual terrain. With the individual subject shattered, the emerging figures are not human beings but geometric shapes resulting from connections among and between bodies that cannot be understood in conventional ways, much less articulated. These forms are perhaps more accurately understood as traces of shapes, for they lack the definition and fixity necessary to produce anything solid.

In this strange and minimal space, traversed primarily by the three figures, desire circulates somewhat randomly—that is, through the figures but without any identifiable source or destination. Yet in some ways desire is less than random, for it moves along heterosexual lines. This seems equally true in *Lol V. Stein* and *L'Amour,* despite the differences in the extent to which structure and control are produced in each.[12] While the three figures of *L'Amour* do not desire in the way Jacques Hold does, the existence of a third party, the surplus of the extra male figure, triggers desire. But desire is not steady or consistent: the triangle first consolidates among the three figures on the beach, but it "warps and reshapes itself, never breaking apart" (8). This slippage within the triangle causes the man who just stands and looks to begin to walk, like the other man who walks up and down the beach, which sometimes produces confusion as to who is who. The movements of these figures apparently result from the force produced by the relations among their bodies—whether they move or remain where they are is determined by these relations, not by conscious control or volition. Their actions and desires originate in some unknowable place.

By taking bodies and desires out of the realm of discursive control, *L'Amour* takes the Lol V. Stein story almost completely out of the realm of individuality and identity. *L'Amour* is, as a result, also out of the realm of psychoanalytic theory as a discourse that attempts to explain how subjectivity comes into being. In fact, it resists assimilation to any such cultural theory or discourse, for, unlike *The Ravishing of Lol Stein,* it does not provide enough structure or control to allow for collusion with oppressive structures. Therefore, of the texts discussed here, *L'Amour* most completely destructures and desublimates desire in order to produce radical exteriority. What it sacrifices in order to do so is not only relevant social or political commentary but a discernible relevance to the world. If the space it produces is outside traditional configurations of power, because it dismantles structures of human significance and meaning in order to suggest a desire existing apart from cultural trappings, its ability to subvert such configurations is quite limited.

In contrast, *The Vice-Consul* puts the representation of desire and the noncoincidence between the body and language into a broader political and historical context: it dramatizes white European oppression of India, a particular historical situation, as a horror that cannot be articulated because it is simply unthinkable. This is not, or not entirely, because of an unbridgeable gap between language and experience but because extreme pain resists verbal articulation in special ways. If *The Ravishing of Lol Stein* dramatizes the effects of Lol's inability to symbolize her suffering and Jacques Hold's unsuccessful attempt to translate the story of her suffering into an authoritative discourse and *L'Amour* asks what a text without traces of social or cultural power might look like, *The Vice-Consul* underscores how the ideology of colonialism is deployed in ways that produce terrible forms of pain and oppression. It returns to the scene of Duras's experience in French Indochina. And *The Vice-Consul* precedes *L'Amour*: the emphasis on the social and political is not, as was the case with Woolf's response to *The Waves* in *Between the Acts,* a move from the abstract to the particular. Because *The Vice-Consul* insists on the reality of pain and oppression beyond its own boundaries, its position on the relationship between language and experience is necessarily different from the extremes of *L'Amour*. In order to insist on the existence of widespread pain, Duras must return to concrete particulars. At the same time the text foregrounds its fictional status, insisting at once on its separation from and relation to lived experience. It begins with Peter Morgan's story of the beggar woman's journey from Cambodia to Calcutta: the first line reads, "She walks on, writes Peter Morgan" (1). The text represents the miseries of imperialism while averring that representation itself is a form of imperialism.

The Vice-Consul takes place in Calcutta, where the white European colonials are surrounded by the unspeakable misery of hunger, leprosy, and madness, and on an island retreat in the Delta, where there are a luxurious European hotel and the French ambassador's villa. Anne-Marie Stretter, for whom Michael Richardson abandoned Lol V. Stein the night of the T. Beach ball, now married for seventeen years to the French ambassador, reappears and in this new context is connected to the "symbol of emaciated Calcutta" (118), the mad beggar woman of whom Peter Morgan writes. Michael Richardson "reappears" as Michael Richard. Anne-Marie is also strangely connected to the Vice-Consul of Lahore, who has committed atrocious murders and is now ostracized from the rest of white society. These three individuals form a textual center that alternately links writing with desire, domination, and death.

Anne-Marie Stretter is unable to give symbolic expression to her pain. In this respect she is much like other Durassian women, including Claire Lannes and Lol V. Stein, but also like the beggar woman who cannot, owing to her madness, even experience let alone represent her pain. Anne-Marie Stretter, like the beggar woman and the Vice-Consul, is mad. Suffering leads to the breakdown of psychic structure and intelligibility: Anne-Marie Stretter absorbs the pain of India in ways that cannot be verbalized. She embodies pain: "I cry for no reason that I can explain. It's as though I were shot through with grief. Someone has to weep, and I seem to be the one" (158). As a result, she seems "at home in this nightmare town" in ways others do not (85). Her pain and madness are the most appropriate responses to such a nightmare. For her, "contrary to popular belief, life [in Calcutta] isn't easy, it isn't hard, it's nothing" (85). Or, as she tells the Vice-Consul: "If one stays, since one can never see things as they really are, one has to . . . contrive yes, contrive a way of looking at them" (92). All the whites feel oppressed by the suffering that surrounds them, and yet, with few exceptions, they seem to think along the same lines as the ambassador, that the situation can be made tolerable, that their "nervous tension" can be cured.

Elaine Scarry argues in *The Body in Pain* that, in contrast to mental pain which can be verbalized in psychoanalysis and in some ways eased, physical pain cannot be put into language; it actually resists articulation or translation. She notes that torture, for instance, is used at particular historical moments by unstable governments or powers in order to break down the experiences and narratives of those who oppose them. This happens when the stories of the opposition are too threatening to their tenuous hold on power. They destroy, therefore, the victims' ability to use language. The white Europeans of *The Vice-Consul* are certainly not torturers of the sort Scarry describes, but they are surrounded by human misery of such unspeakable proportions that it does indeed break down language. In such misery, one, like the beggar woman, has no story to tell: the structures that constitute one's world have collapsed. We cannot know if she even experiences pain, for she lacks the ability to represent it.

In order to maintain their own sanity, power, and privilege, all of which are virtually inseparable in this context, the white Europeans must learn to ignore what is beyond reason, beyond endurance. In this, their culture offers protection and guidance. Unlike the marginalized figures Barnes represents in *Nightwood* who are disenfranchised, the Europeans at the core of Duras's story enjoy almost unlimited power. Walls and fences separate India and the Indians from the luxurious European hotels and embassies. The Indian servant who wakes the "master" (in this case Charles Rossett) from his dream of a woman reading Proust is perceived as a "face with a sly expression [peering] cautiously through the open door" (33). Neither can see the other as entirely human. The one is "master," the other a face—a part not a whole. With the image of a woman reading Proust, and in conjunction with representing Peter Morgan as a writer, Duras suggests that only the privileged few have the leisure requisite to enjoy "the pleasures of the text." In light of the misery which surrounds them, such cultural pursuits on the part of the Europeans seem almost profane. For Charles Rossett, the dream provides a temporary escape from an unbearable reality.

By firing into a crowd of sleeping lepers, the Vice-Consul makes clear just what the European position in India entails. The act is beyond redemption, a refusal of what his culture professes to value above all else—human life. It is madness, but in a way, the Vice-Consul merely does what at some level they all want to do: eliminate the misery, perhaps for their own sake as well as for those who suffer. The Vice-Consul's action, however, is contradictory. It makes clear that the situation, the reality of his privilege and power and of others' pain, is beyond redemption: it cannot be changed by any one person for it is too overwhelming. But his actions also reek of supreme arrogance and power. He makes abundantly clear that all the whites have the power to end human life should they choose. As the ambassador asks, Who is there to care about Lahore? No one. So the colonizers have an unlimited, terrible power.

The figures of Anne-Marie Stretter and the Vice-Consul become equivalent because they both refuse to be blind to or repress the monstrosity of their positions as white colonizers.[13] And yet, within the white colonial culture, their positions could hardly be more dissimilar: she forms the center of desire, he its antithesis. As the wife of the ambassador, she enjoys power and status. The Vice-Consul, removed from his post, his future uncertain, has no status and no social position. Any connection between them is unthinkable from the perspective of white European colonial society. Ostracized by the whites, the Vice-Consul is cast out, forgotten, and ignored in the same way they try to ignore or repress the violence of India. In the fragile oasis of opulence amid extreme poverty, everything that enters the carefully planned world they've created for themselves must be made safe and acceptable, like cocktail party conversation. Surfaces must be maintained, and so the others resent the Vice-Consul because he forces them to notice him—just as they resent being forced to see the incredible pain that surrounds them.

Peter Morgan, the young male who writes the story of the beggar woman, represents public opinion and conventional morality. It is Morgan who steps in gallantly to remove the Vice-Consul from the embassy after his embarrassing outbreak of emotion for Anne-Marie. As he does so, he remarks callously that "a man of your sort is only interesting in his absence" (116). He denies all human connection with or compassion for the Vice-Consul; he denies this other's subjectivity and independence by controlling him. Significantly, this is precisely what Morgan does in writing the story of the beggar woman of Calcutta. On the way out to the island, Morgan describes his project to the others who, except for Anne-Marie Stretter, are willing to contribute their opinions about how her story should be written. Morgan wants to dwell on her filth: "She is as dirty as nature itself, it's incredible. . . . Oh! I want to dwell on that, her filth compounded of everything, and for a long time now ingrained in her skin, a compound of the skin itself. I want to analyze her filth, describe what is in it: sweat, river-mud, scraps of stale foie-gras sandwiches from your Embassy receptions, dust, tar, mangos, fish-scales, blood, everything. I want to disgust you" (145–146). As Michael Richard points out, what Morgan means "is something even more extreme. He wants to deprive her of any existence other than her existence in his mind when he is watching her. She herself is not to feel anything" (146). In short, writing her story becomes a way of controlling her for his own purposes and desires. Because like the Vice-Consul the beggar woman is interesting to Peter Morgan only in her absence, not only is the Vice-Consul linked with Anne-Marie Stretter, he is linked also with the mad beggar woman. They are all three interesting to write about—but terrifying to get close to.

On the trip to the island in the Delta, Charles Rossett, who was selected the night of the party to be Anne-Marie Stretter's next lover, discovers just how terrifying she is, at least from his conventional point of view. He tries to apply his own normative, romantic ideas about how things should work between them and finds she resists them. When he kisses her, he is shocked by a jolt of pain, for she, like the Vice-Consul and the beggar woman, is like death. The island, supposedly a much-needed retreat for white Europeans from the misery of Calcutta, becomes a place of almost surreal horror for Rossett. He realizes just how little he can control Anne-Marie Stretter, and, despite her choosing him as a lover, how little she desires him. Moreover, he begins to realize that, regardless of appearances, she really does desire the Vice-Consul. That this other man could be the object of anyone's desire, given who and what he is, is simply beyond his ability to imagine: "Oh! it's true," he says, "it's impossible, it's absolutely impossible to dwell on . . . the fact of his existence. . . . How can one possibly feel human affection of any kind for the Vice-Consul of Lahore?" (155). When he realizes that Anne-Marie's husband will have the Vice-Consul transferred out of Calcutta because of the force of her desire, he is stunned: "You see," she says, "if I were to force myself to see him, Michael Richard would never forgive me. Nor, for that matter, would anyone else. I can only be the person I am here with you by . . . frittering away my time like this . . . don't you see?" (155). Anne-Marie Stretter's choice of Charles Rossett as her lover is utterly incidental. She has no real desire for him: he is a means for her to fritter away her time, a distraction that enables her to continue an impossible life. When he realizes this, his own desire is thwarted. It is not impersonal choice that he wants; in fact it challenges his way of life and what he values. He wants to be chosen for who he is, but Duras refuses this notion of personal choice.

Although Rossett attributes his loss of desire to her tears, the reasons are much more complex and are related to his unarticulated desire to possess and control—and to his immense frustration when he realizes she cannot be possessed. After she weeps, she goes not to him, whom she has just kissed, for comfort but instead to Michael Richard. At that moment Rossett realizes the truth of the Vice-Consul's words: "She's a woman without . . . preferences. That's what counts. You or me" (136). Like Lol V. Stein, then, Anne-Marie Stretter's choice is impersonal. And unlike Jacques Hold, Charles Rossett cannot accept this refusal to acknowledge his own individuality.

The complexity of Rossett's response to Anne-Marie Stretter, the extent to which he cannot articulate either what happens or his own response, is suggested in the following passage:

> He stops in his tracks, arrested by the memory of Anne-Marie Stretter's tears.
> He sees again Anne-Marie Stretter, rigid under the electric fan—in the heavenly rain of her tears, as the Vice-Consul might say—then suddenly the picture changes. There is something he wishes he had done. What? Oh! how he wishes he had raised his hand. . . . His hand is raised, it is lowered, it begins to stroke her face, her lips, gently at first, then more and more roughly. She bares her teeth in a painful contortion of a smile. More and more she surrenders her face to the impact of his hand, until it is wholly in his power. She is his willing victim. Slapping her face, he cries out that she must never weep again, never, never. She seems at this point to be losing her memory. No one is crying now, she says, there is nothing left that needs understanding. The slapping continues, more and more regularly. It is close to attaining rhythmic perfection.

Anne-Marie Stretter, all of a sudden, is endowed with sombre beauty. Her heaven is being torn down, but she is resigned to it. Smoothly, with marvellous grace, her head moves. It is an effortless movement, as though her head were attached to her neck by a system of carefully oiled and incomparably intricate wheels. It has become, under Charles Rossett's hand, a living instrument.
Michael Richard was watching them. (161–62).[14]

By imagining her as a "willing victim," with Michael Richard standing by as witness and voyeur, watching him take control, Rossett fantasizes he is able, using violence, to make Anne-Marie Stretter into what he wants her to be, a "living instrument" to serve his own desires. As a representative of a certain kind of conventional male figure, Rossett is really more like the Vice-Consul than he might imagine, at least at the level of desires not articulated or known. In this passage his desire to dominate becomes clearer, his rage directed outward toward a weaker other. Like the Vice-Consul, he strikes out in order to assert some power over a misery which he cannot—outside of his own imagination—control. Having to some extent repressed his own pain, having refused to become like Anne-Marie Stretter a porous surface that absorbs the misery of the world, Rossett must forceably keep his protective psychic structures intact.

When Charles Rossett leaves Anne-Marie Stretter's island villa, that area of the island "fenced in for his greater protection" (161), he finds he must traverse a territory even more frightening than that he has just left, for this territory has not been fenced for white Europeans' protection. It is precisely what he thinks he cannot endure—madness, the breakdown of the symbolic order—that threatens him, both at Anne-Marie Stretter's villa and here. Because they are uncharted, the protected areas turn out to be almost as terrifying as the unprotected areas. It is outside in the truly uncharted, uncontrolled space that he encounters the mad beggar woman. Despite the disparity in their social status, the encounter terrifies him. The beggar woman bites off the head of a live fish and advances toward him. In this encounter his guarantees of power—his gender, race, language, and money—do him no good, for they will not serve here as currency. She refuses to acknowledge any of them. The beggar woman does not stoop to pick up the money he throws at her. Refusing his currency, which means nothing to her, she chases him to the hotel, then returns to the sea to pursue other prey.

Duras suggests with this encounter the elaborate cultural supports required to keep the institutionalization of white male power intact. One on one, Charles Rossett has no advantage. With the symbols of the power and privilege of Europe behind him, he does. In fact, it takes only reaching the Prince of Wales Hotel to bring him back to his senses—back to the realm where he can believe in his ability to understand what is happening to him. But with the madness that exists outside this at once fragile and powerful boundary, Duras points to the tenuousness of sanity. The borders between sanity and madness blur. There is much more that is not understood than is understood in the world; what is not understood is perceived as madness, as a threat by the figures who are most conventional.

If Anne-Marie does not allow herself to become Rossett's willing victim in quite the way he imagines, and if she seems in control when she instigates the Vice-Consul's removal from the embassy, it would not be fair to say that in other ways she escapes being precisely what these men want her to be—in Rossett's words, she is indeed a "living instrument." She embodies the pain of India while she serves as a conventional image of feminine grace and beauty in the midst of horror. She is a distraction from the horror as well as a reminder of it, for she is a figure who will take on everyone's pain. In the summary accompanying *India Song,* a text-script-film that repeats and reworks elements of *The Vice-Consul,* Duras describes Anne-Marie Stretter as born of the horror of "famine and leprosy mingled in the pestilential humidity of the monsoon": "She stands in the midst of it with a grace which engulfs everything, in unfailing silence—a grace which the voices try to see again, a grace which is porous and dangerous, dangerous also for some of them" (146). As much as anything, she is an image of Duras's writing, which could easily be described in precisely these terms. In the midst of horror, personified by the beggar woman who exists outside the boundaries of culture and sanity, Anne-Marie Stretter seems graceful, lyrical, and desirable. But Anne-Marie Stretter is not only linked with the beggar woman, she is in fact inseparable from her. Similarly, Duras's writing ravages: the combination of such intense beauty and pain produces something like vertigo. Emotionally and intellectually, one reels from such prose, so "porous and dangerous." Like Rossett, a reader enters a strange landscape where conventional and rational structures no longer apply. It is a place alluring and violent.

The Vice-Consul equates writing with violence and danger: it refuses to purify writing, insisting instead on its terrible powers. As Peter Morgan distances the beggar woman with prose by making her represent what he wants her to represent, so too does Charles Rossett attempt to distance Anne-Marie Stretter by rewriting his involvement with her to enhance his own strength and power, to assert his difference from her. Their actions mirror the Vice-Consul's more outrageous act of violence against unknown lepers. Given these rough equivalences, Duras suggests that the impulses behind representation can be violent and brutal. Both Morgan and Rossett want to distance themselves from others whom they have a great psychic investment in seeing as radically different from themselves. In *Powers of Horror,* Julia Kristeva explains the desire to distance oneself in this way as a desperate attempt to avoid weakness by connecting the frightening other with the concept of abjection. To be abject is to be neither subject nor object: to refuse this non-positionality where boundaries blur is to assert one's own position as subject, to reproduce boundaries and limits.

Because local passions get played out at a global level, *The Vice-Consul* makes a more pointed political statement than many of Duras's other texts. Still, the force of its critique is tempered by the allure of what always remains indeterminant. The magnitude of this unknowable otherness continually threatens any position the writing asserts, making the implicit political imperatives of the text tempered by the power of fascination. Like Anne-Marie Stretter, this writing is poised at the center of eroticism and death.

In *India Song,* Duras translates this powerful fascination into film. *India Song* rewrites but does not cancel out *The Vice-Consul,* much in the way *L'Amour* rewrites but does not cancel out *The Ravishing of Lol Stein.* By rewriting in this way, Duras does not correct the earlier texts, she extends them, producing intertextual cycles that undermine the idea that a text is contained by its own boundaries. *India Song*—at once a text, script, and film—is not, however, as minimally structured as *L'Amour.* Still, like *L'Amour,* it abandons figures of writers or narrators who attempt to control or shape the material. Even Voice 4, who remembers the most about the texts which form the back-drop to *India Song,* does not deploy that knowledge in order to gain authority or mastery. By rewriting *The Vice-Consul* as *India Song,* Duras produces a sense of the impossibility of ever getting the story right. Instead, it is necessary to tell it again and again. In *The Vice-Consul,* Michael Richardson of *The Ravishing of Lol Stein* becomes Michael Richards. In *India Song,* he is Michael Richardson once again. It isn't clear at the end of *The Vice-Consul* that Anne-Marie Stretter intends to kill herself (or if she actually does), whereas in *India Song* this is established as fact right from the beginning in the plot summary Duras suggests should accompany all productions. In *India Song* sirens are heard in the background, recalling *L'Amour.*

There is a radical separation between the voices, who speak of the story being enacted as well as of the incidents that precede that enactment, and the figures and images of which the voices speak. The voices are overwhelmed by their own fascination with what they observe and remember: they speak of their own responses to what they see and try to remember what has happened. They become another story apart from the action of the stage, screen, or text. It is, as Duras writes in her notes, Voice 1's fascination that frightens Voice 2, for the speakers of these voices are lovers and involved in their own passion.[15] The voices' responses reveal as much about them as about the story they remember. In this intertextual series of substitutions, each voice remembers the story in ways that fit his or her own psychic needs. The story they recall is not "a" story at all but fragments of the various texts. Superimposed on such images as Anne-Marie Stretter's breast that resist assimilation to the symbolic structures of their discourse, the voices seem closer to the reader or viewer and less fictional.[16] Because they treat the figures in the story as if they too were real, these fictional figures from the texts seem to cross the boundary separating writing and experience.

The interplay between the voices' rhythms, their silence, the other sounds, and the images produces a deep melancholy. Nothing connects perfectly or falls into place. What remains is longing and desire. No one voice or perspective has authority or attempts to impose its version of the story on the others, though Voice 4, spoken in the film by Duras, remembers the most and so helps Voice 3 to remember. All four voices are enchanted with what they have been unable to forget from the other texts in the Lol V. Stein cycle. What becomes important in *India Song's* rewriting of *The Vice-Consul* is passion: the terrible desire between Anne-Marie Stretter and Michael Richardson overshadows the political commentary of *The Vice-Consul*. In this text, individual emotion is all. It distracts the voices from their own situations or makes those situations more intense. It threatens to absorb and dissolve all forms of rationality, coherence, and significance. Writing is, therefore, not exactly out of relation to subjectivities. It captivates and fascinates. Shot 22 shows "Anne-Marie Stretter's nude breast, surrounded by the black peignoir. Beads of sweat form on the skin as she breathes" (Lyon 23). Lyon states that the image of the breast is about a "fantasy of looking . . . [which] could be said to be the desire to see loss, to see what is by definition that to which the subject can have no access, but through which, at the same time, the subject is marked" (25). For Lyon, the image of the breast traces the middle ground between voyeurism and melancholia, a place where the subject is both excluded and included.

Just as they captivate the voices in *India Song,* Duras's texts captivate their readers. As Kristeva argues, Duras's texts seize us and draw us to "the dangerous brinks of our psychic life" ("Pain of Sorrow" 151). According to Kristeva, these texts "should not be given to fragile readers, male or female. . . . There is no purification at the end of these novels laden with disease, no heightened sense of well-being, no promise of a beyond, not even the enchanting beauty of style or irony that would provide a bonus of pleasure beyond the ill revealed" (140–141). She advises the frail to see Duras's films or plays instead, where the pain is diminished, concealed by a "dreamy charm" that makes them more conventional and artificial. For Kristeva, Duras's texts cultivate the mental and spiritual malaise of the postmodern world—the result of tremendous upheavals in the twentieth century in virtually every facet of cultural, social, spiritual, and political life. Duras's work does not attempt to console or cure—it writes toward a space in which cure is impossible and irrelevant. It does not provide a way to avoid, defer, or experience a cathartic release of psychic pain. As such, to some extent it is the opposite of clinical discourse that would attempt to provide some consolation, compensation, or cure.[17]

Because antithetical to clinical discourses that serve explicit, if sometimes oppressive, social functions. Duras's writing practice and her representations of herself as author contrast with the other writers she represents in her texts: the reporter in *L'Amante Anglaise,* who wants to find out what happened to the head so that the entire female body can be reassembled, the narrative constructed, and Claire Lannes understood and subsequently forgotten, and Peter Morgan, who attempts to control and distance the beggar woman. For Duras, an essential part of the resistance to oppressive forms of convention and tradition involves her refusal as a writer to overdetermine and control her texts, her refusal to participate in writing that dominates its subjects. In this sense, as Marcelle Marini has argued, Duras's work explores territories coded as feminine and excluded by a masculine symbolic. Lol V. Stein remains inaccessible to Jacques Hold, and Anne-Marie Stretter to Charles Rossett, whom she prefers only in the most impersonal way. The beggar woman of *The Vice-Consul* exists in a radical exteriority just as much as in Peter Morgan's narrative, for his narrative does not produce the entire text. And in *L'Amante Anglaise,* Marie-Thérèse's missing head, despite the writer's persistence, is never found. All these events suggest the impossibility of coherence or wholeness—not just of the body but of writing and of texts. What these figures attempt to control is often exactly what eludes them, for no matter what their intent, in Duras the "head" is never among the other pieces. . . .

With *The Lover,* Duras represents herself explicitly as a writer unwilling to assert definitive control over the material. . . .

While it is a work of fiction, not autobiography, *The Lover* blurs such distinctions: the woman in the text seems much like Duras. Duras claims it as her "true autobiography," and indeed many of the woman's experiences in *The Lover* parallel events we recognize from Duras's own life. Like Duras, the speaker grows up in Indochina. Like Duras, the speaker is French; she is a writer; she has a son; she has two brothers, the younger of whom dies during the war from lack of medication; her mother is a teacher; her father dies when she is quite young; she leaves Indochina to attend school in Paris; she drinks "too much" in middle age; and she is roughly the same age as Duras. Moreover, the front and back jacket photos of Duras herself, which also appear in a text she published with Michelle Porte, *Les Lieux de Marguerite Duras,* seem to be presented as photographs of the speaker in *The Lover* when she was young. The speaker describes, for example, the fedora that seems to contradict her small, puny body. Duras wears such a hat in the back jacket photo, and Duras is physically a very small person. Since *The Lover* is at least in part inspired by autobiographical material, one might reasonably expect it to bridge the gap between writing and experience, for Duras is writing about experiences in the world. But such is not the case. Instead of bringing writing and experience into alignment, the text portrays the two as related in complex ways but essentially as separate, distinct, and out of relation.

The photographs on the jacket only frustrate any attempt to separate Duras from her speaker. The essential emptiness of these images is produced by the sense that identity can never be understood in the ways we are accustomed to assuming we understand it. Therefore, and strange to say, the photographs suggest instead the impossibility of reproducing identity in representation. This impossibility is argued by the text itself with a passage describing not the jacket photographs but a photograph of the speaker's mother. Except for the references to age, it might well describe the front jacket photograph of Duras, which is itself minimal and almost featureless and thus seems to have been constructed according to the same conventions:

> All these photographs of different people, and I've seen many of them, gave practically identical results, the resemblance was stunning. It wasn't because all old people look alike, but because the portraits themselves were invariably touched up in such a way that any facial peculiarities, if there were any left, were minimized. All the faces were prepared in the same way to confront eternity, all toned down, all uniformly rejuvenated. This is what people wanted. (96–97)

These images, records of individual subjects that will survive them, leave only traces of those subjects. The individual is eclipsed, at first by the fact of the representation and then by the effects produced by the subversion of representation in the text.

Duras's text is fundamentally about crossing boundaries, deceptions, and displacements. It is the image of her crossing the Mekong River that proves so compelling to the speaker in the present. The image lasts the entire crossing, while the river suggests an unstable region unstructured by the family or social inscriptions of desire, sexuality, pleasure, and pain. It is only in this unstable terrain, this interstice, that the speaker finds an image of herself she can recognize as somehow true to her memory: "I often think of the image only I can see now, and of which I've never spoken. It's always there, in the same silence, amazing. It's the only image of myself I like, the only one in which I recognize myself, in which I delight" (3–4). To cross the river, to separate oneself from family and community, to move from the known to the unknown, provides an escape only while one is moving. It is not, finally, to escape structuring powers—one brings the known into the unknown. Structures are not easily escaped, and, even more, as the speaker suggests, one does not necessarily want to escape them entirely.

Both the beggar woman and a figure upon whom the character Anne-Marie Stretter seems to be based appear in *The Lover*, further complicating relationships among writing, representation, and experience. The obscure reference to an unnamed Anne-Marie Stretter figure in *The Lover* resonates with what we know about Anne-Marie Stretter from *The Vice-Consul* and *India Song:*

> The Lady, they called her. She came from Savanna Khet. Her husband was posted to Vinh Long. Because of the young man, the assistant administrator in Savanna Khet. They couldn't be lovers any more. So he shot himself. The story reached the new posting in Vinh Long. The day she left Savanna Khet for Vinh Long, a bullet through the heart. In the main square in broad daylight.

Because of her young daughters and her husband's being posted to Vinh Long she'd told him it had to stop. (89)

That Anne-Marie Stretter, as well as the beggar woman of Calcutta, should appear, though unnamed, in *The Lover* establishes a connection between it and the Lol V. Stein cycle. In a curious way, this connection makes the Lol V. Stein cycle part of the autobiographical claims of *The Lover,* that paradoxical other space where autobiography and fiction merge, while it makes *The Lover* seem more fictional than autobiographical. That Duras has spoken in an interview of an Anne-Marie Stretter figure in her own life suggests her representations are inspired by an experience which itself disrupted boundaries:

> With the very established, very visible colonial ostentation that surrounded me, this power of woman was not apparent: it was unexpected, it exploded just like that, like a bomb, but silently, you see. This accident wasn't ascribable to anything, nor could it be classified; it was natural, it had the fantastic violence of nature. It was either the cars of the rich or the cars of the poor, the children of the rich or the children of the poor, everything was like that, classified, codified, very clearly. And all of a sudden there was this accident that had nothing to do with the kind of arrangement of white social life in the posts. I think this is what struck me. It overwhelmed me. ("Dispossessed" 80)

This "accident" is a suicide: a young man apparently killed himself for a woman. Whether or not the story Duras heard as a child was true, it continued to haunt her. And this event is strikingly similar to the one she describes in *The Lover* where a young man kills himself for a woman who may have been called Stretter. Although Duras was only seven years old when this incident occurred, it had the tremendous impact of exploding her sense of the normal, conventional structure of colonial life. Because it occurred so many years ago when she was very young, it has the fictional aspect that memories acquire. It exists as a mythical moment, one outside normal experience, which nevertheless structures or influences the way subsequent events are conceptualized.

In *The Vice-Consul* the beggar woman abandons her children as she travels toward Calcutta. (At least in Peter Morgan's version, which draws on a story he has heard about a different beggar woman from Anne-Marie Stretter.) The beggar woman of *The Vice-Consul* also appears in *The Lover,* interwoven with the speaker's memories of her own mother in ways that suggest she felt as abandoned by her mother as the young man probably felt when forsaken by the woman who may have been called Stretter. What's interesting is that Duras adopts the story she had Peter Morgan write in the earlier text: what Duras's readers first encounter as a fiction—and not just fiction but writing that asserts power—seems to solidify into reality. In *The Vice-Consul,* Peter continues a story that Anne-Marie Stretter happens to mention; in *The*

Lover the speaker builds upon Morgan's narrative. She claims to have encountered the beggar woman herself. But her two descriptions of the beggar woman are separated by a fragment in which she remembers her mother, all of which revolve around fear, identity, and madness. The juxtaposition suggests connections between the mother and this beggar woman who abandoned her children. The fear the speaker has of the beggar woman is articulated in the first description, which focuses on a childhood incident when the woman chased her at night. Afraid that to be touched by this woman is to become like her, the speaker flees, refusing the contact. In the second description, we read of the beggar woman's walk to Calcutta, a loose repetition of Morgan's story.

It is curious that along with these two descriptions, perhaps fictional, is an account of something that seems vivid and real. It is as if Duras uses the speaker, who in turn uses the beggar woman, to approach a subject too painful to tackle directly, without such a buffer. She describes her fear of seeing her mother in a certain state of mind. After refusing to name this state she continues:

> There, suddenly, close to me, was someone sitting in my mother's place who wasn't my mother, who looked like her but who had never been her. . . . My terror . . . came from the fact that she was sitting just where my mother had been sitting when the substitution took place, from the fact that I knew no one else was there in her place, but that identity irreplaceable by any other had disappeared and I was powerless to make it come back, make it start to come back. There was no longer anything there to inhabit her image. I went mad in full possession of my senses. (85–86)

The speaker's experience of madness is quite different from the beggar woman's, for the latter seems beyond the capacity to be aware of her own misery. But like the speaker, who feels mad with betrayal and abandonment, the beggar woman is ostracized by family and community, rejected and abandoned by her mother for her illicit pregnancy. She is shunned for the violation of a social code, a transgression for which she pays dearly.

If the speaker is unable to speak directly of her own feelings of being abandoned, she nevertheless seems to displace a psychologically equivalent story onto the beggar woman. In the story of the beggar woman that circulates among these texts, after carrying her child 2,000 kilometers the beggar woman gives the girl away to a white stranger. Here a substitution takes place that is similar to the one she describes when watching her mother. At the same time she justifies her mother's behavior and suggests that her own need for a mother is not the only story that might get told, as if to tell her story without such a qualification would be to betray her mother in some unforgivable way. As Peter Morgan reconstructs the story of this beggar woman in *India Song,* she is devoured by the child she carries inside as she traverses the countryside in search of food. Her desire for food and for her own mother overwhelm her. When she finally eats a fish, she awakens in the middle of the night only to find that she is still hungry—the child has taken this from her as well.[18]

Instead of bringing writing and experience into alignment, this admittedly most autobiographical text insists on the gulf between them in ways both overt and submerged. The displacement of emotion from the mother to the figure of the beggar woman problematizes the gap and does not necessarily reduce it, for the status of the incident with the mother is, of course, open to question too. With such displacements and diversions, the text shapes a collage of fragmentary memories and reflections that proceed not according to the logic of space and time but rather according to some associative logic known only to the speaker. It is a logic based on forgetting, displacing, and substituting. It is not linear, for as the speaker claims, "The story of my life doesn't exist. Does not exist. There's never any center to it. No path, no line" (8). Despite this, however, the speaker does set about the task of representing something about her life: "I've written a good deal about the members of my family, but then they were alive, my mother and my brothers. And I skirted around them, skirted around all these things without really tackling them" (7). The implication is that now that the family is dead these things can be written about more directly. Now she will tackle difficult subjects; now she can be honest. And yet, since the identities of the speaker and those who surround her are constantly called into question, any quest for truth is deflected, any question of finding out the truth absurd.

In addition to all the other identities thrown into question, finally it isn't entirely clear, as Barbara Probst Solomon has noted, who the lover is. Most obviously, of course, it's the older Chinese man. But the younger brother is perhaps the most beloved. This leads Solomon to speculate whether *The Lover* might not be "a tale of incest designed to shock as miscegenation" (418). Solomon suggests that, if read as a story of incest, the text hides the shameful necessity for absolute silence about the true violation by substituting the Chinese lover for the brother. In this way, too, the speaker transfers guilt from herself to the Chinese man, though as Solomon points out, it makes more sense to think that the girl orchestrates the scene of seduction herself. I'm not interested in trying to establish, especially on the questionable basis of *The Lover,* whether Duras did in fact have an incestuous experience with her brother. (Solomon, however, does speculate that Duras's "shameful incestuous affair with her brother . . . gets hidden and becomes obsessively and repetitively displaced by political images throughout her work, not as a device— but because it actually happened in that sequence" [419].) What is more important here in Solomon's argument is its relevance to seeing the associative structure of *The Lover* and its political digressions as a solution to the problem of representing what is simply too transgressive or shameful to represent. This brings us full circle, back to Woolf's internalized boundaries and fears of writing beyond sanctioned subjects and back to Barnes's strategies for telling and not telling. Duras's writing, in addition to subverting its own authority, functions, like Woolf's and like Barnes's, as a coded articulation of the forbidden. Like Woolf and Barnes, Duras both reveals and conceals.

The central contradiction in Duras's work resides in her ability to subvert established modes of representation on the one hand and the problems this subversion and its commitment to nonpositionality raise—particularly for feminists interested in changing material and discursive practices—on the other. Duras questions the ability of language to master or control its subjects. She challenges in a very self-conscious way the authority of the symbolic and its repression of what is unstructured, uncontrollable, and chaotic—in short, of what is, within the terms of the symbolic, equated with femininity. But what this subversion means for female subjects engaged in material practices is problematic. Duras's work enables us to question the connections between femininity as a product of discourse and the experience of women in the world. It enables us to examine the extent to which this discursive equation contributes to the marginality of women. And it enables us to see how identity is constituted by discourses and signifiers dismantled by the real, by what exceeds representation. But it also represents female subjects as necessarily marginal and chaotic within discourse, language, and culture. For these reasons, Duras's writing at once subverts and reinforces conventional notions of what it means to be female.

Notes

1.   Drawing on the work or Deleuze and Guattari, Leo Bersani argues that the effects of a culture of repression and sublimation provide, in themselves, the reason for exploring the possibilities of desublimating desire: "Psychic coherence involves a serious crippling of desire. The viability of the structured self depends on an impoverishment of desire. The desiring imagination's contacts with the world are limited by the need for preserving the intelligibility of a psychic structure. Even more dangerously, the renunciation of desire, as Freud suggested, may increase our sense of guilt instead of assuaging it. And heightened guilt welcomes the potentially ferocious punishments of conscience and of external moral authority. An important psychological consequence of sublimated (civilized) desire may be suicidal melancholy. . . . the endless repetition of desires suppressed by guilt and angry frustration ultimately leads to the fantasy of death as the absolute pleasure" (6).

2.   Winifred Woodhull writes that this text "exposes the political consequences of prevailing forms of symbolic exchange. The apparent accessibility of the media and the 'free speech' they seem to permit prove illusory or are rendered ineffective by the structure of consumption: individuals are organized by hierarchized relations such as the one between the narrator and Claire, and . . . have little in common but their isolation" (7). Woodhull traces this social fragmentation to the symbolic mediation of needs and desires, which, according to Jean Baudrillard, are governed by the logic of the commodity.

3.   Willis explores this impasse with a discussion of Nancy K. Miller and Peggy Kamuf: "For Nancy Miller, it is necessary to maintain a concern for the status of the woman

writing, in the interest of producing connections with the woman reading, with women in the world. . . . For Peggy Kamuf, however, to lay too much stress on the referent is to hypostatize a category of woman to place over against masculine discourse, and thereby to remain within its humanist boundaries" (13).

4. Jacques Lacan, "Homage to Marguerite Duras" in *Marguerite Duras*.

5. This is how Duras describes her meeting with Lacan: "Lacan had me meet him one night in a bar at midnight. He frightened me. In a bar in a basement. To talk to me about *Lol V. Stein*. He told me that it was a *clinically perfect* delirium. He began to ask me questions. For two hours. I more or less staggered out of the place" ("An interview with Marguerite Duras" 129). Duras's description of this meeting with Lacan raises questions about masculine forms of mastery, control, and appropriation. If Lacanian psychoanalysis describes (if not entirely supports) the process by which subjectivity is effected in language as sexist, because male-centered, the meeting as Duras describes it reveals concomitant social practices produced as the result of such male privilege.

6. My discussion of Lacan is very brief and focuses only on some aspects of his thought relevant to my discussion. For a more complete exposition, see Lacan's *Ecrits*. For helpful secondary discussions see Jane Gallop, *The Daughter's Seduction,* or the introductions by Jacqueline Rose and Juliet Mitchell to Lacan's thought in *Feminine Sexuality.*

7. Jardine mentions Michele Montrelay's *L'ombre et le nom* and Christiane Rabant's "La bête chanteuse." Jardine (173) explains that for Montrelay, Lol is "the figure of femininity—not the representation of a woman. She is . . . a figure of Lacan's Real: 'There remains to S. Thala of Lol: two night-bird eyes destroyed by the light, dead from having nothing left to see. An uninhabited body, deserted, fallen to the ground like a stone, reduced to its matter: the Real' (*L'ombre*, p. 18)." Jardine also points out that these writers do little more than echo Lacan's "Homage to Marguerite Duras."

8. Mary Lydon reads Lacan's remarks about Duras differently from Jardine: "What Lacan recognized in Duras' art was not, or not simply . . . that she 'understood his theory,' but that her writing was the artistic embodiment of the real scandal of psychoanalysis: that is, the unconscious and the splitting of the subject that its discovery implied. As Lacan has it: 'the abyss that opened up at the thought that a thought should make itself heard in the abyss' " (262).

9. Duras's textual practice is very much rooted in repetitions with slight variations. Compare the following pair of quotations:

> Lol V. Stein was born here, in S. Thala, and here she spent a good part of her youth. Her father was a professor at the university. She has a brother nine years older than she—I have never seen him—they say he lives in Paris. Her parents are dead. . . . Lol was nineteen when she met Michael Richardson playing tennis one morning during summer vacation. He was twenty-five. He was the only son of well-to-do parents, whose real estate holdings in the T. Beach area were considerable. He did no real work. Their parents consented to the marriage. Lol must have been engaged for six months, the wedding was to take place in the autumn, she had just finished her final year of school and was on vacation in T. Beach when the biggest ball of the season was held at the Municipal Casino.

> Lol spent her entire youth here in S. Thala, her father was of German origin, he was a history professor at the University, her mother was from S. Thala, Lol has a brother nine years older than she, he lives in Paris, she never talks about him, Lol met the man from T. Beach one morning during summer vacation at the tennis courts, he was twenty-five years old, the only son of well-to-do parents who owned a great deal of land in the area, without employment, cultured, brilliant, extremely brilliant, melancholy, Lol fell in love with him at first sight.

10. All translations of *L'Amour* are mine.

11. That this figure is in fact Michael Richardson is suggested more explicitly in the film *L'Amour*. Elisabeth Lyon writes that *L'Amour* "reopens the story of Lol V. Stein in S. Thala with the return of Michael Richardson many years later to the fantasmic scene of the ball. It is from this matrix of madness and fantasy that Duras later drew the film *La Femme du Gange*" (8). If the connection seems clear to film critics, however, it does not seem quite so obvious to Duras's literary critics, who generally treat *L'Amour* more abstractly, as does Sharon Willis in *Marguerite Duras: Writing on the Body*.

12. The heterosexual structuring of desire is unraveled in *India Song* and *Blue Eyes, Black Hair*, where it is also explicitly homoerotic. And if one reads, as I do, against Jacques Hold's structuring of desire in *The Ravishing of Lol Stein*, it is more heterogeneous there too.

13. In *Woman to Woman*, Duras explains her sense of the connections between the Vice-Consul and Anne-Marie Stretter: "There's an equivalence. It's more than an identification; there's an equivalence between Anne-Marie Stretter's pain and the French vice-consul's anger. It flows in her, you see, like a river that's traveled through her; it's as if she's tunneled by this river of pain, if you like, whereas he, by contrast . . . is like an engine of . . . well, of death; he's full of fire, and explosives, finally . . . all that has to get out, burst; it has to get expressed on the outside, be public, loud, whereas the entry . . . Anne-Marie Stretter's entry within India is . . . is carnal. It's internal" (127).

14. The connections Duras sometimes makes between violence and sexuality can be profoundly disturbing. Mary Lydon, in her article about translating this Duras story, writes: "For the anglophone reader with a feminist consciousness, whose aspirations might include a vision of a happy nonviolent sexual union . . . 'L'Homme assis dans le couloir' in particular may be hard to swallow" (261). This story, even more than Duras's other texts, links violence, pain, and pleasure with sexuality, gender, and desire.

15. "Notes on Voices 1 and 2" in *India Song*, 9–10.

16. William F. Van Wert, in an essay where he also discusses his experience teaching Duras's films, writes that "what makes *India Song* such a masterful film is Duras's complex and innovative use of sound. The two voices of *Woman of the Ganges* return for the first half of *India Song*, but are gradually succeeded by two other voices, one of which (a male voice) is fascinated by the fiction at hand and asks the other (the voice of Duras) to help him remember, and her voice, while providing the details, also fears for the safety of the 'partner' voice. . . . these voices are anonymous and the characters within the frame are supposedly unaware of them. For example, Michael Richardson fondles the partially naked body of Anne-Marie Stretter. Duras's notation for the scene is as follows: The hand of Michael Richardson—the lover—stops at precisely that moment (the moment when the second voice declares: "I love you with an absolute desire"), as though this last phrase of the second voice caused him to stop.' Conversely, these women's voices slow down and follow the rhythm of the lover's hand, and their monotone breaks into a lyrical chant" (28).

17. Duras has said that many readers, both male and female, have written to her and said, "Reading your books has made me sick" (*Woman to Woman* 6).

18. In *The Daughter's Seduction*, Jane Gallop criticizes Luce Irigaray for speaking in such writings as "When Our Lips Speak Together" entirely from the daughter's position in relation to the mother. By doing so, Gallop argues, Irigaray makes the mother into a phallic mother, an all-powerful figure upon whom the daughter might depend. The problem with this is that it eclipses the mother's position as a human subject. In contrast, Gallop invokes Julia Kristeva, for Kristeva offers a different perspective in that she at least tries to speak from the mother's position as well. To speak in this way is to explode the myth of the phallic mother, to expose the vulnerability of the mother—who is herself a daughter. The mother exists much as woman does—as a cultural icon upon which we project our needs, fears, blame, and inadequacies. But we do so unfairly, for it is ultimately an empty space. By speaking from the mother's place with

the beggar woman, Duras achieves something similar to Kristeva's exposure of the masquerade of the phallic mother.

19.   Solomon writes that "the sexual exotic, really is the French girl, not the man. In the important first seduction scene she is in control. The fifteen-year-old narrator commands the horrified man to seduce her: 'Treat me like you treat the other woman.' But would a Chinese millionaire's son, who had lived in Paris and known many French women, be weeping and what I call mewling like a stuck pig at the thought of making love to a sexy French girl he had picked up?" She continues by asking: "And why would an adolescent affair with an adoring Chinese man who promises to—and apparently does—love the girl forever permanently ravage and ruin the young girl's face? *What* is the tragedy?" (419).

Le Vice-consul and *L'Amour:* A Word in Default

SHARON WILLIS

The Vice-Consul and *L'Amour* inscribe themselves at the connection between the mother-screen-sign and the cry, in a process which resembles the repetition and delay of mourning, that process by which the subject relinquishes a loved object by draining or displacing the object-cathexis. Freud associates mourning work with incorporation, as a means of relinquishing the cathexis on the lost object by incorporating, internalizing, and idealizing its image. As such, this process is linked to primary narcissism: "The narcissistic identification with the object becomes a substitute for the erotic cathexis. . . . We have elsewhere shown that identification is a preliminary state of object-choice, that it is the first way—and one that is expressed in an ambivalent fashion—in which the ego picks out an object. The ego wants to incorporate this object into itself, and in accordance with the oral or cannibalistic phase of libidinal development in which it is, it wants to do so by devouring it."[1] It is clear from this description that the object of this earliest form of identification, from which later objects are derived metaphorically and metonymically, is the maternal body, or the breast. Hence, the connection Freud establishes between this type of identification and hysterical identification has particular pertinence. Hysterical identification differs from this early prototype, according to Freud, in that the object-cathexis is not abandoned, but "persists and manifests its influence" (250). The hysteric's identification is doubled over by a failure to relinquish; the object is, in effect, both there and not there, both inside and outside. Hysterical identification, then, announces the failure, the delay, of the mourning work.

If the labor of mourning is related to incorporation, it is just as much about decathecting memory traces, in a progressive "forgetting," and about the juncture at which the loss itself is committed to memory. At the same time, the incorporative impulse is always bound up with the negative drive of expulsion/rejection, in the first mappings of the oral stage, where the subject may only accept or refuse/expel nourishment.

From *Marguerite Duras: Writing on the Body* (Chicago: University of Illinois Press, 1987), 96–133. Reprinted by permission.

The complex connection between the two figures, the mother and the cry, is established in Duras' narratives through a certain oral pulsivity of the text. While the tale of the beggar woman traces a repetitive alternance between mother and daughter and daughter as mother, within the frame of starvation, incorporation, and rejection of food, the feminine figure of *L'Amour* obsessively repeats the statement, "I'm expecting a baby. I feel like vomiting" (23; this and all following translations of this text are mine).

The "real" or fantasmatic pregnancy is here connected with "the nauseating movement of the waves, the seagulls that cry and devour the body of sand, the blood" (23). Mer-mère (sea-mother)—the movement of the sea, and the body of the mother, are inextricably bound to the movement of incorporation/rejection. This movement, however, shatters thematic bounds, since the texts themselves effect a cannibalization of the figures and the discourse that appear in *The Ravishing:* the work of mourning becomes a textual condition, a structuring effect as well as a "content."

While *The Ravishing*'s final passages connect hunger and nourishment to forgetting ("Lol is eating, gathering sustenance. I refuse to admit the end . . . Watching her eat, I forget" [174–75]), where incorporation becomes forgetfulness or oblivion of *la faim/la fin, The Vice-Consul*'s opening episodes are concentrated on the biological rhythms of the starving "mendiante," her urges to eat and to vomit. In this case, hunger itself is the locus of a prolonged absence, as the memory of a lack becomes its anticipation. Marcelle Marini calls attention to the text's structuring on this axis, presence-absence of hunger, in connection with the term "mangue" (mango), the mendiante's primary sustenance in the opening passages. The word mango itself condenses the two terms, nourishment and privation, in its phonetic similarity to *mange* (third person singular, or imperative, of "to eat") and *manque:* lack (see *Territoires,* 203).

Extending her line of thought, we might conclude, provisionally, that *Le Vice-Consul* is a text about consuming/incorporating the lack. However, the resonance of "mangue," as it relates to "mange," engages the mother's remembered discourse, the *parole de mère* as nourishing source; "Her mother said: Eat. Don't go grieving your mother. Eat, eat" (5). Indeed, nourishment and the mother's injunction to eat form the juncture of desire and death, for food is also the mother's anticipated means of killing the daughter (" 'If you come back,' her mother said, 'I shall poison your rice. I will kill you' " [1]). This double nature of nourishment extends into the relation of memory to forgetting. The object of the beggar's obsessive fantasies of food is "a bowl of warm rice." Already, the quest for nourishment is linked to death. Such a linkage is found in the primary *clivage* of the pulsional object into "good" and "bad" object, whose fold reflects the duality of the drives—turned toward both life and death. Thus, the "bad" object is food which kills, and which must be expelled.[2]

The obsessive cycle of hunting and finding food is punctuated by the act of expulsion: vomiting the mango. "She vomits, retches, hoping to bring up the child, but all she brings up is sour mango juice" (8). The vomited mango is the failed abortion of the persistent and devouring child. But it is also the *last* object incorporated: "There are flames leaping in the pit of her stomach. She vomits blood. No more sour mangoes for her, only rice-shoots" (9). The last mango and the fish, which becomes the dominant form of nourishment, also put an end to the possibility of satisfying hunger ("the strangest thing of all is that no amount of food can satisfy her hunger {c'est l'absence de nourriture qui se prolonge}" [6]), which, in turn, puts an end to the hunger itself. Not surprisingly, within this context (the chapter which concludes with the line, "The old hunger will never return" [13]), the real stake is forgetting of the mother, and of maternal language. This peculiar gap, then, seems to be the locus of an exploration of a feminine jouissance—in the indifferentiation of mother from child—where the text folds over in the mother-daughter folded into the mendiante figure.

The text slips from a definitive address or appeal to the mother to the word "Battambang," the curious word-object that centers the text. "Who else but you should hear the tale I have to tell? Who else does it concern that I now long more for the food I cannot have than I long for you . . . One day she will go back just to say: I have forgotten you" (10–11). The text poses its own impossibility in the project of returning to the forgotten mother in order to address her: "She tends to forget [elle a tendance à oublier l'origine] that they drove her out because she was a fallen woman [elle était tombée enceinte]" (9). Simultaneous with the oblivion of the origin, the text poses the impossibility of recounting without an origin and without an address, a destination. Such an impossibility is also, more important, the impossibility of recounting the *drive* to eat, the need for food, hunger itself. In this sense, the text operates in suspension of the referent, which is infinitely displaced—the drive cannot be spoken—and yet, inevitably recalled as the limit of the text's own discourse, the body that sustains it.

In place of the *récit,* the story, a history to be unrolled, the text installs the three-syllable proper name, *place* name, "Battambang." "Battambang. She has nothing else to say" (11). The word-object arises at the death of sense in the phrase "I have forgotten you," a phrase already committed to memory, which can never be pronounced without the absolute negation of its own sense. Upon the gap, the space left by memory, appears the word-object Battambang, a punctuation: "All three syllables boom tonelessly [sonnent avec la même intensité, sans accent tonique] as though rapped out on a small overstretched drum" (11).

We may read these words as the sign of an incomplete mourning work, since it is resurgent, vomited up, repeated endlessly, as both appeal and response. For Derrida, the connection to be made between vomiting and mourning intersects questions of representability, a function particularly cru-cial here, since the text opens on the failed effort to narrate hunger.

> Vomit is related to enjoyment [*jouissance*], if not pleasure. It even forces us to enjoy—in spite of ourselves. But this representation annuls itself, and that is why vomit remains unrepresentable. By limitlessly violating our enjoyment, without granting it any determinate limit, it abolishes representative dis-tance—beauty too—and prevents mourning. It irresistibly forces one to con-sume, but without allowing any chance for idealization.
>
> Let it be understood in all senses that what the word *disgusting* de-nominates is what one cannot resign oneself to mourn.[3]

The connection between mourning and vomiting here turns on mourn-ing's function as a displacement of cathexis from the object to its *representation* in the ego; the failure of representation, in this case, signifies the failure of mourning. It is all the more striking, in light of this passage, that the word Battambang serves precisely to de-nominate, to abolish the possibility of nomination within the *récit* of the mendiante, and with it, the *récit* itself. De-nomination is related to problems of representation through a destabilization of limits, of borders determining subject and object. In *Powers of Horror,* Julia Kristeva succeeds in connecting the phobic object with a notion of the abject, which is neither subject nor object; it is not something, but not nothing either. Because the abject is always related to the maternal zone, this notion is particularly pertinent for an analysis of hysterical disgust. Moreover, the hys-terical symptom, product of a conversion, is really another route taken by the anxiety that is displayed in the phobic reaction.

The primal form of the abject, that limit-object, the object that indicates a limit, is rejected food. To expel the food offered by the parents is to reject the sign of their desire: " 'I' want none of that element, sign of their desire . . . 'I' expel it. But since the food is not an 'other' for 'me,' who am only in their desire, I expel *myself,* I spit *myself* out, I abject *myself* within the same motion through which 'I' can claim to establish *myself*" (3). As a limit to the subject position, Kristeva connects vomit to a series of "abjects"—feces, the cadaver—which *indicate* death, the loss of limits, but without signifying or representing anything by themselves.

> In the presence of signified death—a flat encephalograph, for instance—I would understand, react or accept. No, as in the true theater, without make-up or masks, refuse and corpses *show me* what I permanently thrust aside in order to live. These bodily fluids, this defilement, this shit are what life withstands, hardly and with difficulty, on the part of death. There, I am at the border of my condition as a living being. My body extricates itself, as being alive, from that border. Such wastes drop so that I may live, until, from loss to loss, nothing remains in me and my entire body falls beyond the limit—cadere, cadaver. (3)

Having fallen from the body, the abject both poses and menaces its limits, which is why it cannot be made to signify or to represent.

Indeed, the problem of de-nomination conditions the whole textual progress of *The Vice-Consul.* The Vice-Consul himself comes into being under the sign of the word "impossible." His conversational dance with Anne-Marie Stretter, in fact, does no more than explore its own impossibility. "I don't know how to say it," she explains, "the word impossible occurs in your dossier. Is that the appropriate word in this instance? [Est-ce le mot cette fois?]" (100). Her demand that he answer this question produces the following exchange:

> "Is that the appropriate word? Answer me."
> "I don't know myself. Like you, I'm searching."
> "Perhaps there's another way of putting it? [Peut-être y a-t-il un autre mot?]"
> "It's not important now." (100)

An exchange jammed by the question of the word's sense abolishes itself in its own impossibility, in the search for a missing word. And this particular word circulates across the text, reappearing in the discourse of Michael Richard (the character whose name recalls, but does not repeat, that of the lost lover of *The Ravishing,* Michael Richardson): "The word 'impossible' keeps cropping up in his personal file, I believe. What was impossible?" (126). The question's source is anonymous, just as the word in the dossier is authorless, more the property of the object it designates, the Vice-Consul.

Earlier in the text, the Vice-Consul asks the Director of the European Circle, his habitual interlocutor, how he appears: " 'What's my face like, tell me, Mr. Secretary?' asks the Vice-Consul. 'Also impossible,' says the secretary. The Vice-Consul, impassive [impassible], continues talking" (59). The "impossible" stamped on the dossier is equally inscribed on the face. Moreover, the "impossible" is as much the "impassable"—the unmovable, utterly unaffected deadness of the look—as well as the textual impasse of discursive exchange. On the following page, the conversational structure of question and reply collapses on the impossibility of response.

> The Vice-Consul does not expect any reply from the Club Secretary.
> The secretary does not turn a hair.
> "Mr. Secretary," pursues the Vice-Consul, "you have not answered my question."
> "It did not call for an answer, sir. You did not expect any. No one could answer it." (60)

This aborted discursive exchange founders once the unanswerable demand is posed: "Répondez-moi." This demand both imposes the specular structure of these dialogues—where the director repeats the discourse of the

narrative itself—and repeats the perpetual textual impasse, an incommunica-
bility, a failure of exchange.

For Mieke Bal, this communicative impasse, or stagnation, as she calls it,
is a determining textual feature. In Bal's reading of *Le Vice-Consul*, presented
in *Narratologie*, the impossibility of verbal communication is supplemented by
the nonverbal, and reflects the morbidity of the social space of language in
the narrative. Characters or *names,* who lack consistent or solid identity, and
who are determined largely by their discourses, engage in reciprocal mono-
logues, always failing to answer each other, or even to complete sentences.
Messages don't reach their addressees, she argues, but are often replaced by
nonverbal forms, bound to objects. As she puts it, where verbal communication does establish itself in the text, there is an intense concentration on the
phatic function, the simple making contact, a contact established through an
object, for instance Anne-Marie Stretter's bicycle.[4]

To push her analysis in the direction of its own inclination, the word-
message itself seems to become a "dead object," without source or destination, as the text steadily undermines the possibility of even posing those
poles. In their place, Bal argues, the narrative discourse stresses nonverbal
communicative functions: the cry, the look, the gesture, the musical fragment. A glance at this set brings to mind the part object, the detachable
object which confronts the subject with its own loss—the loss in the signifier.
With considerable acuity, she includes in this set, as its very emblem, the
word "Battambang"—the word that stands somewhere between the object
and the cry. For Bal, it becomes a sign through the very repetition that
reduces it, first, to a meaningless form. As such, this empty repetition becomes the sign of something else: the gaps, that which is missing, the textual
obsession. Moreover, "Battambang" stands as the only remaining trace of the
beggar woman's origin, her source.

This word object seems to play out a drama of separation of word from
body, through the part object. Kristeva describes the cry, as part of the anaclisis, in the following manner: "Neither request nor desire, it is an invocation,
an anaclisis. Memories of bodily contact, warmth and nourishment: these
underlie the breath of the newborn baby as it appeals to a source of support"
(*Desire in Language,* 281).

The cry or invocation is one among a system of part objects that constitute and mark the juncture through which the subject passes to enter the discourse of the Other, within which he or she is already passively inscribed. As
object (in the Lacanian sense), the cry operates at the beginnings of representation, still enmeshed in the lost object, which can never be refound because
it has condensed with others to form the hallucinated object, separated from
the pulsional body.

Bal also connects "Battambang" to music. Citing the word's resemblance to the musical fragment of *India's Song*—whose words are forgotten,
another instance of the oblivion of speech, as well as another connection

to the maternal locus, the origin—she emphasizes the function of "Battambang" as the point of interdependence between the two textual *récits,* the story of the Vice-Consul and Peter Morgan's novel. In this sense, it is precisely the voice or cry of the woman permanently out of relation to her maternal origin, and to her mother tongue, that constitutes a juncture and a channel of passage between the two *récits.*

This word-cry also becomes the axis of exchange in the text, at the moment when the mendiante gives her child to another woman. "The girl answers, Battambang . . . Battambang will keep her safe, she will never say another word but that one in which she is enclosed" (22). Indeed, it is the word itself that effects the exchange, functioning as assertion, response, demand and refusal, all at once. This word later centers an "inverted" and terrifying version of this exchange, between Charles Rossett and the *mendiante:*

> She waves toward the bay, and says just one word, the same word, over and over:
> "—Battambang" . . .
> He gets some loose change from his pocket, takes a step or two towards her, and stops . . .
> He does not go any nearer, but stands there, with the money in his hands.
> She repeats the word that sounds like "Battambang." (163)

The exchange, however, remains incomplete, for the woman biting the head off a live fish, posing the Medusa image, causes Charles Rossett to flee. The coin he tosses never reaches her, is never accepted, just as the word "Battambang," tossed toward him, disappears in its utterance. The word, however, acquires the status of the coin tossed without currency, outside any possible exchange of equivalencies. It becomes a "dead" center, a *point mort* for the scene. Such a figure repeats that of the beggar, described by the Vice-Consul: " 'Death in the midst of life {la mort dans la vie en cours},' says the Vice-Consul at last. 'Death following but never catching up. Is that it?' " (139).

To consider the relation between the text's opening sentence: " 'She walks on [Elle marche],' writes Peter Morgan" (1), and one of its final scenes, that of the discussion about Morgan's book among the Europeans at the Prince of Wales, is to disclose the function of the beggar as, simultaneously, narrative and frame, center and periphery, "ground" and "figure." In this respect, the "Elle marche" is also the figure of writing, as it unfolds, doubles, and repeats itself. For Peter Morgan, the desire to write this story is bound up with a kind of death in discourse.

> "In Calcutta, she will be a . . . dot at the end of a long line, the last distinguishable fact of her own life? With nothing left but sleep and hunger, no feeling, no correlation between cause and effect?"

"What he means, I think," says Michael Richard, "is something even more extreme. He wants to deprive her of any existence other than her existence in his mind when he is watching her. She herself is not to feel anything."

"What is left of her in Calcutta?" asks George Crawn.

"Her laugh, drained of all color, the word 'Battambang' that she repeats incessantly, the song. Everything else has evaporated."

"How will you trace her past, piece her madness together, distinguish between her madness and madness in general [sa folie de la folie], her laughter from laughter in general [son rire du rire], the name Battambang and Battambang the place [le mot Battambang du mot Battambang]?"

"Her dead children—because she must have had children—and other dead children?"

"Finally, the exchange, if that's what it was, or, to put it another way, the giving up, was not, in the long run, very different from any other exchange or surrender. And yet it did take place." (146)[5]

Morgan's desire to produce a narrative that arrives at a point that has no point—no destination and no causality—a point of indifferentiation ("How will you distinguish her madness and madness in general"), the merger of definite and indefinite articles, is predicated on the explosion of any causal effects. Moreover, the origin of this *récit* is its indefiniteness, a problem related to the question of memory.

> Peter Morgan is forced to resort to fragments stored in his own memory to fill in the blanks of the beggar woman's forgotten past [voudrait maintenant substituer à la mémoire de la mendiante le bric-à-brac de la sienne]. Otherwise, Peter Morgan would be at a loss to explain the madness of the beggarwoman of Calcutta . . . How long since she lost her memory? How to put into words the things she never said? How to say what she will not say? How to describe the things that she does not know she has seen, the experiences she does not know she has had? How to reconstruct the forgotten years [tout ce qui a disparu de toute mémoire]? (54–55)

Morgan's "false" memory, entering into the place of the beggar's absent memory, constantly entertains the possibility of its own abolition in and through narrative time. How to write *nothing?* How to establish temporality in the absence of memory? Furthermore, this passage discloses one of the most startling of the narrative contradictions: the substitution of one memory for another, of one's memory for another's in the juncture of two *histoires* (in both senses of the word). Indeed, this is the determining problem of the whole text: two *récits* are embedded, but the seams along which the embedding is sutured have no clear distinction or separation.

Although the story/*récit* of the Vice-Consul and that of the mendiante are connected metonymically through the movement of the latter figure from one textual level to the next, they are likewise bonded metaphorically by a textual system of mirrors: the mendiante and the Vice-Consul are both dead centers or dead looks which attract the fascinated gazes of all the other figures. Both are voices or cries that disrupt the system of discursive articulations, while nevertheless stimulating an endless and fragmented proliferation of commentary.

To the extent that Peter Morgan's narrative focuses on a being without existence, except in the look of the other, who "would watch her live [celui qui la regarderait vivre]," his narrative is also captured by what "le regarde" (in the French sense, what concerns it), without ever addressing or even recognizing it.

The precise point of slippage of one narrative into another, the reversal of the capture, is radically indeterminate here. Even more problematically, this same function repeats itself in the dialogic "exchanges" of the Vice-Consul and the Secretary. These exchanges culminate in a substitution of memories. An early dialogue effects the exchange of remembered scenes, *histoires,* of school days, during which the Vice-Consul trades his story of education at Montfort for the Secretary's reminiscences about his experience at a reform school, at Pas-de-Calais, near Arras (85). Subsequently, in the final scene of the text, the Vice-Consul repeats, as is his habit, a memory:

> "My mother looks at her watch: I have not opened my mouth, except for one remark." "What remark was that?"
> "That you were glad to be in Arras."
> "Correct, Mr. Secretary. It's February. Night is falling in the Pasde-Calais. I do not want cakes or chocolates; I only want to be allowed to stay there."
> (106–7)

In this case, memory is displaced, effecting a radical resituation of interlocutors, the exchange of histories. Certainly, this impossible exchange has the features of a transference, in the context of the scene in which the Vice-Consul endlessly repeats and reworks his past, before the almost neutral figure of the Secretary. In more general terms, this transference disturbs the possible positional boundaries that condition the movement of narration: where the speaker/source recounts a history to an addressee. Similarly, the disruption and detachment of memory signals the abolition of its relation to any lived scene, as well as of any property or properness attaching to the subject's identity.

This scene reflects the generation of Peter Morgan's narrative—based on the substitutability of memory, and, ultimately, on its obliteration. Both textual scenes are related to the issue of fixing an impossible narrative origin or source. It is as if the framing story—Peter Morgan's narrative of the beggar woman, with which the text opens—were continually invading, and becoming enfolded inside, the *framed* story. The relationship of margins to the narrative of the Vice-Consul and, metaphorically, that of frame to image, is unstable, contradictory.

Duras' text calls into question the implicit metaphor of figure and ground that such embedding of *récits* installs. Moreover it disturbs the textual relation between controlling narrative voice and its object: narrative *énonciation* to narrative *énoncé*. If the mendiante is nothing but her *histoire* neither is Peter Morgan anything but the story of writing a story. Neither, likewise, is the Vice-Consul anything but the story of the impossibility of telling his story. Just as the story-less beggar crosses the *grillage,* the insistent textual figure for European anxiety to preserve separation from Calcutta, the textual crossing constitutes the explosion of boundaries between narrative layers, and produces an incessant interference among narrative enunciations.

The metaphor of interference is significant here, since these subtexts not only intersect each other, but also merge. Similarly, the textual mirror-effects inevitably produce an indifferentiation among levels and figures. This narrative anxiety is clearly reflected in Peter Morgan's interrogation of his own project, "Comment séparer sa folie de la folie," but it conditions the entire text as well; where does the narration go when it has nothing to recount, when its own origin is absent?

Such a complete inaccessibility of a presumed originary scene accounts for the textual fascination and the "uncanny" effects attaching to the Vice-Consul. The extended ballroom scene, the textual center, which pivots upon the figure of the Vice-Consul, is governed by the indeterminate discursive locus "on," often marked by the conditional, "on dirait que. . . ." The anonymous voices speculate on the blank screen of the Vice-Consul. Yet the scene is equally conditioned by the Vice-Consul's impossible dialogue with Anne-Marie Stretter on the "subject" of Lahore:

> "Why do you speak to me of leprosy?"
>
> "Because I have the feeling that if I tried to say what I really want to say to you, everything would crumble into dust"—he is trembling—"for what I want to say . . . to you . . . from me to you . . . there are no words. I should fumble . . . I should say something different from what I intended . . . one thing leads to another." . . .
>
> "What I want to try and explain, then, is that afterwards, although one knows that it was oneself who was in Lahore, it seems impossible, unreal. It is I who . . . am talking to you now . . . who am that man. I would like you to listen to the Vice-Consul of Lahore. I am he."
>
> "What has he to say to me?"
>
> "That there is nothing that he can say about Lahore, nothing. . . . And that you must understand why." . . .
>
> "I would like to hear you say that you can see the inevitability of Lahore. Please answer me."
>
> She does not answer. (98–100)

The curious alienation effect of this scene reproduces the disembodiment of the utterance that characterizes its discursive context, its surroundings. Further, however, the utterances escape pronominal anchoring—"One knows that it was oneself who was in Lahore." "I would like you to listen [je voudrais que vous entendiez: hear or understand] to the Vice-Consul of Lahore. I am he [je suis celui-là: that one]" (98). The dispossession of the subject pronoun, the intermittence of the speaking "I," is foregrounded in the contradictory expression, "Je suis celui-là," where an incalculable, not to say impossible, distance emerges in the speech act itself. What is at stake here is the very possibility of any identity-within-speech, of an even momentary appropriation of the subject-I, or of an unequivocal *occupation* of that position.

Consequently, the discursive circuit of emission and reception, sending and receiving, that hinges on these pronominal poles is faulty, if not ruptured: "Answer me. She does not answer" (100). (*Répondre:* repondere—to give in return for, satisfy an agreement, agree, to contract, to return, repay, re-echo). As in most dialogic exchanges in this text, there is no return, no reply; nothing comes back to the speaker/sender. Moreover, just as Lahore itself is both inevitable and unrepeatable—it cannot be spoken about, its story cannot be told—this conversation cannot sustain repetition. The next encounter between Anne-Marie Stretter and the Vice-Consul stresses this feature: "You repeated nothing?"—"Nothing" (115).

If their exchange, like the Vice-Consul's story, bears no repetition and provides no return, the Vice-Consul himself appears in the uncanny aspect of a "revenant" (a ghost), whose presence troubles the entire ballroom scene. Yet this figure is the ghostly return of something that was never there. Similarly, both his look and his voice are repeatedly characterized as dead, or empty; they are sourceless, detached: " 'It's true what you said about his voice . . . but it's also true of the way he looks at one [le regard]. It's as though another man were looking out of his eyes. It hadn't struck me before. Perhaps one could say his face is blank [Peut-être il n'a pas de regard].' 'A complete blank?' 'All but, there is an occasional flicker of expression' " (103–4). Or, earlier, "Once again the ambassador seems on the point of moving away and once again he thinks the better of it. He must stay and talk with this man tonight. This man who is looking at him with death in his eyes [cet homme au regard mort qui le regarde]" (92). The Vice-Consul is the petrifying figure of a dead look looking, and failing to feel the look of another upon it. Furthermore, the man himself is described by Charles Rossett as "Oh a dead man. Dead. The word escapes from pursed lips, moist lips, pale at this late hour" (101). Whose lips, whose speech, pass the word "dead," here? The word produces an inextricable confusion of subject and object of discourse, since it hangs detached from both source and aim.

The dead man returned to life is also the echo chamber through which a peculiar foreign voice filters: "She draws away from him a little, but can not yet bring herself to look at him. Later she will say that she was struck by something in his voice. Later she will say, 'is that what is meant by a toneless voice [une voix blanche]?' You couldn't tell [On ne sait pas] whether he was asking a question or answering it" (87). The ambivalent voice, toneless and strange, fails to establish a distinction between the demand and the offer. Later, "people are thinking [on pense]: the Vice-Consul is laughing, but what a laugh! Like the sound track of a dubbed film, utterly lacking in conviction [faux, faux]" (87).

The image here is striking. The Vice-Consul parades the possibility of absolute disjunction between eye and ear, sound and sight, as in a film whose sound track is minutely out of synch with the motion of the image. (Indeed, it is just such a contradiction that Duras will exploit in *India Song*.) The foreignness of the voice (in the sense of a foreign body inhabiting this figure) is figured similarly by Anne-Marie Stretter:

> Anne-Marie Stretter is saying to Charles Rossett:
> "His voice is quite different from what one would expect from his appearance. You can't always tell what people's voices will be like just by looking at them. You can't with him."
> "It's not a pleasant voice. It's almost as though it had been grafted on to him."
> "You mean it's not his voice, but someone else's?"
> "Yes, but whose?" (103)

The image of the voice as false, as grafted on, as coming from another, an elsewhere, is striking, since it connects again with the dead look and the part object—the signifier of lack. Along with the parade of the lack, the Vice-Consul signifies the terrifying possibility of a lack of all lack, the death of desire, the utter detachment from an originary scene. Régis Durand discusses the fascination of the voice in Duras' texts and films in his article, "The Disposition of the Voice," in which he explores the voice as situating the subject in the desire of the Other: "The voice is always anchored in desire. . . . There is no such thing as a neutral voice, a voice that does not desire me. If there was, it would be an experience of absolute terror. But even as it is, and even though it may charm, the voice frightens and disturbs. Is it because the voice gives us nothing to *see,* because it has no mirror image? Speaks to us of loss, of absence?" (203).

The fantasmatic image without an image, the voice both within and with*out* desire, is implicated in the textual network of messages and passages, of slides into indifferentiation that Viviane Forrester so poetically ascribes to Duras' project: a domain without limits or frontiers, a domain "where death itself does not establish the slightest difference" ("Territoires du cri," 171). This is a space that seems to figure the intolerability of pure presence, where, according to Forrester, mirrors *repeat,* rather than reflect. This passage recalls the figure of the mendiante, whose hunger obliterates even the division of the subject in language, reducing language to its own oblivion in the cry. That figure, then, becomes the figure of the too proximate body, pure voice, the collapse of the thetic.

Elsewhere, Duras speculates on the status of voice in her work: "If I don't find the text just as it arose on the page, the written voice, I begin again. . . . You see, I don't try at all to deepen the sense of the text when I read it, no, not at all, nothing like that, what I am looking for is the primary state of this text, as one strives to remember a distant event, not lived, but 'heard about' [entendu dire]. The sense will follow, it has no need of a law" (*Les Yeux verts,* 49). Here Duras proposes a notion of the written voice which refers not to any fantasmatic "pure self-presence" of or through the voice, but rather emphasizes that the voice is continually speaking from elsewhere. The "entendu dire" is distinctly related to the fantasmatic primal scene—what is heard and not understood, except by retroaction. We might therefore characterize the sense of the "entendu dire," "hearsay," or what has been heard, as associated with the "originary scene" and with the family discourse, the fragments of narrative drawn from the family romance, the set of positional relations inscribed in the familial structure.

The cry, however, has a multidimensional status in this text. Like the cry in *Le Ravissement,* of whose absent *scène du bal* this text presents a sort of inverted image (as through a lens inversion), the cry becomes a punctuation in the scene. This is itself a curious inversion, for the cry is unarticulated, unpunctuated voice, which then serves precisely to pierce, interrupt, point the scene.

The peculiarity of the Vice-Consul's voice is at least once described as a suppressed cry: "The Vice-Consul, addressing Anne-Marie Stretter for the first time, speaks distinctly, but with a curiously toneless delivery, the voice pitched a fraction too high [un rien trop aigue], as though he were with difficulty restraining himself from shouting" (97). Here, as in much of the text, it is this "rien," a nothing, an insignificance, that makes all the difference. The cry held back, retained or withheld, will emerge later in the ballroom scene, as its central "event."

The dialogue between Anne-Marie Stretter and the Vice-Consul produces a frame for the suspended central scene, the ambassador's ball, which is then ruptured by the following drama.

> "I shall proceed as though it were possible for me to stay on here with you tonight," says the Vice-Consul of Lahore.
> "There's no hope of that."
> "No hope at all?"
> "None. But there's no reason why you shouldn't pretend there is."
> "What will they do?"
> "Drive you out."
> "I shall proceed as though it were possible for you to prevent it."
> "Yes, what is all this leading up to?"

"It will precipitate things [Pour que quelque chose ait eu lieu]."
"Between you and me?"
"Yes, between you and me."
"When you are outside in the street, shout at the top of your voice."
"Yes."
"I shall say that it is not you who are shouting. No, I shall say nothing."
(113–14)

The retention of the cry is transposed into a desire to be retained, to resist separation. The larger interest, however, is the production of an event, so that something "will have happened." Temporally, the narrative installs the possibility of a "will have happened" upon the ground of the "already there," within the subjunctive mood: that something may have happened—a hypothetical anterior future. For Forrester, *India Song,* the filmic repetition of *The Vice-Consul,* might also be characterized this way, since she describes its story as "an ultimate story, where nothing can happen since it already was" (171). The text, then, poses an anterior future, where something will have already happened, will be past, as if the past were bypassed, where the event can claim no temporal grounding.

Furthermore, the cry, like all utterances in this text, receives no answer: "Someone says [on dit]: 'He is dead drunk.' 'I shall stay here tonight with you!' he shouts. They behave as though they had not heard [Ils font les morts: literally, they play dead]" (115). They "play dead," like Lol V. Stein, who plays dead during the ball scene, where "l'heure trompait," time failed to pass, until the suspension is broken by a cry.

In this case, as in the ball scene, the cry marks separation, interruption, as it ruptures a suspended moment. From this point forward, the Vice-Consul will exist for Anne-Marie Stretter and her friends only as a discursive function, as *story,* the double of the beggar. The last remark exchanged before their separation is Peter Morgan's: " 'It isn't possible,' says Peter Morgan, 'forgive me, but a man of your sort is only interesting in his absence' " (116). The Vice-Consul, then, must be the figure of absence recalled. But he is also the impossible being, as Morgan declares just prior to his ejection (146). This figure—impossible—just as Lahore is impossible (Lahore: "Là-hors," "there outside," Marini), merges with that originary and empty scene, source and end of the narration.

This scene of separation and the cry it produces echoes and repeats itself throughout the textual cycle. For Pierre Fédida, the scene is connected to questions of sexual difference and the body, just as the primal scene and its fantasmatic versions are related to the question of origins: the origin both as birth, and as the origin of difference between the sexes.[6]

Indeed, *The Vice-Consul* is a text that turns on the posing of sexual difference and its effacement in doublings and repetition, in the oscillation of presence and absence. In its most striking movements, these issues are focused by the repeated image of the mirror, the fantasy of a shattered mirror, as a failure or explosion of the moment that is based on the narcissistic and thetic instances. For example, the fascinating rumors about the Vice-Consul turn not to his random shooting into the garden, but to his firing into the mirrors in his house: "There was something else too. The mirrors of his residence in Lahore were riddled with bullets, you know" (72). This notion is repeated in the Europeans' discussion of the Vice-Consul as a "personnage absent." "In Lahore he shattered the mirrors as well . . . 'I'm almost sure,' says Peter Morgan, 'that he felt obliged to do what he did because he had believed all his life that one day he would have to commit himself through action, and after that . . .' " (127).

It is by no means insignificant, then, that Duras filmed the cinematic version of this narrative with frequent use of a mirror as background. The film literalizes, or concretizes, the textual figure of a mirror that only repeats, and does not reflect, since we as spectators would find ourselves before a mirror that repeats images of the figures onscreen, while denying us any narcissistic pleasure in our own anticipated reflection. This is a film, then, that deprives us of a *point de fuite* (vanishing point), as well as of a position of mastery, by inscribing our own absence precisely there.[7]

Concerning the mirror in her films, Duras says: "Yes, it's like holes in which the image is engulfed and then comes back to the surface: I never know where it is going to come out . . . or else a putting into question . . . of the real presence of the word" (*Les Lieux de Marguerite Duras,* 71–72). In this case, the mirror is related to the imaginary—the mirror stage—as well as to incorporation and resurgence. This intermittence of presence may account for Duras' fascination with cinematic re-vision of textuality. If the mirror is an engulfing space, however, Duras' work is all the more emphatic about this function as the locus of loss, loss of speech, sense, and subjectivity.

Anne-Marie Stretter is the figure most present in the text as image or object of desire, for both the Vice-Consul and the mendiante (" 'It's the woman from Savannakhet,' he says, 'It really does seem that she follows her about' " [159]), or as image remembered for Charles Rossett: "He sees Anne-Marie Stretter again [l'image lui revient d'Anne-Marie Stretter] rigid under the electric fan" (161). At most, she is largely the echoing or responding voice, often repeating discursive fragments uttered by others. However, one of the last chapters of the text presents this figure more descriptively: "She stops short of the beach. She stretches out on the ground, resting her chin on the palm of her hand, as she might if she were reading. She scoops up a handful of gravel and throws it. After a time, she stops flinging gravel and lies there, flat on her stomach, with her head resting on her folded arms" (159).

This last image is, precisely, mimed by the textual movement itself, which gathers and scatters fragments; here it interposes the Vice-Consul's "rose reader rose" fantasy with the woman on the beach. If Anne-Marie Stretter's existence as descriptive figure both opens and closes in the movement from inside the Prince of Wales to the water's edge, the entire textual movement of *L'Amour* is suspended on this point, "au bord de la mer." The text reposes the fragment, "reste là," of "S. Thala" and Thalassa, from *Le Ravissement,* where Lol perpetually "reste là." Indeed, to that extent, all of *L'Amour* takes place, takes its place through that phrase, read either as constative or imperative, as description or demand.

This image itself, then, is a fragmented mirror, that disseminates incomplete reflections of the triadic narrative. Moreover, if it can lay claim to the category of *mise en abîme,* its function is unstable, oscillating. In this case, the indeterminacy of the *mise en abîme* effect repeats the textual instability of the source-destination, inside-outside polarities. This question is particularly interesting when applied to the problem of textual mirroring, of a textual mirror scene, which is, in this last figure, particularly bound up with the proximity of "la mer/la mère."

Speaking of Anne-Marie Stretter, as both a narrative and a cinematic figure, and one whose death is much more fully indicated in *India Song* than in *The Vice-Consul,* where it is barely suggested, Duras describes its relation to death: "I don't know if it's a suicide. She meets something like a sea. She rejoins the Indian Ocean, like a sort of matrix" (*Les Lieux,* 78). This almost too transparent passage plays on the homophony of *mer-mère:* the *mer* as origin, as mold, as medium and enclosing mass—matrix. More interestingly, perhaps, Duras herself rediscovers and determines the particular resonance of this play in all of her work, beginning with one of her first novels, *Un Barrage contre le Pacifique.* "I've always been by the edge of the sea {au bord de la mer} in my books . . . I was involved with the sea from an early age, when my mother bought the flood plain, the land of *Un Barrage contre le Pacifique* and the sea swept through it all and we were ruined" (*Les Lieux,* 84).

Here we need only remark the potential pun's effect. "J'ai eu affaire à la mèr[e] très jeune dans ma vie {I was involved with the sea}"; "j'ai toujours été au bord de la mèr[e]." Moreover, the early narrative, *Un Barrage contre le Pacifique,* is explicitly concerned with the invading presence of both the sea and the mother. Until recently the only overtly autobiographical text of Duras' corpus, this novel establishes the historical referent of the mother's purchase of land in a tidal plain and the ensuing struggle to protect it from the seasonal flooding, as the simultaneous annihilation of time/history. The sea overwhelms all barricades and stops time, prevents advance through time. Its invading propensity abolishes all construction, causing the family's bankruptcy. Simultaneously, however, the family itself crumbles to ruin under pressure of the mother's suffocating investment in her children and her ponderous inertia, which abolishes any future.

Marcelle Marini takes up the question of the phrase "au bord de la mer" in her extended analysis of *The Vice-Consul, Territoires du féminin avec Marguerite Duras.* As she points out, "au bord de la mer[e]" is precisely the feminine territory, always in vague proximity to the mother. The phrase itself implies both separation and proximity, and hence poses the problem of limits, boundaries. For Marini, *Le Vice-Consul*, like most of Duras' texts, meditates on the question of femininity as that which is, not repressed or censored, but rather foreclosed by the symbolic order. Consequently, she sees these texts as an elaborate search for the signifier of woman's desire, for the Name-of-the-Mother, which would guarantee an access to subjectivity as feminine, and hence, a feminine access to history, as well as to History. Alternately, Marini sees this text as a reinscription of a positive mythology of femininity, where the story of the mendiante may be read as privileging the maternal axis of the family discourse. But, again, she also reads the textual inscription of what she calls "cryptograms of the feminine sex," traced by the mendiante's trajectory, with the result that "the text figures what language does not allow it to say" (188).

For Marini, these issues condition Duras' narrative project in general, thereby accounting for the curious triangulations that subtend it. She sees the intervention of the masculine term, or of death, as the institution of a certain separation between feminine doubles, and as figuring a textual movement from the imaginary dyad to the symbolic order (*The Ravishing, L'Amante anglaise,* etc.). For her, this obsessive figuration and refiguration is linked to the ambivalence of the mother-daughter relation. Concerning what she calls "the myth of the beggar-woman," she contends that it plays out the ambivalence of the mother-daughter dyad. At its core is the combination of hostile, aggressive feelings, desire, identification, and the fantasmatic menace of absorption into the maternal body that conditions the mother-child dyad. What can be seen as specifically feminine here is what is known as the female Oedipus: the extra turn that girls must take through the Oedipal drama, in Freud's estimation. Since the female child is not so intensely the object of an incest prohibition which forbids sexual access to the mother, her separation from this figure and, hence, her attainment of enough distance from the mother to "separate" the fields of desire and identification along gender lines is more complicated, more slowly achieved. At the other end of the trajectory through which gender position is acquired, she will herself become a mother, will occupy the maternal body as a speaking subject. The narrative of the beggar woman seems peculiarly intent on exploring the threats, murderous aggression, and desire that characterize the mirror stage, lived in overwhelming proximity to the mother's body.

Examining the maternal fatality of this text, or perhaps better, its morbid maternity—all the characters are, one way or another, motherless, and the mendiante produces children that are continually abandoned—Marini relates it to the problem of feminine access to the symbolic in general.

> The reading of this text shows sufficiently that [the woman] is caught between the impossibility of symbolizing her relation to the maternal body as imaginary body—as the sustenance from which she separates herself—, and as feminine

body where she must represent herself, and, on the other hand, the impossibility of abandoning it except by alienating herself as subject and becoming affiliated with paternal values that are only valid for a male subject. (227, my translation)

To this particular bind, Marini proposes a very specific elaboration and emphasis. She finds that the narrative of sexual difference, with its fictive "historical" temporalization, needs a beginning and an end "proper" to the feminine—one that, in a sense, redeems or restores a lost past. That is, she calls for a feminized narration, which is nonetheless a linear narrative organization. Such a reading, it seems, would contradict Duras' narrative project in its demystification of narrative origins.

Marini's analysis is more complicated, however, at other points. For instance, speaking of the mendiante's journey, which she nonetheless characterizes as a "search for the maternal signifier," she situates its contradictory consequences: as the struggle to separate an archaic fantasmatic image of the mother from an "alienated" image of woman, and from an image of anticipated femininity, a space where a woman might find her "proper" place (*Territoires*, 199). Here the tensions residing in Marini's own text are evident, for indeed, the utopic feminine territory she proposes is never attained in Duras' text or her own, which remains fixed, anchored in in its own bind, between the two possibilities. Part of the problem, posed more strongly in Marini's text, although hinted at in Duras', is the dream of a "proper" femininity, a place where Woman comes into her own, an ideal and homogenized, though different, identity. This myth can only constitute the "other side" of a mythological "masculinity." Increasingly, in her more recent texts, Duras' narrative strategies seem aimed at disclosing the mobility of gender positions, in their discursive construction.

However, Marini will push at the limits of Duras' text, remythologizing the feminine, in what she characterizes as a radically different form of exchange, the exchange of the infant among women. As she reads it, the moment of exchange is the institution of genealogy and symbolization in and for the feminine. The possibility of exchanging the child, for her, puts an end to the specular fascination of the imaginary, what she calls "la fascination mortelle," while it introduces the subject, the beggar and mother, into intersubjectivity (257).

It seems to me, however, that the "fascination mortelle" is here displaced onto the narrative progress itself, as the text imagines the infant suspended on the point of death. Moreover, this scene of exchange signals the beggar's complete withdrawal from linguistic space into muteness: the word "Battambang" emerges to mark this point of separation. Further, the complex exchange only serves to open the space of its own repetition, since the beggar will repeat the conception, production, and abandonment of children throughout the story.

If anything, in fact, this scene seems to be the institution of the text's perpetual plying between "here" and "away." The proximity of the infant, the "semblable," the image, is rejected, cast off, abandoned, installing a rhythm of presence and absence. Furthermore, Marini's assertion that this scene marks a passage from imaginary to symbolic will apply equally well to the beggar's violent "symbolization" in the last scene of the text. For it is she who has the power to make the cut, biting the head off the fish—the Medusa's head that menaces Charles Rossett.

In focusing on the so-called mythic figure of the beggar, Marini's text makes a utopic detour, occluding the possible significance of the Anne-Marie Stretter figure, the "speaking" double (or perhaps triple, given the specular balance struck with this figure by the Vice-Consul) of the beggar. Such an occlusion may be related to Marini's more general tendency to find in the Vice-Consul a thematic reflection or performance of certain issues of feminist theory. But, indeed, such a move leads her to veer away from the last appearance of Anne-Marie Stretter, who is precisely, in her place, which is no place, a space "au bord de la mer," in default of separation, where distance is indeterminate.

As regards the orality inscribed in the narrative image of the beggar: it figures the movement of separation from the mother, the presence-absence, the offer and withdrawal of the breast, the zone of hallucinatory satisfaction giving way to representations, where one eats the object or eats the "nothing," the part object. But it is precisely this "nothing" or not-thing, which is already something—the cut already inscribed in the imaginary plenitude of the mirror stage—that is important here.

What if Anne-Marie Stretter were the figure of this unassimilable, irrecuperable lost object? Addressing the fascination this figure holds for her, Duras gives the following "description" of Anne-Marie Stretter.

> She has exceeded all presumptions concerning intelligence, knowledge or theory. It's a despair . . . In embracing what is most general in the world, the generality of the world, she is most herself. In being the most entirely open to everything, Calcutta, misery, hunger, love, prostitution, desire, she is most herself. When I say "prostitution," I mean prostitution passes through her like hunger, like tears, like desire; she's a hollow that receives, things inhabit her. (Les Lieux, 74)

This is a figure without properties, without property, without properness. Perhaps, in fact, Anne-Marie Stretter is the mirror that swallows, permitting no reflection, allowing no image to realize itself. Further, this infinitely receptive space has particular resonance for Duras, as she says in Les Yeux verts: "I've come to envision a master-key image, indefinitely superimposable upon a series of texts, an image that would have no meaning in itself, that would be neither beautiful nor ugly, that would only take its meaning from the text that passed over it" (49).

This paradoxical image would then be both figure, and the ground upon which individual narratives produce their figures—on the order of a screen—receiving projections, yet superimposed on the textual surface: a *passe-partout,* a pass-key, master-key. Such an image explodes the relationship of priority that traditionally governs the pair, figure and ground, routing it through the triadic organization, image-projector-screen, and establishing an utterly reversible directionality for that process. Furthermore, this characterization of the image renders radically problematic the status of the image as a function of representivity. Again, I might describe Duras' textual production as more closely related to mourning work, or to its incompletion, than to any specific reproduction of the Lacanian mirror stage's fantasmatic structures. Consequently, the textual process at once poses and undermines the notion of repeatability, subsuming it under the repetition itself.[8]

We might return to Duras' figuration of the maternal, in order to elaborate some of the complexities it involves. To Marini's purely feminine realm of exchange, we may juxtapose Jane Gallop's argument about Kristeva's strategy for speaking of the mother, in *The Daughter's Seduction.* Gallop focuses on a statement of Kristeva's in *Polylogue,* concerning the mother and the phallus: "That the very subject poses him/herself in relation to the phallus has been understood. But that the phallus is the mother, it is said, but here we are all *arrêtés* [stopped, arrested, fixed, stuck, paralyzed] by this 'truth.' "[9] Analyzing this formulation, Gallop goes on to suggest that it has particular pertinence when applied to the idea of an exclusively feminine space.

> The idyllic space of women together is supposed to exclude the phallus. The assumption that the "phallus" is male expects the exclusion of males to be sufficient to make a non-phallic space. The threat represented by the mother to this idyll might be understood through the notion that Mother, though female, is nonetheless phallic. So, as an afterthought, not only men, but Mother must be expelled from the innocent, non-phallic paradise. The inability to separate the daughter, the woman, from the mother then becomes the structural impossibility of evading the Phallus. (*The Daughter's Seduction,* 118)

In a precisely tuned argument, Gallop proposes that the Kristevan enterprise consists in exposing the fraud and the ideological status of the phallus, precisely by repeating and stressing the term "Phallic Mother": "The Phallic Mother is undeniably a fraud, yet one to which we are all infantilely susceptible. If the phallus were understood as the veiled attribute of the Mother, then perhaps this logical scandal could expose the joint imposture of both Phallus and Mother" (117). Such a strategy may work, according to Gallop, because, after all, the phallus is that which functions-as-veiled, and therefore, is most "phallic" precisely where it is most veiled: in the mother. For this reason, Kristeva's most subversive move may be in the theatricalization of the phallic mother: "not merely to theorize the phallic mother, but to theatricalize her, give her as spectacle, open the curtain" (118).

We might begin to see Duras' narrative cycle as a similar type of performance, or spectacle. Parading, alternately, the figure of the woman as lack—Lol V. Stein, the beggar—and the woman as phallic mother, the narcissistically full, self-referential body—Anne-Marie Stretter, Tatiana Karl, the beggar's mother—the texts reinscribe and disfigure a certain imposing libidinal economy. It is surely no accident that Anne-Marie Stretter on the beach, one of the three "vanishing points" of *The Vice-Consul,* emerges and disappears on the site where Lol V. Stein's absence must be marked, or remarked. Such a reading finds some confirmation in the reappearance of the unnamed Lol V. Stein of *L'Amour.* No doubt, however, it is particularly significant to note as well that these polarities are peeled away from discursive gender-binding, as demonstrated by the Vice-Consul and the traveler of *L'Amour.*

We must also investigate the maternal within at least one other structure of triangulation, as constituted by the intervention of the symbolic in the imaginary at the mirror stage itself. Colin MacCabe presents a convincing account in "Theory and Film: Principles of Realism and Pleasure": "The infant verifies its reflection by looking to the mother who holds it in front of the mirror. It is the mother's look that confirms the validity of the infant's image and with this look, we find that at the very foundation of the dual imaginary relationship, there is a third term already unsettling it. The mother verifies the relationship for the child, but at the cost of introducing a look, difference where there should be only similitude."[10] This is to say that the process by which the subject identifies the imagined plenitude of the specular image as his or her own image, the totality of his or her body, itself only takes place through the intervention of the Other's look.

Such a version of this scene then locates the force of intervention as already there in the imaginary dyad. Furthermore, because it stresses the imbrication of imaginary and symbolic, it obviates the possibility of theorizing the relation between the two on the model of chronological narrative development, from one phase to another. Additionally, for my purposes, it has the advantage of establishing the constitutive intervention of the third look within the "narcissistic" space.

In a slightly different vein, Marini sees the narrative project of *The Vice-Consul* as a shifting of the form of triangulation, since the origin is doubled in the organization mother–father–daughter, and mother–daughter–daughter of the daughter, or mother of the mother. The second triangle remains unclosed, in constant displacement, pivoting around one point, a movement Marini sees as marked out in the zigzagging pattern of the beggar's itinerary. This narrative disturbs any fixed triangular base and instead puts that structure in constant motion, transfiguration, exchange among poles, as in the opening passage of *L'Amour:* "Because of the man who is walking, constantly, with equal slowness, the triangle is deformed, reformed, without ever breaking" (8).

The "closing" piece of the narrative cycle, *L'Amour,* repeats Lol V. Stein in the veiled figure of Elle. This is a text without memory—"There is no more ball" (127)—a text, rather, of cancelled memory, which folds over on *The Vice-Consul* to become one of the two wings of a frame, as anticipated by the V that interrupts Lol V. Stein's name and figures the radical break of the ball itself. *L'Amour* is a text without memory, but one which activates a purely textual memory, a reenactment of the text already read. The uncanny effect produced by the already-read might be figured "metonymically" by the following fragment of dialogue between Il and Elle.

> She looks, beyond the hotel and the gardens, at the continuous succession of space, the density of time. She adds: "That trip to S. Thala, you know." . . .
> "I have never come back [revenue: come back, not retournée: gone back] there since I was young."
> The sentence remains suspended for a moment, then it ends [elle se termine].
> "I've forgotten." (107–8)

The logical explosiveness of this passage that evokes both memory and the telling, in order to obliterate them, establishing their impossibility, also performs this impossibility in producing an aporia. "The sentence ends," or "she finishes," one reading allows. But it has no beginning. Grammatically, "I've forgotten" is a complete sentence, as is the preceding one. The hiatus framed by these two sentences is the "suspended sentence," which does not exist until it is spoken, at which moment it is no longer suspended, except by the written text. Moreover, this phrase itself constitutes a contradiction when juxtaposed with the previous *ne:* "je n'y suis jamais revenue": "I have never come back here" (implied: where I am). "I have forgotten"; the assertion of forgetfulness here is precisely the sign of the repetition.

In fact, *L'Amour* is about suspense—the suspended phrase, the word suspended outside syntax, the suspended look which sees nothing and comes from nowhere. The *récit* itself is suspended, hung on the frame of two cries. "For a moment, no one hears, no one listens. And then there is a cry . . . A scream. Some one cried out near the sea wall. The scream has been uttered and it was heard in the whole space, full or empty" (12). On the following page appears the explosive passage: "The story [l'histoire]. It begins. It began before the walking at the seashore, the scream, the gesture, the movement of the sea, the movement of the light. But now it becomes visible. It is on the sand that it already settles, on the sea" (13).

The story gives itself as an autonomous inscription, suspended, in a sentence of its own: "L'histoire." "It begins": the story begins after the text has begun, only to begin by telling us that it has already begun, before. It has begun anticipating the cry already emitted. It has, in effect, just remembered, only to forget again, its own beginning—its own anteriority.

The space produced by the cry, in this context, has the same status as the space created by the step.

> The triangle is breaking up, reabsorbing itself. It just broke up: for, the man is passing, one sees him, one hears him.
> One hears; the steps space themselves out. (9)[11]

The step spaces itself, makes space. The step passes; but this step is not only a "step," it is a "pas," negation, as well. The text takes place, makes its space, under the sign of this "pas," the terminal fragment of the negative formation "ne . . . pas," which itself operates as a frame.[12] This step is the step we never "hear" coming, just as we don't hear the story coming, since we know we are already reading it.

If the story hangs on the two cries, the second of these obliquely fulfills the anticipation of the first: "An isolated cry: the mother. She screams that they must leave" (99). Is this the cry—now articulated, developed, and differentiated—that can put an end to the reverberations of the first one, which emanates from nowhere? Or perhaps it is the sirens on the preceding page which it simply voices. "Fire alarms blast throughout the city" (98). At stake here is the impossibility of framing, since *The Ravishing* also pivots on a cry, and a delayed one at that. Indeed, we might speculate that *L'Amour* gives voice to that unvoiced, unpunctual cry of the anterior text, its "generative" moment.

It is precisely the domain of suspense, however, that stages the "continuous succession of space, the density of time," that paradoxical reversal of attributes—density or volume to time, and sequentiality to space. If we consider this operation in light of the function of suspense in general, we may see how, in this case, it explodes the limits narrativity poses for itself. Barthes addresses the issue of suspense in connection with the logical time that governs the production of narrative sequence.

> "Suspense" is clearly only a privileged—or exacerbated—form of distortion: on the one hand, by keeping a sequence open (through emphatic procedures of delay and renewal), it reinforces the contact with the reader (the listener), has a manifestly phatic function; while on the other, it offers the threat of an uncompleted sequence, of an open paradigm (if, as we believe, every sequence has two poles), that is to say, of a logical disturbance, it being this disturbance which is consumed with anxiety and pleasure (all the more so because it is always made right in the end). (*Image-Music-Text,* 119)

L'Amour's operative suspense serves only to produce this curious phatic function, the "wink" at the reader, or better, the glance, which fascinates and hangs us up—suspends us. No resolution can be accomplished. The text explodes the anticipation of the two poles of sequence. This is suspense without the "pay-off."

As a temporal function as well, this suspense is overwhelming. I might read it in terms of Colin MacCabe's very concise characterization of the most elementary parameters of narrative.

> Narrative is propelled by both a heterogeneity and a surplus—a heterogeneity which must be both overcome and prolonged. The narrative begins with an incoherence, but already promises the resolution of that incoherence. The story is the passage from ignorance to knowledge, but this passage is denied as process—the knowledge is always already there as the comforting resolution of the broken coherence (every narration is always a suspense story). Narrative must deny the time of its own telling—it must refuse its status as discourse (as articulation), in favor of its self-presentation as simple identity, complete knowledge. (17)

This narration is, by contrast, only a suspension, not a story. Because of its character, it abolishes the possibility of coherent polar juxtaposition: story-discourse; *énoncé-énonciation;* writing-reading. If, indeed, the "story" is only the passage itself, between foreclosed source and destination, then it "presents" only the process of articulation: "les pas," steps, beats, pulsation. Furthermore, this text need not deny the time of its telling; its telling *is* its time. But this is also a story which cannot tell time, which denies the possibility of "telling time."

In this connection, it is no accident that the text figures writing itself, but as a "dead letter," caught and suspended, without a trajectory. "Le voyageur" himself is suspended on the immobilized trajectory implied in his name. The letter he writes is central to the text, constituting yet another repetitive mechanism.

> The man takes a piece of paper, he writes: S. Thala, S. Thala, S. Thala.
> He stops. He might be hesitating between the written words. He begins again. Slowly, with certainty, he writes: S. Thala, September 14.
> He underlines the first word. Then he writes again. "Don't come any more, it's not worth it."
> He pushes the letter away. (22)

In this first instance, the letter begins on a repetition, and on a hesitation between words. Curiously, the passage lacks the "hesitations between the words" that are constituted by punctuation. Only the second beginning of the letter can establish even the most primary references: place and time. Finally, the letter *éloignée* is only distanced, not sent. And, indeed, it *can*not be sent.

The last instance of the letter's appearance establishes it as never sent. Its message is already clear to the wife, to whom it is perhaps addressed. " 'I wrote to you. The letter is still there.' She puts the letter back on the table" (88).

This scene turns on the letter's exchange, its repositioning, its return to the table: used and reposed. But it remains, textually, unread, still a "dead letter"—voided of meaning in the scene of the encounter. And the subject/message of the letter is simply death: the death of the love relation, the intersubjective relation, as well as the possibility of its writer's suicide. In this regard, the figurative quality of the letter is most articulated in its second appearance, the one that is framed by the other two in the repetitive structure; or, read in another way, the point of the triangle framed by its occurrences. This scene is the simultaneous writing and reading of the letter's message:

> The traveler pushes the letter away, remains there. . . .
>   He resumes the letter. He writes.
>   S. Thala, September 14.
>   "Don't come any more, don't come, tell the children anything at all."
>   The hand stops, resumes:
>   "If you can't manage to explain to them, let them invent." He lays down the pen, picks it up, again.
>   "Don't regret anything, nothing, silence all your sorrow, don't understand anything, tell yourself that you will be all the closer to"—the hand lifts, resumes, writes "comprehension."
>   The traveler pushes the letter away. (42–43)

This scene, the scene of inscription of the word "S. Thala," also inscribes, or marks out the space of, S. Thala. In the coming and going, the posing and reposing—"lays down the pen, picks it up again"—the scene articulates a pulsating repetition: "pushes the letter away, resumes it." The repetition here is automatic, since a puppet hand, detached from the writing subject, is the agent of writing. Furthermore, this rewriting of the first instance of the letter adds nothing, produces nothing, it merely reinscribes the first message: the admonition not to come, not to return, not to seek. The promise of sense that binds us in the narrative pact is abolished in the destruction of the letter's circuit, *destinateur-destinataire*. In its ultimate failure to make these poles cohere, such a letter inscribes only death—the abolition of desire in repetition—the collapse of temporal and spatial boundaries.

The full impact of the scene of the letter's writing-reading is situated on the level of the narrative pact or promise, that is, where it concerns the reader. For the ultimate destabilization and displacement wrought by this text concerns the reader's position, implicating his or her desire in its movement. In a sense, the text's repetitions serve to abolish the space and time of a desire: the desire of reading.

In this respect, the moment of discovery, recognition, or recall of the "generative" figure, Lol V. Stein, is remarkable.

> She holds the mirror out to him, shows it to him.
>   "He gave me this before leaving."
>   She opens her bag: again. She puts the mirror back in it.

> He looks: the bag is empty, it contains only the mirror.
> "A ball." . . .
> She turns around, smiles at him.
> "Yes, after." She returns to pure time, to contemplating the ground—"after,
> I was married to a musician, I had two children." (113)

The recounted facts are indeed those of Lol V. Stein's story. And this is the first time we may establish the connection, which serves to identify Elle through the continuity expressed by this repetition, the recall. The ball, the empty center, source of her story, is also the source of this story; like the ground contemplated, it, too, returns us to "pure time." "Pure time" is the time of narration. Without direction and without the *articulation* necessary for measure, this can only be dead time, a time of death.

It is the conspicuous presence of the mirror that renders the scene even more strange. The mirror itself is almost uncanny; "the bag contains only the mirror." A mirror is enfolded in an empty handbag, and serves as an object of exchange, a gift, spectacle, memento ("he gave it to me before leaving"), and as threshold between a before and an after. Furthermore, this very scene is enfolded in a text which, like the bag, is empty, except for its repetition of images. The mirror, however, becomes a sort of lost object, suspended as it is, like the look that characterizes all these scenes, or the sourceless reverberating cry. This mirror reflects nothing; it only recalls another look. Here, we are reminded of the mirror-as-ground of *India Song,* the mirror that reflects only our absent place as spectators.

It seems that *L'Amour,* in its *mise à mort* (the putting to death) of narrativity, simultaneously inscribes our absence or impossibility as readers. This is the function of the omnipresent and floating pronoun "on," the "on" who "hears the steps space out" (10), and the "on" that governs the last passage of the text.

> One hears:
> For a moment she will be blinded.
> Then she will begin to see me again. To distinguish the sand from the sea, then, the sea from the light, then her body from mine. Afterwards she will separate the cold from the night and she'll give it to me. Only afterwards will she hear the noise, you know . . . of God, . . . of this thing? They are quiet. They survey, keep watch on the exterior dawn. (143)

It is not insignificant that the last word of the text should be "extérieure," emphasizing an obscure exteriority. The poetic or metaphoric deviation implied by the connection of "extérieure" to "dawn" is disturbed by the possibility of the literal effect. Exterior to whom or what? To these anonymous third-person pronouns, "ils," to the scene, to the text, or to its reading?

Such an effect is linked to the problem posed by the anchoring of narrative voice in "on." "On entend" controls the last passage, which then slides into the final sentences, which, presumably, "on" does not hear, and which exist on another narrative plane. The instability of this "on" is further augmented by its recalling the "on" of *The Vice-Consul;* this "on" is sometimes an anchor of the narrative level of discourse, in opposition to the *récit,* and sometimes textually localized as an individuation of the collective voice and eye of the European community which seems to observe the other textual figures.

The "on" of *The Ravishing* and *The Vice-Consul* is always both an anchor and a relay, since it acts as a switch point between narrative levels: from the diegetic "on entend" to the more abstract "on dirait": "as if" or "one *would* say." In such a construction, what "one would say" is already problematized. What one would say, one probably doesn't say. The "said" itself becomes discursive subject, either as the ground of hypothesis, the disturbance of the possibility of speech, or as the "already said," and, hence, the "already heard," the "heard tell," of rumor or cliché—collective, unspecified discourse.

Moreover, this last signal passage is anticipatory—"she will be blinded and then she will begin again." The "on" hears a projected discourse whose own source is unsituated, a passage overheard and not located. The "on" is further problematized, since its "overhearing" doubles ours. As readers, we maintain precisely the position of one who overhears. Moreover, "on" as a narrative anchor point is already shattered and fragmented as a pronominal function: "we," inclusive, implying complicity; "one," anonymous, possibly veiling the inclusive gesture, a more generalized collective; the loosely floating "they," noninclusive. The shattered image, the dispersion, projected by "on" then produces a set or series of relays through which our position as readers establishes itself, but as always destabilized, displaced. Duras' later texts will bring into play the "you"; *Savannah Bay* carries an initial envoi: "Savannah Bay, c'est toi [it's you]." Similarly, much of *L'Homme atlantique* is written in the second person—to a male other. Such reader-positions repel our investment even as they seem to solicit us all the more directly.

Régis Durand explores the cinematic version of this textual function, embodied (or disembodied) in the "off" voices. For him, the disruption of connection between voice off and figure on screen throws into question the convention of voice as "expressive," as exteriorizing an interiority.

> Because of this different logic and circulation of desire, *India Song* is perhaps the first cinematographic and textual disposition of another scene, in which reader/spectator, writer/director, text/film, characters/actors are equally implicated, equally affected; where no central, omnipotent subject pulls the strings, orders and reorders . . . desire runs from one object, one "person" to another, carrying danger and death to all (including the viewer). ("The Disposition of the Voice," 109)

Durand goes on to emphasize the problematical status of the relation between language and the voice, through which Duras, as he puts it, works to "cancel, displace, the subject as referent. The question she asks is: What happens when voices are freed from the conventions of what E. Benveniste calls written/spoken discourse, in order to become something that does not concern you, even though it affects you deeply? Marguerite Duras approaches the exploration of pure desire, pure intensity and horror" (110).

Such a displacement occurs through the dislodging of subject from "grammatical person," and of pronominal shifters from their function as discursive anchors. Paradoxically, however, the textual displacement also admits the possibility of cancellation of our subjectivity as readers, transforming that conventionally controlling position to the status of grammatical person, implicated within the play of textual relays. In a Lacanian sense, moreover, the speech/voice that "does not concern you, even though it affects you deeply," is precisely the function of "ça regarde," in the sense of "ça vous regarde," the look that looks at you.

Here we may connect Durand's version of Duras' project with her own meditation on the status of textual discourse, a meditation which refuses or fails the boundaries between written and spoken, as well as written and *read* language. In *Les Yeux verts,* a special edition of *Cahiers du cinéma* devoted exclusively to her work, Duras writes consistently of the relationship between her narratives and her films. The following passage is exemplary for its dissolution or occlusion of a distinct boundary between forms.

> Reading aloud suggests itself in the same way that it suggested itself to you alone, the first time, without voice. That slowness, that undisciplined punctuation is as if I were stripping the words, one after another and I discover what was underneath, the isolated word, devoid of all relationships, of all identity, abandoned. Sometimes nothing, barely a space, a form, but open, for the taking. But everything must be read, the empty space too, I mean to say: everything must be found. (49)

The ins and outs of this passage, its gaps and its breakdowns, serve to dislocate the relationship of writing to voice, reading to writing, as well as the relationship of before and after. Sense becomes a sort of *après-coup.* But it is also the *après-coup,* retroaction, or repetition of an impossibility, "the primary state of this text," which is already written, spoken, articulated, even in "that undisciplined punctuation." The "isolated word . . . devoid of all relationships, of all identity," in this context, must be that impossible disengagement of sound from sense, voice from body, reading from writing. What is at stake, then, is a perpetual work of binding and unbinding. Indeed, Durand's "pure desire, pure intensity and horror" suggests that the disruptive quality of these texts is related to a different economy of narrative binding or suturing—a circulation of intensities.

Because it occurs across repetition effects, which produce an internal network of attachments, the text called *L'Amour,* along with the cycle of which it is one circuit, escapes immobilization and legibility. This text establishes a desiring textual body in the unintelligibility of the word at its head, just as it forecloses the pleasurable immobilization purchased by suspense, in favor of another pleasure.

Just what that other pleasure is can only be determined approximately as the suspension of suspense in repetition, a failure to satisfy or consolidate our investment. Durand describes the uncanny quality of voice-over, the transposition of the voice in Duras' films, as related to a failure to satisfy our urge for investment: "Those voices . . . are radically cut off from our demand, our need to fasten on to them and invest them with our desire" (108). A similar failure to consolidate sites of investment is effectuated in Duras' novels, through unceasing translation and repetition, of trauma and of the circulation through subject positions by which the narrating instance continually signals its own dispossession. The voice that speaks through these texts is never localized, but rather wandering, translating itself from text to text.

In the narrative domain, which maintains a relation of reciprocal translation with the filmic in Duras' production, we may read this function in the incessant translation which never succeeds in bringing back the "same," but which nevertheless provides no stable difference, but only a heterogeneity achieved through alterations. In this regard, we might speculate that these texts elaborate a different narrative syntax, where repetition produces more disjunction than coherence.

The voice itself comes increasingly to the fore in all of Duras' work. In her films it floats, unanchored to the narrative movement, continually failing to sustain or assure the fullness of the image through a consistency of shared reference. Just as the work of the voice undermines the frame—the fixation of the image as centered and coherent in the midst of filmic sequentiality, process, loss of image—it also signals a lack in the representation. It calls to us from another, absent space, the space outside the frame. Simultaneously as it disturbs the placement and consistency of the image, however, this voice "off" also destabilizes the form of address. We are not consistently hailed by the film; it speaks to an indeterminate set of addresses from a mobile position. In so doing, it frustrates any simple, comfortable recuperation through identification with the *narrated* subjects—the figures in the film—or with a spectator position that accedes to knowledge, assurance, or stability through a narrative resolution. Instead, dividing the filmic space explicitly into "on" and "off" screen, the voice stresses the absence in representation, and our absence to the film.

We find a similar strategy at work in Duras' text *Le Navire Night,* the narrative of an entirely telephonic relationship between a woman who claims to be dying and a young male telephone operator. This is narrative reduced to a dialogic *scene,* but on a one-way circuit, since only one speaker—the woman—calls, and the other—the young man who does not have her telephone number—is called. This is a text of voices, where the two interlocutors are framed by other speakers who pose questions: " 'No image on the text of desire?' 'What image? I don't see what image.' 'Then there is nothing to see. Nothing, no image.' "[13] All that is constructed is a set of repeated appeals, lures, demands, punctuated by interruptions—the nights without calls. It is as if each call merely served to bridge or breach, momentarily, the telephonic gap. Here we have the narrative reduced to a figuration of the *fort-da* spool, where the voice vibrating through the telephone line is the object reeled in and tossed out. But around and through this established and ruptured connection (telecommunications—contact without touch), is absence—absence of the space and the body from which the voice emanates, absence across which it carries, the absence of any possible image to accompany it.

What then is the reader's position? On what level does the text appeal to us? We need to frame our examination of the text with a consideration of the instance of reading. That is to say, how does the experience of dissatisfaction that Durand describes relate to the disjunction within repetition that is produced by the collision of trauma and pleasure, as they work on the woman reader's position? How do we, as readers, operate in response to the continual trauma of loss and refinding that is elaborated in the textual structure and that is also mapped in the varying degrees of legibility the text offers—its oscillation between overdetermination and blankness or muteness? My point is that these texts map a different set of positions for the reader to invest, as well as to occupy, thereby performing the sort of displacement Barthes calls for in "Plaisir/Ecriture/Lecture": "Bourgeois culture is in us; in our syntax, in the way we speak, perhaps even in a part of our own pleasure. We can not pass into the non-discursive because the non-discursive doesn't exist . . . the only battle . . . is not always a triumph, but we must try to displace languages. One tries to create . . . a new space where the subject of writing and the subject of reading don't occupy exactly the same place."[14]

In this regard, we may feel ourselves participating in and performing a displacement of reading and writing positions, precisely through the loss of subject-effect in the narration. Among the most striking instances of this loss/dispossession of narrating instance appear when Duras' discourse occupies the textual zone coded for suspense: the murder mystery, the narrative of crime and its investigation, involving narrative movements from breach or disturbance of order, through crisis, to resolution by certain transformations. If we see resolution as mastery which involves the solution of the mystery and the restoration of order, then suspense, delay of pleasure, allows for the meticulous production of coherence among dispersed details, with the result that the pleasure in narrative closure is doubled: as both pleasure in knowledge-mastery and in the construction of a consistent subject *for* knowledge.

If suspense is suspended, the reader's position shifts abruptly, if not violently; such a shift forces the reader's consideration of his or her stance. This disruption is the subject of the following investigation, which follows the trail of Duras' continually returning figures, as the oral thematics of the Lol V.

Stein "cycle"—*The Ravishing, The Vice-Consul,* and *L'Amour*—is translated into a "detective story" frame.

Notes

1. Sigmund Freud, "Mourning and Melancholia," *S.E.,* 14:249–50.
2. Cf., for example, the exposition of Melanie Klein's theory of "good" and "bad" objects in Jean Laplanche and J.-B. Pontalis, *The Language of Psychoanalysis,* trans. Donald Nicholson-Smith (New York: Norton, 1974), 187–89.
3. Jacques Derrida, "Economimesis," *Diacritics* 11, no. 1 (1981): 22–23.
4. See Mieke Bal, *Narratologie* (Paris: Klincksieck, 1977), 79.
5. As for the final parenthetical phrase, the French has "the *word* Battambang for the *word* Battambang." The distinction to be made is between word and word, not name and place. The translation has, "her madness from madness in general," but the words "in general" are too *specific* here; the problem is not only to separate the specific from the general, but also the part from the whole, while each of these terms remains undetermined.
6. Pierre Fédida, "Entre les voix et l'image," in *Marguerite Duras,* 158–59.
7. Cf. Copjec, 46–47, where she connects the filmic function of the mirror with the central reception scene of *India Song,* where the mirror suspends both Anne-Marie Stretter's image and her gaze, figuring her death.
8. See Copjec for a meticulous explication of the repetition mechanism in Duras' films.
9. Kristeva, *Polylogue* (Paris: Seuil, 1977), 204. Also cited in Jane Gallop, *The Daughter's Seduction* (Ithaca, N.Y.: Cornell Univ. Press, 1982), 117.
10. Colin MacCabe, "Theory and Film: Principles of Realism and Pleasure," *Screen* 17, no. 3 (1976): 15.
11. Note the construction "on": "on l'entend, on le voit," which may be read "he is heard, seen," "one hears, sees him," "we" or "they hear, see him." As such, it introduces a pronominal displacement and a mobility of subject and object within the very grammar of the sentence which cannot be reproduced in translation, but which are the mapping, in germ, of this text's movement. Such a syntax itself reproduces the moving triangle that rotates around its three points.
12. On the question of "pas," see Jacques Derrida, *La Carte postale,* 317, for example. This passage is a prolonged speculation on the pun that discloses a connection between repetition and negation, in the repeated "ne . . . pas" in Freud's text, with respect to its inability to advance.
13. Marguerite Duras, *Le Navire Night* (Paris: Mercure de France, 1979), 30, my translation.
14. Roland Barthes, "Plaisir/Ecriture/Lecture," in *Le Grain de la voix* (Paris: Seuil, 1981), 153–54.

Writing Sexual Relations

LESLIE HILL

In her texts of the 1980s and 1990s Duras embarked on what amounts to a complex restatement of many of the concerns that were at the centre of her earlier work.[1] Once again, as in the 1950s and 1960s, the theme of the couple predominates. But in the prose and theatre of the 1980s, the couple, though still usually made up of a woman and a man, is in many respects more unconventional and irregular than ever before. In her play *Agatha,* for instance, written in 1981, and filmed the same year under the title *Agatha et les lectures illimitées,* Duras stages a story explicitly devoted to an incestuous relationship between brother and sister. In the piece, sexual desire, hovering perpetually on the brink of ecstatic consummation, albeit only by proxy or in retrospect, prepares to enact that which, in normal circumstances, and in most known human societies, lies far beyond the pale of exclusion. *Savannah Bay,* Duras's next play, produced in 1983, though not concerned with incest, is in other respects very similar; what it shows, mediated and refracted through the words of two women, separated by two generations, is a mythically conjectural love story, part fiction, part remembrance, involving a man and a woman, both of whom commit suicide as an expression of the intensity of their desire for each other. Here, as elsewhere, even despite the birth of the couple's daughter—if not in fact as a direct consequence of it—no marital or familial institution seems adequate to contain their overpowering love for each other (*SB,* 60). And much the same theme, though framed in more conventionally melodramatic terms, is in evidence in *La Musica deuxième* (1985) with its story of two recent divorcees lingering nostalgically but dangerously in the vivid afterglow of their now spent and impossible relationship.

But perhaps more provocative—at any event more controversial—than any of these tales of thwarted but overwhelming heterosexual passion is Duras's short *récit,* halfway between a novel and a playscript, entitled *La Maladie de la mort* (1982), together with the longer narrative that amplifies and reworks it, *Les Yeux bleus cheveux noirs,* written in 1986.[2] In both these texts, Duras explores the sexual relationship between a homosexual man—though

From *Marguerite Duras: Apocalyptic Desires* (London: Routledge, 1993), 137–58. Reprinted by permission.

159

not explicitly named as such in either text—and a compliant heterosexual woman; the two are joined together in a contract that could well be described as prostitutional, were the pair, at least in the 1986 text, not also to be bound by their common—though mutually exclusive—desire for the inaccessible stranger to whom the words in the title refer. Duras also makes it clear that the woman in the first story is not primarily in search of money (*MM, 23*), but that something more is at stake that has to do with the question of the relation between sickness, death, and desire which the words, *La Maladie de la mort,* seem to suggest. But in turn, Duras implies, that relation itself hangs on the more radical conundrum of the very possibility of sexual relation between the two differentiated, adversarial bodies whose mutual dealings Duras in her narrative nonetheless endeavours to articulate or relate.

In all Duras's writings of the 1980s, relations between the sexes are of vital importance, but they also prove to be intensely fraught and precarious. In many instances, the prospect of union seems out of the question from the outset; and for some of the partners even the possibility of a shared present or future is excluded. To this extent, these stories of incest, suicidal passion, male homosexuality, separation, or divorce all display a prolonged and deep-seated crisis affecting the inner logic of sexual relations; and what Duras's texts describe, rather than a sequence of euphorically transgressive love idylls, is a series of sexual relations that seem to be like so many failures of sexual relation. The simple bliss of unencumbered happiness is nowhere apparent, and each text tends instead to inscribe or retrace a sexual or affective catastrophe culminating only in irreparable loss, mourning, solitude, aggression, or despair.

But throughout Duras's work, states such as these function less as signs of bodily fiasco than as figures of sublime or catastrophic disclosure. As such, they obey what in Duras is a familiar logic of apocalyptic inversion or reversal. For desire here survives undeterred by the cultural taboos that, for instance, forbid sexual relations between brother and sister; and it refuses to be intimidated by the puzzling asymmetry produced by the co-existence of divergent, mutually antagonistic sexual orientations or object choices within the same couple. On the contrary, such difficulties seem inseparable from the very origin of desire itself; and their effect is not to diminish the power of love but rather to provoke, sustain, and radically intensify it. Thus, the bars on sexual satisfaction encountered by Duras's couples seem rarely imposed on them from the outside; on the contrary, desire itself in Duras is always already animated by the inaccessibility of the object it seeks and the necessary impossibility of ultimate gratification.

What is most clearly common to all the love relations that Duras describes in her late texts is an abiding, though paradoxical, sense that relations of desire between sexually differentiated bodies are somehow founded on the very impossibility of such relations.[3] Bodies in Duras remain irreducibly separate and irreconcilably different; but in so far as the goal of sexual desire is to erase these boundaries between bodies, and thus fuse self with other in an undecidable merging of identities, it is evident that the absence of relation between self and other, like the separateness of bodies themselves, instead of blunting desire, is its necessary and indispensable precondition. It is only ever when there is no possibility of relation between self and other that the other may be grasped as radically different, and thus genuinely desirable. Desire here is no longer regulated by received notions of sex or gender identity or by criteria of crude orgasmic efficiency; instead, in Duras, it often turns out, as *L'Amant* most clearly shows, that the most sexually desirable of other bodies is that very body with which, for reasons of cultural custom, social or personal circumstances, or even sexual orientation, no relationship is possible.

The logic of desire at work here is an ecstatic and often violent one, and one of the most incisive demonstrations of what it entails is provided, among Duras's works of the 1980s, by her two films of 1981, *Agatha et les lectures illimitées* and *L'Homme atlantique*. The first of these, a version of her—by then still unperformed—play *Agatha,* is in the form of a dramatic reading of the dialogue from that text, spoken off-screen by the voices of Duras and Yann Andréa;[4] while on the image track, amidst a series of largely static shots of the beach, sea, and sky at Trouville, punctuated periodically by the intervention of an empty black (or blank) frame, Bulle Ogier and Andréa are seen to embody, intermittently and without ever speaking on screen, the roles of the two protagonists. For these interior shots, the film uses the empty entrance hall in the Hôtel des Roches noires in Trouville (where Duras's own flat is situated and where, a decade before, she had already set *L'Amour* and *La Femme du Gange*).

Having finished *Agatha et les lectures illimitées* in May, Duras followed it, only six months later, with the release of a second film based on the same visual material, *L'Homme atlantique*. The text was subsequently published, with minor variations, early the following year. This second film, which at forty-one minutes is less than half the length of its predecessor, is made up of an off-screen commentary spoken solely by Duras, while in the role of the eponymous *L'Homme atlantique* Duras casts none other than Yann Andréa, to whose image the film is seemingly addressed, and who, of course, opposite the author, had read the part of the incestuous brother in *Agatha et les lectures illimitées* and had appeared in the earlier film, though for no more than a few frames, wearing the same black sou'wester as he does in *L'Homme atlantique*. Using the same tactic as when making *Césarée* from the abandoned footage belonging to *Le Navire Night* in 1979, Duras did not film any new material specially for *L'Homme atlantique,* but decided to utilise the shots jettisoned after the final editing of *Agatha et les lectures illimitées* earlier in the year. As in the previous film, these shots are intercut with a series of empty black frames, but in *L'Homme atlantique* these interruptions are far more extensive than before. Their duration is extremely variable, and while in some cases the empty frame is held for little more than one or two seconds, at other moments the state of invisibility is imposed on the film for considerably longer; and Duras ends the film with a black empty frame which is held for 14′40″, during which time the author's offscreen voice reads the equivalent of nine and a half pages of published text (*HA*, 22–31).

As this brief description suggests, the relationship between the two films is a complex one. The many points of visual similarity between the movies are offset by striking divergences between the two spoken texts. In this respect, though in a different register from before, the making of *L'Homme atlantique* recalls the apocalyptic rewriting of *India Song* as *Son nom de Venise dans Calcutta désert* in the mid-1970s. As with the earlier film, there are a number of specific ways in which *L'Homme atlantique* both recapitulates and radicalises its predecessor. In *Agatha et les lectures illimitées,* for instance, one key sequence, interrupted and resumed several times over, shows the figure of Bulle Ogier, doubling on the image track in the role of the sister, as she enters from the left, and crosses the hall of the Hôtel des Roches noires on her way towards the windows positioned to the right of the screen, which face out to sea; behind her, the camera, just before it begins to pan to the right to keep her in shot, can be seen reflected, together with the film crew, in the large wall mirror at the back of the frame. Ogier herself, like the room's many empty chairs and internal pillars, is also replicated as an image in the mirror, in which, some minutes later, it becomes clear that a second, parallel mirror, mounted on the opposite wall, is also visible; meanwhile, between these two sightings of mirrors, the camera lingers on the windows that overlook the beach, positioning the sea as a distant image within their rectangular frame.

Throughout this whole sequence the effect is a disorientating one of infinite visual regress (not unlike the scene described ten years earlier in *L'Amour* [*AM*, 56]). The use of the two parallel mirrors, showing the camera photographing itself photographing itself, invites the sense that the object being viewed is vertiginously out of control, no longer properly contained or held in place by the frame that surrounds it. Moreover, there is a dizzying sense of the abysmal uncertainty affecting the status of the images on the cinema screen, and it is at times unclear whether these are real images, or simply reflections of images, or indeed reflections of reflections of images (at one point, for instance, there are three different versions of Bulle Ogier visible simultaneously within the same frame). From the very outset, too, Duras uses the frequently opaque or dimly translucent windows as a visual frame-within-the-frame, drawing attention to the failure of the camera to reach beyond the severely imposed limitations of its own monocular vision. The result is a peculiar tension between the frame itself and the object—often the sea—that it aims to enclose. And in the end, it is as though the camera, frustrated at the possibility of being able to record only a plethora of narcissistic reflections, is appealing, beyond the frame, to some other dimension invisible to the human eye. That other dimension, as far as *Agatha et les lectures illimitées* is concerned, is not hard to find: it is the dimension of the human voice.

Speech, clearly, is not subject to constraints of visibility; and it is thus inevitable that it should be in the voices delivering Duras's text that the difficulties of vision explored in the sequence described above are overcome, albeit on the condition that what the voices enact should itself remain hidden from sight, like some clandestine secret that ought not to be disclosed. This, of course, is exactly what is at issue in the film. For throughout this whole interrupted sequence, as Bulle Ogier passes from the mirror to the windows and to the second mirror and back again, what the voices of Duras and Andréa are reading—from the play *Agatha*—is a story of incestuous identification between brother and sister. In the story, each of the two siblings, independently, visits the converted château—or house of assignation—that reminds them of their childhood, in part because it overlooks a river and has a piano (*AG*, 24–35); as the woman begins playing a favourite Brahms waltz on this piano, she is aware of her brother listening from the floor above. Unable to play the waltz correctly, she abandons the attempt (reminding viewers of Anne-Marie Stretter, that other musician in Duras who also despaired of her piano-playing). As she gives up, her brother appears—unseen by the viewer—in the doorway, and resumes the waltz on the piano in her stead, while she, in turn, now leaves the room, only to find herself in the reception hall a little further off, gazing at her own reflection in a mirror; as she listens, it is as though she can see their two bodies merging simultaneously in the glass. Music, as often in Duras, becomes a vehicle for displaced erotic communion, and the woman's body is overwhelmed by a surge of ecstatic physical desire: for a few moments, she says, "j'ai perdu la connaissance de vivre" ("I lost all sense of being alive," *AG*, 30).

The story offers a pointed commentary on the relationship between sound and image in Duras's film. For just as the scene recounted by Duras and Andréa off-screen tells a story of literal separation and metaphoric fusion, so the film, overlaying the mirror image on screen with the theme of the mirror on the soundtrack, is able to create in the viewer a powerful, if imaginary sense of the metaphorical identification taking place in the film between the body of Bulle Ogier and that of the fictional Agatha, even though all that is shown on camera is the isolated figure of Ogier facing the mirror. Image and spoken word refuse to match, but they do converge metaphorically; so the film is able temporarily to suspend the effect of their separation without annulling it. What the film does, therefore, is to enact or re-enact the impact of the Brahms waltz on the sister recalling her bodily identity with her own brother. Though the violence of the desire between brother and sister is not displayed on screen directly, it is performed invisibly by the impossible merger between screen and sound effected within the film itself. To the extent that it can articulate that which escapes representation, speech here is given priority over image; but what is more important is that all realist coincidence between vision and sound is withheld, its very possibility denied, even as Duras invites her spectator to imagine their impossible conjunction. And it is that impossibility which gives incestuous desire its awesome power, its "force si terrible" (*AG*, 12). As the text later puts it, spoken to the brother by his sister's voice: "Je vous aime comme il n'est pas possible d'aimer" ("I love you as it is not possible to love," *AG*, 30).

Some five minutes after the beginning of *L'Homme atlantique* there is a scene similar to the one from *Agatha et les lectures illimitées* that I have been describing. A human figure enters from the left, is filmed against a wall mirror by the camera that is visible as a reflection within the image that it is itself recording. The camera pans to the right, showing a silhouette looking out to sea through the windows; and it then turns to the left, where it encounters the mirror again. Throughout, unlike before, the figure on screen is not that of Bulle Ogier, but of Yann Andréa, and it is in part as though Andréa is still continuing—though in the wrong film—in his earlier role of the incestuous brother from *Agatha et les lectures illimitées,* revisiting the hall of the Hôtel des Roches noires and retracing his sister's steps in a belated lover's homage to her. Separate sequences from different movies fuse together even as they remain at a distance. Cinema, Duras's voice announces on the soundtrack, is at the limit here of what it is capable of recording (*HA,* 12–13), and it is certainly the case that the shot, at 3′15″ the longest genuine take in the film (if one excludes the black frames), is initially as confusing as the sequence from *Agatha et les lectures illimitées* which it cites and largely reproduces.

This reprise of one film by another provides, of course, another neat allegorical fable of incest as a merging of two siblings as one, but in some respects the reworking of desire implicit in *L'Homme atlantique* is more disorientating than this. For in the film, unlike its predecessor, there is no recognisable narrative structure with which to make sense of the image of Andréa replicated in the mirror alongside the abysmal reflection of the camera and crew. Though the text of the film, as read by the voice of Duras, is addressed to an unnamed second person—"vous"—with a precise date—15 June 1981—it is impossible to tell who this addressee is. Even within the film itself there is no reliable match between the image of Yann Andréa and the person referred to by the text, so that, when the voice declares: "La mer est à votre gauche en ce moment" ("The sea is now to your left," *HA,* 14), this turns out conspicuously not to be the case. As a result, no reliable subject-object axis sustains the relation between spoken text and image, and the shifting transferential dynamic of desire in Duras is such that it is impossible to decide, when viewing the film, whether Andréa is still doubling up as Agatha's brother, or whether, alternatively, he is acting out his own biographical role as Duras's publicly accredited companion, or whether he is not simply an extra appearing in an experimental film. What is important about the image of Andréa in *L'Homme atlantique* is that it fulfils all these possibilities at one and the same time; Andréa's role, like an ocean breaker, so to speak, is to stand in for himself amidst the multiplicity of other men he both is and is not. This, at any rate, is what the viewer is told by the voice of Duras: "dans le déferlement milliardaire des hommes autour de vous," she says, "vous êtes le seul à tenir lieu de vous-même auprès de moi" ("amidst the surging millions of men around you, you are the only one to take the place of yourself beside me," *HA,* 10).

In this way, if *L'Homme atlantique* reprises *Agatha et les lectures illimitées,* it does so only with the effect of ruining its precursor's residual claims to narrativity. Projecting desire beyond the realm of story-telling, it amplifies its apocalyptic, catastrophic intensity. As a result, what Duras articulates in *L'Homme atlantique* is no longer in the form of a recognisable narrative, save possibly a private scenario of desire, abandonment, and loss, but rather in the shape of an impossible dialogue between an invisible speaking voice and a silent—often absent—screen image. To an extent, this asymmetry was already implicit in *Agatha et les lectures illimitées,* but here, with *L'Homme atlantique,* the separation of image and voice becomes more radical than ever before, since for the first time in Duras's cinema the gap between image and sound is now aligned with the fissure of sexual difference itself.

In *L'Homme atlantique,* the divorce between female and male lapses into an impossible, failed dialogue between voice and image. All communion between the sexes, as between text and screen, is found to be desperately lacking or wanting; but this is a clue that the very impossibility of such communion is itself a spur for turning it into a miraculous actuality, the name for which, in Duras, is love itself. In *L'Homme atlantique,* one might say, it is the impossibility of the relationship between sight and sound that paradoxically makes such a relationship possible, even though, at the very same time, it has the effect of deferring that possibility and making it perpetually unavailable. The paradox is one that applies not just to Duras's film but also to relations between the sexes. (And this convergence between cinema and sexuality is no doubt the reason why, later in *L'Homme atlantique,* life is described by Duras as a photographic phenomenon, ["ce phénomène photographique, la vie," *HA,* 25].) The voice of Duras puts it as follows in the film, addressing an empty, black frame in which, immediately after, the image of Yann Andréa reappears: "C'est à votre incompréhension que je m'adresse toujours. Sans cela, vous voyez, ce ne serait pas la peine" ("It is your failure to understand that I am appealing to. Otherwise, do you see, it would all be pointless," *HA,* 18).

While the asymmetrical, failed relationship between image and voice in the film places male and female on either side of an unbridgeable divide, other elements of the film point to the fact that this apparently irreconcilable state of opposition between the sexes is only one aspect of the economy of desire *L'Homme atlantique* strives to articulate. This is evident at various moments in the film when Duras has recourse to the theme of the ocean, as she does, for instance, at the end of the film, when, during the final empty frame (lasting 14′40″), in the gaps between her own spoken words, the sound of the sea is heard on the soundtrack, building first to a roar and then fading away. The effect is repeated four times. With regard to *L'Homme atlantique* as a whole, the motif is not unlike the use of thunder at the end of *Détruire, dit-elle,* and here, as there, what it announces is the promise or arrival of an unnamed force which seemingly has the power to fuse bodies together and overwhelm the state of separation that exists between them. By introducing into the film a third element, the ocean, which is neither male nor female and without identity or determinate shape, Duras unsettles the binary opposition between the sexes which the film otherwise appears to endorse. Faced with the presence of the ocean on both the soundtrack and image track, the viewer is invited, also, to reflect on the title of the film, which shortly after the unexpected sound of the ocean ends—though not in the 1982 published version—with the words: "Vous êtes l'homme atlantique. Vous l'ignorez" ("You are the Atlantic man. You are unaware of this").

But who or what is this Atlantic man? Part of the answer has evidently to do with what, earlier in her text, the author names as the Atlantic object, "l'objet atlantique" (*HA,* 12), which is none other than the ocean itself. Readers of Duras will remember that this is not the first occurrence of the Atlantic ocean in her work, nor is it the first occasion there has been an unnamed Atlantic man. Already in the author's second novel, *La Vie tranquille,* published in 1944, there is an Atlantic man, or at any rate an anonymous man who drowns in the Atlantic (*VT,* 172–5). The incident happens while the narrator, Françou, is in a small town called T . . . on the Atlantic coast, where she has gone to grieve for her brother, Nicolas, who earlier in the book committed suicide in remorse at causing the death of his uncle (*VT,* 111–15). (Shortly after her arrival, as though in anticipation of *Agatha,* almost forty years later, Françou finds herself staring at herself in a mirror; the person she sees is like some alien character, both brotherly and malevolent ["à la fois fraternel et haineux," *VT,* 122], silently challenging her identity.) Some days later, lying on the beach, Françou watches a man swimming, and sees him laugh; later she realises that her grief for her brother has begun to subside, and she returns to her hotel, to discover the following day that the man has disappeared, presumed drowned, at which point she is obliged by the hotel proprietor to leave the resort.

In the novel in which it figures, the episode may seem at first sight to have little connection with the rest of the plot; but it is clear that the scene serves as a belated, transferential frame for the ambivalent feelings of desire, guilt, and loss, associated for Françou with the death of her brother, Nicolas. As such, the episode is more than just an isolated reference in Duras's work to the dangers of submersion. On the contrary, it seems to have set in motion, throughout a series of texts, a remarkable spate of deaths by drowning, many of which are suicides, and among the victims of which may be counted characters like Anne-Marie Stretter in *India Song,* or the two desperate lovers in the play *Savannah Bay,* and several others. Even more common than deaths by drowning in Duras are references to the fear of drowning, which recur with surprising frequency, and are particularly in evidence in the texts of the 1980s, notably *Agatha, Savannah Bay, L'Amant,* and *La Douleur.*

The Atlantic ocean, for Duras, seems to fuse together two conflicting yet equally compelling motifs: the theme of incestuous identification with the brother, and the theme of death, loss, and guilt. Both meanings lie at the centre of *L'Homme atlantique,* as they did in *Agatha et les lectures illimitées;* and it is no doubt because the two are never properly disentangled by Duras in the film that *L'Homme atlantique* presents the viewer with such a problematic and disconcerting impression of desire fused with aggression, or violence with amorous intensity. "Je suis dans un amour entre vivre et mourir" ("I am in a state of love between living and dying," *HA,* 31), affirms the voice of Duras towards the end, and if it is true that *L'Homme atlantique* records the narrator's abandonment by the man to whom the film is addressed, the film also constitutes an ecstatic message delivered to that inaccessible other. Desire here is nothing other than the very process of its own exhaustion or extinction; as Duras's voice puts it to her lover: "Tandis que je ne vous aime plus je n'aime plus rien, rien, que vous, encore" ("Even as I no longer love you I no longer love anything, not anything, except for you, still," *HA,* 27).

Slightly earlier in the film, by way of glossing its title, Duras, in her role as narrator, suggested that, for her part, she saw no difference between her lover and the sea; she tells him:

> Vous et la mer, vous ne faites qu'un pour moi, qu'un seul objet, celui de mon rôle dans cette aventure. Je la regarde moi aussi. Vous devez la regarder comme moi, comme moi je la regarde, de toutes mes forces, à votre place. (*HA,* 14)

> (You and the sea are as one for me, a single object, corresponding to my part in this adventure. I am looking at it too. You must be looking at it just as I am, just as I am looking, with all my strength, from where you are standing.)

Coming as it does at the end of the mirror sequence described above, the passage condenses the many transformations of desire at work in the film: the identification of the narrator's lover (in the masculine) with the sea (in the feminine); her fusion with him as she takes his place and both are bound together in a common predicament, facing this undifferentiated element, the sea, to which they both already belong yet which still remains somehow separate from them, and inaccessible; and, with this motif of the sea, the implied equivalence of desire and death, love and mourning. Yet none of the mergers promised here seems as yet to be complete, and something still resists the imperious and assertive violence of Duras's prose. The result is a dual, contradictory dynamic by which the libidinal loss of self is constantly offset by the irreducible singularity of the film's differentiated bodies and the asymmetry of their possible relations.

In *L'Homme atlantique,* as in the *Aurélia Steiner* stories, what the theme of the sea serves to articulate is both the engulfment of bodily difference and the perpetual reaffirmation of that difference. Much the same sense of oscillation is implicit in the rise and fall of the waves heard on the soundtrack of the film. It follows that the sea, if it is an object of desire, is arguably not a determinable object from which the narrator or lover may be detached; and that if it is a body, it is a body with which the only relation is one grounded in ambivalence, with the result that the narrator is left moving back and forth, irreconcilably, without the possibility of a stable position, between a fear of death by drowning and a yearning for bodily submersion. Here, the sea is no doubt itself already no more than a metaphor for that most primal and archaic of all ambivalent love objects in Duras's writing, one that, throughout the whole of her work, she describes with an equal measure of violent anger and intense desire, as she made plain herself, barely three years after *L'Homme atlantique,* in *L'Amant:* the body of the mother.[5] In Duras's case, as *Un barrage contre le Pacifique* had established in 1950, the identification between the sea and the mother (in French, "la mer" and "la mère") is no idle pun; and its re-emergence in many of the texts of the late 1970s and early 1980s confirms that, in *L'Homme atlantique,* as in several of the texts that follow, what is at stake for Duras is not the success or failure of desire for this or that body in preference to another, but, more radically, the very ground on which these choices are made, the enigma of what it is that drives bodies to separate at all from each other, only for those selfsame bodies then to struggle endlessly and painfully to reverse the process in the pursuit of impossible love.

As this association with the mother suggests, the sea in *L'Homme atlantique,* though it is named in the text as an object, is less an object than a kind of ever-changing, indeterminate environment which necessarily escapes all properly mimetic representation. But, at least in the film version of *L'Homme atlantique,* it nonetheless retains its own distinct and persuasive visual emblem. This is clear when, at the point corresponding to the passage cited above, a cut in the image track of the film intervenes just before the viewer hears the second sentence: "je la regarde." The frame that follows immediately after is an empty black image lacking in all definition. Such frames, by the end of *L'Homme atlantique,* entirely overwhelm the film and submerge it in darkness. As they do so, they seem to signify in a double manner: they point on the one hand to the absolute separation of bodies, of male and female, image and voice, and lament the loss of all properly cinematographic space in which the two might have been joined together; but they also promise, in apocalyptic mode, the possibility of a catastrophic merger of the unseen with the unspoken, of the visible with the invisible, and thus, at last, of male with female. (It comes as no surprise to realise that, in almost all Duras's texts of the 1980s, erotic communion is signified by the motif of characters intently looking, with their eyes closed.) What is accomplished at the close of *L'Homme atlantique,* is an act of erotic fusion, in which intense libidinal engulfment becomes inseparable from deathly submersion.

In *L'Homme atlantique,* all images except absent ones are pushed to a point of exhaustion; all that survives, functioning precariously as a sign of bodily and sexual difference but also, if it were to fall silent, presaging the imminent loss of difference, is the sound of the human voice, itself, in this guise, working arguably as yet another avatar of the maternal body. But less, here, is also more, and this rediscovery of the radical extremity of the human voice, towards which the ending of *L'Homme atlantique* points, is a feature central to much of Duras's later work. Indeed, following on from her experience with films like *La Femme du Gange* and *India Song,* Duras seems, in the latter half of the 1970s, to have taken a renewed interest in the aesthetic possibilities of the speaking voice. This in turn was instrumental in persuading her to resume writing for the theatre after an interruption of nearly ten years, with the result that, from 1977 onwards, Duras became increasingly involved in work for the stage, publishing *L'Eden Cinéma* in 1977 and *Le Navire Night* two years later (though this second piece was also a film script); *Agatha, Savannah Bay,* and *La Musica deuxième* followed in quick succession. These last two plays Duras also directed, to mixed reviews, for their Paris opening; in 1981 she provided Sami Frey and Delphine Seyrig with a new version of her adaptation of *La Bête dans la jungle* (based on the Henry James short story *The Beast in the Jungle*),[6] and in 1985 brought out a French version of Chekhov's *Seagull*. Earlier, in January 1984, at the Théâtre du Rond-Point, Duras organised a series of dramatic readings from her work, in the course of which a number of non-theatrical texts—including *L'Homme atlantique, L'Homme assis dans le couloir,* the three versions of *Aurélia Steiner,* and four other short pieces—were read on stage by a small group of actors.[7]

Surprisingly, the common thread that runs through all these different theatrical activities, whether on the level of the texts themselves or the mode and manner of their performance, is a concern in Duras's work that seems to be at the opposite extreme to what the theatre is usually held to offer: the act and theme of reading. Admittedly, the term is used by Duras in a rather idiosyncratic way, and the particular significance of reading in relation to the theatre is perhaps best revealed by the unusual, elongated title given to the film *Agatha et les lectures illimitées.* "Unlimited" readings, the audience is told, are "personal" readings (*AG,* 63); and in the text of the film (and play) this is explained by the acknowledgement that the names of the characters, Agatha and Ulrich, are borrowed from Robert Musil's novel, *The Man Without Qualities:* the unnamed brother and sister of Duras's text, the explanation runs, reading Musil or some other story while still children, seem immediately to have recognised themselves as the incestuous siblings in the text and thereby, so to speak, become a direct embodiment of the text they were reading.[8]

If incest in Duras is a merger of two into one, then the act of reading, as dramatised in *Agatha et les lectures illimitées,* constitutes a similar loss of boundaries and a process of fusion between reader and writer, with both mingling their bodies in the text they share as though in an ecstatic union exactly parallel to incest itself. The process is one that *Agatha et les lectures illimitées* endeavours not only to describe but also to enact. For Duras's film reminds the viewer from the outset that it, too, is based on a reading—an off-screen recitation of the play *Agatha* by Marguerite Duras and Yann Andréa—and to that extent is itself constituted as an act of apocalyptic fusion with its own text. As though to demonstrate the fact, the opening shot of Duras's film, presenting itself as an ecstatic re-embodiment of the author's own writing, is taken up with the movement of the camera scrolling down the first page of the printed Minuit text of *Agatha* (and the same gesture is repeated, with later pages, three times more in the film).

In the stage directions given in *Agatha,* the two protagonists (who, in the film, are never visible on screen) are described at one point as having to appear, stiffly, with closed eyes, as the "récitants imbéciles de leur passion" ("mindless narrators of their own passion," *AG,* 19). The phrase describes exactly what is at stake here; for what it affirms is that Duras's actors, in the course of the performance, are themselves transformed into depersonalised vehicles for the sublime intensity of the text. Their fate is to be dissolved, as they speak, into the act of reading that alone sustains their existence as performers. The act of reading, for Duras, is an act of powerful fusional identification, yet it stands at the opposite extreme to any naturalistic, psychological representation of sexual passion. What it affirms, instead, for Duras, with regard to both theatre and cinema, against all forms of realism, is an apocalyptic refusal of representation. The plays Duras writes may at times resemble love stories, but their aim is to disable any psychology of desire; exploding the bounds of inwardness, they therefore promise—and enact—the catastrophic ruin of psychological explanations. And it is in accordance with the ensuing overwhelming devastation that, in all her later plays, from *L'Eden Cinéma* to *Savannah Bay* or *La Musica deuxième,* Duras points to the need for stage sets that are open, empty spaces, lacking in intimacy or detail, allowing the intensity of the text being read to touch each last corner of the theatre with its incandescent power.

Reading, as Duras understands or practises it, is an embodiment of the written text that aims—impossibly—to dispense with both representation and performance, and, reaching beyond theatrical illusion, to arrive at a mode of textuality that is pure affirmation or event, shunning all ready-made, prior narrative space or temporality, reliant only on its own sublime virtuosity. Implicit in the endeavour is Duras's rejection of theatre in its conventional form; and this refusal of stage representation is itself a concern that lies at the centre of her two most controversial works of the 1980s, the *récit* entitled *La Maladie de la mort,* together with the longer narrative that reprises and reworks it, *Les Yeux bleus cheveux noirs.* Both texts explore the effects of a sexual contract by which a woman, explicitly said not to be a prostitute, agrees, in return for money, to spend a given number of nights with an unknown man who explains he has never had experience of desire for a woman; in both versions the story culminates in an ecstatic moment of sexual intercourse, the result of what the woman in *La Maladie de la mort* terms "une faille soudaine dans la logique de l'univers" ("a sudden fissure in the logic of the universe," *MM*, 52), while, in the later book, as the woman cries out, it is not only logic, but Duras's own prose as well that falters in its attempt to describe the intensity of the woman's orgasm (*YB*, 132; 101). Duras concludes in both cases with a familiar apocalyptic motto: "Cela est fait" ("It is done," *MM*, 53), or, alternatively: "Tout était fait. Autour d'eux la chambre détruite" ("It was all over. Around them, the room, destroyed," *YB*, 143; 110).

Common to both *La Maladie de la mort* and *Les Yeux bleus cheveux noirs*, in addition to their obvious similarities of character and plot, is the contradictory relationship each entertains with the theatre. Initially, neither text was written for the stage. But, at the end of *La Maladie de la mort*, Duras suggests in a note, as she had earlier with the published versions of *Détruire, dit-elle* and *India Song*, that this work, too, might be done on stage (*MM*, 59–61); Duras stipulates, however, that the text be performed as a reading by a male narrator (distinct from the—absent—male protagonist), while the woman in the story would speak her text from memory in the usual way. But despite the recommendation, the text as it stands is in the form less of a stage script than a peremptory address in the style of *L'Homme atlantique*, delivered by an anonymous first-person voice ("je" [*MM*, 15]) to the man (addressed as "Vous") decreed by the woman who agrees to sleep with him to be suffering from the malady of death mentioned in the title; the woman herself is referred to throughout in the third person (as "elle").

The published text of *La Maladie de la mort* makes little concession, then, to the possibility of a future stage performance of the work. Duras's note in this respect appears to have been no more than an afterthought or, at best, a statement of intent; and it is perhaps not surprising therefore that, in reality, though *La Maladie de la mort*, when first published, seemed already to have taken into account the eventuality of a stage version, no such adaptation in fact occurred. Duras explained why, when, in an article in *Libération* in November 1986, entitled "La Pute de la côte normande," she described her difficulties in devising a satisfactory stage adaptation of the text, which she eventually abandoned, and went on to insist that the text as published could not be represented, only read on stage (*PCN*, 7). Eighteen months later, during a television interview with Luce Perrot, she reiterated her refusal to commit herself to a stage adaptation of the text and illustrated her point by reading *La Maladie de la mort* aloud to the camera on her own.

If *La Maladie de la mort* is a text that promises itself to the theatre only ultimately to withdraw from the arrangement, *Les Yeux bleus cheveux noirs* questions the possibility of stage representation in more explicit textual terms. For though the book is in the form of a continuous narrative, almost

three times the length of *La Maladie de la mort,* the story it recounts is that of
a stage performance, interspersed with hypothetical stage directions, as
though to suggest that the published text could in fact be used as a script for
a real theatrical production. But that performance, it is implied, would only
ever occur in the sense that reading the book already, in advance, renders it
redundant, if not in fact null and void. To read *Les Yeux bleus cheveux noirs* is to
be a spectator at an event which is already both more and less than a theatrical occasion in the conventional sense: "La lecture du livre," writes Duras, "se
proposerait donc comme le théâtre de l'histoire" ("The reading of the book
will act as theatre for the story," *YB,* 38; 25).

Duras's qualifications of the possibility or impossibility of theatrical representation of *La Maladie de la mort* and *Les Yeux bleus cheveux noirs* may seem
anecdotal. But an important series of issues is at stake. The contradictory
relationship that exists between Duras's two texts and the question of their
theatrical adaptation re-enacts a paradox that goes to the heart of Duras's
writing. For if Duras, as she reports in "La Pute de la côte normande," eventually failed to honour the agreement to provide theatre director Luc Bondy
with an adaptation of *La Maladie de la mort,* it is because text and theatre for
Duras, despite their reciprocal fascination, resist one another according to a
relationship of mutual exteriority; and if no theatrical adaptation of *La Maladie de la mort* proves to be adequate to the written text, it is because Duras's
own writing denies the possibility of any preconceived or ready-made—and,
thus, theatrical—space of representation in which male and female might
appear together and thus allow a stage performance to take place. As far as
the lovers in Duras's text are concerned, given their asymmetrical object
choices, the situation is of course much the same; and though the contract
they conclude obligates them to one another, what it primarily serves to
demonstrate—more readily than any sense of prior community—is their radical incompatibility. The relationship between text and theatre in *La Maladie
de la mort,* then, provides an implicit gloss on the question of relations
between the sexes in Duras. The encounter between them, whether sexual or
textual, is arguably always already a missed encounter; the only mode of relationship that Duras's text allows one to envisage is in fact a non-relationship.

But while *La Maladie de la mort* and *Les Yeux bleus cheveux noirs* both fall
short of—or exceed—the possibility of theatrical representation, they survive
nonetheless as written texts that, though irreducible to theatrical representation, may at times be read on stage in a place which may be a theatre. To this
extent, both texts include the possibility of theatre while also outstripping it.
The theatre functions here for Duras as an internal limit, one which it is the
role of writing, like the unlimited readings referred to in *Agatha,* constantly
to subvert or overwhelm. Writing here functions as an apocalyptic refusal of
all generic closure or specification; so, while allowing the possibility of theatre, it also disallows it as an unwarranted limitation if not in fact a return to
some earlier state. And when Duras does eventually come to posit—in a fic-

tional, written text—a theatrical space in which the relation of male and female might occur, as she does in *Les Yeux bleus cheveux noirs* (*YB*, 151–2; 116–17), it follows that the theatre in question should turn out to be inspired by an indestructible concrete wall, set amidst the Normandy cliffs like a relic from the last war, surrounded by the violence of the sea raging below, as though to suggest that the inescapable impasse of relations between the sexes will always be overwhelmed by the unrelenting, oceanic fury of desire itself, but also that no final reconciliation will ever be on hand to resolve this antagonism between elemental force and human architecture.

Duras refuses to adhere to the conventions and limitations required by stage production by affirming the apocalyptic violence of her texts. To that extent, the relationship between writing in Duras and the theatre is a transgressive one. In *La Maladie de la mort* and *Les Yeux bleus cheveux noirs,* however, the writer goes one step further in transgressing the apparent object and purpose of her own narrative. For by articulating in fictional terms an account of the libidinal asymmetry of the sexes and the nonrelationship that exists between them, Duras's writing has already forged a relationship between the sexes, albeit one ultimately founded on the impossibility of unification or identity, and in so doing her own text already exceeds and contradicts the position it had initially aimed to establish. Thus, even while Duras explores a situation of radical incompatibility between the sexes, that separation is simultaneously already in the process of being questioned and effaced by the very fact of writing itself.

Writing therefore, by virtue of its existence, is an act that constantly transgresses its own boundaries and divisions. It is towards the end of *La Maladie de la mort* that this becomes most clearly evident. For in closing, as the series of meetings between the male protagonist and the woman come to an end with the woman's anticipated but nevertheless abrupt departure, *La Maladie de la mort* alludes to the possibility that the protagonist might somehow be able to fashion their time together into some coherent narrative. But the tale he tells, that very evening, in some bar, remains a dubious and uncertain one, which he subsequently abandons, or retells with a laugh, as though to indicate that it could not possibly have taken place, or simply that the whole saga was mere fabrication (*MM*, 54–5). Much the same comments, of course, might be seen to apply to Duras's own text, but by affirming them within her own writing, as a set of possibilities which the text itself incorporates, Duras's text outstrips or transgresses them too, and the result is a mode of textuality that is uncontrollably in excess of whatever it may itself be saying. To write in Duras is already to affirm the excess and extremity of desire, if only in the form of the desire to write. Embodied in *La Maladie de la mort* is a writing that enables theatre yet overwhelms it, just as it allows narrative but steps beyond it; and as it does so, by virtue of its own existence, it affirms the inescapable necessity of love, desire, and communion at the very moment that it may be suggesting their radical impossibility.

In this way, then, as Blanchot argues in his account of *La Maladie de la mort* in *La Communauté inavouable,* if Duras's text describes a sexual impasse, it also offers the prospect of a lovers' community.[9] Such a community would rely on no prior institution or legislative order, but merely on a singular, unrepeatable contract between two antagonistic, asymmetrical bodies. To this extent, the sexual contract between Duras's two protagonists in both *La Maladie de la mort* and *Les Yeux bleus cheveux noirs* is not a simple external circumstance, to be read primarily as a moral indictment of prostitution or, more broadly, of the inequality of relations between men and women in contemporary society, as some readers have perhaps too quickly assumed. Rather, it functions as a metaphor for the possibility that has somehow enabled these texts to be written even in the absence of any prior, ready-made code governing relations between the sexes. What it figures therefore is the necessary price paid and the debt exacted in order that a sexual relation might in fact take place; it signals difference as well as negotiation, separation as well as transaction, loss of self as well as mutual positioning; it binds together that which resists all binding, and fuses as one that which cannot ever be fused.

The sexual contract enacted in *La Maladie de la mort* and *Les Yeux bleus cheveux noirs* is not unique in Duras. It resembles all the other sexual contracts in Duras's work, of which there are many, as for instance between Suzanne and the philanderer Agosti in *Un Barrage contre le Pacifique,* between Anne-Marie Stretter and her admirers in *India Song,* between the youthful Duras and her Chinese lover in *L'Amant,* between Véra and Michel Cayre in *Véra Baxter,* or between the two lovers in *Le Navire Night.* "The crucial thing is money" (*NN,* 49), declares the narrative voice in this last work, referring to the extravagant presents given to the young man by his unseen lover; and there, as in *La Maladie de la mort,* it is clear that the sexual bargain is more nearly akin to an unaccountable gift than an act of exploitation, and that it serves to stimulate desire rather than to inhibit it. It supplies a provisional structure to love that ensures relationship while also limiting its terms. What the contract enables is the impossible—ecstatic—relation of terms that are themselves without relation.

In *La Maladie de la mort,* the sexual contract that makes the text possible seems inseparable from the title of the work, for it is by seeing the signs of that so-called malady on the man's body that the woman in the text initially agrees to the bargain her future partner proposes (*MM,* 23). But what is this "malady of death"? At first, what the phrase seems to dramatise most clearly is the sexual gulf between the two partners in the story. The man, the reader is told, has never touched a woman before (*MM,* 9–10, 34); and it is in response to this lack of desire that the woman whom he requires to sleep with him summarily pronounces him dead, declaring, disdainfully, twice over: "C'est curieux un mort" ("It's strange, being dead," *MM,* 35, 45). A page later, Duras confirms this association between death and sexual difference by writing of the man: "Vous fermez les yeux pour vous retrouver dans votre différence, dans votre mort" ("You close your eyes to return to your difference, your death," *MM*, 36). But when asked by the man to explain what she means by "la maladie de la mort," she replies that the malady is deadly in two important respects:

> In that whoever is suffering from it does not know that he is carrying it, death, that is. And also in that he would be dead with no previous life to die to, with no knowledge at all of dying to any life.

Though it evokes ignorance and sterility, death in Duras resists being enclosed in any simple binary paradigm. It is not the crude opposite of life; it is arguably more like an indeterminate state of existence that precedes life or death in the usual sense, and is inherent in both living and dying as the precondition and final destination of both. Moreover, though it names sexual difference, death in Duras's text does not belong simply on the side of the male body, for the man sees it, too, displayed on the woman (*MM*, 36), while in turn it is the woman who repeatedly uses the figure of death to describe the jealous intensity of her desire. Towards the end, just before she delivers her second verdict to the man, the woman asks him:

> Do you not know, have you never known the wish to be on the brink of killing a lover, keeping him for yourself, yourself alone, taking him, stealing him, in the face of all laws and systems of morality?

To be filled, as is this woman, with murderous desires like these, to be sensitive, as she is, to all the symptoms of death indelibly written on her partner's body, is not to be opposed to the malady of death, but to be profoundly and irrevocably contaminated by it. To this extent, the only malady that death evokes in Duras's text is none other than the malady of desire itself.

If death, in the case of the male protagonist, figures the lack of desire, it also serves as proof of the work—or worklessness—of desire in his female partner. The infernal absence of desire is little different here from its consuming presence; like death, it has an inexhaustible circularity, and though the man and the woman are not at first sexual objects for one another, they become bound together by the same desperate necessity, for which the only name available is desire itself. Duras confirms as much by the complex relations of similarity and difference that she elaborates throughout her text with regard to the pounding black sea visible from the flat (*MM*, 27) and the billowing white sheets on the bed (*MM*, 30) in which the pair pursue their failed erotic encounter. For though the couple cannot agree whether the sea is black or white (*MM*, 46), the ocean nonetheless, as for the woman and her lover in *L'Homme atlantique*, symbolises the possibility of love and fusion for which they both yearn. After all, bodily fluids are just as much a sign of desperate lamentation as a token of sexual excitement (*MM*, 7). And at the end, just before an apocalyptic dawn arrives to seal the final separation between them (*MM,* 53), what the pair discover together, as the culmination of the chaste, unconsummated union that has been theirs, is the impenetrable night (*MM,* 53) into which the man finally penetrates in spite of everything, and within which the woman welcomes him at last, in an impossible, but ecstatic act of intercourse.

In *La Maladie de la mort* the malady of death names both sexual difference and the inescapable circularity of desire. By that token, in Duras, it necessarily also names the act of writing, and it comes as no surprise to learn how, as Yann Andréa recounts in *M.D.,* writing *La Maladie de la mort* put its own author's survival severely in the balance. In this and other ways, the desire the text enacts might best be termed an apocalyptic desire, one which accentuates to the point of intolerability the bodily differences that exist between male and female, but only in order to arrive at a more radically catastrophic, purer affirmation of the sublime relationship of non-relationship on which Duras here confers the implicit name of love. Nowhere perhaps, in the whole of the author's work, is the revelation of the simultaneous impossibility and necessity of that relation rendered so powerfully and with such disturbing violence. Destroyed here is any complacent attachment to the stabilities or fixities of sexual identity; writing *La Maladie de la mort,* for Duras, becomes the only authentic, radically affirmative manner of living out revelation, community, love, death, and desire.

Notes

1.   The works by Duras I am referring to in this chapter are as follows: *Agatha* (Paris, Minuit, 1981); *L'Homme atlantique* (Paris, Minuit, 1982); *La Maladie de la mort* (Paris, Minuit, 1982); *Savannah Bay* (Paris, Minuit, [1982] 1983); *Les Yeux bleus cheveux noirs* (Paris, Minuit, 1986); and *La Pute de la côte normande* (Paris, Minuit, 1986). The film, *Agatha et les lectures illimitées,* based on the earlier stage play, was released in 1981, closely followed by the film version of *L'Homme atlantique.* In this chapter all translations from *La Maladie de la mort* are my own.

2.   *La Maladie de la mort,* together with *Les Yeux bleus cheveux noirs,* is one of the most fiercely debated of recent texts by Duras. See, for instance, Marcelle Marini, "La Mort d'une érotique," *Cahiers de la compagnie Renaud-Barrault,* 106, September 1983, 37–57; Maurice Blanchot, *La Communauté inavouable* (Paris, Minuit, 1983), pp. 51–93; Sharon Willis, "Staging Sexual Difference: Reading, Recitation, and Repetition in Duras's *Malady of Death,*" in Enoch Brater (ed.), *Feminine Focus: The New Women Playwrights* (New York, Oxford University Press, 1989), pp. 109–25; and George Moskos, "Odd Coupling: Duras Reflects (on) Balzac," *Contemporary Literature,* 32, 4, Winter 1991, 520–33.

3.   There are no doubt echoes here, for some readers, of Lacan's dictum, as glossed at length in *Le Séminaire, Livre XX: Encore* (Paris, Seuil, 1975), to the effect that sexual relations do not exist (as Lacan puts it: "il n'y a pas de rapport sexuel"). In Lacan's account of love there is, however, an almost Jansenist-like austerity and pessimism far removed from the apocalyptic tone adopted by Duras.

4.   Yann Andréa is a major participant in much of Duras's work during the early 1980s. In addition to his involvement in *Agatha et les lectures illimitées,* Andréa also appears on

the image track of *L'Homme atlantique* and reads, together with Duras, the off-screen dialogue making up the soundtrack for *Dialogue de Rome* (1982); he is a powerful, if unnamed presence in a number of later fictional texts, too, including notably *La Maladie de la mort, Les Yeux bleus cheveux noirs* (which Duras dedicates to him), and *Emily L.* Duras recounts how her relationship with Andréa came about in *Yann Andréa Steiner;* she seems to have begun introducing him in public as her accredited companion during her 1981 visit to Montreal (as the volume *Duras à Montréal* records). However, this was not the first time that Duras incorporated one of her current companions or former lovers into her work. Dionys Mascolo, Duras's partner of the 1940s and 1950s, has an acting role in *Jaune le soleil, Nathalie Granger* and *La Femme du Gange,* and reads one of the narrative voices in *India Song* and *Son nom de Venise dans Calcutta désert. L'Homme assis dans le couloir,* Duras revealed in 1980, also originated as a homage to a particular lover, according to a principle she first voiced in an interview with Jeanne Moreau in 1960: "Ce que je peux offrir à un homme," Duras told her, "le mieux que je puisse lui offrir c'est ce que j'ai écrit à partir de lui" ("The best thing I can give a man is what I have written on the basis of knowing him"). See "La Comédienne et la romancière," *Afrique-Action,* 17 October 1960.

5.   The importance of the maternal body as an image of ambivalence is a central and recurrent one throughout the whole of Duras's work, as she herself admits, for instance, in *L'Amant* (*A,* 34-5; 28–9). This has tempted some critics, like Julia Kristeva, in her *Soleil noir: dépression et mélancolie* (pp. 229–65), to ground the whole of their interpretation of Duras on the question of the difficulty of separating from the mother. However, Kristeva's case, persuasive though it may seem, is not aided by gaffes like her analysis of the opening pages of *Le Ravissement de Lol V. Stein,* in which she misconstrues the arrival of Anne-Marie Stretter as referring to Lol's mother!

6.   Duras first adapted the story for the stage in collaboration with James Lord in 1962, before rewriting it, on her own, for the 1981 revival. The text of the new version is given in Duras's *Théâtre II* (Paris, Gallimard, 1984), and she describes her revisions in "Le Château de Weatherend (*La Bête dans la jungle*)," *L'Arc,* 89, October 1983, 100–2. James's tantalisingly apocalyptic story already displays something of the same asymmetry in the relation between the sexes as *La Maladie de la mort;* interestingly, in *Epistemology of the Closet* (Berkeley, University of California Press, 1990), Eve Kosofsky Sedgwick takes the story in this respect to be paradigmatic of what she describes as homosexual panic in a number of early twentieth-century texts. In reworking in *La Maladie de la mort* the situation explored in James's story, Duras would seem to be committing herself to a rearticulation of the relationship between homosexuality and heterosexuality which seriously challenges the separation between them and thus the whole notion of sexual identity founded on object choice.

7.   For a helpful description of Duras's involvement in the theatre, see Arnaud Rykner, *Théâtres du nouveau roman: Sarraute, Pinget, Duras* (Paris, Corti, 1988).

8.   On Duras's reading of Musil, see *E,* 35–6, and "Une des plus grandes lectures que j'ai jamais faites," *La Quinzaine littéraire,* January, 1982, 16–31. The incestuous relationship between Ulrich and his sister Agatha constitutes one of the main centres of interest in the unfinished third section of Musil's novel. At one point, for instance, the pair are on holiday together, staying in a hotel by the sea, where they rediscover the pleasures of naturism, as though they were children again; they eventually decide, however, to stay in their hotel bedroom. "Alors," Duras will have read in Philippe Jaccottet's standard French translation, "pour les corps, le miracle se produisit. Soudain Ulrich fut en Agathe ou Agathe en lui" ("Then, for their bodies, the miracle happened. Suddenly Ulrich was inside Agatha and Agatha inside him"). See Robert Musil, *L'Homme sans qualités,* translated by Philippe Jaccottet, 2 vols. (Paris, Seuil/Points, 1956), II, 834.

9.   *La Communauté inavouable,* pp. 52–4. Duras's own reaction to Blanchot's reading of *La Maladie de la mort* was a surprisingly hostile and defensive one, and also extended to Peter Handke's German-language film version of the text. See Marguerite Duras, "Dans les jardins d'Israël il ne faisait jamais nuit," *Les Cahiers du cinéma,* July–August 1985, 374.

The Poetry of Marguerite Duras

MICHAEL BISHOP

I have written incomprehensible books and they have been read.[1]

Music also is the divine. You have to look a great deal to find it in writing, I have found it.[2]

If Victor Hugo hesitated to push his generic perception of the poetic beyond versified form, and if Verlaine, too, winced somewhat at the idea of the latter dissolving into free and assonanced verse, their broader degenericized aesthetics, like the renewed conceptions and practices of contemporaries Baudelaire, Mallarmé, Rimbaud, and Lautréamont, allowed for the embrace of factors vastly in excess of the banally generic or formal. Poetry thus became free—the surrealists, the cubists, the New Novelists, and New Wave cinematographers readily understood this in their different ways—not just to radically diversify its forms, as Rimbaud had demanded of the yet poetically "divine" Baudelaire, but also to become that "act and place," as Bonnefoy writes, of a (self-)expression, of a mode of thought and being utterly liberated precisely from preexistent constraints of referential order, semantic structure, representational modality. To speak of the poetry of Marguerite Duras, in effect, becomes possible and, I should argue, essential, in three ways, which I shall further compact down to two: first—and this will be the main thrust of my endeavor here—Duras's complex perception of writing and, specifically, her own written production coincides in many respects with both structural and conceptual factors generally admitted as crucially pertinent to an understanding of modern and contemporary French poets, from Baudelaire, Rimbaud, and Mallarmé to Char and Du Bouchet, Dupin and Hyvrard. Questions of incomprehensibility and unknowing, paradox and simplicity/complexity, will thus be initially assessed, followed by matters of atemporality, structure and rhythm, gathering and disparateness, indeterminacy, and irreducibility. For each of what will emerge as

This essay was written especially for this volume and is published here for the first time by permission of the author.

these modes of the poetic, various subfactors central to Duras's aesthetics will also come into focus. The second and shorter part of this study takes what is indubitably a manifest and visual rendering of the poetic, *Césarée* (*Caesarea*), and seeks to offer it a reading it has not as yet received.

NINE DURASSIAN MODES OF THE POETIC

1.   The Incomprehensible

"Painting, written texts," Duras tells us in *La Vie matérielle* (*Material Life*), "are not produced in utter clarity. And always words fail to express things, always" (*VM,* 35). The obscurity and opaqueness that result from this felt unspeakableness of the real should not be deemed, however, to constitute a negative element in the poetics of the incomprehensible she holds centrally pertinent to her work. As she indicates in *Écrire* (*Writing*), "I have written incomprehensible books and they *have* been *read*" (*E,* 44, my emphasis). Readability and comprehensibility are thus not quite synonymous. "*L'Amant* is difficult," Duras affirms, "*La Maladie de la mort* is difficult, very difficult. *L'Homme atlantique* is very difficult, but is so beautiful that it isn't difficult. Even if one doesn't understand. Besides one can't understand such books. It's not the word. It's all a matter of private relationship between book and reader" (*VM,* 119–20). Incomprehensibility clearly does not prevent, nor even in a sense problematize, reading—the "difficult" is simultaneously "easy," Duras makes clear in the same commentary (*VM,* 119), and her allusion to the beauty of the incomprehensible shows that the former is not merely a compensation for the latter but is perhaps implicitly intrinsic to it: what is not at stake in this poetic mode is some reductive intellectualization conceivably available. As with Yann Andréa, the "unreadable, [the] unpredictable" also remain the locus for Duras of the "unlimited."[3] The loved, the beautiful are not flatly reducible, this being precisely their infinitely expandable, creative (*poiein:* to make, create) merit. To "speak without understanding," as Sabana says in *Abahn Sabana David,*[4] comes about partly because of the strangeness of life itself, partly because of a felt noncoincidence of language's symbolism with being. But in neither case does incomprehensibility block meaning. "I write . . . things that I do not understand," Duras insists in *Yann Andréa Steiner,* while insisting equally that "I leave them in my books and reread them and then they take on meaning."[5] Language thus is not radically distinguishable from nonlanguage in Duras's view: all, ultimately, is writing and all writing has meaning, manifest, revealed, intuitable, or latent. The self-inscribed meaning of the fly dying in her house at Neauphle-le-Château, although "incomprehensible" at the time of witness, remains felt, lived, immediate though blinding, and "one day, perhaps, in the centuries to come, we might read this writing, it would be deciphered too, and translated. And the vastness of a [previously] unreadable poem would unfold in the sky" (*E*, 55). The *poietic* element of the incomprehensible thus lies deep within the mystery of phenomena Duras is in no hurry to decode according to intellectually, rationally provisional norms of penetration. This explains exactly why, in *L'Homme atlantique*, she can write, so tellingly, so delightfully paradoxical in manner, that "it is to [the reader's] lack of comprehension that I always address myself."[6] Théodora Kats can even push this logic to a desire not to "see, know, understand" (*YAS*, 48), and we can thus come close to appreciating this desire.

2.   *Not Knowing*

Growing out of the above, but also constantly feeding its logic and reality, is a widespread poetics of unknowing or not knowing endlessly woven into the imaginary structures of Duras's œuvre and conceptually central to both her aesthetics and what might be thought of as the ethics of her creation. Endless characters of novels, theater, and scenarios thus confess their seeming stalematedness: *I don't know, I no longer know, I forget, perhaps, I'm not sure,* and so on; and, from beginning to end of her long career, Duras tended to refuse all simplistic, normative conceptions of what the act of writing is and what, therefore, its logic might be. "I've spoken a great deal about writing", she confesses in *La Vie matérielle*, "I don't know what it is" (*VM*, 37). And in *Écrire*, we read, "If one knew something about what one is about to write, before writing, one would never write. It wouldn't be worth it" (*E*, 65). The lucidness Duras thus demands of the writer (cf. *E*, 64) is thus centered on the need to appreciate just to what degree creation (: the *poietic*, I stress) "is the unknown" (*E*, 64), is the experience, the traversal of an unknown. This is true, for example, of Lol V. Stein in the book of that name: "Nobody can know her," Duras perhaps astonishingly, but so perceptively, asserts, "neither you nor I" (*E*, 23). And if meaning is intuitable in a global sense, so that we can know meaning is rife, abundant and livable without being able to sift it through into its component specific *significations,* we can appreciate how the film and acting crew of *Le Vice-consul* could weep freely "without knowledge of the meaning" of their tears (*E*, 25–26). Unknowing in such circumstances can authorize a closeness, an intimacy despite incomprehension, despite doubt as to rationalizable meaning—indeed, perhaps because of them. Doubt, not surprisingly, can be equated by Duras with writing and reading: "Doubt is writing. So it is the writer, too. And with the writer everyone writes" (*E*, 26)—how could it be otherwise, for writing, as we have just seen, plunges writer and reader into the "unknown," into a living of our unknowing *both* as intellectual aporia *and* as emotional-cum-aesthetic access to that strange and wondrous meaningfulness of the opaque, the inexplicable. Duras puts it beautifully in *La Vie matérielle:*

"That not knowing how to say things, which remains largely unelucidated, is perhaps what would come closest to the meaning of life in every sense of the term" (*VM*, 130). It is thus hardly unacceptable to the reader if, in concluding *Écrire*, Duras resorts to metaphor—writing is wind, like life itself, moreover: an act of passing, fleeting presence, enigmatic yet livable, shareable ontic mystery. An unknowing traversal of the unknown, yet occasioning, as in *Les Yeux bleus cheveux noirs,* that sensation so often of "seeing for the first time."[7]

3.   *Paradox, Betweenness*

Little wonder, then, that Duras's entire œuvre is lit with the darkly illuminating light of paradox. *L'Été 80* thus can speak of the tensions, the imbrications of passion and indifference; *L'Amant* slides into one the separate experiences of pain and laughter;[8] the "basic pessimism" that Duras attributes to her psyche (cf. *VM*, 54) needs to be read in the light of that soft, beauteous smile so constantly haunting her imagination—in, for example, *L'Eden cinéma* or *La Pluie d'été;* gentleness and provocation intermingle inextricably in *L'Homme atlantique;* endless loss seems to be integrally bound up with Duras's very modes of recognition and recuperation; fear and the pall of "shame [that] covers my entire life" (*VM*, 26) never blunt love, even though the latter is filtered through the former and, in a certain sense (only), stymieing its full expression; an abiding solitariness, alienation even, cannot disallow Duras's equally persistent if shaky sense of the divine (cf. *YAS*, 95); mourning, as *Yann Andréa Steiner* amply shows, always is silhouetted against "the splendor of the sea," a certain "grace" of being, within and without (*YAS*, 51).

Paradoxes such as these, then, proliferate within Duras's books, revealing a will, better an instinct, that orients her not at all toward gratuitous oppositions but rather toward a multiplicity, a teeming simultaneity of consciousness that, without articulating itself as such, hints at that kind of synthesis hypothesized by Breton in his 1924 manifesto: "Everything leads us to believe that a certain point in the mind exists from which life and death, the real and the imaginary, past and future, the sayable and the unsayable . . . cease to be perceived in contradiction." Moreover, the same paradoxicality (*paradoxos:* that which is counter to common opinion, strange, extraordinary) colors Duras's pronouncements on the logic of writing and the written. In part, we have seen this already, but it is useful to note rapidly a number of characteristic designations. The "openness" of the book thus leads to a "darkness," Duras maintains in *Écrire* (35)—no doubt the darkness of the paradoxical light of the incomprehensible penetrated by our unknowing. Writing is at once "impossible" and actual (cf. *E*, 64), practicable though deeply rooted in an aesthetics-cum-ethics of impotence and ignorance, Duras feels. The descriptions and evocations that may emerge, even in a quasi-journalistic set of texts such as we find in *L'Été 80*, provide at best a relativity of meaning well understood by poets, and even certain novelists, of the modern period. The *"search"* that is writing, but also life itself, may thus offer what we term a "story," but, as *Les Yeux bleus cheveux noirs* suggests (cf. *YB,* 30)—and we are not much removed from Mallarmé's ontological equations here—such narration or fiction remains pretty well synonymous with "nothingness" (or perhaps that *wind* that blows through writing).

While, then, the swarming paradoxes that people both Duras's imaginative universe and her extensive meditations on life and the creative impulse may be said to promote enigma and lectoral problem, complicating via contradiction and inverse correlation our reading of world and word—while this, then, is true, it is equally true that Duras's paradoxes foster obscure harmonies and challenging reconciliations that, as Derrida has argued, our Western philosophy has not tended to prefer to generate. The consciousness of living a "betweenness" wherein difference yet is downplayed and suffused with an *all*-embracing (if vulnerable, almost unlivable) love has long been emblematized for me by Duras's beautiful declaration in *L'Homme atlantique:* "I am in a love between living and dying" (20). To be, to write, *between,* and with this possible/impossible love, is not to resolve enigma, opposition, paradox. Rather it is, lucidly, to embrace the blind gropingness of one's articulations and, synthetically, *poieti-cally,* rather than analytically, to embrace the moving experience of being.

4.   Simplicity, Complexity, Equivalence

There is much, of course, in all of Duras's work that we justifiably feel is bathed with a simplicity of great beauty and bare though thickly virtual emotion. In *La Maladie de la mort (The Malady of Death)* we read: "You look again. The face is abandoned to sleep, it is stilled, it sleeps like her hands . . . You go back out onto the terrace before the black sea. There is within you a sobbing you cannot explain . . . You return to the bedroom. She is sleeping. You don't understand . . . Then it is almost dawn. Then there is in the room a dark brightness of uncertain color . . . She is sleeping. You switch off the lights. It is almost bright."[9] Such narration seems so close to what we think of as the real that it becomes, as it were, tautological, near-absolute in its descriptive hugging of the contours of "truth" and "fact," just as the first sentence of the following passage from *Les Yeux bleus cheveux noirs* seems to have reached a pinnacle of transparent self-evidence: "She is a woman. She is sleeping. She appears to be doing so. One doesn't know. Appears to have gone completely off to sleep, with her eyes, her hands, her mind" (*YB,* 23–24).

The simplicity of such absolute, definitive narration abounds in Duras and examples like these could be multiplied a thousandfold. And indeed, conceptually too there is a certain obsessiveness, focus, single-mindedness about Duras's creations and explorations that would have us read her as a writer of excessive modesty, economy, and underelaboration. Does she not go as far as to affirm in *La Vie matérielle* that "all the women of my books, whatever their age, derive from Lol V. Stein" (32)? And yet, of course, we have just seen to what extent Duras is given to paradox, to what extent nothing is, or can be, simple, in a world of unknowing and the incomprehensible. Com-pli-cation (the multiplying of the folds or *plis* of being and meaning) thus—naturally: for this is not a contrived manoeuvre—goes hand in hand with simplification. The words "She is sleeping" or even "You go back out onto the terrace" always exceed, as a poet such as Bonnefoy has sought to show, in mystery and strangeness, the very signs they deploy. If *Aurélia Steiner* is three separate but identically titled and textually overlapping texts—scenarios, poems, films—it is because the "simple," at once intrinsically and as it were extrinsically, never ceases to overflow its only apparent bounds into that unspeakably complex "limitlessness" that was, for example, Yann Andréa's (*PCN*, 19), but is, too, the property of all that is. Sleeping can, finally, only ever be the "appearance" of sleep, as we saw earlier (*YB*, 23–24). Love—in, say, *Emily L.*—is always only lived *as, like:* here "as despair":[10] "simplicity" slips into relativeness, relatedness, loses its absoluteness, endlessly opens up its folds, its infinitely creatable (: *poiein*) folds. The dying mother's silence at the close of *L'Éden cinéma* bursts the bubble of its potentially banal absoluteness, as Duras stunningly, exquisitely, opens up its meaning cosmically: "It must not have been to us, her children, that our mother presumably would have liked yet to speak but beyond us, to others, to others and yet others still, who knows, to whole races, to the world."[11] And what Duras terms the "concomitancy" of phenomena and the "resembling, transporting difference" (*leur différence ressemblante, transportante*)[12] at the heart of such concomitancy—such factors manifestly complexify the "simple" and can even urge upon us a poetics of what she thinks of as the astonishing but felt *equivalence* of distinct phenomena, ideas, emotions, words. Take, for instance, this striking passage in *L'Amant,* where the *poietic,* what we create and use to create, is deemed malleable to an improbable degree:

> Collaborators, the Fernandez. And I myself, two years after the war, member of the French Communist Party. The equivalence is absolute, definitive. It's the same thing, the same pity, the same call for help, the same debility of judgement, the same superstition let's say, which consists in believing in the political solution to a personal problem. (*AT,* 85)

This element of Duras's *poiein* thus tends to deconstruct radically categories of all kinds, caught as she lucidly recognizes herself to be in the liminal text of *La Vie matérielle* in the relativity and becoming of her own thought and articulation: "The book at most represents merely what I think sometimes, some days, about some things" (*VM*, 7). And, in this de-absolutizing swirl, another type of equivalence may also emerge, that of the seemingly intrinsic pertinence or *poietic* (: i.e., to do with our creation, our doing) merit of our "subject-matter." "From anything whatsoever," Duras decrees in the same text, "a dog run over, set in motion human imaginative power, our creative reading of the universe, that strange yet common genius, and do it from a dog that has been run over" (*VM*, 113). The negligible, the insignificant, the absurd, raised back up, resurrected, to the level of grace, divineness (cf. *AT*, 117), high meaning, in the midst of a "metonymic" or "synecdochic" seeing allowing for a transmutation of part into whole, derisory fragment of being into infinitely expanding locus of ontological urgency and felt pertinence. An equivalence, moreover, remaining as ever, and as *Les Yeux bleus cheveux noirs* affirms (p 54), at the intersection of knowing and unknowing.

5.   *Atemporality, Finitude*

Nobody will deny that the poetic, in Duras, depends enormously on lived experience, emotions, specific places and moments, relationships, a sense of *présence* and finitude to which poets such as Char, Frénaud, Bonnefoy, or Du Bouchet would readily subscribe. The fortuitous and the aleatory, the ephemeral and the mortal, thus, not surprisingly, find expression via a privileging of the present tense or, to a lesser degree, the perfect and the imperfect, both implicitly or explicitly related to our ever-nascent, ever-mortal finitude, now. On the other hand, what may appear to be as flagrantly there and available as it is fugacious and provisional is endlessly undercut, not just by those factors of the *poietic* with which we have dealt to date but also by a consequent insistence in Duras on aspatial and achronological factors, on amoral and a-epistemological factors, on other elements that would push the "events" related to that brink of the atemporal, the mythical, where, in effect, all fiction, all imagination may be more truly said to "happen." A few examples will suffice to demonstrate these subtle shifts and fusions. *Abahn Sabana David,* sunk deep though it may be into the history of the Second World War, nevertheless rides buoyantly over temporality; where, when, how, remain open-ended issues and, as such, raise the relevance of the book above what might otherwise have drowned its universality. *La Pluie d'été,* too, like the film from which the book emerges, *Les Enfants,* although visibly and avowedly crafted from teeming finite detail,[13] slips easily out of its temporal and spatial frames, humorously shedding the skin of Ernesto's age and entering a realm of pertinence suspended between Ecclesiastes and the "time of the Kings of Israel" (*PE,* 149) and a future where only "the inexplicable . . . music . . . for example" (*PE,* 117) may counter a loss of hope and an unthinkable divineness. *Césarée (Caesarea),* too, but without the compensatory lightness of *La Pluie d'été,* bursts the bubble of time, transmuting past and present into one vast and moving experiential gestalt. If these instances could be endlessly duplicated throughout Duras's œuvre, we should not forget that she is well aware of the limits that need to be respected in the atemporal universalizing of the finite. "When nothing happens any more," she writes in *La Pute de la côte normande,* "history/story is truly beyond the reach of writing and reading" (18). Atemporality, in short, requires a grounding, in lived event, in narrated happening: without such palpable rooting, its mythical, emblematic power wilts, the infinity of the finite cannot be authenticated and tumbles into pure abstraction, a conceptuality emptied of its life.

6. *Structure, Rhythm, Unfinishedness*

Duras's entire creative production is an immense reservoir of repetitions, reprises, reworkings, reimaginings. Thus can one work, say *L'Éden cinéma,* reframe, modify, reemphasise another, *Un barrage contre le Pacifique;* thus can film and *récit* mutantly embed themselves one into the other; thus can one single work structure itself in parallel fashion around a series of thematic nodes in constant mirrorlike yet contradistinctive interplay, as in *La Maladie de la mort* or *Hiroshima mon amour, Abahn Sabana David* or *Émily L;* thus can individual Durassian sentences, when viewed either rhythmically or strictly from a semanticolexical point of view, manifest significant patterns or repetition, with or without variance or development. Such structural or rhythmic textual modes of course remain crucial to all creation or *poiesis,* whether that of Mallarmé's *Un coup de dés,* Perse's *Anabase,* or Michaux's *Paix dans les brisements.* And Proust, Sarraute, Robbe-Grillet, Beckett, and Simon have shown us the differing manners that give rhythm, and with rhythm, ebbing and flowing palimpsestlike meaning, to our modern prose. Punctuation is a critical and dramatizing element in such structuring of meaning, as in this passage from *Écrire* (53):

> The fly was dead.
> The queen-fly. Black and blue.
> That one, the one I had seen, was dead.

Silence emerges as a major structuring tactic, whether via the simple ellipsis or rather ellipses of the above or the larger lacunae that space out scenes, decontextualizing them, yet sealing them too, invisibly in that white unspokenness modern poetry is so familiar with. Discontinuities and accumulations thus fuse their logics; abruptness and circularity meet in the same rhythmic gesture; erasure and intensification flow easily within the same sentence or paragraph. Two final points, however, to conclude an analysis that could extend fruitfully to full book length: first, the various structurings and many resultant rhythmic units in Duras do not engender books that may be deemed neatly finished and climactically achieved. Just as Francis Ponge moved from a poetics of aesthetic "infallibility" and closure to one of open, osmotic *parole,* so Duras shifts from works such as *La Vie tranquille* to, say, *Les Yeux bleus cheveux noirs*, *La Pluie d'été*, or *Yann Andréa Steiner*, marked by rhythmic fluidity of *forme* and *fond*, a nonclosure that provokes expectancy and free meditation. Second, lest we imagine for a moment that repetition and reworking are banal, Duras, we should remember, never loses sight of what, in *L'Homme atlantique*, she terms an "inalienable royalty," an "irreducible difference" (*HA*, 12) that in effect mark all ontic experience and creative molding thereof. What we may think of as structure—we shall return to the point in 8. below—is far from synonymous with constraint, systematization, congealment of vision.

7.   *Embrace, Music*

It is, I believe, in order to understand the *poietic* power of Duras, important to add to our interwoven consideration of factors of paradox, "betweenness," equivalence and rhythmic structuring governing her aesthetics and global consciousness, a sense of two other notions that recurrently orient and nuance the latter. The first of these involves a gathering into a unified and unifying notional space of those kinds of highly disparate elements that, in *La Pluie d'été*, Jeanne believes her brother Ernesto tends to bring together: "Ernesto had had to gather," she thought, "the martyrdom of the [burnt] book and that of the tree's solitariness into one and the same destiny" (*PE*, 15). Duras here is not only interested in the oddity of this paradoxical restructuring into quasi-equivalence but, as often elsewhere, appreciates that this gathering is synonymous with ontic embrace: it brings together the ragged, bereft things of being in a gesture of compassion and, amazingly—for a writer so alert to pain, suffering, madness, absurdity, and her characters don't desert her here—what she terms, in the same book, and despite the sobbing of Jeanne, "the adoration of life" (*PE*, 92). Such loving embrace of all that is certainly creates a structure in which, as with the relations between Jeanne's mother and father (cf. *PE*, 76), what is at stake is the gentle, transcendent seizure of all immanence, of all that composes the huge psychic gestalt perceived. That such an embrace is coextensive with the *poietic* action of the written text hardly needs to be stressed at this point. Writing, creation, *poiein*, *is* the embrace of the disparate, of all disparates, for Duras. Like all embrace, however, it gathers, holds in joinedness, in a mode of unity that for Duras also evokes the averbal, nonanecdotal, nonjudgmental mode of music. It is no surprise to find, still in *La Pluie d'été*, that the "greatest happiness" of Ernesto's Vitry family, the moment truly suffused with laughter and softness, is sparked by the mother's singing of the Russian lullaby, *La Neva*, and their collective immersion in song and music (cf. *PE*, 70). Nor is it surprising that, in the dour and disenchanted future world Ernesto peers into as he speaks with the journalist, the enigmatic residual virtue of music is conjured up in a strangely beautiful exchange of glances.

8.   *Freedom, Innocence, Indeterminacy*

Poiein: to create, to make, to be free to do ... There is a fine passage at the beginning of *L'Éden cinéma* where Duras describes the mother, "object of the narrative": "The others touch her, stroke her arms, kiss her arms. She lets them: what she *represents* in the play exceeds what she *is* and she *is* not responsible for this" (*EC,* 12). If, in effect, Duras could easily have chosen to insist upon the excess of being over its representation, here she delightfully inverts the relationship and shows, *too,* how representation—if one *wants it so,* as Bonnefoy might say—always remains equally in excess of being. Free, that is; infinite, open, as endlessly innocent of limitations we might carelessly impose upon representation as being itself. The closing scene of *L'Éden cinéma* I have already evoked, in which the mother's mute speech is similarly sensed to transcend all manifest destination, quickly freed from its tight mortal spheres of address (cf. *EC,* 150). And throughout the book/scenario, the mother constantly recuperates her innocent, mythical identity in the midst of quotidian banality. Such freeing of the self or the other finds parallel expression in the scene of arhythmic dancing: "Violent music. / Their cadence is irregular. / They dance, drift apart, come up close again, with a freedom ever renewed. / The mother and the corporal are in unison. They spin about, disappear from sight, come back into view. / Everybody's deep childlikeness. The clearest thing is the joy of it all" (*EC,* 38). Music, freedom of movement, joinedness and difference, ever-becoming pattern of being, joy, childlike innocence, unspeakable meaning ... Duras recently, in *Écrire,* made a point of stressing her refusal of fixity and orchestration. "Never any programming," she argues, "there has never been any in my life. Never. Neither in my life nor in my books, not once" (*E,* 40). The matter is truly significant to her, for she continues to insist that what she "reproach[es] books for, in general, is that they are not free" (*E,* 41). Too "organized, regimented, conformist" (*ibid.*), most books avoid the disorder, the "indecipherable innocence" (*E,* 37) her own work seeks to favor, sacrificing the "wild," primal surges (cf. *E,* 28, 38), the cries and screams of (dis)articulation Duras finds so revealing. To create, to give oneself to the *poietic* is not to immerse oneself in one of Barthes's semiotic systems—Barthes may have been a good friend of Duras, but his work could not enthuse her, brilliant as it may be (cf. *YAS,* 21). But, as she writes in the opening paragraph of *Écrire,* "[M]ais écrire des livres encore inconnus de moi et jamais encore décidés par moi et jamais décidés par personne" (15–16). Writing, the *poietic,* as an act and a place of indeterminacy, undecidableness, giving us books strangely feasible yet ever innocent, free, unstabilizable.

9.   *The Unthinkable, Hero(in)ism*

The creative, poetic impulse in Duras, then, it is not unreasonable to agree with her, is akin to that energy triggering the "volcanic" overflow that pushes consciousness toward obsession, vision, and even a form of "madness" yet lucid and compassionate (cf. *E, 29*). And, although we have spoken of notional synthesis and mythical unifying, there is something always rather unaccountable in Duras that brings us full circle to what I initially termed the incomprehensible and here call the unthinkable. For the freedom, the innocence and the indeterminacy that persist in characterizing Duras's aesthetics and her human, telluric, and cosmic vision tend ever to *reopen* the *question* of being and writing her work originally poses. To write even one whit in the light of a poetics of madness—but Duras's belonging is strongly felt—is to unravel constantly the very syntheses and reconciliations, however beauteous, as they are felt and formed. Thinking in Duras is thus always an *un*thinking, *poiein*'s doing always an *un*doing, splendidly honest as they may be. But this is not because of human and authorial impotence alone, for (un)thinking the (un)thinkable is always related, beyond personal relativity, to that ever-upwelling invisibleness or unimaginableness that, precisely, *positively* connotes and motivates being, and Duras's writing of being. If, as she writes in *Les Yeux bleus cheveux noirs,* "no external definition is forthcoming to say what they are in the process of living through" (63), the tackling of this unthinkableness remains what, consciously, preoccupies Duras throughout her vast œuvre. It is an act, a hero(in)ic act, that seems to correspond to that equally heroic imperative that even the totalitarian Gringo of *Abahn Sabana David* found impossible to gainsay:

He said: Be joyful towards and against everything. (30)

A heroism shared, Duras tells us in *La Pluie d'été,* by all human beings (*PE,* 147); a heroism heroically sung out of poetic instinct, blind but telling creative impulse, embracing the weak and the suffering, the gentle and the violent, the terrified and the smiling.

CÉSARÉE

Césarée (Caesarea) is, of course, not the only Duras text that may be deemed generically, formally, a poem. *Les Mains négatives (Negative Hands),* the first *Aurélia Steiner* text, and others reveal similar modal inclinations that lend themselves additionally to cinematographic portrayal. My intention here, moreover, is not to demonstrate the intrinsic poetic qualities of *Césarée* but, quite simply, to offer it a reading it has not as yet, to my knowledge, been accorded. The films titled *Césarée* and *Les Mains négatives* "were written from takes not used in *Le Navire Night,*" Duras tells us, "then made with these takes."[14] A strange creative beginning, but one, as we have seen, very much in keeping with Duras's fused *poietic* model of rhythmic reprise and radical difference. The fact, moreover, that *Césarée* the film, in choosing to give us Parisian scenes of the Tuileries,

Maillol female statues and one statufied queen being restored on the near-deserted Concorde square, both departs from and elliptically evokes the main body of *Césarée* the text, may be read equally as in conformity with Duras's typically modern aesthetics of metaphoric and referential distance and pertinence or *justesse,* as Pierre Reverdy called it. The title of the poem-film, although seemingly specific—if one ties to it later loose allusions to "the Queen of the Jews," her incomprehensible repudiation and the destruction of (the temple in) Jerusalem—nevertheless remains open both referentially (: there were many towns named Caesarea throughout the Middle Eastern region some 2,000 or so years ago) and, more importantly, semantically, symbolically (: from the outset the word is litanized, musicalized, emblematized, losing its absolute temporal, historical attachment in a blurring of time, an eternalization and pluralization of the meaning of what Caesarea once witnessed and still, for Duras, lays bare, as a trace, before our contemporary gaze and meditation). The poem is written in 26 textual blocks that we may think of either as unrhymed free verse or as visually, poetically sculpted prose. These blocks, ranging in length from 1 to 10 lines, are full of syntactic compactions, repetitions, variably functioning punctuation, highly divergent line lengths, shifting tenses, insistent yet gentle rhythms, great mixtures of descriptive and contemplative modes, historical and psychological perspectives. My remaining analysis will be concise and will center upon systematic assessment of each block or stanza.

1: "*Césarée* . . .": Simplicity, sereneness, and concentration dominate. The focusing and repetition take us both into that Durassian will for immanence, her plunge into experience now in touch yet with its implicit depth, and into a realm beyond specificity, accessed via incantation and the dreaming, musing state the latter promotes.

2: "*Il n'en reste que la mémoire de l'histoire* . . .": A poetics at once of the minimal, the residual trace and of the maximal, "the totality," is characteristically elaborated. One word represents a vastness of event, experience, meaning. Just as the deserted, ruined place speaks, spectrally, a fullness.

3: "*Le sol* . . .": Duras affirms here her unambiguous rooting in the things of the earth, the plain yet strange presence of things—white marble dust and sand mingling, blatantly yet mysteriously there, finite yet infinite in their so easily bypassed implication and movingness.

4: "*Douleur* . . .": The obsession, the extreme consciousness of pain we know to be an integral part of Duras's universe: the pain of motherhood, parenthood, childhood, human fragility and death, war, the terrible difficulties of love, and so on. Here, it is the pain of "separation," of manifest love once more capsized, foundering upon the rocks of all that presses in upon it. Understatement, implicitness, and simple expressive forcefulness typically reign.

5: "*Césarée* . . .": Haunting, litanical, barely modified (*ainsi* becomes *encore;* one *Césarée* drops) repetition allows the name of the place to ring out, quietly yet sonorously representative of all it historically and symbolically says and can never say.

6: *"L'endroit est plat . . ."*: Duras returns to minimal, essential descriptive detail: the flatness of the ancient—and still alive, haunted—terrain; the sea, ever-present in Duras's work, that pounds and reduces, and that opens upon other vistas, lands, origins, possible futures; the ruins of Caesarea, blue—a color of so much fascination in Duras: eyes, sea, sky, at times, dying fly, the "negative hands"—cast down before the sea, emblems at once of creation and destruction, vitality and decline.

7: *"Tout détruit . . ."*: Duras solemnly acknowledges this decline, the violence of being as she sees it, yet never advances toward the rhetorical, the moralizing. All is suspended in six isolated words of bare reflection.

8: *"Césarée . . ."*: The litany resumes as place and person—Caesarea and "Queen of the Jews"—fuse their femininity and their pertinence. Duras proceeds, by ellipsis, striking minimalism, and accumulation, to develop, in parallel with the story of destruction of place, the story of Berenice's seizure and exiling "by him": neither Berenice—heroine of Racine, beloved of Duras for the "divineness" of his writing (cf. *VM*, 82)—nor Titus is named, but their story of passion and sunderment flashes across the space that now lies deserted in the face of infinity. Let it be said, too, that "his" passion, though seemingly returned, is steeped from the outset in the violence of capture, possession, domination of "her."

9: *"Lui . . ."*: If Duras names, she is also the poet/writer of unnaming, of the unsaid, the unsayable or that which transcends, while being rooted in, the specifities evoked. Titus is not just unnamed, he becomes man, all men: *lui,* him, the abandoning, exiling one. He remains "he who had destroyed the temple of Jerusalem," and in so doing, he who scattered the Jews into a definitive diaspora. But he becomes, too, that *he* who "criminally" sacrifices the other, human difference, spiritual or religious alterity, to political, temporal advantage. All, for Duras, implicitly and, one might say, this side of judgment.

9: *"Et puis répudiée"*: A single line becomes a full stanza. The reference skips back over the previous stanza, "Lui . . . ," and the interplay between the monolithic masculine pronoun *lui* and adjectival past participles in the feminine (stressing received, imposed action) continues: *captured, carried off, exiled . . . , and then repudiated.* Repudiation, seen in this context, is less surprising than some historians seem to regard Titus's action, taken under pressure from the Roman Senate.

11: *"L'endroit s'appelle encore . . ."*: The same leitmotif returns, but with a changed order of elements. Duras characteristically comes back time after time to the irresistible pull of simple presences, a calm but astonished sense of the strange palpableness of our earthly mystery via a single word, a single name, endlessly giving us that "totality" she speaks of in the second stanza.

12: *"La fin de la mer . . ."*: This time, the sea returns to fill Duras's imagination. Two lines suffice, both paratactic, incomplete, opening upon the infiniteness they contain within their insistence on finitude: the sea's "end," its crashing against the desert shores, like a simultaneous emblem of implacable ephemeralness and fresh, ever-eternal happening.

13: "*Il ne reste que l'histoire . . .*": A poetics of minimal residualness—that of our "story/history," our narration, of things—and a poetics of complete-ness, totality, combine inextricably. What is minimal is equally "everything," "the whole thing": Durassian fiction is, indeed, one that, despite *and because of* incomprehensibility and unknowing, succeeds in drawing everything from next to nothing—while showing that the former still is mere residue, trace, "nothing more than"—here—"this marble rubble beneath our feet / This dust. / And the blue of drowned columns."

14: "*La mer a gagné sur la terre de Césarée*": Duras plays here more mani-festly on temporal factors. The stanza's opening line takes up a more histori-cized perspective, stressing the sea's encroachment on "the land of Caesarea," ever reminiscent of *Un barrage contre le Pacifique*. Lines 2–5, however, although discreet, adopt a more lyrical tone and thrust us into the long-past yet, in Duras's mind's eye, still-living streets of Caesarea's little port nearly 2,000 years ago (: the sack of Jerusalem took place in 70 and Titus put aside Berenice, sister of Herod Agrippa, in 75): their dark narrowness suddenly giv-ing out on to sun-drenched squares packed with farmers, merchants, and sailors. In lines 6–9 Duras continues to see, in the dust of today, the life of yes-teryear, the still half-sensed thoughts of Caesarea's inhabitants and "peoples."

15: "*Elle, la reine des Juifs . . .*": Via continued reprise and development, ellipsis and a transparency that still prefers not to name the protagonists of a story that thus attains to its universal, mythical, dimensions, Duras edges her way to a more complete picture of this hero(in)ic saga of love, pain, physical and emotional apogy, and trauma. The rhythm is at once serene and oddly staccatolike, each line either a single word or a handful, one quietly cascading over the other, time often being, as it were, effaced by the erasure of almost all finite verb forms.

16: "*Au fond du navire repose dans les bandelettes blanches du deuil*": Duras equates loss of love with loss of life and, white being in these parts of the world the color of mourning, implicitly renders funereal the entire locus and ambi-ence: the dusty land and the brilliant light become means of symbolic burial rather than of caress, revelation, and embellishment. Such pain, as Duras expresses it, is felt worldwide, and this is, of course, true both historically—as a historic moment whose ripples spread to all corners of the Roman Empire, and emblematically—all women knowing their "political" vulnerability, the poten-tiality of their "repudiation" according to a still-ubiquitous dominant mascu-line ethos. The "seas"—*les mers:* never far from *les mères*—ironically spread this destruction and fear of love, of intimacy, of otherness, of the feminine.

17: "*L'endroit s'appelle Césarée*": Duras dips into tautology, for the articula-tion of the self-evident symbolically speaks the totality of its representations. *Césarée,* moreover, is the (French) sign of this mere trace, this residue, here and now.

18: "*Cesarea*": Like the previous one-line stanza, this litanizes meaning, transforms the story into a blazon of extraordinarily condensed power. But this time, we shift from French sign to Roman sign, sliding through endless centuries via one small white space separating and joining Berenice and Marguerite Duras's loving contemplation of her.

19: "*Au nord, le lac Tibériade, les grands caravansérails de Saint-Jean-d'Acre . . .*": After this second incantatory evocation of Caesarea—Duras prefers the alternative modern spelling Cesarea—she offers a telescoped yet full geographic and demographic contextualization of the then-vibrant port, showing its strategic pertinence and the natural and cultivated wealth immediately surrounding it. Why? we might ask. No doubt in part to show that the pain, the trauma, the political fears, fade into and emerge from this larger landscape. No doubt, therefore, to contrast their intensity with the creative potential available in closed and open imaginative perspectives. Such abundance, such prospects, such teeming and splendid otherness, everywhere only reinforce the sense of loss in this "story" as in ceaseless other stories that will not be sung this side of eternity.

20: "*Elle était très jeune, dix-huit ans, trente ans, deux mille ans . . .*": With exquisite sensitivity, and a charming provocativeness that returns in *La Pluie d'été*'s treatment of age, Duras concertinas time to dwell rather upon the deeper atemporal pertinence of (one) woman's story. But she does so quickly to return, via rhythmic reprises, to the specific historical grounding of Berenice's exiling and "repudiat[ion] for State reasons." Such traumatizing refusal of the found beauty of love always in effect leaves "her," woman, "very young," innocent, quite rightly unprepared.

21: "*Arrachée à lui . . .*": Separation, the destruction of love, is, for Duras, a profound violence—perhaps, as it were, fatal, in the Durassian *univers imaginaire,* relentlessly pressing—but she insists here upon the degree to which it both runs contrary to desire and instinctive embrace of the other, and is, finally, synonymous with death. Love may be impossible in Duras, but its absence maims and kills.

22: "*Au matin devant la ville, le vaisseau de Rome . . .*": With the same considerable economy and understatement, Duras achieves great affective but unsentimental intensity. The inestimable dignity of woman, of this woman, of endless millions of women throughout time, faced with adversity, emerges; it is the speechlessness of innocence, the incomprehending persistence of love before the dismissal of love.

23: "*Dans le ciel tout à coup l'éclatement de cendres . . .*": Duras seeks to link here the demise of Berenice and the eruption in 79 of Mt. Vesuvius burying Pompeii and Herculaneum. Nothing is explicit, however; all remains at the level of sheer imaginative and affective juxtaposition: a physical devastation seen in the distant sky over the sea, from the place of psychical devastation.

24: "*Morte . . .*": After the active verb *en meurt,* in stanza 21, Duras gives us the stark and irreversible past participle, followed by the ambiguous "has everything destroyed"—is this Berenice's action, and if so, to what does it refer? Or is it another reference to Titus's destruction of the love that bound him all too briefly to a woman who reciprocated it? In effect, the line defies all clear attribution. It lacks subject, even if the following line would bind it to the "Queen of the Jews." Its force thus is generalized and underlines the fact that destruction is everywhere, an immense psychic gestalt love is (still) not able to transform.

25: *"L'endroit s'appelle Césarée . . ."*: The same quiet understatement is recycled from stanza 17 and, indeed, the opening lines. The final thrust of the third line, "There is nothing to be seen any more. Except for everything," is a typical and wonderful expression of Duras's creative, *poietic* genius: taking up once more the equation of residue or fragment and totality—the possibility of seeing the most intense and complete pertinence in the most derisory trace of being—Duras invites us to contemplate the near invisible, the marginally, only intuitively available meaning of our existence. Where everything lies full and mysterious.

26: *"Il fait à Paris un mauvais été . . ."*: We are thrown—a few words are enough to achieve it—from the torridness of Palestinian heat imagined, perhaps lived, to the present of the film *Césarée* from which, bizarrely, emerges the poem *Césarée*. A present yet *merged with* that of the poem, which is a story of woman and man, their difficult being-together, their beauteous and destroyed love, in the powdery light of Caesarea, in the mists and hesitations of a Parisian summer.

Notes

1. Marguerite Duras, *Écrire* (Paris: Gallimard, 1993), 44; hereafter cited in the text as *E*.

2. Duras, *La Vie matérielle* (Paris: P.O.L., 1987), 82; hereafter cited in the text as *VM*.

3. Duras, *La Pute de la côte normande* (Paris: Minuit, 1986), 19; hereafter cited in the text as *PCN*.

4. Duras, *Abahn Sabana David* (Paris: Gallimard, 1970), 31.

5. Duras, *Yann Andréa Steiner* (Paris: P.O.L., 1992), 31; hereafter cited in the text as *YAS*.

6. Duras, *L'Homme atlantique* (Paris: Minuit, 1982), 18; hereafter cited in the text as *HA*.

7. Duras, *Les yeux bleus cheveux noirs* (Paris: Minuit, 1986), 53; hereafter cited in the text as *YB*.

8. Compare with Duras, *L'Amant* (Paris: Minuit, 1984), 78; hereafter cited in the text as *AT*.

9. Duras, *La Maladie de la mort* (Paris: Minuit, 1982), 26–29.

10. Duras, *Émily L.* (Paris: Minuit, 1987), 40.

11. Duras, *L'Éden cinéma* (Paris: Mercure de France, 1977), 150; hereafter cited in the text as *EC*.

12. Duras, *L'Été 80* (Paris: Minuit, 1980), 67.

13. Compare with Duras, *La Pluie d'été* (Paris: P.O.L., 1990), 154–56; hereafter cited in the text as *PE*.

14. Duras, *La Navire Night et autres textes* (Paris: Mercure de France, 1979), 14.

Selected Bibliography

Baudelaire, Charles. *Oeuvres complètes*. Paris: Gallimard, Pléiade, 1961.

Bishop, Michael, ed. *Thirty Voices in the Feminine*. Amsterdam: Rodopi, 1996.

Blot-Labarrère, Christiane. *Marguerite Duras*. Paris: Seuil, 1992.

Bonnefoy, Yves. *Le Nuage rouge*. Paris: Mercure de France, 1977.

Borgomano, Madeleine. *Duras: une lecture des phantasmes*. Petit Roeulx: Cistre, 1987.

Char, René. *Oeuvres complètes*. Paris: Gallimard, Pléiade, 1983.

Du Bouchet, André. *L'Incohérence*. Paris: Hachette, 1979.

Dupin, Jacques. *Dehors*. Paris: Gallimard, 1975.

Duras, Marguerite. *Césarée*. In *Le Navire Night et autres textes,* Paris: Mercure de France, 1979.

————. *La Vie tranquille*. Paris: Gallimard, 1944.

————. *Un barrage contre le Pacifique*. Paris: Gallimard, 1950.

————. *Le Vice-consul*. Paris: Gallimard, 1965.

————. *Abahn Sabana David*. Paris: Gallimard, 1970.

————. *L'Éden cinéma*. Paris: Mercure de France, 1977.

————. *Le Navire Night et autres textes*. Paris: Mercure de France, 1979.

————. *L'Été 80*. Paris: Minuit, 1980.

————. *La Maladie de la mort*. Paris: Minuit, 1982.

————. *L'Homme atlantique*. Paris: Minuit, 1982.

————. *L'Amant*. Paris: Minuit, 1984.

————. *La Pute de la côte normande*. Paris: Minuit, 1986.

————. *Les Yeux bleus cheveux noirs*. Paris: Minuit, 1986.

————. *La Vie matérielle*. Paris: P.O.L., 1987.

————. *Émily L.* Paris: Minuit, 1987.

————. *La Pluie d'été*. Paris: P.O.L., 1990.

————. *Yann Andréa Steiner*. Paris: P.O.L., 1992.

————. *Écrire*. Paris: Gallimard, 1993.

————. *Les Mains négatives*. In *Le Navire Night et autres textes,* Paris: Mercure de France, 1979.

Frénaud, André. *Haeres*. Paris: Gallimard, 1982.

Guers-Villate, Yvonne. *Continuité/discontinuité de l'oeuvre durassienne*. Brussels: Université de Bruxelles, 1985.

Hill, Leslie. *Marguerite Duras: Apocalyptic Desires*. New York: Routledge, 1993.

Hugo, Victor. *Poésie III*. Paris: Seuil, 1971.

Hyvrard, Jeanne. *La Baisure/Que se partagent encore les eaux*. Paris: Des Femmes, 1985.

Mallarmé, Stéphane. *Oeuvres complètes*. Paris: Gallimard, Pléiade, 1945.

Michaux, Henri. *Chemins cherchés Chemins perdus Transgressions*. Paris: Gallimard, 1982.

Perse, Saint-John. *Oeuvres complètes*. Paris: Gallimard, Pléiade, 1972.

Reverdy, Pierre. *Cette émotion appelée poésie*. Paris: Flammarion, 1974.

Ricouart, Janine. *Écriture féminine et violence: Une étude de Marguerite Duras*. Birmingham: Summa, 1991.

Rimbaud, Arthur. *Oeuvres complètes*. Paris: Gallimard, Pléiade, 1963.

Schuster, Marilyn. *Marguerite Duras Revisited*. New York: Twayne, 1993.

Tison-Braun, Micheline. *Marguerite Duras*. Amsterdam: Rodopi, 1986.

Verlaine, Paul. *Oeuvres poétiques complètes*. Paris: Gallimard, Pléiade, 1962.

Willis, Sharon. *Marguerite Duras: Writing on the Body*. Urbana: University of Illinois Press, 1987.

The Theater and the Sacred:
A Religious Pagan

LILIANE PAPIN

In her interview with Xavière Gauthier, Marguerite Duras, apparently for the first time, uses the word "religious" concerning *Le Ravissement de Lol V. Stein.* This work is widely known as the matrix from which *L'Amour, India Song* and *La Femme du Gange* have been drawn. All are linked in one way or another to the central episode of the dance.[1] In these books Duras began to resort to a dissociation of the levels of narration.

The word "religious" is always suspect in our society. Not long ago Artaud complained that all one had to do was to pronounce it to be taken "for a sacristan."[2] In that same interview Marguerite Duras explains that all the books written at the time of *Le Ravissement* and after represented an upheaval for her. They are books that she "can no longer avoid," that make her "fear to lose all her readers." In other words they are books that "delight" her too.[3] On that level, her writing draws from religious experience since it escapes conscious control and becomes the instrument of a Revelation.

A little later, in the same interview, she again defines the word "religious" as the "transgression of oneself into the other" and as "the urge stronger than oneself that silences logical reason."[4]

Those are definitions that one can apply to the writing experience as seen by Marguerite Duras, and, as we have seen in the preceding chapter, to the love experience of her characters. It is on that level that one finds coincidence and displacement regarding the Judeo-Christian tradition and where one can truly speak of Duras as a "religious pagan."

As in the Christian tradition, Love is the driving force and the essence of the sacred. With Duras, however, it is no longer Love of God but pagan love tied to a woman and her power of fascination.

There is a religious dimension in (Marguerite Duras) . . . a blending of eroticism touching the flesh of the woman. It passes through whatever can be

Liliane Papin, *L'Autre scene. Le Théâtre de Marguerite Duras* (Saratoga, Cal.: Anma Libri and Co., 1988), 76–87. Reprinted by permission. Translated by John W. Kneller.

upsetting and beautiful in something in the woman that is indefinable—and then to death. It merges . . . as if death closes in on life. As if death loved life.[5]

Consider Anne-Marie Stretter as she takes her walk. All eyes turn toward her—Michael Richardson, the vice-consul, the embassy guests—while the "voices" describe her. She attracts, she fascinates, she is the focal point of attention and admiration, yet she chooses death. Her death is not at all dramatic. It seems to complete the cycle. It closes the circle. She simply walks into the ocean until the water engulfs her, until life and death come together.

This dimension of love is not the only place where Marguerite Duras joins Christian tradition. Clearly, there are also in her world the elect who are the meek of the earth. They are the women, the children, those who have nothing or who, indifferent to wealth and possessions, can distance themselves from them and give up everything without looking back. Vera Baxter is a case in point. She is rich (thanks to her husband), but she cannot get used to the idea of money. She does not know how to possess money. She cannot decide to rent a summer villa whose rental price seems exorbitant to her, though her husband has often told her that she need not be concerned with the price and that they can financially afford what she wants. She belongs to Duras's "innocents," those who are innocent in the original meaning of the word, like the beggar of *India Song,* like Lol or Claire Lannes. Also innocent are the characters whose travels take them to the nocturnal edges of madness and who are in a state of "virginity" regarding the world, for example the vice-consul, "the virgin man of Lahore."

Duras meets Christianity wherever it is subversive—primitive Christianity founded on a need for love and selflessness and promising the kingdom of heaven to the children, the poor, and the innocent. The difference, however, is the absence of God from this religious vision. Duras's characters discover "the new grace of a heaven without God," a religious meaning without any idea of a supreme authority, any need for obedience or any feeling of remorse and guilt.[6] Their itinerary does, however, recall Christ's *via dolorosa,* the Christian interpretation of what is surely the essence of a fundamental religious experience. It is a rite of passage that inevitably fulfills itself in sorrow and sufferance, where one dies in oneself and is reborn in another person by accepting death and self-denial.

All the great cosgomonic myths repeat on the collective level the individual initiatory journey of the hero's descent into hell. We find the same design in Duras. All her characters come back from a voyage that is in some way a descent into hell. They all seem certain that for a beginning to take place they must endure total destruction. That is what the traveler of *Le Camion* says clearly: "Let the world go to ruin, that is the only political situation."[7] Those are the thoughts of Alissa and Stein who try to help Elisabeth Alione to get by the destruction phase. The title is also clear: *Détruire, dit-elle.*

That is also what the beginning of the two women of *Yes, peut-être* in a world destroyed by the bomb seems to suggest.

Duras intrinsically links the political vision with the religious vision, as in the end of *Yes, peut-être,* where the play ends with the image of two women reciting the beginning of a "materialist bible." Political liberation seems inconceivable if it does not bring with it the renunciation of the "I," of individuality and the loss of identity.

For her part, Marguerite Duras achieves this task in her writings, by agreeing to be only the depository of broken recollections and memories, the receptacle of constantly unfolding time, "an echo chamber crossed by a word."[8] Her manner is to remain open, to lose herself in other memories and other recollections so that the "transgression of self into others" may take place.

Her characters have to an extreme extent the faculty of losing themselves in their surroundings, in persons and in things. During her long hours on the garden bench, Claire Lannes is in communion with the air, the wind, the insects, the swarming mass of "matter" and water, just as the beggar woman of Calcutta is in perfect harmony with the rhythm of the days and the heat. They reach the state of mind and spirit that Marguerite Duras, by her own admission, envies: "the courage to do nothing."[9] That statement is far from being a simple author's phrase, if we bear in mind that in all the countries and religions of the world it is in fact the state of mind and spirit that all the great mystics wish to attain: the renunciation of possessions and material wealth culminating in the renunciation of self.

This religious aspect of Duras's thought has important repercussions in her writing. The most important aspect is doubtless the fact that we are placed in the "after" of the event. The text, the play and the film are set right away in a ceremony, a commemoration of past events. We attend the re-presentation, the recommencement of a primordial act, and the textual space is a ritual and sacred place from which all profane activities of everyday life are excluded. Everything is created, everything is born from the magic of the voice and the narration. That is already true in a play like *Le Square* and becomes particularly evident in *L'Eden Cinéma* and *India Song,* because in these plays the characters are already dead and on stage they portray their own images and reflections. They are truly shadows summoned from the grave not only by the power of ceremony, the power of the voice and the writing but also by the spectators' desire to listen to and look steadily at their own story in the game of distance put on in the performance through word, image or gesture.

It is hardly surprising that Duras's texts have so quickly attracted the attention of theater directors. Of all the arts, theater is the one whose ritual character is the most immediately present and evident, though the realist and positivist tradition have made of it a profane and rational activity. We know the efforts of contemporary directors from Copeau to Barrault, including

Grotowski, Artaud and many others, to find that lost dimension of the theatrical act, performance as rite. Of all the media, theater is, it seems, the form that best respects this religious dimension of Duras's writing. The fact that she has often chosen film while preferring the "pure" text is not a contradiction.

True, film is more malleable. In it one can do without the presence and the "weight" of the actor and let the creative power of the audience go to work. The two films, *Son nom de Venise dans Calcutta désert* and *L'homme atlantique,* are the ultimate experiences in Duras's works of her desire to let the spectator make his or her own narration. In the first film, images lacking human presence provide the narrative. In the second, the screen remains dark most of the time. It is also true that nothing can replace the "pure," the imageless text, the act of reading or writing, the direct, personal contact with the page and the story. Still, theatrical space is the only place where the exchange "ceremony" can be realized through the actor. Spectators and actors share the same fictional space, the one where doing, representing, and believing are depicted.

Only with *L'Eden Cinéma* does Marguerite Duras seem to have succeeded in completely mastering this ceremonial and ritual aspect of the theater and to have integrated it into the web of the text. Here Marguerite Duras makes theater *with* theater and makes full use of its ritual possibilities. That is undoubtedly why she believes, as we shall see in the interview at the end of this study, that *L'Eden* is the only play on a level with what she has accomplished in film. One does not always necessarily agree with an author. For my part, I believe that many of her plays deserve to be defended against her. Yet if she has expressed this opinion, it is, I think, because with *L'Eden* she succeeded in recapturing the sacred dimension of writing *by* and with theater. In that film she achieved what she had accomplished with a film like *Le Camion,* for example, where she used what she calls "the preludial conditional of children . . ." who say "we would have been, we would have done, we would say that," who see no gap between the word and the act and who magically become what they utter.[10] Similarly with *L'Eden* she found a ceremonial of the spoken word.

In that play, the characters are split in two, multiplied and off center. The actor at once becomes the spectator and author of his own character, since he is the one who takes on the narration. No longer is there any pretension to realism. We are in the fictional and sacred space of myth, where progress is no longer possible, where time is cyclical and can only recommence, turn back on itself and relate again and again the primordial, past event. In *L'Eden,* the story is no longer to be told, it is simply to be said. The Mother and Joseph are dead, we are in the presence of ghosts who play at being characters and performers in a legend.

With *Savannah Bay,* a play that Marguerite Duras had not yet published at the time of the interview, a play in which all the great Durassian themes crystallize out into their purest, most condensed form, she pursued the exploration of the ritual space of theater. It is a play that she wrote for Madeleine Renaud, a "Durassian" character par excellence, because in it this great actress lost herself evening after evening in a thousand different personalities, haunted by characters and memories that were not her own. With *Savannah Bay* and Madeleine Renaud, Duras closes a loop. The woman who plays Claire Lannes in *L'Amante anglaise,* the Mother in *Journées entières dans les arbres* and *L'Eden* becomes both the subject and the object in the plays in which they act. Marguerite Duras has completely mastered the ritual of representation and has rediscovered ritual space, the space of the ceremony of writing.

The words "rite" and "ceremony" when applied to theater necessarily call to mind the name of Artaud. Reading *Le Théâtre et son double* we discover more points in common between him and Duras than we might at first suppose. How can we not think of *L'Amante* when Artaud passionately declares that there is something sublime and poetic in certain crimes that have no discernable or known causes and that we need to use these crimes in the theater. Like Duras, he thought it necessary to explore the mysterious and dark regions of the human soul and make the spectators participate in the scene. But Artaud thought that to recapture a "total" theater one had to get rid of language. To reinvent a language of signs similar in preciseness to the language of the Balinese theater that so impressed him (an experience that he did not, however, bring about in his play *Les Cenci*). To awaken spectators from their apathy, he wanted above all to "shock" them, to show them evil at work in torture scenes or in crimes on stage before one's eyes. On that level Duras's approach is the opposite.

It is true that Artaud could not foresee the fantastic development of the visual image in our society and consequently the loss of the power of suggestion. Crimes, perversity and sexuality in all their forms have become the basic ingredients of the horror and pornographic film industries and are far from arousing the "primal terror" that he envisioned.

With Duras, on the other hand, we find a wholly Racinian restraint. Like Racine, her theater is most of all a theater of the Logos and the Spoken Word. On stage nothing happens in spite of emotions at their paroxysmic state. Murders occur "in the wings," while, on stage, only narrative and description take place. As in Racine also, Durassian writing quite naturally leans toward extreme condensation. She freely respects the unities of time, place and action. Where Artaud sought to quicken the means and effects of reaching the spectator, she prefers to reduce them. She uses words—even in expressing what is indescribable or irrational—when she explores abnormal psychic regions. If Artaud dreamed of a theatrical language that would do without words, it is because he most feared facile psychologisms and rational explanations that can so easily reduce the mysterious to the known. As we have seen, it is a fear shared by Duras, but she succeeds in avoiding the pitfall by tying language to what is its constituent part and its opposite: silence.

Words in her plays are never used as simple instruments of translation or transpositions of events or emotions. Hers is a creative language that never seizes things in the heat of the moment to transcribe them, but always at a distance and indirectly, altered according to what they tell. In that "after" where sorrows and joys are evened out by memory. Facts take on the clarity and purity of stones transformed into diamonds covered with the patina of their own legend. In this way she succeeds in creating a paradoxical language of silence. All the "blanks," all the "missing sights" that she scatters throughout the text amount to so many hollow places into which our imagination loses itself, as if caught by the force of the empty space. Here language is multiplied ad infinitum. What is said is always accompanied in continuing echoes by the weight of what is "unsaid"—an undeniable sign of a poetic language.

Marguerite Duras is a poet. Her art relates to Verlaine's or Mallarmé's, to those poets who have sought the maximum poetic weight of words. She may be intuitively aware of the poetic force of words, of their resonance, of the suggestive power of truncated sentences, of rhythms that have been cut off and taken up again, of everything that can come to the surface of the text.

When Duras takes up a text or a theme a second or third time, it is never to add, but to condense and reduce. Her books become shorter and shorter. Her themes ever more compact. The best example of this transformation would surely be the evolution that takes place from *Un Barrage contre le Pacifique* to *L'Eden Cinéma* and finally to *Agatha*. It is as if, in going from one text to the other, Duras has succeeded in grasping ever more tightly what was essential for her. Looking back over time, her comment on the dialogue that she wrote for *Hiroshima, mon amour* was that it was "too wordy" (*"trop bavard"*). Nevertheless this minimal writing is constant in her style. In *Le Square,* for example, the event that was apparently the most important in the life of the traveling salesman is also the one about which he speaks the least. We the spectators reconstitute this man's love story by the scraps of sentences scattered here and there. He speaks of a city whose light he has not forgotten and where he experienced great happiness. Later, he says simply: "I was no longer alone. Then, again, I found myself alone."

That is, one might say, a "typical" sentence of Marguerite Duras. The present moment is as if rubbed out, already transformed by time, by the banal yet unique story buried in a past that only the spoken word can briefly bring to the surface again. At another time in the text, he admits that he was once very unhappy, that he wanted to die. He fell asleep on the side of a road and for a moment thought that he would never have the strength to get up again and go on. We realize that all these bits of information concern the same story. The city light, the moment of intense happiness and the moment of despair are scattered memories of the love story that he has known.

Nevertheless, the emotion that this restraint can create in a member of the audience is almost unbearable. It is there, present and underlying, on the surface of the words, the text and the skin. Everything is continually under-played in the concrete sense of the word, as in *L'Eden* where the Mother's children, strange phantoms of a lost past, play out a story in which suffering, anger, despair, the tragedy of hunger and death are said with the same smile, the same detachment, without raising the voice and without pity. The narra-tion escapes the present. It is free from the weight and emotions of profane duration.

In any religious ceremony, time becomes sacred by the very fact that it escapes chronological duration and linear development. It is cyclical. Its essential characteristic is its ability to repeat itself over and over again and recommence indefinitely the primordial act. Religious and sacred time is the ageless time of memory and myth. For that reason theater has always been associated with the religious ceremonies from which it descended. With the-ater we go directly into another reality, but different from film, the ceremony takes place before our eyes and the actors are transformed at the very moment that we look at them.

This is the aspect that the realistic theater strove to eradicate by trying to make theater and reality coincide, by asking actors to play as if the audi-ence were not there and *to be* the characters that they are portraying. Duras, on the other hand, like Genet or Becket, uses all the possibilities of temporal or spatial dislocation permitted by the theater. As we have seen, she creates theater *with* theater, with her ceremonial. In *L'Eden Cinéma* the children face the audience and ask it to pay attention to what will follow for that is when the "immortality" of the Mother begins. That is when her personal story will cease to belong to her and disappear into the collective story, the great recap-tured, lost legend of the struggle against death and the elements.

What then is the primordial act that Duras continues to seek and to recommence through all these legends and voices?

We soon realize that it is about the pain of division, about human beings constantly cut off from themselves while they long for unity. Separation is always the same, whether it takes place between the Mother and the children as in *L'Eden* or *Des journées entières* or between two lovers as in *Lol V. Stein, India Song* or *L'Amante anglaise*. It occurs when the personality splits and then separates from itself in loss of memory, in madness, or in Claire Lannes's inability to relate to her crime. Yet the narrative itself causes this separation, makes it complete. It seizes upon a story and the subject becomes an object. The story ceases to be personal as it becomes collective and attains the dimen-sion of a myth.

The separation also occurs between the writer and the book, the writer and the play. The unity is broken when the word is on the page or is uttered, when the "I" is dislocated. As we have seen, women seem best able to accept that separation, not only because they have experienced it biologically but also because they are the most separated from themselves, their image, their name and their history. The obliterated birth name of Anne-Marie Stretter on the tombstone comes to mind. When the separation is accepted there is a sudden calm. The journey of the young woman of *Hiroshima, mon amour* illustrates particularly well the transformation that takes place. At the age of eighteen, when she has her first love affair with the young German soldier and he is killed, she bangs her fists bloody against the walls of a cellar. Her rebellion is not against society. It is against herself. She already feels that the memory of their love and his death will escape her and she beats herself black and blue in order not to forget. Still, when she meets a new lover in Hiroshima, she knows that this memory will escape her, that it will probably merge into the memory of the young German soldier. This time she does not fight. The experience is painful, but she has learned that she can possess nothing, not even her own story and her memories. She refuses to remain in Hiroshima longer than planned, in spite of her lover's pleas. She knows that the pain will stop. She no longer fights against the passage of time.

That is no doubt Marguerite Duras's journey. In *Un Barrage contre le Pacifique,* the struggle of the Mother is present. It continues throughout the story in her cries and her tears. In *L'Eden Cinéma* everything has become calm, everything is finished. We are in narrative space. At the end of the play, however, only the children are separated, not Joseph and Suzanne. We know that Joseph is dead but everything takes place as if Marguerite Duras had not yet found the strength to write about the sorrow of her brother's death. It is in *Agatha* that the last separation takes place and the young woman brings it about. The autobiographical aspects of these texts are unmistakable and they have been acknowledged by Duras herself. All that time had to pass for her to close the wound opened by the death of her young brother.[11]

Eighteen is always an important age and number in all the writings of Duras. It is the age of the woman of Hiroshima at the death of her lover. It is the age of Aurélia Steiner, Suzanne and the young woman of the Square. It is also the time that has elapsed when the man in *Un Homme est venu me voir* returns. Duras has never revealed the experience in her personal life to which this age relates—whether it was her age when her brother died or her age when she left home. Yet in her writings this number functions as the age of separation from oneself, the age of the first love and the first forgetting, the age of childhood and innocence, the age when adulthood begins. It is also the time necessary for a new generation to be born and for historical events to belong completely to the past, since the young adults have not experienced them. It is the time necessary for the time of the story, the narrative and the myth to begin.

Duras's writings achieve a sacred dimension in the abolition of secular time and place. This remark may at first be surprising since she is also a writer of the "singular" who never pauses to look at social groups or great historical upheavals. *Hiroshima, mon amour* speaks of Hiroshima only in the past and through a love story between two individuals, two isolated voices neither one of which has *seen* Hiroshima at the time of the bomb. Yet she never considers the individual story apart from its legend, its collective state of flux, just when other memories take hold of it. Individual reality is present, but enlarged and broadened, transformed by the narrative. It is all of modern history, all the great catastrophes, the fears and failures of our civilization implacably reflected in that reality. The Mother's story does not symbolize colonialism, it *is* colonialism, it is indissociable from it, because it is what gives it its particular form, its contour. *Yes, peut-être* is not only a play written about the Vietnam war, it is a play in which the terror of two young women becomes the essential horror of all past and future wars. It has no center of gravity, no precise origin. The text carries us away and continues to resonate, to open different spaces, to take us to other places and other times. Suddenly truth and falsehood, the real and the imaginary, the past and the future cease to be contradictory.

This dimension of Duras's writing is particularly important to consider in a theatrical work and in the choice of staging. To be "faithful" to her writing, we must not forget that she does not try to set her plays in a fictional present, but rather to free them from it. That is the only way one can portray Duras at her maximum strength and respect the religious aspect of her narrative.

Notes

1. *Les Parleuses,* p. 177.
2. Antonin Artaud, *Le Théâtre et son double* (Paris: Gallimard, 1964), p. 109.
3. *Les Parleuses,* p. 177.
4. *Les Parleuses,* p. 178.
5. Hélène Cixous, *Cahiers Renaud-Barrault,* no. 89 (Paris: Gallimard, 1975), p. 13.
6. *Les Yeux verts,* p. 23.
7. *Le Camion,* p. 25.
8. *Les Parleuses,* p. 217.
9. Marguerite Duras et Michelle Porte, *Les Lieux de Marguerite Duras* (Paris: Editions de Minuit, 1977), p. 91.
10. *Le Camion,* p. 7.
11. *Duras filme,* film vidéo avec Marguerite Duras, Bulle Ogier, Yann Andréa et l'équipe de tournage de *Agatha et les lectures illimitées,* produit et réalisé par Jean Mascolo et Jérôme Beaujour.

What Alissa Knows . . . Mutants Mutating:
Destroy, She Said Terrorizes Psychology

SHARON SPENCER

Destroy, She Said is Duras's most perplexing work, text and film both, and the one about which least has been written, even by dedicated and comprehensive interpreters of her oeuvre. Without the rich conversation "Destruction and Language" by Jacques Rivette and Jean Narboni appended to the text, an unwary reader might be hopelessly lost in the tangle *inside* the hotel/hospital grounds, without ever having to risk penetrating the dangerous and frightening forest on the other side of the gate. Duras says, "There are ten ways to read *Destroy;* that's what I wanted" (92). Perhaps she is alluding to the 10 days during which Max Thor observes the mostly recumbent Elisabeth Alione.

Ten there may be, but in a modest approach I wish to offer one reading of this text that occupies a unique space in Duras's world. When asked, "To what extent do you feel more or less tied to adaptations of your own novels?" she replied, "*Destroy* cancels out the rest of them" (13). Later, in the same three-way discussion, she said, "[A]s for *Destroy,* I was really quite comfortable. Even though I was afraid. And at the same time, completely free. But frightened to death of being free" (133). Duras, perhaps without intending to do so, composed a work that challenges the parameters of contemporary psychology in a definitive manner that is at once emphatic and radical. With Beatrice Wood, 104-year-old active sculptor, Duras might have wanted to proclaim, when she realized the implications of what she had done in creating *Destroy,* "I shock myself."

The setting of *Destroy, She Said* is a spare and vaguely defined space, a sanatorium or a hotel situated at the edge of a forest that is said to be one of its attractions. Although the text refers to this space as a "hotel," it is obviously an unusual sort of hotel. Alissa explains to Elisabeth, " 'We're here by mistake. We thought it was just an ordinary hotel. I can't remember who recommended it. . . . Someone at the university, I expect. They especially mentioned the forest' " (39).

This essay was written especially for this volume and is published here for the first time by permission of the author. Copyright reserved.

Here, three vaguely defined "characters" stalk a fourth, who is more clearly outlined. In order of appearance, they are Elisabeth Alione, a convalescent who is asleep most of the time; Max Thor, a discouraged professor of history whose only interest seems to be covertly observing Elisabeth Alione; Stein, a devotee of the hotel, who seems to have no interests, at least until he meets Thor's wife, Alissa; and Alissa, the proverbial "loose cannon," the young woman, or girl, who will bring total destruction (according to the two men).

Most of the "action" takes place in the dining room. Outside, there is a lawn apparatus for croquet and an invisible tennis court (no players are ever seen; only the sound of the balls is heard). The overwhelming feature of this landscape is the forest (recall that the lovers in *The Ravishing of Lol V Stein* hold their erotic encounters at the Hotel du Bois—Forest Hotel). The setting of *Destroy* is another version of the Hotel du Bois. A path leading away from the hotel toward the forest terminates at a gate, yet another of this work's ambiguous symbols, for one can pass from the forest to the hotel grounds (to safety) or from the grounds to the "dangerous" forest. Even though the forest is considered, at any rate by Max Thor's university colleagues, one of the hotel's attractions, early in their exchange Alissa and Elisabeth agree that this forest is "dangerous." Alissa offers her opinion that it is "dangerous" *because* "they're [everyone except herself and Stein] afraid of it" (19). To enter this forest is an act of daring. There is much talk of going into the forest, but only two of the four *perhaps* enter it. This is a speculation on Max Thor's part, but the forest seems a dark and tangled zone where erotic trysts take place, trysts that inevitably involve what conventional people call "adultery."

The thrust of the "action" is Alissa's effort to persuade Elisabeth Alione to go into the forest with her. The latter at times seems tempted and ventures toward it, but at the last minute she always retreats in fear. At one point the two men, who become interchangeable, discuss whether they should "let" Elisabeth Alione go into the forest with Alissa. They agree that they should not (later, there is talk of Alissa's "killing" Elisabeth). The ambiguity of this contretemps is fascinating; if Alissa's proposed excursion into the forest is for purposes of seduction, then the men may be using their protective attitude toward Elisabeth as a pose to guard their own claims on Alissa. In *Destroy* jealousy is always a submerged, unarticulated subtext, in spite of the work's pretense of presenting a revolutionary model of nonpossessive sharing of lovers.

The interactions of *Destroy* (it cannot and should not be called a novel) take place in gorgeous bright hot July weather. Its palette is dominated by blue: the sky, the light in the dining room, the bright blue of Alissa's eyes and, at times, of Elisabeth's. The window, essential in any text by Duras, is located in the dining room and serves as a vantage point from which various characters observe other characters; sometimes the observers are in pairs and sometimes the subjects of observation are in pairs.

In *Destroy,* the quarry is Elisabeth Alione, a housewife from Grenoble who has come to the hotel to recover from an amorous misadventure. Solitary, usually sleeping, she is the object of Max Thor's passive yet persistent obsession. Considerably less interesting to Stein, she becomes of paramount importance to Thor's wife, Alissa. Alissa, who fears Thor may love her less now than before, is jealous of Elisabeth Alione. Moreover, in the reckless puritanical fervor of judgmental youth, Alissa wishes to change Elisabeth Alione's life, which she denounces. Elisabeth herself is a frightened woman, both by her own admission and as evidenced by her having shown her husband a letter from her lover, the better to ensure the security of her marriage and her accustomed lifestyle: Paris every October, bridge on Sunday afternoons.

Elisabeth Alione is a pallid version of the daunting seductress Anne-Marie Stretter. She is also a variation on a powerful archetype that is often found in Duras's fiction, that of the sleeping beauty. A convalescent, she is a sleeping beauty whom Max Thor "watches . . . from the balcony as she sleeps. She is tall, and looks as if she were dead" (4). Later, "she sits in profile facing the windows. This makes it easier for him to keep watch on her.

"She is beautiful. But it is invisible.
Does she know?"
"No. No."
The voice dies away over by the gate into the forest (5).

Elisabeth Alione's "story," which Alissa does succeed in drawing from her, though only by innuendos, is not unusual. In the time-honored tradition of Emma Bovary, she has had an affair with a younger man, a doctor, conceived a baby, and allowed her lover to interfere with the pregnancy with the consequence that the baby, a girl, was born dead. After she confesses this drama to her husband, Bernard, Elisabeth Alione must face the fact that the doctor attempts suicide, humiliated and probably threatened as well by Bernard. It is this betrayal of her lover that Alissa uses to intimidate and dominate Elisabeth.

The suicide attempt of a spurned lover also links Elisabeth Alione with Anne-Marie Stretter, who is held responsible for the ruined lives of both Michael Richardson and the French Vice-Consul. There are other supporting details for this identification. Like Anne-Marie Stretter (originally, Anna Maria Guardia of Venice), Elisabeth has an Italian name; it is her husband's name. Elisabeth's own name, ironically, is Villeneuve. Both women usually wear black, associated, on the one hand, with seduction and, on the other, with death. The difference, and it is a crucial one, is that Elisabeth, though fascinated and attracted by her suitors, evades all three attempts to make her "cheat" (as Max Thor urges during the croquet game).

"Stein says you're insane," Elisabeth says.
"Stein will say anything."
Alissa laughs. She turns back into the room and comes over.

"The only thing that will ever have happened to you . . ." she says.
"Is you," Elisabeth says. "You, Alissa" (65).

Less powerfully, Elisabeth Alione concedes when teased by Max Thor that she'd "been watching [him] for ten days," that "there was something about [him] that fascinated [her], put [her] in a turmoil . . . something interesting . . . [she] couldn't make out what it was. . . . 'Yes,' Elisabeth says at last" (80). This "yes" must be seen as more than a concession. It is forceful; Elisabeth Alione's usual response to the goads launched at her by the weird triumvirate is "silence."

Flirting with but avoiding seduction, rescued finally by a phone call to her husband, Elisabeth Alione urges Bernard to leave the hotel. Ironically, and unexpectedly, he is moderately receptive to the trio of lovers. He actually offers to stay on for another day—to be "loved" by Alissa?

The by now familiar triangle—ever an erotic one in Duras's creations, at least initially—is formed by Max Thor, whose name is seemingly ironic, for this personage is a self-effacing history professor who is ever and never in the process of becoming a writer. He frequently professes intense love for his much younger wife, whom he met when she attended one of his classes, only to fall asleep (he apparently admires this in the same mood as Anne Desbaresdes covertly admires her son's obstreperous attempts to undermine his piano lessons). Thor, who identifies himself as a Jew, is, despite his love for Alissa, obsessed by Elisabeth Alione:

> She has changed her position on the chaise-lounge. She has turned over and gone to sleep again, her legs stretched out and parted, her arm bent up over her face. Until today he had avoided going past her. Today, coming back from the far side of the grounds, he does just that, he walks past her. His footsteps on the gravel pierce the stillness of the sleeping body, make it start. The arm lifts slightly, and two eyes gaze at him from under it, unseeing. He walks by. The body goes still again. The eyes close. Stein was coming down the steps of the hotel absent-mindedly. They pass each other. "I tremble all the time," says Stein in a sort of trembling uncertainty (11–12).

In spite of this "trembling uncertainty," Stein provides the work with a formidable presence and a forceful energy, second only to Alissa's.

Stein, a German Jew, as his name indicates, is endowed with no profession. Like Thor, he says he is "in the process of becoming" a writer. "Becoming a writer" is a familiar condition to anyone who tries, seriously tries, to write. An intriguing joke associated with Stein is the Rosenfeld theory. " 'Alissa only believes in the Rosenfeld theory,' Stein says" (40). " 'Sometimes,' Alissa says, 'Blum teaches the Rosenfeld theory' " (77). The humor—rather heavy handed—derives from the trio's assumption that Bernard Alione is an anti-Semite, the sort who would unconsciously use one Jewish name in place of another. Blum is Stein. The Rosenfeld theory is never described.

Bernard Alione looks at the three friends and asks, "Who are you?"

"German Jews," Alissa says.
"That's not what I . . . that's not the point. . . ."
"I think it must have been," Max Thor says gently.
Silence (70).

Stein shares with Thor the confidence that he has returned to the hotel because

"This place has memories for me. They wouldn't interest you. I met a woman here."
"And she hasn't come back?"
"She must have died."
He says everything in the same monotonous voice.
"There could be other explanations," he adds. "But that's what I think."
"But you came back in the hope of finding her?"
"Oh no, I don't think so. You mustn't think it was a . . . oh no. But she kept me interested a whole summer. That was all."
"Why?"
He pauses before answering. He rarely looks anyone in the eye.
"I couldn't say. It was a question of me—me and her together. Do you see? Shall we go over by the windows?"
They get up and cross the empty dining room. They stand by the windows. Yes that's where she was [ambiguous pronoun *she*, the woman Stein is haunted by, Elisabeth Alione, or both]. She [Elisabeth Alione] is walking around the tennis courts, dressed in black today. She's smoking. All the guests are outside. He [probably Stein] doesn't look out into the grounds.
"My name's Stein," he says, "I'm a Jew."
There she goes, past the porch. Now she's gone.
"Did you hear what I said my name was?"
"Yes—Stein. It must be quite cool now" (7–9).

Stein, who returns to the hotel every year because of a woman who "kept him interested" for a whole summer, initiates a friendship with the laconic Thor and instantly becomes captivated by Thor's wife, Alissa. After meeting her only briefly, he remarks, " 'You didn't tell me Alissa was insane.' 'I didn't know,' says Max Thor" (21). Thor offers absolutely no resistance to Stein's avowed instant attraction to Alissa. (Perhaps he actually welcomes Stein's attentions, hoping that Alissa will be distracted from his silent courtship of Elisabeth Alione.) " 'Did you want Alissa as soon as you saw her?' Stein asks. " 'No,' Max Thor says. 'I didn't want anyone. And you?' 'As soon as she walked through the door,' says Stein" (38).

In fact, in an act that alludes retrospectively to the saturated levels of voyeurism in *The Ravishment,* Thor leaves the bedroom window open so that

Stein, prowling the grounds, is free to observe the nightly lovemaking of Thor and Alissa.

"We make love," Alissa says. "Every night we make love."
"I know," says Stein. "You leave the window open and I see you."
"He leaves it open for you. To see us."
"Yes."
Alissa has put her childish lips on Stein's hard mouth. He speaks like that.
"Do you see us?" Alissa says.
"Yes. You don't say anything. Every night I wait. Silence clamps you to the bed. The light stays on and on. One morning they'll find you both melted into a shapeless lump like tar, and no one will understand. Except me" (31–32).

In spite of, because of, or in addition to his love for Alissa, Max Thor is totally intrigued by the dormant and apparently ill Elisabeth Alione. He is so intrigued, in fact, that he writes her: " 'Madame,' he [Stein] reads, 'Madame, I have been watching you for ten days. There's something about you that fascinates me, puts me in a turmoil, and I can't, I simply can't, make out what it is' " (14). Transforming himself from observer to observed, Thor later reverses roles and approaches Elisabeth Alione (she is about to leave the hotel with her husband, Bernard): " 'You'd been watching me for ten days,' he says. 'There was something about me that fascinated you, put you in a turmoil . . . something interesting . . . you couldn't make out what it was.' 'Yes,' Elisabeth Alione says at last" (80).

Alissa, the youngest of the quadrangle, is both the most awesome and the most confused, as well as confusing. Though Thor says she was 18 when he met her two years earlier in his class, she is described as 18 during the interactions shadowscaped in the text. According to Duras's Note for Performance, she is supposed to be "petite," and Elisabeth Alione is described as "tall." But when the two women admire and adore themselves, the one in the other, the two together in a mirror, Alissa "murmurs, 'I think we look alike. Don't you think so? We're the same height.' They smile" (63). At one moment full of bravado, immediately after she and Elisabeth have agreed on the "dangerous" nature of the forest, Alissa says, " 'Destroy' " (19).

Clearly, Alissa wants to destroy Elisabeth. She reveals jealousy when she reproaches Thor for murmuring the name "Elisa" in his sleep. In a passage so bizarre that it almost appears a mistake, something that should have been edited out, Alissa confesses, " 'I'm afraid.' Alissa goes on. 'Afraid of being abandoned, afraid of the future, afraid of loving, of violence, of numbers, of the unknown, of hunger, of poverty, of the truth' " (45).

Duras's intent was that Alissa be terrifying precisely because of her youth and her childlike spontaneity, which embraces an innocence that can be deadly (as when she attacks Elisabeth Alione's integrity for showing the young doctor's letter to her husband). Alissa is more a principle than a character, the principle of destruction. She would readily destroy Elisabeth, not only because of Thor's obsession with this woman but also because of the falseness and hypocrisy, the emptiness of Elisabeth Alione's life, which Alissa says is "fascinating and terrible" (62):

> Elisabeth doesn't notice anything, neither the icy hand nor the pallor [apparently, Thor's]. She tries to remember, but can't.
> "I'd got you [Stein and Thor] mixed up," she says, smiling.
> "Let's go into the forest," Alissa says.
> She starts to go, followed by Stein. Max Thor doesn't appear to have heard. Elisabeth Alione waits. Then Max Thor moves toward Alissa as if to stop her. But Alissa has already set off.
> Then all three turn toward Elisabeth Alione. She hasn't moved.
> "Come along," Alissa says.
> "Well. . ."
> "Madame Alione's afraid of the forest," says Alissa.
> "In that case we can stay in the grounds," Max Thor says.
> Alissa comes back to Elisabeth and smiles at her.
> "Choose," she says.
> "I don't mind going into the forest," she says.
> The two women set out, preceded by Stein and Max Thor.
> "Let's stay in the grounds," Elisabeth Alione says.
> Silence.
> "As you like," Alissa says.
> Silence. They retrace their steps.
> "To go back to what we were saying," Stein says.
> "Total destruction" (43–44).

The men are unified in this as in all else: Alissa is powerful. Moments of comedy (perhaps unintentional on Duras's part) occur when Alissa and Stein read a letter together:

> She picks the letter up slowly and opens the envelope.
> "Stein, look at it with me."
> Side by side, almost indistinguishable from one another [!], they read:
> "Alissa knows," Stein reads. "But what does she know?" Quite calmly Alissa puts the letter back in the envelope and tears it up.
> "I wrote it for you," says Stein, "before I knew you'd guessed."
> They go over, arms entwined, to the bay windows (31).

In a reprise a day later the two men are in the dining room looking out through the bay windows.

> "How quiet," Stein says. "You can hear them breathing."
> Silence.

"Alissa knows," Max Thor says. "But what does she know?"
Stein doesn't answer (33).

What they *think* Alissa knows is, of course, never revealed by this ever-elusive text. Actually, Alissa doesn't "know" anything. She *feels* everything, and she acts on her feelings. This is why she is able to galvanize and rejuvenate the others. The men also agree on Alissa's capacity for destruction:

"Total destruction will come first through Alissa," Stein says. "Don't you agree?"
"Yes. And do you agree she isn't altogether safe?"
"Yes," Stein says. "Alissa isn't altogether safe."

"Safe" is, of course, an ambiguous term. Does it mean that Alissa is endangered in some way, or that she is dangerous to other people? The men believe that she is dangerous to Elisabeth, and Elisabeth, indeed, is at times frightened of her. However, the text indicates that Alissa is always secure in the love of both men in spite of her moments of doubt, caused by Max Thor's passive yet relentless pursuit of Elisabeth Alione. The endangered person, however, is always Elisabeth.

Max Thor and Elisabeth Alione are watching Alissa and Stein "move slowly and evenly, as if dancing, away across the grounds."

"Where are they going?" Elisabeth Alione asks.
"Into the forest, I expect," Max Thor says, smiling.
"I don't understand. . . ."
"We're Alissa's lovers. Don't try to understand."
She thinks this over. And begins to tremble. . . .

After stating, "I love Alissa desperately," Max Thor proclaims, "I'd like to understand you. Love you."

She doesn't answer.
Silence (58).

But when Elisabeth Alione learns that the confusing and scandalous trio of lovers is leaving the hotel, she becomes frightened; her ambivalence toward them is arresting, because they both comfort and threaten her.

"Here comes Stein," Max Thor says. "We're leaving tomorrow morning."
"I'm frightened," Elisabeth Alione says. "I'm frightened of Alissa. Where is she?"
She looks at him, waiting.
"We've nothing to say to one another," says Max Thor. "Nothing."
She doesn't move. He doesn't speak. She goes off. He doesn't turn around.
Stein approaches (59).

Alissa is admirably dangerous, or perhaps she is merely pretending to be spontaneous in her attractions. On the surface, she is alluring yet risky because she dares to love everyone: both Thor and Stein. She offers to love Elisabeth Alione, who is frightened and backs away in terror. Finally, Alissa assures Bernard Alione "with incomparable gentleness, 'you know, we could love you too.' 'Really love you,' Stein says' " (75).

At times Alissa's offhandedness evokes laughter. It is the same sort of laughter with which adults greet brazen proclamations by children who have not yet been scorched by the bonfires of life, not even when toasting marsh-mallows. She brushes off cataclysmic statements with breathtaking insou-ciance: When Max Thor says, " 'You're insane, Alissa. Insane,' " she replies, " 'I surprise myself too' " (45). Later Elisabeth Alione tells her she's insane. Alissa breezily responds, " '[t]oo bad' " (64).

Equally bizarre is her dismissal of the idea of killing Elisabeth Alione. First, she aggressively unmasks the other woman:

> "I'm just thinking about what you told me. It was because you showed your husband the letter that you were ill. You're ill because of what you did."
> She gets up.
> "What's the matter?" Elisabeth Alione asks.
> "Disgust," says Alissa. "Disgust."
> Elisabeth Alione gives a cry.
> "Do you want to make me desperate?"
> Alissa smiles at her.
> "Yes. Don't say any more."
> "No, let's not talk any more."
> "It's too late," says Alissa.
> "For what?"
> "To kill you." She smiles. "It's too late."
> Silence.

Alissa's response is ludicrous. After her presumptuous and savage attack on Elisabeth Alione, whom she barely knows, she dismisses the idea of killing her with the casual remark that it's "too late." This misplaced nonchalance can only evoke laughter, weird laughter at that. But for some sensitive persons it may incite shock.

The concatenation of proclaimed loves and lovers in *Destroy* threatens credulity and, at times, does invite laughter. Max Thor pursuing Elisabeth, Stein pursuing Elisabeth Alione and Alissa (maybe Thor as well), Alissa pursuing Max Thor, Stein, *and* Elisabeth. Even more outrageous is the suggestion that Alissa and Stein are difficult to distinguish from one another; more understandably, Max Thor and Stein are difficult to distinguish from one another. And finally, the mirror scene is designed to show that Alissa and Elisabeth (the similarity in names is almost too obvious, as is the ironic use of

Thor for the timid Max) are interchangeable. The paradox of a music like Stein, stone, also creates a response of wonder.

Since the late 1950s, Duras was experimenting with superimposed, interchangeable, and fluid identities. This experimentation reaches its climax in *Destroy;* however, it becomes even more radical in a different way in the twin biographies written by her and Yann Andréa Steiner (a subject for a possible future exploration). There are, of course, various ways of interpreting this fluidity and interchangeability. If the context is realistic fiction or film, then it seems obvious that Duras has brought to the surface of her readers' awareness and understanding a commonplace psychological phenomenon: the way in which all humans expand and elaborate their experience of life by identifying with other people and experiencing through empathic fantasy what the other(s) is experiencing. Already we are very far from a crude definition of *voyeurism,* a term that oversimplifies and degrades Duras's fictional project. Nonetheless, it is true that when Lol lies in the rye field behind the Hotel du Bois she is vicariously experiencing the sexual commerce between Jack Hold and Tatiana, which is but a substitute for Lol's original trauma, or ravishment, her abandonment by Michael Richardson, who has no power to resist the instantaneous sexual undertow exerted by Anne-Marie Stretter. This is voyeurism in its simple dictionary meaning: sexual desire concentrated on seeing sexual organs and sexual acts.

In later works the dubbing and overdubbing of characters by one another assumes a profundity that is much more enveloping than voyeurism. The nature of identity is challenged by an equation between emotional engagement with others and one's own being, which as these engagements and identifications shift and change, change and shift, transform the identities of the observers/participants. Certainly this seems so with *Hiroshima, Mon Amour, The Vice-Consul, India Song,* and of course *Destroy, She Said.*

In *Destroy* the blurring and crossing over of identities become truly extreme and invite the question: What ideology drove Duras to move directly against the European ideal of individualism, originating during the Renaissance and reaching its most extreme manifestation (one wants to say "manifest destiny") in the twentieth century in the United States? Much has been written about the dangers of megalomaniac individualism, most notably by Dostoevsky, Gide, and Camus. The counterargument, of course, is that of Marxism, but even more especially of Confucianism, the ancient and fertile soil in which Chinese Communism took root and flourished. As an idealistic Marxist who, like so many others, was compelled to reject the living Communism for the theoretical and messianic, Duras was quite clearly deeply stimulated by the student movement of the late 1960s in France and the U.S.

Moreover, Duras was a product of French culture, though she may have come to it late because of her early life in Indochina. How could she *not* have absorbed at least elements of the stance of the Dadaists, the shock troops of modernism, and the surrealists, who devoutly believed that they had corrected the chaotic, may we say anarchistic, tendencies of Dada with a positive program for total liberation of the human person (actually, the human *male* person) to include, even to *stress,* erotic liberty?

Indeed, to Duras as to many others, the student protests, the general expansion of the demand for egalitarian standards of life that were articulated by the young seemed to renew the hope in the viability of revolution that had been brutally annihilated, to say the very least, by Stalinism and German national socialism. Neo-Dadaism and neo-Surrealism to some extent drove the student movements of the 1960s and early 1970s. Duras responded to young people's demands for social change by quickly writing *Destroy* and by quickly producing an extraordinary film (on a budget of $44,000). And yet, having experienced disillusionment with the evolution of civic life in France, most especially the Communist Party, she had attained a wisdom that saw both the hopefulness and the terrible dangers of youthful exuberant revolutionary zeal: hence, Alissa and the principle of destruction.

What is truly shocking about *Destroy* is not the sexuality of multiple and shifting partners, this to include multiple and shifting genders, but the thrust of the book and the film toward a theory of identity in which the Western ideal of "self," of individual, introspective, aware, knowledgeable identity, is simply trashed. So much for psychoanalysis! In *Destroy* gender essentialism has no significance whatsoever. And there are various kinds of love: erotic love, soul love, sisterly/brotherly love, incestuous love, and yes, even married love. Sex is a pleasure, a pleasant, perhaps even a *necessary* pleasure. But it is an accessory. It is disposable.

These loves exist in a context in which there is an aspiration to expand the parameters of love far beyond the monogamous monofocus of Western life. Two men may be considered interchangeable, two women may be considered interchangeable, a man and a woman may be considered interchangeable, and two men and a woman may be considered interchangeable. Two men and two women doesn't work only because Elisabeth is too terrified to become part of the community of lovers.

Destroy is an enterprise that makes one catch one's breath! But before its aspirations can be achieved, the "old" ways of thinking and living must be destroyed. Hence, Alissa. Even though she yearns to change her life, Elisabeth Alione is too frightened to let go of the foothold on stability she has achieved through a conventional marriage to a conventional man. Max Thor is too rigid and too stupid to change anything, especially himself. But Stein can do anything whatsoever; this is because, even though he is in the same age group as Thor, he is a mutant, a sudden and unexpected manifestation of a new form of life.

Alissa is fearless in her inner dynamism and she wants, she sincerely wants, to know: " 'How can one live?' Alissa cries softly." The appearance of the Alione family, a nightmare of bourgeois complicity, elicits a repetition of this plea: " 'How can one live?' Alissa breathes. 'What will become of us [a deliberately open pronoun expanding from Stein and Alissa to their immediate group and to all the people of France, Europe, or the world]?' Stein asks." Most of us, like Elisabeth Alione, just go on "the same as before . . ." (59). But Duras did not go on "the same as before." Besides the deeply meaningful relationship with Yann Andréa Steiner that enhanced the latter part of her life, Duras evolved an evolutionary radical aesthetic in which such conventional literary terms as *narrative strategy* are just as trivial and inadequate as is *voyeurism* to describe the viewing of sex acts in her novels and films.

Duras is always creating at her most exciting pace and with the greatest lyrical resonance when her characters and situations blend erotic with sociopolitical themes. *Hiroshima* is truly great, and it is great for many reasons, but most tellingly it entwines outrage and compassion with suffering and with love. This is also true of *India Song*, which, without the relentlessly present subtext provided by the lepers and the Woman from Savannakhet, could appear to lack depth. Anne-Marie Stretter and the Asian beggar woman are situated at extreme poles of reality. But they are both women. And they both suffer, although in different ways. The counterpoint of the film's extraordinary music articulates and enhances both their differences and their profound sameness. *The Lover*, a great triumph for Duras in every way, in spite of her dislike of the film version, blends sociopolitical and erotic themes with a poignancy and skill that reveal Duras's artistry at its most inspired. Without doubt, it is a masterpiece, and one that is, in part, dependent for its greatness on its richness of themes and innuendos.

No one who either loves or detests Duras's writings and films can forget her early life in French Indochina. Fluent in Vietnamese and very proud of what she called being "Creole," she was shocked and disappointed when her mother explained to her that she was not Vietnamese but French. Certainly the circumstances of her early life would and did nourish a strong identification with the marginalized, oppressed, colonized people of Indochina, fertile soil indeed for an admiration of theoretical socialism and even for political activism on its behalf. But there is something much deeper that must have affected Duras's concept of human identity and its obligations. This is the simple fact that she was steeped in the traditional value system of Asian societies: that the group, the community, the family, *always* demand a loyalty far more urgent and profound than the shallow wants and needs of any individual. Traditional life, not simply in Asia but in traditional societies worldwide, exigently requires that the human self serve the community. Hence, Stein.

Alissa, the destroyer, Stein, the creator. Both indispensable to any dialect of radical social transformation. The forest is the place where one can easily become lost in erotic indulgence, hidden away from the eyes of the judgmental defenders of conventional morality. Yes, it is dangerous, dangerous because in the forest people enjoy delights they have been taught they are not permitted to enjoy without suffering. Overcoming one's inhibitions in the name of pleasure is not easy. (Just ask Elisabeth Alione.) And when people dare to do it, they often suffer crippling guilt. Some even commit suicide when the beloved for whom they have risked everything proves unreliable, selfish, shallow, and faithless. Duras knows this and reminds us of it again and again. The French Vice-Consul does not "go crazy" in a vacuum. He *is* one of the lepers he shoots at, and he knows it. But the question Stein asks, " 'What will become of us?' " is urgent. The interchangeable mutants have freed themselves. But what are they going to do with their freedom?

Listen to music, one is tempted to say, in a frivolous mood. Because in this otherwise magnificent and brave text, the ending comprises words, just words. Duras has made her adoration of music work for her in all her other writings and films, but in *Destroy* it is unconvincing and flat. In a text in which silence is such a major persona, music might perhaps have sustained the perfect note of frightening and mysterious resonance. But in *Destroy, She Said,* when music enters it is introduced too abruptly, and one wonders— Bach—the composer associated with Teutonic Lutheranism! One might argue that Protestantism was historically revolutionary, yet in a text that aspires to suggest the real possibility of contemporary revolution, Bach is a surprising choice indeed. The music is too traditional and too measured. It is asked to bear the weight of a gigantic messianic enterprise, but it seems a classic deus ex machina, a contrived resolution, almost an act of the author's desperation.

One would not presume to suggest a substitution, another composition to bring to a satisfying sense of expectation and promise this superb text. Perhaps the music need not be named at all, as indeed it is not in the text. The image of the music penetrating the forest is captivating and arouses genuine hope in the reader who has given herself over to the rhythms of Duras's dance of words:

> "It's going to do it, it's going to get through the forest," Stein says. "Here it comes."
> They speak in the intervals of the music, softly, so as not to wake Alissa.
> "It has to fell trees, knock down walls," Stein murmurs. "But here it is."
> Yes, here it is, felling trees, knocking down walls.
> They are bending over Alissa.
> In her sleep Alissa's childlike mouth widens in pure laughter.
> They laugh to see her laugh.
> "Music to the name of Stein" she says. (85)

Works Consulted

Duras, Marguerite. *Destroy, She Said and Destruction and Language: An Interview with Marguerite Duras.* New York: Grove Press, 1970. (First published in France as *Detruire, dit-elle,* Paris: Minuit, 1969.)

————. *Yann Andréa Steiner.* New York: Charles Scribner's Sons, 1993. (First published in Paris: P.O.L., 1992.)

Schuster, Marilyn R. *Marguerite Duras Revisited.* New York: Twayne Publishers, 1993.

Vircondelet, Alain. *Duras.* New York: Dalkey Archive Press, 1994. (First published in France by Bourin, 1991.)

Le Vice-consul and India Song: Dolores Mundi

Deborah N. Glassman

> Les personnages évoqués dans cette histoire on été délogés du livre intitulé *Le Vice-consul* et projetées dans de nouvelles régions narratives.
>
> —*India Song*, p. 9

Le Vice-consul reconjugates many themes as well as several formal devices dear to Duras. The anonymous narrator does not identify with any particular point of view or character. Within the cast of characters, another narrator, a male writer, is in the process of writing an imagined biography of a mad beggar-woman cast into exile by her mother. His framed narrative is set within the primary diegesis and erodes the boundaries between story and plot. Tale-telling, as is so often the case in Duras's work, grows from the desire to appropriate and domesticate experience, here, the attempt of colonial whites to participate in the suffering of India, to both know and deflect its horrors. The eponymous hero of the novel grapples with his inexplicably painful visions, is unable to give them verbal form, and is overcome by his passion for Anne-Marie Stretter in whom he sees a partner of the soul. His scream is the language closest to his desires; he never covers the distance between himself and Stretter, however. He is repugnant to the consulary world of which he is an unsettling member. A white leper, his exile and future in the administration are the main preoccupations of the French Consul.

The film, *India Song*, retains the diegetic universe and cast of characters of *Le Vice-consul*—indeed there are direct citations from the novel—with some important differences. The beggar-woman of the novel is only a voice on the sound track in the film. The voices recall Lol's story—uttering several sentences from the novel by way of which Duras was obliged to pass before making *India Song*[1]—and Stretter's seduction of Richardson at the ball is said to be the originary moment of their couple. Stretter is the visual center of the

Margeurite Duras: Fascinating Vision and Narrative Cure. Rutherford: Fairleigh Dickinson Press, 1991, 62–92.

film in which Duras kills her off.[2] The ambassadorial reception occupies a major portion of the film's visuals but is only one of the short "chapters" in the novel. Where the novel sets storytelling *en abîme* by using the biography of the beggar-woman to erode the edges between the novel and its framed narrative, the most visually arresting of the Indian Cycle films multiplies and dislocates visual and narrative frames. There is a constant play of door frames, window frames, picture frames, and mirrors; mirrored space disrupts temporal and spatial signposts. Most importantly, the sound track is unsynchronized with the images. Sound track and images clearly relegate the narrative universe of *Le Vice-consul* to the past tense in *India Song*. Taken together, these two works allow us to explore what Marie-Claire Ropars has called the "circulation défective de [c]es texts," as Duras explores the new narrative regions offered in the cinema.[3]

LE VICE-CONSUL

"Elle marche, écrit Peter Morgan" (9) (She walks, writes Peter Morgan) reads the first line of the novel. Peter Morgan, a white man in Calcutta, is writing a biography. His biography, of another character in the novel, begins with an exile. She is a young peasant, pregnant, unmarried, and about to be banished from her family and home. Her expatriation is more correctly an exmatriation, for her mother issues the order that she lose herself in a place where nothing is familiar and everything is hostile. Inflexible, the mother warns her daughter not to return. "Si tu reviens, a dit la mère, je mettrai du poison dans ton riz pour te tuer" (10). (If you return, said her mother, I will put poison in your rice to kill you.) The young girl comes to envisage her exile as a road of maternal abandonment. "Dans la lumière bouillante et pûle, l'enfant encore dans le ventre, elle s'éloigne, sans crainte. Sa route, elle est sûre, est celle de l'abandon définitif de sa mère" (28). (In the boiling and pale light, the child still in her womb, she moves on, without fear. Her road, she is certain, is that of the definitive abandonment of her mother.) From her home on the plains of the Tonlé-Sap, a lake in present day Cambodia, the young woman wanders north, following an impossible itinerary through Cambodia and Thailand and over the Cardamome mountains, to India. Nearly starving along the way, her strength diminished by the fetus, she steals food and takes lovers to survive. She loses her hair and badly cuts her foot. When she imagines her mother's reaction upon seeing her return, she is paralyzed. Her mother's look freezes her in her steps, a maternal Medusa paralyzing her victim.

> Elle a peur. La mère fatiguée la regardera venir depuis la porte de la paillote. La fatigue dans le regard de sa mère: Encore en vic, toi que je croyais morte? La peur la plus forte, c'est celle-là, son air lorsqu'elle regardera s'avancer son

enfant revenue. Tout un jour, elle hésite. Dans un abri de gardiens de buffles, sur la rive du lac, elle reste sous le regard, arrêtée. (26)

She is afraid. The tired mother will see her returning from the door of the hut. Fatigue in the mother's look. "Still alive, you whom I believed dead?" The strongest fear is that one, her demeanor when she watches the daughter who has returned coming towards her. An entire day she hesitates. In a buffalo keeper's shelter, on the lakeshore, she remains beneath that look, frozen.

Paralyzed by a look, this daughter slowly goes mad. In her madness, she begins to inhabit her hallucinations. As if to escape the cruelty visited upon her, she imagines her sisters and brothers and a beneficent mother.

Elle voit des frères et soeurs perchés sur une charrette, elle leur fait signe, ils rient eux aussi en la montrant du doigt, ils l'ont reconnue, elle se prosterne encore, reste, reste visage contre terre et se trouve devant une galette posée devant elle. Quelle main la lui aurait donnée sinon celle de sa mère? (27)

She sees her brothers and sisters perched on a cart, she waves to them, they too laugh, pointing at her, they have recognized her, she prostrates herself again, remains, remains with her face against the ground and finds herself before a cracker placed in front of her. What hand would have given it to her if not her mother's?

The image of the prodigal's return and a caretaking mother fades and the young woman abandons in her turn, what has abandoned her. In a gesture recalling that of the heroine of *Hiroshima, mon amour,* who declares her defiance by claiming to forget, the beggar-woman imagines another return home. She will be disdainful. "Elle reviendra pour lui dire, à cette ignorante qui l'a chassée: Je t'ai oubliée" (21). (She will return to tell her, to tell this stupid woman who drove her out, I have forgotten you.)

When her child is born, the young girl tries to give it away at the marketplaces that she haunts in the search for food. She beseeches other women to take her baby but they ignore or shun her, too poor to help or repulsed by her festering foot and apparent madness. She does not speak their language, but shows the infant in the hope that she will be understood. Eventually, a white woman takes the baby, at her daughter's insistence. They return to their home, trailed by the beggar-woman, mad now, who has completed her exile from Tonlé-Sap. Near the gates of the house from where she observes uncomprehending, a doctor arrives. The white woman is distressed, the child is dying, but the mother repeats only "Battambang" in singsong fashion, and laughs.[4] Relieved of its referential value, the name becomes mythical; the word becomes a song. The sonorous husk of the word alone remains like a corpse to attest to the past. Language become song signals the beggar-woman's madness; no record remains of the memory of her trauma, vaporized.

The beggar-woman is a typically Durasian heroine. She is a figure in which sexuality and maternity are conjugated with violence and death, memory and language abolished by madness. The musicality of language and of a musical rather than a signifying logic, what some have seen as the poetic orality of Duras's writing, is in the ascendancy at specific moments in Duras's texts.[5] These are moments of feminine madness or of definitive loss, as when the heroine of *Hiroshima, mon amour* bids her lover farewell in a hypothetical future when their story would be "no more than a song." The cycle of maternal castigation and abandonment, madness and dispossession in an unjust social universe circulates through the texts of the Indian Cycle and is a recurrent theme in Duras's writing.

Like Jacques Hold, Peter Morgan is a narrator who writes a madwoman's story as a gesture of appropriation. With her pain he will be initiated into the pain of Calcutta. "Peter Morgan est un jeune homme qui désire prendre la douleur de Calcutta, s'y jeter, que ce soit fait, et que son ignorance cesse avec la douleur prise" (29). (Peter Morgan is a young man who wishes to partake of Calcutta's suffering, to throw himself into it, that it be done and that his ignorance cease with the possession of pain.) Hold revels in the suffering of the Indias, as he claims the others do. "Je m'exalte sur la douleur aux Indes. Nous le faisons tous plus ou moins, non? On ne peut parler de cette douleur que si on assure sa respiration en nous . . . Je prends des notes imaginaires sur cette femme.—Pourquoi elle?—Rien ne peut plus lui arriver la lèpre elle-même . . ." (157). ("I exalt in the suffering in the Indias. We all do more or less, don't we? We cannot speak of this suffering unless we are sure that it breathes in us. I am taking imaginary notes on this woman." "Why her?" "Because nothing more can happen to her, leprosy itself.") This framed narrative would be his initiation.

The beggar-woman is the perfect subject for Morgan. She embodies the suffering of India; her madness defines an end-point for suffering. She is someone to whom nothing more can happen. Moreover, she will never dispute Morgan's version of her biography for she no longer speaks. Her only language is the chant of her exile and madness, the single sound, Battambang. If Peter Morgan has free reign to represent her exile and madness, he must supply a language that she herself no longer possesses, and this language, like the imagination that Morgan must also employ, can be none other than his own. The act of narration, then, the male story of a madwoman's road to her madness, is less an enterprise of representation than one of pure fabrication and substitution. In the place of biography is the bios of the writer; the writer's desire shapes what has lost its form, resubjectifies the subjectless. "Peter Morgan voudrait maintenant substituer à la mémoire abolie de la mendiante le bric-à-brac de la sienne. Peter Morgan se trouverait, sans cela, à cours de paroles pour rendre compte de la folie de la mendiante de Calcutta" (73). (Peter Morgan would now like to substitute the bric-a-brac of his memory for her destroyed memory. Without this, Peter Morgan would find himself short of the words to describe the madness of the beggar-woman of Calcutta.)

Typically, Duras places a male character in the role of a narrator who imposes a narrative form on a woman's abolished memory and paralyzed imagination. The female subject is absent from these biographies, which the male narrator misreads. Morgan does not write his story as an effort to cure the beggar-woman, as did Jacques Hold, nor to possess her in the sense that Lui tried to possess Elle, but to cure himself of his ignorance. And he will reiterate the abandonment of his subject, the abandonment with which Duras's narrators characteristically meet their own limits and which, here, echoes the mother's gesture. For if he can describe her filth, her excesses, her past, her trail of dead and abandoned children, he abuts the onset of her madness. "Je l'abandonnerai avant la folie, dit Peter Morgan, ça c'est sûr, mais j'ai quand même besoin de connaître cette folie" (183). (I will abandon her before madness, says Peter Morgan, that is certain, but I nonetheless need to know this madness.) Unlike Hold, Morgan refuses to be fascinated by his subject. He imposes a narration on the trauma of madness and suffering, which is not narratable. His fiction-making activity is a bald gesture. His language and his reason supplant that which has been destroyed.

Michael Richard, Stretter's lover, claims to understand Morgan's fiction and his narrative narcissism. "Je crois que ce qu'il [Richard] veut dire, dit Michael Richard, c'est plus encore, il voudrait ne lui donner d'existence que dans celui qui la regarderait vivre. Elle, elle ne ressent rien" (182). (I believe that what he means, says Michael Richard, is even more, he wants her to exist only in the person who would watch her live. She, she does not feel anything.) For Morgan, according to Hold, the insensible beggar-woman comes to life only insofar as a spectator sees her. "Elle serait à Calcutta comme un . . . point au bout d'une longue ligne, de faits sans signification différenciée? Il n'y aurait que . . . sommeils, faims, disparition des sentiments, et aussi du lien entre la cause et l'effet?" (182). (In Calcutta, she would be something like a . . . point at the end of a long line, of events without any differentiated significance? There would only be . . . sleep, hunger, the disappearance of feelings, and also of the link between cause and effect?) If Morgan acknowledges his own limits and refuses to follow his heroine into her madness, Charles Rosset is less well able to sustain a distance between this mad siren and himself.

Charles Rossett pursues his own version of a rite of passage by facing head-on this cohabitant of sweltering Calcutta. He does so with fascination and horror. At the river where she washes herself and eats, he watches her. She plays to her audience, decapitates a live fish, and offers it to Rossett.[6] Like Morgan, who cannot tolerate the tale of the woman's madness, Rossett discovers that the sight of a woman's madness is more than he can bear. Veritable medusa. "La folie, je ne la supporte pas, c'est plus fort que moi, je ne peux pas . . . le regard des fous, je ne le supporte pas . . . tout mais la folie . . . ." (206). (Madness, I cannot stand it, it is stronger than me, I cannot . . . the look of a madperson, I cannot stand it . . . everything but madness.) This feminine spectacle of madness horrifies and fascinates, intolerable spectacle of the madwoman.

If the first half of the novel focuses on the tale of the beggar-woman and finishes the story of her madness, the second half focuses on the co-star of the feminine constellation, Anne-Marie Stretter. Stretter and the beggar-woman are linked. They are said to share the secret of suffering. Stretter suffers. "Elle sait qu'ils sont là, tout près, sans doute, les hommes de Calcutta, elle ne bouge pas du tout, si elle le faisait . . . non . . . elle donne le sentiment d'être maintenant prisonière d'une douleur trop ancienne pour être encore pleurée" (198). (She knows that they are there, near, without doubt, the men of Calcutta, she does not move at all, were she to . . . no . . . she gives the impression now of being a prisoner of suffering too old to cry about still.) Her acclimation to India has never been complete for when she traveled up the Mekong toward Savannakhet to meet M. Stretter near the Laotian border seventeen years ago, she fell ill. Her husband feared that she was unable to bear the suffering of India. It was during that trip that Stretter caught sight of a beggar-woman selling her child. She told this story to Morgan. This is their second link.

Music is the shared language of the feminine characters. Like the beggar-woman whose only language is her song, Stretter's Venetian dialect inflects her voice and overpowers the sense of what she says. "Charles Rosett perd le fil de ce qu'elle dit, il se met à l'entendre sans l'écouter—la voix, de cette façon, a des inflexions italiennes qu'il découvre" (191). (Charles Rosett loses the train of what she is saying, he begins to hear her without listening to her—her voice, in this fashion, has Italian intonations which he discovers.) Stretter was a musician, a talented pianist, the very hope of Venice. Her lover, Michael Richard, an English tourist in Calcutta, was on the verge of leaving India when he chanced to hear Stretter's piano playing from the street outside her residence. Soothed and intrigued, he listened for several evenings before entering the guarded house to meet her. Language and music are two poles, the one of signification and the other of passion, abolished memory, and suffering. The beggar-woman stands at one end of the spectrum; Stretter straddles the two.

Stretter and the beggar-woman are paired by their sexuality. Stretter is an easy woman who inflames the desire of those around her where the beggar-woman has been punished because of her extramarital pregnancy. And typical of Duras's work, feminine sexuality is never evoked without some accompanying violence. Both characters incite real or imagined physical violence. With respect to Stretter, violence occurs at the level of taletelling, erupting systematically into the visual field. One example involving Charles Rossett situates the intersection between perception and fantasy at the periphery of sadism. This imagined scene carries the mark of fantasy, for it is imagined as perceived by Michael Richard.

L'image lui revient d'Anne-Marie Stretter droite sous le ventilateur—dans le ciel de ses larmes, dit le vice-consul, puis tout à coup l'autre image. Il voudrait l'avoir fait. Quoi? Qu'il voudrait, ah, avoir dressé sa main. . . . Sa main se dresse, retombe, commence à caresser le visage, les lèvres, doucement d'abord puis de plus en plus sèchement, puis de plus en plus fort, les dents sont offertes dans un rire disgracieux, pénible, le visage se met le plus possible à la portée de la main, il se met à sa disposition entière, elle se laisse faire, il crie en frappant: qu'elle ne pleure plus jamais, jamais, plus jamais; on dirait qu'elle commence à perdre la mémoire. . . . Michael Richard les regardait. (202).

The image of Anne-Marie Stretter erect beneath the fan comes back to him—in the heaven of her tears, says the vice-consul—then suddenly the other image. He would have wanted to do it. What? That he would have wanted, ah, to have raised his hand. His hand is raised, falls, begins to caress the face, the lips, softly at first then more and more briskly, then more and more strongly, the teeth are bared in an unflattering smile, painful, the face puts itself as much as possible within reach of the hand, it offers itself completely to him, she is passive, he yells while striking: that she never never cry again; she appears to begin to lose her memory. Michael Richard was watching them.

At the ambassadorial reception, Rossett again watches Stretter. The intensity of his gaze appears to immobilize her and Rossett imagines this initiate into the pain of India as dead. Vision or fantasy?

Il la regarde longuement, elle s'en aperçoit, s'étonne, se tait, mais il continue à la regarder jusqu'à la dèfaire, jusqu'à la voir assise à se taire avec les trous de ses yeux dans son cadavre au milieu de Venise, Venise de laquelle elle est partie et à laquelle elle est rendue, instruite de l'existence de la douleur. (191)

He looks at her for a long time, she becomes aware of it, is surprised, stops talking, but he continues to look at her to the point of undoing her, to the point of seeing her sitting, having stopped talking, with the cavities of her eyes in her cadaver in the middle of Venice, Venice from which she left and to which she returned, instructed in the existence of suffering.

Stretter, like the beggar-woman whose madness Rossett is unable to contemplate, generates a violent fantasy as she becomes the spectacular object of a male gaze. Anne-Marie Stretter. Aging but still strikingly beautiful, attentive to her two daughters, the elder of whom already resembles her, indulged by her husband and attended to by a coterie of indolent and properly dressed international bureaucrats and businessmen who gather around her at the French Embassy, she remains the mesmerizing center of the Indian Cycle. "Elle est plate, légère, elle a la rectitude simple d'une morte" (197). (She is flat, light, she has the simple rectitude of a corpse.) Stretter, siren of death.

The eponymous vice-consul of the novel is an unusual male character in Duras's universe. Like the beggar-woman, he is a figure of exclusion and incomprehension whose inability to adapt to the misery of India results in his eventual ostracism. Jean-Marc de H. is more properly the ex-vice-consul of Lahore. He has been removed from his post for having shot at lepers at night in the gardens of Shalimar. M. Stretter and his staff pore over his files hoping to find something in his dossier to explain his behavior. They find few details in his biography: educational successes, his parents' deaths, juvenile escapades, none provide insight into his actions in Lahore. Duras mocks the would-be psychologists in search of a larval state of madness and suggests, moreover, that biography is fundamentally a fiction with little power to illuminate and much less to cure.

Despite his momentary lapse, the vice-consul remains perfectly cordial and able to sustain polite conversations with other members of white Calcutta. Even if, as Morgan claims, white Calcutta would participate in the suffering of India, the character that has partaken of that suffering becomes as incomprehensible as the suffering itself. The Europeans cannot assimilate the vice-consul any more than the suffering of India, or the beggar-woman's madness.

Like most of the other male characters, and despite the noteworthy absence of other feminine liaisons, Jean-Marc de H. conceives a special sympathy for Anne-Marie Stretter. He would be initiated into passion by her. This passion has no language. "Parce que j'ai l'impression que si j'essayais de vous dire ce que j'aimerais arriver à vous dire, tout s'en irait en poussière . . .—il tremble—, les mots pour vous dire, à vous, les mots . . . de moi . . . pour vous dire à vous, ils n'existent pas. Je me tromperais, j'emploierais ceux . . . pour dire autre chose . . . une chose arrivée à un autre" (125). (Because I have the impression that if I were to try to tell you what I would like to be able to say to you, everything would dissolve in dust . . .—he trembles—, the words to tell you, you, the words . . . from me . . . to tell you, you, the words do not exist. I would make a mistake, I would use words . . . to say something else . . . something which happened to someone else.) Exiled in this passion, mistrustful of language at the frontiers of passion, he will not be invited into Stretter's circle. Rather, she offers him a geographical metaphor of trauma. "Je crois qu'il faut que vous pensiez à une chose c'est que, parfois . . . une catastrophe peut éclater en un lieu très lointain de celui où elle aurait dû se produire . . . vous savez, ces explosions dans la terre qui font monter la mer à des centaines de kilomètres de l'endroit où elles se sont produites . . ." (129). (I believe that you must think of something, which is that sometimes . . . a catastrophe can explode at a great distance from the place where it should have exploded . . . you know, these explosions in the earth which make the sea rise up at several hundreds of kilometers from the place where the explosions happened.) The vice-consul responds to his rejection with a yell, a language of suffering that is not language.

Not surprisingly, the tale of two exiles finishes inconclusively. Typical of the Indian Cycle texts, the novel that recounts the mesmerizing power of the feminine and charts the inability of language to imagine its own limits opens into a visual form, a film. Just as Duras plays with the boundaries of narration, fiction, and fantasy, and with the borders of memory and language in *Le Vice-consul,* she complicates these relationships in *India Song* in terms proper to cinema; the new narrative regions she explores thwart traditional definitions of time and space.[7]

INDIA SONG

In a typically elliptical remark about the nature of the cinematic medium, Duras claims that the camera writes more completely than the pen.

> En somme, oui, ça pose la question du cinéma, là, de l'image. On est toujours débordé par l'écrit, par le langage, quand on traduit en écrit, n'est-ce-pas; ce n'est pas possible de tout rendre, de rendre compte du tout. Alors que dans l'image vous écrivez tout à fait, tout l'espace filmée est écrit, c'est au centuple l'espace du livre. Mais je n'ai découvert ça qu'avec *La Femme du Gange,* pas avec les autre films.[8]

> To sum up, yes, it raises the question of the cinema, there, of the image. One is always overwhelmed by writing, by language, when you translate into writing, right; it is not possible to render everything, to take everything into account. Whereas in the image you write completely, all of the filmed space is written. But I only realized that with *La Femme du Gange,* not with the other films.

Duras gives much attention here, and she is not the only one, to the image, the filmed space. For if *India Song* has attracted no small amount of interest in certain circles, it is in large measure due to the formal pyrotechnics of splitting sound and visuals. This technique was used already in *Hiroshima, mon amour.* Later, Duras experimented on her own with the relationship between sight and sound in *La Femme du Gange,* the film that made *India Song* possible. "En réalité, *India Song* est consécutif de *La Femme du Gange.* Si *La Femme du Gange* n'avait pas été écrit, *India Song* ne l'aurait pas été."[9] (In fact, *India Song* follows *La Femme du Gange.* If *La Femme du Gange* hadn't been written, *India Song* would not have been.) Duras claims that the sound track is completely independent of the sounds and images in *La Femme du Gange,* and that she maintains this disjunction in *India Song.*

> *La Femme du Gange,* c'est deux films: le film de l'image et le film des voix, les deux films sont là, d'une totale autonomie, liés seulement, mais inexorablement, par une concomitance matérielle. . . . Les voix parlent dans le même lieu que celui du tournage du film de l'image, mais pas dans la partie de ce lieu retenu par la caméra. Elles se parlent. Elles ignorent la présence du spectateur. Il ne s'agit donc pas d'un commentaire. Ce ne sont pas non plus des voix off,

dans l'acceptation habituelle du mot: elles ne facilitent pas le déroulement du film . . . elles l'entravent.[10]

La Femme du Gange is two films, the film of the images and the film of the voices, the two are there, completely autonomous but tied together, inexorably, by a material concomitance. The voices speak in the same place in which the shooting occurs, but not in the same space where the camera focuses. They speak to each other. They ignore the presence of the spectator. It is therefore not a question of a commentary. These are not off voices, either, in the traditional sense of the word, they do not facilitate the film's unfolding, they create obstacles for it.

Are the visuals really independent of the sound track? There is some debate around this question and persuasive claims for a relationship of montage rather than radical disjunction.[11] And as we shall see, this question raises the other, familiar one, of images and narration. But before entering into that debate and exploring the film, it is important to clarify the terminology. What is a *voice off*, in the traditional meaning of the term? How and to what end does Duras pose her challenge? To answer requires some appreciation of the traditional relationship of sound to image from which Duras departs, that of classic narrative cinema.

On and Off: Sounds and Images

On and off sound are defined in terms of the image.[12] The visibility or invisibility of the sound source at the moment of the sound's perception defines on and off, respectively. Light is projected through a dark space and reflected onto a flat screen where it is interpreted as a piece of a diegetic universe extending beyond the boundaries of the screen. Sound can support the illusion of a completely visible diegetic universe, and it can rupture it, making palpably clear that something is beyond vision, and may never be visible.[13] Sounds seem to come from some part of either the visible images (on) or the invisible (off) part of the diegesis. But on and off inadequately differentiates that category of sounds emanating from somewhere other than the diegetic universe.[14]

Michel Chion, one of the best writers on the subject, proposes three terms for describing the relationship of sound sources and images, hoping to account for sounds independent of the diegetic universe. These are off, off screen (hors champ) and in.[15] In the first two cases, the sound source is not visible. The source of off sound is located in another time and space (voice-over or movie music, for example) while an off screen sound source belongs to the diegesis but is temporarily out of sight. Chion calls off and off screen sounds acousmatic. He maintains the traditional definition of in—a sound whose source is visible on screen. Beyond clarifying the terminology, Chion explores the analogies between sound and image, and develops the notion of an aural equivalent of point of view, or point d'écoute. Not only does he ask "where do the sounds come from?" but also, "who listens?"[16] Who listens raises the question of identification. Where point of view provides a visual vehicle for spectatorial identification, the point d'écoute—hearing something that a character hears, or does not—aurally determines a spectator's identification. Chion's analogy between the processes of identification set in place by an image and sound is intriguing. But, he argues, the analogy between theoretical tools for describing images and sounds falters when it comes to the material supports. We can say that the screen is the place where we see the images, but how do we define the place of sound? Sounds come from the speakers which diffuse them, and give a variety of impressions of localization, depending on the technology of the sound system.

Sound has always been a troublesome element for this relatively new art form.[17] From its inception, cinema has been conceived of as a visual medium. The bias remains, even today, and is responsible, in part, for the relative theoretical inattention accorded the phenomenon of sound in the movies.[18] History and technology are one part of the picture; the camera could record images and a projector reproduce them before appropriate sound recording and reproducing instruments were developed. As of the late 1920s, sounds could be recorded and reproduced while the visuals were projected. When the technology was in place, sound changed the nature of the movies. Early filmmakers and theoreticians, in one of the most important polemics in the history of film, heatedly debated the consequences of allowing images to talk synchronously.[19] The argument raged around the status of the image and, consequently, around the nature of the art form itself. Including sound in a fundamentally visual medium would reduce it to little more than filmed theatre, some argued. Language would subjugate images that would thus be relegated to the status of illustrations. Dialogue would be in the ascendancy.

If sound changed the nature of the art form, synchronized sound changed the nature of cinematic realism. The simultaneity of a sound with the visibility of its source reinforces the illusion that the screen image is a real, complete world. Visibly moving lips and slamming doors, accompanied by audible voices and slamming sounds, better help the spectator penetrate the space of the fiction. The sound-space relationship is a crucial one in the creation of the cinematic illusion. Crucial as well for cinematic pleasure, without which a filmgoer would probably not pay good money to go to the movies.

Today's filmgoer is a sophisticated consumer of films, familiar with the technology by which images and sounds are recorded, edited, reconfigured and projected.[20] Notwithstanding his understanding of the operation of the illusion, the spectator willingly relinquishes critical distance to be absorbed by a film. Absorption is pleasurable, and accepting the three dimensionality of the world projected onto the flat screen is the first gesture toward it.[21] If pleasure is a motive for yielding to the filmic illusion, the vehicle is identification. Identification was recognized early on as a particularly powerful effect of this art form.[22] More than a simple identification between viewer and camera, several levels of identification between spectator and spectacle are possible.[23] The pleasure of spectatorial identification is complex.[24] The spectator identifies with the image and pleasure waxes. Complete absorption would be intolerable, however, for the film over, the illusion ended, where would the spectator be? Thus, displeasure and denial follow. The illusion is recognized as such and critical distance reestablished. For spectatorial pleasure to be preserved and jouissance held at bay, the illusion must be denied and the impression maintained that identification can be arrested by an act of will. The fiction can thus function and the pleasure of identification enjoyed and contained in the oscillation between spectatorial absorption and denial.[25]

That spectatorial pleasure arises from an illusory identification with an image has provoked some comparison with the mirror phase.[26] But, as Metz has pointed out, the screen is not a mirror and the spectator's body will never be reflected there. Cinematic identification has been decried by some as voycurism. Feminists have noted that the image offered for visual consumption is often one of the female body. The spectator, regardless of gender, thus identifies the camera as a male gaze and identifies with this gaze. The complex processes at work of identification and denial at the cinema, and the pleasure of watching a scene unwatched, have linked the magic of the movies to the process of sexual differentiation.[27] Laura Mulvey has argued persuasively that the particular power of the cinematic image to induce spectatorial identification, and its strong form of fascination, inheres in its evocation or recapitulation of earlier, psychological structures.[28] Indeed, this is suggested elsewhere in Mannoni's elegant argument about the comic illusion.[29]

Classic narrative cinema possesses a number of techniques designed to preserve spectatorial identification undisturbed. The necessarily fragmentary diegetic universe—fragmented as much by the screen and camera as by sounds coming from off screen—is palliated by a number of shooting techniques. Nothing on screen accuses the spectator in his role as spectator. Shot-reverse shots suture the spaces of the diegesis. A travelling camera can similarly appear to aggregate the pieces of the diegetic universe. Deep focus, favored by Bazin because it allows the spectator to penetrate into the depth of the image and explore it, uses time as an ally in creating the illusion of a coherent, homogenous world even beyond the screen. The conventions of classic narrative cinema have established the norm.

Duras does not respect these conventions. She refuses to make narrative cinema. She uses sound and shooting techniques to confuse time and space rather than support any illusion of reality. The image-sound relationship disrupts the spatial and temporal signposts in the service of the illusion. The new narrative regions into which she casts her characters resist easy denomination by traditional narrative designations. The sounds of *India Song,* including more or less audible human voices in several languages, animals, rain, tides, and music, are a mixture of acousmatic and off. But they occupy an ambiguous space off, off screen, temporally elsewhere. Ambiguous, but not, as Duras claims, radically off and disjunctive. On more than one occasion, the images seem to be commented upon by the voices. The voices of visible characters seem to be audible on the sound track even if no lips move visibly. Despite her claim of independent sounds and images, Duras's images appear to fascinate the voices. The visual cues instruct us to understand the images as nostalgic rather than representational; where is this visible space located? From where and in what time frame do the voices speak? No synopsis or discussion of this film can ignore its formal pyrotechnics. These formal experiments notwithstanding, Duras's films alternately absorb and bore the spectator. She does not escape—and rather, invites—the spectatorial fascination inherent in this art form.

India Song has been described as a film in the nostalgic mode; the images are silent, the languorous and sole feminine center of male attention is treated like a Hollywood star, the cast is dressed in evening wear of the late 1930s.[30] Everything is calculated to enrapture. The cast of characters is penetrated by an odd air of distraction, the result of hearing the sound track played while the cameras were turning. This simple, material fact would argue for Duras's claim of an independent sound track. Separation is a technical reality, but the relationship of sound track and images creates a montage effect. To argue for a radical disjunction is to ignore that the images constitute a "foyer de fascination" for the spectator as well as for the voices on the sound track.

Synopsis and Segmentation

Segmentations of this film rely on the sound track. The most scrupulously detailed of these divides *India Song* into prologue, story, and epilogue, according to the voice changes.[31] The prologue, dominated by women's voices, opens on a sun slowly setting over a green, rolling landscape. A female voice singing in Laotian laughs. Two young female voices begin a dialogue while the song's audibility fades. Off space is immediately stratified; the single voice and the couple's voices seem not to occupy the same space. The couple speaks about a beggar-woman from Savannakhet. Voice 1: "Une mendiante," and Voice 2: "Folle." They remember her story: Voice 2: "Ah! oui, je me souviens. Elle se tient au bord des fleuves. Elle vient de Birmanie." Voice 1: "Elle n'est pas indienne. Elle vient de Savannakhet. Née là-bas." ("A beggar-woman." "Mad." "Ah, yes, I recall. She keeps to the river banks. She comes from Birmanie." "She is not Indian. She comes from Savannakhet. Born there.") We take the singing and laughter suddenly to be those of the beggar-woman, relegated to an indeterminate past whose relationship with the voices is unclear. Is she audible to them? Remembered by them? The beggar-woman is linked to Anne-Marie Stretter and Calcutta. The two voices recount their story in the past tense. "A Calcutta, elles étaient ensemble," Voice 1 says. "La Blanche et l'autre?" ("In Calcutta they were together." "The white woman and the other one?") The immobile camera continues to frame the setting sun. The sounds change and a piano plays a song that becomes the theme. What is the source of the piano music? Is it off or off screen? Does it occupy the same space or time as the voices or the beggar-woman? Again, off space thickens as the piano music marks a shift in images. In an interior shot, a turbaned servant places flowers next to a photo of a young woman (one of at least three photos by Boubard shown atop the piano). The immobile camera frames the piano and flowers, and incense slowly wafts through the still image. We follow the servant in the mirror as he retreats and exits into reflected contiguous space, rear left into the penumbra, his path marked by the lit candle he carries. The somber image prepares us for the announcement that Stretter is dead and the piano and photo take on the significance of an altar. A slow, close-up pan of a dress, jewels, and wig follows. The voices recall Lol and the ball and recall, as well, that Stretter ravished Lol of her lover.

> V1: Michael Richardson était fiancé à une jeune fille de S. Tahla, Lola Valérie Stein. . . .
>
> V2: Le mariage devait avoir lieu à l'automne. Puis il y a eu ce bal . . . ce bal de S. Tahla.
>
> V1: Elle était arrivée tard à ce bal . . . au milieu de la nuit . . . habillée de noir. . . .
>
> V2: Que d'amour ce bal, que de désir. . . .

> V1: Michael Richardson was engaged to a young girl from S. Tahla, Lola Valérie Stein. . . .
>
> V2: The marriage was supposed to take place in the fall. Then there was this ball . . . this ball of Tahla.
>
> V1: She came to the ball late . . . in the middle of the night . . . dressed in black. . . .
>
> V2: Such love this ball, such desire. . . .

The voices comment on the light, the monsoon, the dust, and the smell of leprosy in Calcutta. "Où est-on?" ("Where are we?") asks Voice 2. Excellent and appropriate question posed in the present tense and to which the image seems to respond. A scaling château comes on screen. A voice intones. "L'Ambassade de France aux Indes." The camera penetrates (into what is, in fact, another château) and a voice asks: "De quoi avez-vous peur?" a pan left stops on a photo of a young woman. Stretter's name is pronounced. How else to understand the image than as one of Stretter? "Morte là-bas aux îles. Trou-vée morte." ("Dead there, in the islands. Found dead.") Simple sentences follow. The voices shift to a past tense, and then, in a characteristically Durasian move, to the present tense. "Ils dansaient." ("They were dancing." "They are dancing.") In the counterpoint, the image shifts. A male character, back to a mirror, watches a couple, reflected in a mirror, dancing. Stretter? Despite the photo, despite the announcement of her death, the images incarnate the name. Inevitably Stretter. The couple stops. All three characters slowly leave the room. In a long shot, we see a sole male character. The name of the vice-consul is pronounced. Virtually the entire cast of characters from *Le Vice-consul* has appeared or been named in this prologue. The voices's reference to Lol Stein broadens the time frame and geography of the novel.

Loud music opens the second part of the film, the story. Dance tunes seem to emanate from the space of the visuals. "Avant, il y a ceu ce bal." ("Before, there was this ball.") The story concerns the ambassadorial reception at which the vice-consul will make his desire known to Stretter and she will dance with her various admirers. The feminine voices of the prologue remain audible. A number of new voices (including those of the actors on screen and Duras herself) become audible. Occasional sentence fragments stand out clearly against more muffled background voices. The theme song and rhumba (by Carlo Alessio) as well as Beethoven's Diabelli Variations are audible at well-paced intervals.

The transition from the story to the epilogue is not as aurally evident as that from prologue to story. A very long shot (almost six minutes) of five immobile characters opens the third part of the film, and the voices tell us that we are in the islands. Stretter and her coterie plus one sojourn at the Prince of Wales Hotel. A light intensifies, dims, and intensifies again as the voices speak in the present tense. "Ici" punctuates their conversation as if they were cohabitants of in space. The news of Stretter's suicide concludes the epilogue. In the final shots we see Stretter alone in a darkened room. She rises and exits through French doors rear left, her red hair haloed by the light. After the voices have spoken of the lovers' pact of a double suicide, they recount her drowning, and the subsequent discovery of her peignoir, found washed ashore. The final shots pan a French map of Indochina while the beggar-woman's song and laugh are again audible.

The space of the film, like the space and temporality of the voices, is stratified. On and off screen together occupy the screen thanks to mirrors. For example, in Shot 7 the camera focuses on a clock atop a mirrored mantle. The mirror reflects a second off-screen mirror obliquely, whose reflection we see. An infinite regression of chandeliers appears in this contiguous, virtual space. Duras projects her characters into this new narrative region, illusory, repetitive and insistently imaginary.

The interplay of voice and image challenge traditional narrative. Not because they are radically separate, but because they are ambiguously linked.

The voices seem to converge on the images, drawn to them. As if demonstrating the lesson of *Le Ravissement de Lol V. Stein,* the female voices of the prologue are contaminated by their storytelling. Fascinated, they reiterate the mortal passions of the ball whose drama they intone. When Voice 1 asks: "Sur quoi pleurezvous?" Voice 2 answers: "Je vous aime jusqu'à ne plus voir, ne plus entendre, mourir." (1: "What are you crying about?" 2: "I love you to the point of blindness, deafness, death.") Narrator or player in the drama? Narrative frontiers are blurred.

Numerous examples of the sound-image relationship suggest that rather than rupture, there is, as Ropars insists, montage between sound track and images. "De quoi avez-vous peur?" is answered with a shot of a photograph and the name, "Anne-Marie Stretter." Characters at the reception dance in time to the music. Similarly, and also at the reception, we see Stretter and Rossett and Stretter and the vice-consul. Lips unmoving, the characters seem nonetheless to be speaking because we hear a conversation between them. The montage is persuasive. So too is the image of the vice-consul's departure and his audible screams. Verb tenses, adverbs, voice changes, counterpoint of question and (visual) answer, souvenirs serving as narrative commentary, all these strongly suggest a montage of image and sound track. The difficulty of the temporal relationships between images and voices or sounds, however, remains. The images suggest that they are reflections of a past, but how past with respect to the sounds? The voices are audible but their relative temporality stratifies off screen space and time and skews, at moments, the temporality of on screen images. The desire of the voices to wrest the story from the past inflects the film with a palpable nostalgia.[32] The melancholic mode and peculiar space of the on and reflected images, the stratified temporality of the voices, the immobile camera, all these constitute an arsenal in the service of non-narrative, non-representational cinema. Taken together with the delectation in framing, this use of image and sound reflects a fantasmatic activity. At its center, the disruptive and fascinating character of Anne-Marie Stretter.

Fantasme . . . scénario imaginaire où le sujet est présent et qui figure, de façon plus ou moins déformé par les processus défensifs, l'accomplissement d'un désir inconscient.[33]

Fantasy . . . an imagined scene in which the subject is present and in which an unconscious desire, more or less transfigured by the defenses, is realized.

La fascination du récit fantasmatique . . . le récit-cadre celui qui, comme le cinématographe, change sans cesse de point de vue . . . rend impossible la localisation de l'énonciation: qui voit, qui regarde?[34]

The fascination of a fantasmatic tale . . . the story-frame that, like the cinematographer, ceaselessly changes point of view . . . rendering the localization of the enunciation impossible: who speaks? who is looking?

Mirrored Space

At the center of the Indian Cycle and often literally at the center of the images in *India Song,* Anne-Marie Stretter exerts a powerful visual fascination. At the same time, she figures a resistance to narrative representation. Object and figure of a properly fantasmatic structure at once within the diegesis and for Duras herself, Stretter is a character of excessive powers.[35] The following stills suggest that the mirrored space in which Stretter's image is doubled, introduces into the already illusionistic space of the frame, an off screen, adjacent space that is visible and visibly a fiction. Often framed in the mirror or in doorways or by other characters, Stretter draws characters and camera toward her, organizes gazes and disrupts spatial frontiers. She arrests movement, but explodes representation.[36]

A photograph elicits the name Stretter. We see Delphine Seyrig, well-known star of French cinema. Seyrig becomes Stretter. First appearing in shot 9 dancing with Michael Richardson, she and her partner are observed by a spectator leaning against the mirror, his back to his reflection. We understand that he is watching the couple dance before him even if they are reflected behind him in the mirror. Its edge is discernible to the spectator's left. Anne-Marie Stretter stands between the two men, the object of gazes (the camera's, the spectator's, the film spectator's). But what is the status of this scene? Where is the couple? In contiguous, reflected off screen space or in a space imagined by the spectator? Are they remembered? By whom? From whose point of view is this shot organized? The status of the image with its double frames of screen and mirror, recalls that of the ball scene in *Le Ravissement de Lol V. Stein;* unattributable, indistinguishably fantasy or fiction, an insistent scene that figures itself, a scene in which a spectator, unobserved, is observed observing.[37]

Shot 69 is a variant of Shot 9. Stretter appears on screen with another male character while Michael Richardson sits to the right in the same space, his back to a small mirror. The mirror obliquely reflects some piece of the space to the left of the couple. Richardson sits on the ledge, framed by the embrasure, looking away from the couple. At the center of the image, Anne-Marie Stretter sutures on and off. She looks at the other man who embraces her, both reflected and beheld by Richardson. Our gaze is relayed by his as, immobile, he looks ahead, apparently into the contiguous space whose reflection we see on. The complexity of the image, the relay of gazes, and the multiplicity of frames are set in motion by Stretter.

Shot 18 is a veritable explosion of spaces and frames. The camera, posed at a slight oblique to the mirror, reflects the room with the piano in which entries and exits proliferate. It is only when Stretter, dressed in a black peignoir, traverses the image from off screen that we understand that we are watching reflected space. This is a peculiar space, contiguous to and extending on space, it is both on and elsewhere. Stretter's space. She moves in front of the mirror laterally while penetrating the deep space reflected in the mirror at the center of the frame. These spacial ambiguities trouble temporal correlatives. Stretter's reflection precedes her entry; when she enters the frame, the shot is reassessed. Stretter plays with frames, eluding and multiplying them, disrupting clear spatial and temporal boundaries, confusing point of view, making its localization impossible.

When we see Shot 39, we hear characters speaking without seeing their lips move. Stretter stands obliquely to a mirror, her reflection at the center of the image, between her and the male character. Stretter is doubled, reflected, she occupies an ambiguous space. The dance scene that follows pays tribute to the fantasy of the ball. The couple observed by the spectator, observed by the mirror, inhabits an illusionistic space dislocated by its multiplication. Like the multiplication of Lol's fantasy, this scene figures an internal duplication. The mirror deepens space and Duras projects the dance into that fantasmatic and fascinating territory of illusory, elusory repetition.

Over ten minutes long, Shot 52 is one of the longest and most elaborate of the mirror shots. It beautifully demonstrates the seduction of illusionistic space and the derealization of "real" characters. Stretter has entered from the right and is looking to the right. Only when we see her enter the space do we comprehend that we have been watching her advance from off to on space; her reflection, mistaken for her presence, is now doubled by it. As she turns, she averts her gaze and stands obliquely, shoulder left, to the mirror. She will continue to turn her back to the camera into the mirror as she watches the vice-consul approach.

The drama unfolds in the mirror (frame 1). We watch as Stretter watches as the vice-consul advances toward her reflection (4). The distance between them is never closed. Stretter retreats to a deeper space than that of the vice-consul (6), but not before the reflection has opened up an impossible space of encounter. Playing reflection against "real," making off screen on screen and conjoining it with an on that looks into the reflected off become on, multiplying reflections and exposing their seductive illusionism of the mirror, Duras demonstrates the disruptive fascination of Stretter. The character figures the gaze, fascinates the spectator by engaging him in a fantasmatic activity that is properly Duras's own.

Fascination and Fantasy: From Oeuvre to Biography

No other shibboleth is so often used to describe the effect of Duras's works on readers and filmgoers as the term *fascination*. Fascination is a theme and an effect with a performative dimension in Duras's texts. Characters are fascinated and fascinate each other, reader and spectator are similarly absorbed. Can this radicalized moment of an identificatory process lay bare an earlier and fundamental structuring moment of the subject? Isn't this fascination the measure of the fantasy text?

The Indian Cycle characters are fascinated and fascinating. Lol Stein, fascinated by Stretter who takes her lover and her place, is entirely dispossessed. For Lol, fascination is to be taken in the strongest sense, a question of identity, of the life and death of the subject. The beggar-woman, like Lol, is dispossessed by a mother figure, and her biographer is stopped in his tale by her horrifying madness. Unlike Lol's biographer this narrator is not enraptured. The beggar-woman evokes Stretter, the element of suture and the figuration of fascinating fantasy in the Indian Cycle.

Fantasy is a subject's interrogation of his or her biography.[38] Duras's fascination with Stretter begins in Indochina where Stretter, a woman she sees but never meets, becomes an idealized alternative to a mad mother. The image is fissured but Stretter remains a fascinating figure for Duras. Observed through the lens of Duras's biographical fascination, the Indian Cycle becomes a thematic and formal experimentation with the content and structure of fantasy as scene and text.[39]

Notes

1. "Il a fallu que je passe par Lol pour arriver à *India Song*." (I had to go through Lol to get to *India Song*.) "Couleur des Mots," Conversation avec Dominique Noguez following taped version of *India Song* published as a set of six films and accompanying commentary.
2. "Je l'ai fait se tuer pour m'en débarrasser." (I had her kill herself to rid myself of her.) Ibid.
3. Ropars-Wuilleumier, "Contretextes," p. 82.
4. On the sound track of *India Song,* the beggar-woman sings *Savannakhet* and not *Battambang.*
5. Théophano-Artémis Hatziforou, in "Présence de la voix: A propos de *L'Homme Atlantique* de M. Duras," observes that "A propos de M. Duras on n'a que trop souvent parlé de ravissement et de fascination: d'une écriture fascinée et fascinante. Quelque abusive qu'une telle attitude puisse paraître, elle trouve son explication dans une imprégnation sonore qui dépasse l'entendement immédiat, projetant les textes vers le supra ou l'infra-verbal . . . un texte oral." *Hors cadre* 6, pp. 94, 102.
(There has been too much discussion of ravishing and fascination, of a fascinated and fascinating style of writing style with respect to M. Duras. This excess can be explained by the total sonorousness of her work, which eludes immediate comprehension, projecting these texts toward a supra- or infra-verbal state—an oral text.)
6. See Marini's discussion of this scene in *Territoires du féminin.*
7. Published as a "texte théâtre film" in 1973, commissioned by Peter Hall for the British National Theatre, then later recorded for French radio and finally released as a film in 1975. See Duras and Gauthier, *Parleuses,* p. 185.
8. Duras and Porte, *Lieux,* p. 91.
9. Ibid.
10. Duras, *India Song,* p. 10.
11. "Ainsi découpée, l'éconciation verbale ne peut trouver de support diégétique à l'image. . . . Plus l'image se tait . . . plus l'attention se porte sur l'énoncé des voix, seule base

sémantique quand la représentation fait défaut. La tentation serait grande de conclure à une possible disjonction, et de suivre en cela les propositions mêmes de Duras. . . . Mais c'est là précisément que le sépartisme rencontre ses limites: qu'une même piste sonore puisse engendrer deux films radicalement différents ne désigne pas seulement la polysémie d'une bande-son capable de supporter deux types de lecture; la possibilité d'une telle représentation indique plus fortement que l'écriture du film détruit l'identité de la bande-son: plus le film s'écrit, plus la structuration filmique procède de l'articulation ménagée par la structure interne à ces énoncés, pour une bande-son montée, jamais de bande à part." *Le Texte Divisé,* pp. 140–41.

(Thus separated, the verbal enunciation is not supported by the image. As the image becomes increasingly silent, attention is increasingly accorded to what the voices say, the only semantic base when the representation falters. It would be tempting to argue for a possible disjunction, and to agree with Duras. But it is here that separatism encounters its limits: that a single sound track can generate two radically different films affirms the polysemism of a sound track capable of producing two types of readings; moreover, the possibility of such a representation reinforces the identity of the sound track. As the film is increasingly written, the filmic structuration increasingly moves toward an articulation overseen by the internal structure of what is said. For an articulated sound track, never an independent sound track.)

See also, Chion who argues that in "un film comme *India Song* . . . Marguerite Duras supprime presque complètement le son in tout en usant largement du son horse-champ: on n'entend parler les personnages qu'une fois qu'on les a vus sortir. Mais c'est ce 'presque' qui en fait toute la force. Apparemment, en effet, le film ne fait entendre que du son hors-champ (les voix des protagonistes sortis du cadre, l'orchestre invisible du bal de la réception à laquelle nous assistons)—ou bien du son off (d'autres voix qui parlent au pas) des personnages que nous voyons ou une musique de piano de Beethoven. Il y a cependant, au coeur du film, une illusion de son in quand on voit le couple d'Anne-Marie Stretter et du Vice-Consul qui danse lentement . . . et qui se parle. On pourrait presque croire voir remuer les lèvres mais il n'en est rien: les bouches et Delphine Seyrig et Michael Lonsdale, les acteurs, restent closes. On ne sait si l'on entend une conversation imaginaire ou télépathique, ou s'ils se sont dit ces choses-là ailleurs ou dans un autre temps. . . ." (Chion, *Son au Cinéma,* pp. 40–41.

(In a film such as *India Song* . . . Marguerite Duras suppresses in sound almost entirely while using a good deal of off screen sound: we hear characters speak once we have seen them leave the screen. But it is this "almost" which creates the effect. The film, apparently, only lets us hear off screen sound [the voices of the characters, outside the frame, the invisible orchestra at the ball of the reception which we see]—or off sound [other voices speaking in time] of characters we see or of piano music by Beethoven. There is, however, at the heart of the film, one illusion of sound in when we see Stretter and the vice-consul dancing slowly . . . and speaking to each other. We can practically believe that we see their lips moving, but it is not the case. The mouths of Delphine Seyrig and Michael Lonsdale, the actors, remain closed. We do not know if we are listening to an imaginary or telepathic conversation, or if they have spoken to each other elsewhere or in another time.)

12. "In a film, a sound is considered 'off' (literally off the screen) when in fact it is the sound's source that is off the screen, therefore an 'off screen voice' is defined as one which belongs to a character who does not appear (visually) on the screen. We tend to forget that a sound in itself is never 'off': either it is audible or it doesn't exist." Christian Metz, "Aural Objects," *Yale French Studies* 60 (1980): p. 29.

Michel Chion asserts that "*{J}amais le son en lui-même . . . servirait à situer le son, lequel est naturellement chose diffuse, mêlée, aux frontières indécises.* Nous conserverons donc, dans cette étude, des critères de localisation et de regroupement des sons choisis *en fonction de l'image et de ce qu'elle indique,* parce qu'il n'y en a pas d'autres possibles ou plutôt parce que le cinéma, c'est un jeu qui—même chez Godard, Duras ou Michaël Snow—se joue comme ça, par rapport à l'espace d'un écran investi comme lieu de pas-tout-voir." Chion, *Son au cinéma,* p. 30.

(*Sound in itself never situates the sound which is naturally diffuse, mixed, with unclear boundaries.* We will keep the criteria of localization and regrouping of sounds *as a function of the image and what it indicates,* because there are no other criteria or, rather, because cinema is a game that—even in Godard's, Duras's or Michael Snow's work—is played like that, with respect to the space of the screen invested as a place where not everything is seen.)

13.   Noel Burch, writing about the dialectic of on and off space in *Praxis du Cinéma,* explains the impossibility of their being simultaneously on screen—that is, the impossibility of the cinema's presenting a whole world. He refers to Bonitzer, *"Voici," Cahiers du cinéma* 273 (February 1977).

14.   "[T]ous ceux qui ont posé ou qui ont discuté cette distinction n'ont pas manqué de dire qu'elle était incomplète, et que la musique du film, par exemple, ou la voix-off du commentateur-narrateur n'ont pas le même statut que la musique du pianiste invisible qui est le voisin des personnages . . . ou que la voix du personnage que le changement d'axe de la caméra a rejeté en dehors du champ, mais non de l'action, et qui continue son discours." Chion, *Son au cinéma,* p. 32.

(Everyone who has raised or discussed this distinction has said that it was incomplete, and that film music or the voice-over of a narrator/commentator, for example, do not have the same status as the music of an invisible pianist who is next to the characters . . . or the voice of a character moved off screen by a different camera angle but still in in terms of the action, and who continues what he is saying.)

In *Praxis du Cinéma,* Burch introduces a temporal dimension by offering the terms imaginary and concrete to define a sound corresponding to an image which was once off, but easily imaginable as continguous to on space, and then on.

15.   "*Son hors-champ,* seulement celui *dont la cause n'est visible simultanément* dans l'image, *mais qui reste pour nous situé* imaginairement *dans le même temps que l'action montrée et dans un espace contigu à celui que montre le champ de l'image;* . . . *son off,* seulement celui qui *emane d'une source invisible située dans un autre temps et/ou un autre lieu* que l'action montrée dans l'image (musique du film, voix-off du narrateur racontant l'action au passé.) Ce qui, avec le son "in" dont nous conservons la définition courante, nous donne trois cas: un cas de son "visualise" et deux cas de son 'acousmatique'. . ." Ibid.

(Off-screen [hors-champ] sound is only that sound whose cause is not simultaneously visible in the image, but which remains, for us, imaginarily situated in the same time as the action we are seeing and in a space contiguous to the space shown in the field of the image; off sound, only that which emanates from an invisible source situated in another time and/or place than the action shown in the film [film music, voice over of the narrator telling the story in the past tense]. With in sound, whose generally accepted definition we retain, we have three cases: a case of visualized sound and two cases of acousmatic sound.)

16.   Ibid., chap. 3, "Le point d'écoute."

17.   Panofsky remarks that "film art is the only art the development of which men now living have witnessed from the very beginning." "Style and Medium in the Motion Pictures," p. 15.

18.   The literature exploring and theorizing the relationship between film and language, between films and novels, between filmic organization and linguistic structures, is extensive. Michel Marie puts it succinctly. "Aujourd'hui encore, alors que la parole est au centre de l'écriture filmique tant chez Marguerite Duras que chez Jean-Luc Godard, Jean-Marie Straub, elle garde toujours sa tache originelle, sa connotation impure au sein de l'idéologic critique envisagée globalement: le film, cela reste l'image." "Le Film, la parole et la langue," p. 69.

(Even today, where language is the center of filmic writing as much in the work of Marguerite Duras as that of Jean-Luc Godard and Jean-Marie Straub, it retains its original stain, its impure connotation, as the heart of a globally conceived critical ideology: film remains the image.)

19.   Eisenstein's statement, signed by Pudovkin and Kuleshov as well, strongly urged contrapuntal sound in order to preserve the integrity and hegemony of the image. "[E]very adhesion of sound to a visual montage piece increases its inertia as a montage piece, and increases the independence of its meaning. Only contrapuntal use of sound in relation to the visual montage piece will afford a new potentiality of montage development and perfection. The first experimental work with sound must be directed along the line of its distinct non-synchronization with the visual images." *Film Form*, p. 258.

20.   Jean-Louis Baudry describes this process of transformation, or work, as cinematographically specific, that is, as differentiating cinema from other systems of signification. See Baudry, "Ideological Effects of the Basic Cinematographic Apparatus."

21.   "S'il existe une idéologie de la représentation, à laquelle souscrirait en quelque sorte mécaniquement le cinéma, on pourrait en pointer le symptôme le plus radical et en même temps le plus inaperçu dans la disposition première qui fait de tout individu un spectateur, et qui consiste, au cinéma, d'abord à investir la surface de l'écran d'une fictive profondeur." Bonitzer, *Regard et la voix*, p. 9.

(If there is an ideology of representation to which cinema would mechanically subscribe, its most radical and least noticed symptom lies in the primary disposition which makes of every individual a spectator. At the cinema, this consists of initially investing the surface of the screen with a fictive depth.)

22.   "In the cinema the camera carries the spectator into the film picture itself. We are seeing everything from the inside as it were and are surrounded by the characters of the film. . . . Nothing like this 'identification' has ever occurred as the effect of any other system of art and it is here that the film manifests its absolute artistic novelty." Balázs, *Theory of the Film*, p. 48.

23.   "Le miroir est le lieu de l'identification primaire. L'identification au regard propre est secondaire . . . mais elle est fondatrice du cinéma et donc primaire lorsqu'on parle de lui: c'est proprement l'identification cinématographique primaire. . . . Quant aux identifications aux personnages avec elles-mêmes leurs différents niveaux (personnage hors-champ, etc.) ce sont les identifications cinématographiques secondaires, tertaires, etc.; si on les prend en bloc pour les opposer simplement à l'identification du spectateur à son regard, leur ensemble constitue, au singulier, l'identification cinématographique secondaire." Metz, *Signifiant imaginaire*, p. 79.

(The mirror is the site for primary identification. Identifying with a look is secondary . . . but it is a founding gesture when it comes to the cinema, and therefore primary. . . . Regarding identification with characters each with their different levels [off screen character, etc.] these are secondary, tertiary identifications, etc. If we take them as a whole to oppose them simply to the identification of a spectator with his own gaze, they constitute a secondary cinematographic identification.)

24.   "Ce 'recul' critique ressemble beaucoup à une défense contre 'l'impression de réalité,' contre la puissance d'assertion dont on crédite le cinéma. C'est une défense, dans la mesure où le geste en reste liée, et même aliène, à 'réalisme' du détail, du décor, etc. appuyant la 'vraisemblance' du récit, qui obsède le cinéma classique. . . . Le réel constitue la borne idéologique autour de laquelle tourne la critique, la lecture dévisée et bloquée, entre l'hésitation névrotique et le tourniquet fétichiste (le déni) où alternent les paradigmes du 'vrai' et du 'faux.' Cette alternance du 'judgement' de la lecture et de sa dérive, c'est à dire de sa productivité, définit sommairement le mécanisme de la captation spec(tac)ulaire; la 'prise de distance' est un moment nécessaire de la représentation, qui permet de prévoir, de tolérer et de maîtriser les chutes de 'crédibilité.'" Bonitzer, "Le hors-champ (Espace en défaut)." p. 15.

(This critical distance greatly resembles a defense against the "impression of reality," against the strength of assertion with which the cinema is credited. It is a defense insofar as the gesture is tied to and even alienates the "realism" of the detail, the decor, etc., emphasizing the "verisimilitude" of the tale which haunts classical cinema. The real is the ideological boundary around which the criticism turns, a reading divided between a neurotic hesitation and a fetichistic [denial] where paradigms of "true" and "false" alternate. This alternation of the "judgement" of the reading and its straying, that is to say, its productivity, summarily defines the mechanism of spec[tac]ular captation. Setting oneself at a distance is a necessary moment in the representation that allows the spectator to foresee, tolerate, and master the breakdowns of credibility.)

Similarly, Metz claims that "[p]our comprendre le film de fiction, il faut à la fois que je 'me prenne' pour le personnage (= démarche imaginaire), afin qu'il bénéficie par projection analogique de tous les schèmes d'intelligibilité que je porte en moi, et que je ne me prenne par pour lui (= retour au réel) afin que la fiction puisse s'établir comme telle (= comme symbolique): c'est le *semble-réel.*" *Signifiant imaginaire,* p. 80.

(In order to understand the fiction film, I must take myself for the character [= imaginary procedure] so that he benefits, by analogical projection, from all the patterns of intelligibility which I possess, and at the same time that I do not take myself for the character [= return to reality] so that the fiction can be established as such [= as symbolic]: it is the *seems-real.*)

Laura Mulvey also suggests an oscillation between two spectatorial positions of identification and denial. "[T]he cinema has structures of fascination strong enough to allow temporary loss of ego while simultaneously reinforcing the ego." "Visual Pleasure and Narrative Cinema," p. 10.

25. See the excellent discussion regarding theatrical illusion in Mannoni, "L'illusion cominque ou le théâtre du point de vue de l'imaginaire," *Clefs pour l'Imaginaire,* pp. 161–84.

26. "La fonction du stade du miroir s'avère pour nous dès lors comme un cas particulier de la fonction de *l'imago* qui est d'établir une relation de l'organisme à sa réalité. Ce développement est vécu comme une dialectique temporelle qui décisivement projette en histoire la formation de l'individu: le *Stade du Miroir* est un drame dont la poussée interne se précipite de l'insuffisance à l'anticipation—et qui pour le sujet, pris au leurre de l'identification spatiale, machine les fantasmes qui se succèdent d'une image morcellée du corps à une forme que nous appelerons orthopédique de sa totalité,—et à l'armure enfin assumé d'une identité rigide tout son développement mental." Lacan *Ecrits I,* "Le Stade du Miroir comme formateur de la fonction du Je," pp. 93—94.

(I am led, therefore, to regard the function of the mirror-stage as a particular case of the function of the *imago,* which is to establish a relation between the organism and its reality. This development is experienced as a temporal dialectic that decisively projects the formation of the individual into history. The mirror stage is a drama whose internal thrust is precipitated from insufficiency to anticipation—and which produces for the subject, trapped by the image of spatial identification, a succession of fantasies extending from a fragmented body-image to a total form that I will call orthopedic—that will mark the armor of a rigid identity that is ultimately adopted.)

27. In his *Three Essays on Sexuality* of 1905, Freud links scopophilia to touch and makes the eye an erotogenic zone. Later, he argues that this produces pleasure in watching spectacles. In the "Fourth Lecture on Psychoanalysis," he argues that "instinctual components of sexual pleasure . . . occur in pairs of opposites, active and passive . . . most important representative of this group [are the] active and passive desire for looking, from the former of which curiosity branches off later on and from the latter the impulsion to artistic and theatrical display." *Standard Edition* 11, p. 44.

28. Mulvey argues that "the fascination of film is reinforced by pre-existing patterns of fascination already at work within the individual subject and the social formations that have moulded him." "Visual Pleasure and Narrative Cinema," p. 6.

29. "En poussant les choses jusqu'au bout, on en viendrait à admettre que, chez l'adulte, les effets de masque et ceux de théâtre sont possibles en partie grâce à la présence de processus qui s'apparentent à ceux de la négation *(Verneinung);* qu'il faut que ce ne soit pas vrai, que nous sachions que ce n'est pas vrai, afin que les images de l'inconscient soient vraiments

libres. Le théâtre, à ce moment, jouerait un rôle proprement symbolique." Mannoni, ibid., p. 166.

(Taking things to their limit, we would agree that for the adult, the effects of a mask and of the theatre are possible thanks, in part, to the presence of processes related to those of negation {Verneinung}. It is necessary that it not be true, that we know that it is not true, in order to free unconscious images. Thus, theatre would play a properly symbolic role.)

30. Bonitzer defines the mood of this film as nostalgic. "La musique, le parfum, le rêve dont ces noms sont chargés, et la date, 1937. Voyons, mais ce charme, quel est-il? Mais oui, bien sûr, cela crève les yeux: la mode rétro! La mode rétro. Rétro veut dire nostalgique." *Le Regard et la voix,* p. 149.

31. Marie-Claire Ropars Wuilleumier's precise segmentation differentiates prologue (30 minutes; shots 1–27) from story (57 minutes; shots 28–58) from epilogue (23 minutes; shots 59–72) based on the changes of voices on the sound track. Grange proposes three divisions, based on the changing position of the narrators with respect to the image: contiguous in Part I, unified with the image in Part II, and distant from the image and transparent in Part III. See Grange, "Un système d'écriture," pp. 51–59. Marie offers an analysis of the film based on the degrees of distance between the voices and a potential speaking subject, suggesting "une typologie marquant cinq degrés de distance vis à vis d'un éventuel sujet de l'énonciation externe ou interne à la fiction . . . voix de narrateurs . . . intemporelles . . . voix des invités anonymes . . . des personnages désignés par la bande sonore . . . personnages présents à l'image ne parlant jamais (Michael Richardson) . . . personages présents à l'image censés dialoguer . . . " Marie, "La parole dans le cinéma contemporain," p. 46.

(A typology indicating five degrees of distance with respect to an eventual speaking subject exterior or interior to the fiction: intemporal narrative voices; voices of anonymous guests; characters designated by the sound track; characters whom we see but who never speak [Michael Richardson]; characters whom we see and whose ostensible voices we hear.)

32. Chion describes the impression of a strong bond between sounds and images as nostalgic. "L'image ici n'accueille jamais aucun son, mais en même temps tous les sons semblent se presser sur ses bords, nostalgiques d'un lieu qui les délivrerait de leur errance. Le champ filmé, dans *India Song,* agit pour les sons comme *foyer de fascination* autour duquel ils sont réunis sans pouvoir s'y perdre. . . ." Chion, *Son au cinéma,* p. 42.

(The image never receives any sound, but at the same time all the sounds seem to rush to its edges, nostalgic for a space which would deliver them of their wandering. The filmed space, in *India Song,* acts like a foyer of fascination around which the sounds converge, unable to lose themselves in it.)

33. Laplanche and Pontalis, *Vocabulaire de la psychanalyse,* p. 152.

34. Clément, *Miroirs du Sujet,* p. 100.

35. Clément argues that "le fantasme (a). . . la fonction d'un cadre, la structure d'une logique. Objet d'évocations rêveuses et point de fuite de la littérature, le fantasme est devenu l'axe d'une possible formalisation analytique. [L]e fantasme . . . est scène. . . . Le scénario implique une fixité, un récit, un déroulement régle: en même temps, le mot même induit la notion de scène constitutive à la structure fantasmatique. Le scénario se présente comme une succession de scènes." Clément, *Pouvoir des Mots,* pp. 89–90.

(Fantasy has the function of a frame, the structure of a logic. The object of dreamy evocations and the vanishing point of literature, fantasy has become the axis of a possible psychoanalytic formalization. A fantasy is a scene. The scenario implies a story, a logical unfolding, a permanence. At the same time, the word suggests the notion of a scene which establishes a fantasmatic structure. The scenario offers itself as a succession of scenes.)

36. "The gaze in itself not only terminates the movement, it freezes it. . . . What is . . . that time of arrest of the movement? It is simply the fascinatory effect, in that it is a question of dispossessing the evil eye of the gaze, in order to ward it off. The evil eye is the *fascinum,* it is that which has the effect of arresting movement and, literally, of killing life. At the moment

the subject stops, suspending his gesture, he is mortified. The anti-life, anti-movement function of this terminal point is the *fascinum,* and it is precisely one of the dimensions in which the power of the gaze is exercised directly. The moment of seeing can intervene here only as a suture, a conjunction of the imaginary and the symbolic." Lacan, *Four Fundamental Concepts,* pp. 117–18.

37.   In the chapter on *La Ravissement de Lol V. Stein,* I situated Lol at the periphery of the Imaginary and Symbolic. Recalling this, it is interesting to note Clément's remarks about Lacan's definition of fantasy. "Ainsi le fantasme est à la conjonction de l'imaginaire, reflet instable et du symbolique, cadre obligé du langage. C'est ce que Lacan désigne par la formule ꟼ a . . . ◊. Ce poinçon est le cadre du fantasme, ce qui dans les scènes hystériques se représente par la porte entrouverte, la lucarne dans la nuit, la fenêtre géante; cadre du désir. . . . Il fonde un rapport impossible entre le sujet et l'objet du désir: identité et non-reciprocité absolue, dans laquelle le sujet est déterminé par un objet auquel il ne peut avoir aucun accès." Clément, *Miroirs du Sujet,* p. 99.

(The fantasy is thus at the intersection of the imaginary, unstable reflection, and of the symbolic, necessary frame of language. This is what Lacan means by the formula $a . . . ◊. The diamond is the frame of the fantasy, which is represented in hysterical scenes by an open doorway, a light in the night, an enormous window: the frame of desire. It establishes an impossible relationship between the subject and object of desire: identity and absolute non-reciprocity in which the subject is determined by an object to which there is no access.)

38.   Laplanche and Pontalis suggest that fantasies figure a subject's answers to the questions of his or her origins. "Fantasmes des origines dans le scène primitive, c'est l'origine de l'individu qui se voit figurée; dans les fantasmes de séduction c'est l'origine, le surgissement de la sexualité; dans les fantasmes de castration, c'est l'origine de la différence des sexes." Lapanche and Pontalis, "Fantasmes originaires," p. 1854.

(Fantasies of origins in the primal scene are figures of the individual's origins; in seduction fantasies, it is the origin, the surge of sexuality; in castration fantasies, it is the origin of sexual difference.)

39.   "[L]e fantasme n'est texte qu'en partie; il a à se formuler comme texte, sous la forme d'un énoncé insistent dans le discours su sujet . . . mais cet énoncé, sur lequel une sémiotique peut intervenir, n'est sans doute que le résultat de l'operation fantasmatique, indissolublement texte et scene." Clément, *Pouvoir des Mots,* p. 91.

(A fantasy is only a text in part. It must be formulated as a text, in the form of an insistent énoncé in the subject's discourse. But this énoncé, upon which a semiotic operation can intervene, is doubtless the result of a fantasmatic operation, indissociably text and scene.)

The Politics of Marguerite Duras

Jeanine Parisier Plottel

Successful French women writers often create a fashion vogue of their own. In the nineteenth century, George Sand was notorious not only as the author of *La mare au diable* and *François le champi* but also through the photographs that show her wearing trousers and smoking a cigar. At the turn of this century, Colette was often identified with the demure "col Claudine," a Gibson girl collar that was the Paris rage when her Claudine novels were best-sellers. In the last 20 years, Marguerite Duras dominated Left Bank cafés because of the fashion she promoted: black vest, straight skirt, turtleneck sweater, and in winter, short boots.

One is tempted to establish connections between fashion style and literary style. Yet clothes make statements that are political rather than literary. George Sand's costume may reflect her socialist aspirations of equality between men and women. Colette and her friend Polaire, the *"belle-époque"* actress devoted to Sappho, were photographed in identical schoolgirl costumes reminiscent of boarding-school uniforms. The concept that one's identity was not necessarily what it appeared to be suggests current feminist ideology about the indeterminacy of gender.

Duras, who always wore the same outfit, presented to the world a mask of utter banality. Her costume was an effigy of the politics of an "everywoman" who readily acknowledged she drafted political books from the very beginning. The clue here is that for several decades the young and not so young adopted for their codes of dress the principle of sameness that guided Duras. Not a skirt, vest, and short boots, but jeans, shirts, leather jackets, and athletic shoes. Everywhere everyone wanted to look alike, and surface uniformity reigned from Lahore to Los Angeles and Savannah Bay.

It is extravagant to claim that all those who dress in a similar way share a common political view. Yet what is political is the fact of adopting a standard costume. In this spirit, it is hardly excessive to suggest that in France at least, Duras's political perspectives, often characterized by the words "sameness" and "triteness," were identical to the collective emotions of her contem-

This essay was written especially for this volume and is published here for the first time by permission of the author.

poraries. The political spheres of her works integrated and incorporated the sentimental cultural references of her age.

Like everyone, probably neither more nor less so, Duras was often wrong and readily admitted her errors. "I have often been wrong. I claim this right."[1] We will presently examine some of these errors, at least the most obvious ones. Duras herself made a distinction between opinions expressed in so-called creative works, for example *Un barrage contre le Pacifique; La vie tranquille; Hiroshima, mon amour; Le ravissement de Lol V. Stein; Le vice-consul; Le square; L'Amant;* and points of view in her books culled from newspaper articles and interviews, for instance, *Outside* and *La vie matérielle*. These works of journalism, Duras warns, are not exhaustive or definitive. "None reflect my general thoughts about a given topic, because I have no general thoughts about anything except social injustice. At most, the book [*La vie matérielle*] represents my thoughts sometimes, some days, about some things. Therefore it also represents what I think. I do not carry within myself the tombstone of totalitarian thinking; I mean definitive thinking. I have avoided this sore."[2]

Indignation, anger, and rage about social iniquity and unfairness were constants and invariants defining Duras as a representative of the cultural left. This left believed that suffering, exclusion, poverty, madness—all negative traits of the human condition—had prerogatives for redemption and reintegration extending beyond laws and the social order. In the July 1986 issue of *Esprit* devoted to Marguerite Duras, Paul Thibaud makes the point by the very title of his essay "Les ambiguïtés de la compassion" that, having achieved power when François Mitterand, a longtime close friend of Duras, was elected president of France, this left was forced to abandon its ideals and its illusions in the practice of power. Nevertheless, it clung to its sentiment about the sanctity of the disfranchised condition with quasi-religious fervor. The vice-consul of France to Lahore who shoots bullets at night in the gardens of Shalimar, where lepers and dogs seek shelter, comes to mind as the metaphor embodying this perspective in Duras's world.[3] He could not bear such misery and affliction, and gunning down the victims expressed his disgust. The vice-consul may also stand for French colonialism. At its best, this doctrine had as its ideal ensuring the access of populations under its tutelage to the heritage of the French Revolution, to liberty, equality, and fraternity. Faced with unspeakable suffering, this high-minded and lofty creed eventually reached a point of no return. Shooting it down became the honorable solution and the sign of its impotence.

Marguerite Duras inherited this legacy. It is all too often forgotten that the French colonial enterprise of the first half of this century was itself a bequest of the nineteenth-century French left. There was no greater enemy to colonial expansion, for instance, than Georges Clémenceau, a radical Republican, therefore a man of the French right, the French chief of state during World War I. In 1885, for example, he ruthlessly attacked promoters of French Indochina and caused the fall of Jules Ferry's leftist cabinet. Historically, for the most part the French left championed the colonial conquests, and the French right opposed them.

Students imbued with current pseudo-Marxist ideology assume that French colonialists were wealthy exploiters of working-class natives. How far removed from the truth! In Duras's books, the archetypal character who was a victim of colonialist greed and corruption is *"la mère,"* a paradigmatic mythical personage whose early curriculum vitae coincides with the one of Marguerite's real mother, Marie Legrand, the *mère* of *Des journées entières dans les arbres* and *Le barrage contre le Pacifique* who was the daughter of Flanders farmers. In *Le Barrage* Duras wrote *"paysans,"* and in "Mothers," an essay written much later, the term used was *"cultivateurs,"* a more current term that has replaced the more pejorative and conservative *"paysans."* She was a good student, and state scholarships allowed her to pursue the course of studies required to become an elementary school teacher. At the age of 25, between 1905 and 1910, she came to the country then called French Indochina, where she taught French and arithmetic to Annamese children.[4] In *Barrage,* *"la mère"* is the victim of Pierre Loti's quest for exoticism and adventure. She was carried away by the posters of colonial propaganda whose slogans she believed: *"Engagez-vous dans l'armée coloniale!"* "Enlist in the colonial army!" *"Jeunes, allez aux colonies, la fortune vous y attend."* "Young people, go to the colonies, where fortune awaits you."

Indochina became her country and her daughter's in much the same way that French Algeria was Camus's country and his mother's. She was closer to Vietnamese and Annamese than to other whites.[5] Her children—in *Le barrage* and in *L'amant*—see themselves as transitional children, to borrow a Melanie Klein idea, between the Indochinese reality and the values infused by French culture. Until she was 14 or 15 Marguerite's only friends were Vietnamese. She and her little brother, *"nous juifs,"* she wrote, were little skinny children, *"des petits créoles plus jaunes que blancs,"* "little Creoles more yellow than white," and *"la mère"* called them *"sales petits Annamese,"* "dirty little Annamese." The forbidden mangoes with which they filled their bellies seemed to turn them into children of another race. They would not eat bread, the most French of all French staples, only rice; they spoke a foreign, Oriental language, and they walked barefoot. When they were about 15 years old, people began asking whether they were their father's children. "Look at you! You are mulattoes! We never answered. There was no problem: we knew my mother was faithful and that the metis mixture came from elsewhere. We belonged to the land of mangoes, to the black waters of the South, to rice plains. We knew it."[6]

My own hunch is that eventually they would learn to eat apples, the French fruit that does not melt in one's mouth the way a mango does. They may have disliked them, but apples were their dominion because they were French children. Their *mère* was right. In spite of her denials, Marguerite as a young woman did not totally reject prevailing convictions about France's civilizing mission. Here, I should like to cite a book she published in 1940, under her real name, Marguerite Donnadieu, with Philippe Roques, a member of Georges Mandel's cabinet who was killed in 1942 trying to cross the Spanish frontier from France.[7] It is a book that Duras admirers find embarrassing. The title itself, *L'Empire Français,* which bears the prestigious Gallimard imprint and appeared in its collection "Problèmes et documents," is suspect today. About 10 years ago, I myself found a copy of it in a secondhand bookstall on the rue de Bourgogne in Paris, a neighborhood that houses many retired military officers, and my copy was inscribed to General Pellet.

At the onset, let us confirm what has been noted by Duras's biographer,[8] that the chapter on Indochina carries the mark of the creator of *Le barrage* insofar as one finds an emphasis on the beauty of its great rivers, Mekong, Tonlé-Sap, and Red River. Unlike the vain efforts of *"la mère,"* who tried to dam up the waters of the Pacific, in Tonkin, "an admirable network of dikes and canals, the technical organization of draining allowed it to become a region of intensive farming able to supply the needs of a high density population."[9] Otherwise, lyrical Alain Vircondelet's analysis of the book resorts to an interpretation linking loss of the land with loss of the father:

> She must have been grieved by the loss of the land of her childhood from within the flesh. How else are we to understand this book written in collaboration with Philippe Roques, and published in 1940 by Gallimard, called *L'empire français,* and signed with the name Marguerite Donnadieu, not found in any bibliography, except as the last call for the Father, the last concession to the disavowed name? Yes, how else can one interpret this hymn to the "mother country," to "sweet France," to the "Colonizing glory" to "French treasures of goodness and intelligence," this homage to Mendel [sic], to Bugeaud, to Colonel Mangin, to Marshals Lyautey and Joffre, to Gallieni except as the ultimate forgiveness for the burial of the Father?[10]

Revision of this evaluation is needed. Placed in its historical context, the book's significance has little to do with such oedipal fantasies. The clue here is to be found in the authors' preface, in the "Avant-Propos." They stress that the French empire is important because it can count on young and fresh forces in case of national danger: "The Empire is all made. The war completed it. If, until now, it has too often been but a theme for speeches, from now on the German menace and racist doctrine have made it conscious of its definitive reality."[11] At the time, the young woman was employed by the colonial ministry administered by Georges Mandel, a leading antifascist figure of the Third Republic. The preface reflects his views and his office's pragmatic attempt to avoid what was to prove the most humiliating defeat ever suffered by a major European power.

Today, few persons remember Mandel, who began his career on Premier Georges Clémenceau's staff and was a particularly honorable official of the

French Third Republic. Between the world wars, he opposed the pro-German policies of many conservatives. In May and June 1940, he advocated the same course of action set forth in the Roques/Donnadieu foreword, namely continuing to fight the Nazis from the French colonies in Africa rather than surrender. It was for this purpose that he, who like his mentor Clémenceau had no use for France's "colonizing mission," created the idea of the French empire.

Is it possible that *L'empire français,* written by two members of his office's staff, was designed and perhaps commissioned as a propaganda piece by the minister of colonies? It was well known that Mandel, a good speaker, could not wield a pen. There is a legend that when Clémenceau read an article Mandel wrote for *L'Aurore,* he advised him that henceforth he should take care to write only short sentences. He was told to "put down the subject and the verb, but consult me when you come to the predicate."[12] Because of his poor writing, he had other people write on his behalf. *L'Empire français,* which articulates Mandel's tenets of continuing to fight the Germans from French colonies in Africa rather than surrender, is a book perhaps written at his behest and surely under his patronage. Circumstantial evidence may be found in the attacks on both Mandel and Roques by the vicious best-seller of the occupation, Lucien Rebatet's *Les décombres.*

Mandel's own political stance suggests he acted according to the principles set forth there. He was against the Armistice. When it was announced, General Spears wanted to fly him, his daughter Claude, and his companion, the actress Béatrice Bretty, to the relative safety of London. He refused the offer, and he sailed from Bordeaux aboard the *Massilia* to Casablanca, where he attempted to set up a resistance administration with himself as premier. Philippe Pétain had him arrested almost immediately at his hotel, the Excelsior, and had him arraigned at the Riom trials. In November 1942, Vichy handed him to the Nazis, who imprisoned him in Oranienburg. He was transferred to Buchenwald, where he remained until July 4, 1944, when the Nazis sent him back to France, where he was assassinated by Joseph Darnand's militia.

In this historical context—why not think of the film *Casablanca?*—Vircondelet's appraisal of the orientation of the authors should be amended. The book's objective, it would appear, was to stress the prominence of the strategic reserves of the French empire and perhaps to influence public opinion. It contained numerous pages warning about the power of the Third Reich's propaganda machine. The reader was reminded, for example, that Hitler's *Mein Kampf,* which defined his colonial policies, called Africans who would fight for France half-monkeys. It was to the credit of both Roques and Donnadieu that Mandel was praised highly and held in high esteem.[13]

L'empire français belongs to the Duras journalism mode. Like her other essays of this genre—she wrote a regular column for *L'Observateur,* and in 1985 and 1986 for a short-lived periodical *L'Autre Journal*—these pages carry the stamp of their time, "*l'air du temps.*" Rather than ridicule and dismiss her work in this realm, why not concede that Marguerite Duras was an excellent propagandist? She was also on the right side of history.

My opinion may seem subjective, so I should elaborate and attest that she was on the same side of history as Winston Churchill. Here is what the Englishman wrote in his *History of the Second World War* about his last meeting with Mandel in Tours on June 13, 1940, a meeting that took place a month after the "*achevé d'imprimer*" of *L'empire français*. When the prime minister landed at the Tours airport, an airport that had been heavily bombed, the degeneration of affairs was obvious, and there was a sense that resistance was hopeless. When he met Mandel at the headquarters of the still-legitimate French government at the prefecture, the

> faithful former secretary of Clémenceau, and a bearer forward of his life's message, seemed in the best of spirits. He was energy and defiance personified. His luncheon, an attractive chicken, was uneaten on the tray before him. He was a ray of sunshine. He had a telephone in each hand, through which he was constantly giving orders and decisions. His ideas were simple: fight on to the end in France, in order to cover the largest possible movement into Africa. This was the last time I saw this valiant Frenchman. The restored French Republic rightly shot to death the hirelings who murdered him. His memory is honored by his countrymen and their Allies.[14]

Britain and the United States hoped that France would not capitulate to the Germans, but in the words of the official record "would remain in the struggle, with her fine Navy, her great Empire, her Army still able to carry on guerilla warfare on a gigantic scale."[15] Against this backdrop, *l'empire français* takes on the dimension of being an antidote to works of defeatism and pious treachery characteristic of 1940 publications. It is doubtful that it was much read or circulated, and in spite of its anti-German stance, it does not seem to appear on any of the notorious Otto Lists, compilations of titles that the Nazis wanted banned and destroyed.

By 1941 Mlle. Donnadieu was working at the Cercle de la Librairie, a Vichy publishing entity. Much remains to be learned about its role and function. In general, this organization was charged with coordinating various aspects of French publishing, including editing *La Bibliographie de la France*, distributing paper, and coordinating these activities with the German *propagandastaffel*. In his book, *L'edition française sous l'occupation*, Pascal Fouché states that he was unable to gain access to any archives. It was difficult for him to obtain a clear picture of its workings, but the sense is there was much cooperation with the enemy. Should one criticize a young writer in her twenties who needed to earn a living for taking a job created by authorities with an enigmatic mission? She was probably paid very little. In order to be able to buy black-market butter, cigarettes, and coffee, she wrote novels under various pseudonyms, none of which has come to light.[16]

The war years did not spare her. In May 1942 she gave birth to a stillborn baby fathered by Robert Antelme, whom she had married shortly after the outbreak of hostilities. In December of the same year, her brother died in Indochina, which was then under Japanese occupation. By 1943, she had followed Robert, his sister, and their friends Georges Beauchamp, Dionys Mascolo, who was also her lover, and François Mitterand in their resistance activities. Here is what Dionys Mascolo remembers, at "the risk of simplifying somewhat":

> This commitment to the Resistance took place only in September 1943, late in the war. Meanwhile, in the Spring of 1943, I had met Robert Antelme. Marguerite Duras and he already lived in rue Saint Benoît when a Christian friend of Robert Antelme and François Mitterand suggested to Robert that he enter in Mitterand's resistance movement, the "Mouvement national des prisonniers de guerre et déportés." Marguerite, Robert, and I joined together on the same day, in the presence of Mitterand and that friend.[17]

Now that much has been learned about Mitterand's activities during the war, one is naturally curious about the part played by his friend Marguerite. According to the late French president, it happened that he needed a safe apartment, and his friend Georges Beauchamp, who lived in rue Saint-Benoit, introduced him to Robert Antelme and the others. Robert's sister Marie-Louise lent him the room he needed. In retrospect, various accounts of the period now familiarly call this group the *"bande à Antelme."* At first Marguerite was given no information about the group's activities. In her interview with Mitterand on July 24, 1985, she gave the following account of how she became implicated in the Resistance:

> There is something that I . . . who forgets everything remember vividly: it is the first time we saw each other here, in this apartment. It was late in the evening. There were two of you. You sat in front of the living room fireplace, on either side of the heater, the kind made with old oil drums which burns newspaper compressed into balls. I do not know whether I gave you something to eat. The three of you spoke together, but very little. And suddenly the room was taken over by the smell of your English cigarette. I had not smelled that scent for three years. I did not understand. I said: "But you are smoking an English cigarette!" You said: "Oh, I am sorry." You took the pack of cigarettes out of your pocket, along with the one you were smoking, and you threw everything in the fire. Immediately, the three of you began talking about something else. That evening I asked Mascolo if it was what I was thinking, London. He said he did not know. An explanation as to the origin of the English cigarette was never given me. But that night, I understood that we had joined the Resistance, that it had been done.[18]

A few months later, on June 1, 1944,[19] Marie-Louise and Robert were arrested in rue Dupin[20] by the Gestapo along with two other comrades, Paul Philippe and Minette de Rocca-Serra. Only Robert would come back.[21] A little more than a month later, at the beginning of July 1944, Robert had not yet been deported to Germany and was being held at the Fresnes prison. It was that month that the events described in the piece of La douleur, "Monsieur X, dit ici Pierre Rabier," took place. Pierre Péan, the biographer of Mitterand's youth, raises the issue of whether Marguerite was considered reliable by the "bande à Antelme." The answer is tentative at best, and a conclusion cannot be provided.

At the beginning of July Mascolo informed his comrades, including Mitterand, that Marguerite had gone to Gestapo headquarters in rue des Saussaies to obtain permission to send a package to Robert. My own reminiscences may be in order here: during World War II, packages were mailed and smuggled everywhere by everyone—from one zone to another, one city to another, through official channels and underground ones. They were shipped at the beginning of the war and long after the war ended; some reached their destination, many did not, but those who had the means to send them did, often knowing they would never be received. So there is nothing odd or suspect about this move. After a very long wait, Marguerite approached a man who turned out to be French and to have arrested and interrogated Robert. He asked her whether her husband belonged to the Resistance, and she denied he did. Accounts of her meeting with this man, whose real name was Charles Delval, are found not only in La douleur but, according to Péan, also in the judicial inquiry of Delval's trial after the liberation, and they are supposedly preserved in File 3W at the French Archives Nationales. In passing, one should note that it may be unclear whether this Delval was French or German. In his interview with Duras in 1985, Mitterand claims that his real name remains a mystery, but Péan's research disproves this.

Portions of these archives are reproduced by Péan. I myself tried to secure access to the file, but I was told that a special "dérogation," a dispensation, would have to be granted, a dispensation applying to all documents pertaining to archives of trials following the liberation of France. The various sources cited by Péan—the socialist Edgar Morin, for instance, a good friend of the Antelmes, and Jean Munier, whose Resistance name was Commandant Rodin—do not today look too kindly on Marguerite's dealings with Delval, whom they tried to assassinate at various times.

What should be added to Duras's account is the testimony of Rabier/Delval's wife, Paulette Delval, whom Péan interviewed on the telephone on March 29, 1994. According to Paulette's testimony, Marguerite and Dionys interrogated both Delvals in rue Beaubourg—the date is unclear, possibly it was during the summer of 1944—and Marguerite wanted to cut off Paulette's hair.[22] Dionys was quite smitten by Paulette, a beautiful 27-year-old woman, and he did not allow Marguerite to do this. What Duras did not reveal is that Paulette and Dionys had a relationship whose structure was symmetrical to the Delval/Rabier/Duras couple. According to Péan, as the months went by, September, October, November 1944, the two began having an affair, which lasted several years.[23] Paulette's child was born in June 1946—Charles Delval had been shot in the yard of the Fresne prison at the beginning of 1945—and Marguerite's child by Mascolo, the following year. The question of the paternity of Paulette's child is shrouded in ambiguity, an ambiguity that is only an appearance, because in real life the truth is known by the persons concerned.[24] In this light, Duras's concern for the wife and child of the man "here called Rabier," a concern that led her to postpone publication for many years, appears a mere literary device.

Marguerite testified at the Delval trial twice. The first time, her passionate testimony moved the state attorney to request the death penalty. She then asked to testify again, and she tried to rectify the record at a time when her husband was still in Germany, and she did not know whether he was alive. She told the court the story of how Delval/Rabier failed to arrest the Jewish father of the little boy whose drawings had moved him.[25] What was her motivation? Regard for justice? Astonishment at the bitterness of revenge? A few months later, she would attempt to resolve her anguish and confusion by joining the Communist Party. Toward the end of her life, when she expressed indignation at and compassion for the condemnation and execution of Robert Brasillach in 1945, she seemed to have suffered amnesia about this chapter in her life and her own quest for retaliation and vengeance.

It is striking that the chronology of events narrated in "Monsieur X. dit ici Pierre Rabier" and in "La douleur," the tale that gives the volume its name, are inverted. The incidents of the second tale, which took place in June and July 1944, preceded those of the first, which took place the following year, after the liberation of the Nazi concentration camps. By reversing the order, the narrator elicits far more compassion from her audience than would have been the case had she followed a historical temporal sequence. In other words, reading about Robert L.'s return from Dachau makes us far more tolerant toward the implications of the other episodes. Our moral sense is laid in abeyance.

In Duras's July 24, 1985, interview with him, Mitterand corroborated many episodes. He confirmed that when he accompanied the American General Lewis to the just-liberated Dachau, he chanced upon a dead and dying heap of bodies. He suddenly heard someone whispering his name. After looking down, he discovered that Robert L., Marguerite's husband, Robert Antelme in real life, was the one uttering his name. Because Robert L. was ill with typhus, he had to be quarantined and could not leave the camp. Morland/Mitterand returned to Paris, obtained an American uniform and appropriate false papers, and returned to Dachau together with L., or Dionys Mascolo. He smuggled Robert out of the camp and brought him back to Paris.

We see why the war and its atrocities continued to haunt the memories of Duras and her generation, why these were often present in her books even when there was no actual allusion to them. In a Canadian interview, Duras confirmed that her ordeals during the war and the existence of concentration camps branded her so that they perpetually permeated her writings.

In a 1981 Montreal press conference, to the question of whether she felt herself implicated by concentration death camps, she answered that they had remained within her always. "You know," she stated, "everyone who lived through the war the way I did, became that way." To the response from her interviewer that she wrote only about love, she replied, "I don't know whether one can say that. I write. I write in that former dimension, even though the words are not stated, even though they remain far away. Writing in such a global aggregate . . . Writing of Jews in any other way is impossible. But speaking about it is difficult for me."[26]

La douleur and *L'amant,* which had not been published at the time, shed diffuse light on how she experienced events that have continued to haunt her writing, making up for the blindness and lack of insight of her compatriots, to paraphrase a well-known title in academic circles. She readily acknowledges, for example, that the destruction of European Jewry eluded her:

> You must have lived through things like that in your life, world events that elude you. It seems to me compulsory. I had Jewish friends; I had a Jewish lover, two of my best friends were Jewish, they had Jewish children, I had a very dear friend who was a Jewish writer. All at once, they had a yellow star. And I did not think about it.[27]

The sections of *La douleur* describing the narrator's ordeal as she waited for news of her husband, Robert L., are admirable. The account of his rescue and his return from the dead confirm that humanism and redemption are inherent to the act of survival. These pages constitute an absolute and conclusive testimony of the horrors that swept over the most civilized European nations half a century ago. When read against the backdrop of Duras's life and works, they shape the ambiguities underlying creative endeavors dealing with the dread, terror, suffering, and revulsion that draw their substance from the occupied France of the 1940s. Most of Duras's compatriots had friends and family, or at the least acquaintances—a neighbor, a colleague, or a schoolmate—who had disappeared one day in Pitchipoï, the euphemism for places of no return beyond the Rhine. And after the war, when those who had held high positions under the occupation were discredited, many of us counted friends and acquaintances there too. Marcel Ophuls's *Le chagrin et la pitié* presented this with great tact. The film showed for instance how a man of high society with impeccable demeanor, Christian de la Mazière, a gentleman, belonged to the French Waffen SS. In a similar spirit, in the same building where *"la bande à Antelme"* was engaged in subversive activities, Ramon and Betty Fernandez entertained the high society of collaborationist Paris. Both circles included Marguerite. Her position was to tally into the final score of atrocities, the horror of Hiroshima, horror among horrors. But it was not by describing the atomic bomb dropped on Hiroshima, that the film *Hiroshima, mon amour* captured the ensuing destruction and devastation. Duras believed horror could not be depicted by describing it. The horror stored in ashes of memory was to be restored only through the personal history of exemplary protagonists. In the film, our sense of atrocity is derived from the girl from Nevers whose head has been shaven and her Japanese lover.

When Duras appeared on Bernard Pivot's *Apostrophes,* she reiterated the belief stated in *L'amant,* to wit that collaborators and members of the French Communist Party, to which she belonged, are completely equivalent. In the context of her experience with this party, but with no reference to the Delval/Rabier affair, she stressed it was unfair for Brasillach to have been executed while she herself was whitewashed.[28] Followers of totalitarian systems seek political solutions to personal problems caused by their own inadequacy, despondency, feelings of impotence and worthlessness. For those who suffer from the malady of death, the malady of those who belong nowhere, the outcasts, the misfits, the pariahs, those who, like the girl from Nevers in *Hiroshima, mon amour,* are crazed with infamy, those who are hungry, in pain, there is no solution. In one of her last books, *Yann Andréa Steiner,* Duras asked herself why a young man came to settle down with a woman *"âgée déjà, folle d'écrire."* Here is what she says:

> Perhaps it is the same as usual, the same everywhere, nothing at all, and you came simply because of your despair, the way you are every day of your life, and certain summers at certain times of day and night when the sun leaves the sky, for instance, and every evening sinks into the sea forever, you, you can't help wanting to die. I know that.
>
> I see both of us lost in the same type of nature. Sometimes, I am filled with tenderness for the kind of people we are. Unstable, people say, a little crazy. People who never go to the movies any more, nor to the theater, nor to any receptions. People of the left, you see, that is the way they are, they do not know how to live, they find Cannes disgusting and the same goes for great Moroccan hotels. Movies and the theater, all the same.[29]

At the end of the day, in Duras's world, the harvest of the left was scant, a fashion gone astray. In this realm, to quote her words, the legacy of her politics resembles the fashion look she exemplified: *"Je suis la banalité. Le triomphe de la banalité."* She was commonplace itself, "the triumph of the commonplace."[30]

Notes

1. "Je me suis pas mal trompée. Je revendique ce droit." "Avant-propos," in *Outside* (Paris: P.O.L., 1984), 13.

2. "Aucun ne reflète ce que je pense en général du sujet abordé parce que je ne pense rien en général de rien, sauf de l'injustice sociale. Le livre ne représente tout au plus ce que je pense certaines fois, certains jours, de certaines choses. Donc il représente aussi ce que je pense. Je ne porte pas en moi la dalle de la pensée totalitaire, je veux dire: définitive. J'ai évité cette plaie." *La vie matérielle,* 7.

3. *Le Vice-consul,* (Paris: Gallimard, 1965), 94.

4. "Mothers," *Marguerite Duras* (Paris: Albatros, 1979), 99.

5. Michelle Porte, *Les lieux de Marguerite Duras* (Paris: Minuit, 1977), 56.

6. "Les enfants maigres et jaunes," 1976, *Outside,* 278.

7. Francisque Varenne, *Georges Mandel mon patron* (Paris: Editions Défense de la France, 1947), 167.

8. Alain Vircondelet, *Marguerite Duras* (Paris: François Bourin, 1991), 93.

9. "Un admirable réseau de digues et de canaux, une organisation technique de dragages a cependant fait du Tonkin une région de culture intensive qui pourvoit aux besoins d'une population très dense." *L'empire français,* 108.

10. "Inconsolée, elle devait l'être, intérieurement, charnellement, de cette terre de l'enfance, l'Indochine, car comment comprendre autrement ce livre obscur publié en collaboration avec Philippe Roques en mai 1940 chez Gallimard, intitulé *L'Empire français* et signé sous le nom de Marguerite Donnadieu, absent de toute bibliographie, sinon comme le dernier appel crié au Père, la dernière concession au nom renié? Oui, comment interpréter autrement cet hymne à la 'mère patrie,' à 'la douce France,' à la gloire colonisatrice, aux 'trésors de bonté et d'intelligence de la France,' cet hommage à Mendel, Bugeaud, au colonel Mangin, aux maréchaux Lyautey et Joffre, à Galliene encore, sinon comme l'ultime pardon avec l'ensevelissement du Père?" Vircondelet, 93.

11. "L'Empire est fait. La guerre l'a achevé. Si, jusque-là, ce n'était trop souvent qu'un thème à discours, désormais la menace allemande et les doctrines raciste lui ont donné conscience de sa réalité définitive."

12. Quoted in Varenne, p. 180: "Dorénavant, faites des phrases courtes, un sujet et un verbe. Pour le complément, vous viendrez m'en parlez."

13. *L'empire français,* 108.

14. Winston Churchill, *Their Finest Hour* (Boston: Houghton Mifflin, 1949), 179.

15. Churchill, 187.

16. "Avant-Propos," in *Outside,* 12.

17. *Lignes,* 21 (Paris: Editions Hazan, Janvier 1994), 179. This issue of *Lignes* is dedicated to the memory of Robert Antelme: "Cet engagement dans la résistance n'a eu lieu qu'en septembre 1943; tardivement, donc. J'avais fait la connaissance, entre temps, au printemps 1943, de Robert Antelme. Marguerite Duras et lui habitaient déjà rue Saint Benoît qu'un ami chrétien de Robert Antelme et de François Mitterand a proposé à Robert d'entrer dans le mouvement de résistance de Mitterand, le 'Mouvement national des prisonniers de guerre et déportés,' et nous avons adhéré ensemble, Marguerite, Robert et moi, le même jour, en présence de Mitterand et de cet ami."

18. Entretien Marguerite Duras et François Mitterand. "Le bureau de poste de la rue Dupin," *L'Autre Journal,* #1 (26 février-4 mars 1986), 36–37: "Il y a une chose [. . .] dont moi qui oublie tout je me souviens de façon lumineuse: c'est la première fois qu'on s'est vus, ici, dans cet appartement. C'était tard dans la soirée, vous étiez deux. Vous vous êtes assis devant la cheminée du salon, de part et d'autre d'un poêle, de ceux qui étaient faits avec des vieux barils à huile et dans lesquels on brûlait du papier journal compressé en boulets. Je ne sais plus si je

vous ai donné quelque chose à manger. Vous avez parlé ensemble tous les trois, mais très peu. Et tout à coup la pièce a été envahie par l'odeur de la cigarette anglaise. Il y avait trois ans que je n'avais pas senti cette odeur. Je n'ai pas compris. J'ai crié: 'mais vous fumez une cigarette anglaise!' Vous avez dit: 'oh pardon . . .' Vous avez pris votre paquet dans votre poche et la cigarette que vous fumiez et vous avez tout jeté dans le feu. Immédiatement vous avez parlé d'autre chose tous les trois. Le soir j'ai demandé à Mascolo si c'était bien ce que je pensais, Londres. Il a dit qu'il ne savait pas. Je n'ai jamais eu d'explication sur l'origine de la cigarette anglaise. Mais j'ai compris ce soir-là que nous étions entré dans la Résistance, que c'était fait."

19. June 1, 1944, is the date given by Duras in *La Douleur,* 87. Péan's book gives a muddled chronology, but the date seems to be May 30, 1944.

20. Péan gives 5, rue Dupin as the address for Robert and Marguerite and rue Saint-Benoit as the address of Marie-Louise Antelme, Robert's sister.

21. See Pierre Péan, *Une jeunesse française* (Paris: Fayard, 1994), 417. Marie-Louise was deported to Ravensbruck and died of typhus a few days after the end of the war, on May 10, 1945.

22. Péan, 467.

23. Ibid., 470–3.

24. Ibid., 473.

25. Ibid., 472.

26. *Marguerite Duras à Montréal.* Textes réunis et présentés par Suzanne Lamy & André Roy (Montreal: Editions Spirale & Editions Solin, 1984), p. 27.

Q. Est-ce que vous vous sentez impliquée par les camps de concentration, les camps de la mort?

M.D.: C'est là, en moi, pour toujours. Vous savez, tous les gens qui ont vécu la guerre comme je l'ai vécue, deviennent comme ça. C'est impossible autrement.

Q. Et pourtant vous n'écrivez que sur l'amour.

M.D.: Je ne sais pas si on peut dire ça. J'écris. J'écris dans cette dimension-là, même si les mots ne sont pas énoncés, même s'ils sont lointains. Ecrire dans cette espèce de globalité. C'est impossible d'écrire sur les Juifs autrement. Mais ça m'est très difficile de parler de ça.

27. *Marguerite Duras à Montréal,* 27: "Vous avez vécu des choses comme ça dans votre vie, des événements mondiaux qui vous échappent. Il me semble que c'est obligatoire. J'avais des amis juifs, j'avais eu un amant juif, deux de mes meilleurs amis étaient juifs, ils avaient des enfants juifs, j'avais un très cher ami qui était un écrivain juif. Et puis tout à coup, ils avaient une étoile jaune. Et je n'y ai pas pensé."

28. "Je me suis dit que je vais retrouver la fraternité à l'intérieur du parti. Collaborateurs, c'était pareil. La collaboration offrait des occasions . . . La violence offrait à d'autres gens des aventures pareilles. Un autre voisinage. C'est une occasion de changer de direction." My own transcript.

29. "Peut-être que c'est comme d'habitude, que c'est partout pareil, que ce n'est rien, que tu es venu simplement parce que tu étais désespéré, comme chaque jour de ta vie tu l'es et aussi pendant certains étés à certaines heures des jours et des nuits quand le soleil quitte le ciel par exemple et qu'il pénètre dans la mer chaque soir pour toujours, toi tu ne peux pas t'empêcher de vouloir mourir. Je le sais, ça.

Je nous vois perdus tous les deux dans la même sorte de nature. Il m'arrive d'être prise de tendresse pour la sorte de gens que nous sommes. Instables, disent les gens, fous un peu. Des gens qui ne vont plus au cinéma, ni au théâtre, ni aux réceptions. Des gens de gauche, voyez, ils sont comme ça, ils ne savent plus vivre. Cannes ça les dégoûte et aussi les grands hôtels marocains. Le cinéma, et le théâtre tout pareil." Yann Andréa Steiner (Paris: P.O.L., 1992), 76–77.

30. "Je suis la banalité. Le triomphe de la banalité." *Ecrire* (Paris: Gallimard, 1993), 45.

Selected Bibliography

PRIMARY SOURCES

Novels/Novellas

Les Impudents. Paris: Plon, 1943.

La Vie tranquille. Paris: Gallimard, 1944.

Un Barrage contre le Pacifique. Paris: Gallimard, 1950. Translated by Herma Briffault under the title *The Sea Wall* (New York: Farrar, Straus & Giroux, 1985).

La Marin de Gibraltar. Paris: Gallimard, 1952. Translated by Barbara Bray under the title *Sailor from Gibraltar* (New York: Grove Press, 1967).

Les Petits chevaux de Tarquinia. Paris: Gallimard, 1953. Translated by Peter DuBerg under the title *The Little Horses of Tarquinia* (London: Calder, 1960).

Des Journées entières dans les arbres, followed by *Le Boa; Madame Dodin; Les Chantiers.* Paris: Gallimard, 1954. Translated by Anita Barrows under the title *Whole Days in the Trees* (New York: Riverrun, 1984).

Le Square. Paris: Gallimard, 1955. Translated by Sonia Pitt Rivers and Irina Morduc under the title *The Square,* in *Four Novels* (New York: Grove Press, 1965).

Moderato cantabile. Paris: Minuit, 1958. Translated by Richard Seaver, in *Four Novels* (New York: Grove Press, 1965).

Dix heures et demie du soir en été. Paris: Gallimard, 1960. Translated by Anne Borchardt under the title *10:30 on a Summer Night,* in *Four Novels* (New York: Grove Press, 1963).

L'Après-Midi de Monsieur Andesmas. Paris: Gallimard, 1962. Translated by Anne Borchardt under the title *Afternoon of Monsieur Andesmas,* in *Four Novels* (New York: Grove Press, 1965).

Le Ravissement de Lol. V. Stein. Paris: Gallimard, 1964. Translated by Richard Seaver under the title *The Ravishing of Lol. V. Stein.* (New York: Grove Press, 1966).

Le Vice-consul. Paris: Gallimard, 1965. Translated by Eileen Ellenbogen under the title *The Vice-Consul* (London: Hamish Hamilton, 1967).

L'Amante anglaise. Paris: Gallimard, 1967. Translated by Barbara Bray (New York: Grove Press, 1968).

Détruire, dit-elle. Paris: Minuit, 1969. Translated by Barbara Bray under the title *Destroy, She Said* (New York: Grove Press, 1970).

Abahn Sabana David. Paris: Gallimard, 1970.

L'Amour. Paris: Gallimard, 1971.

Ah Ernesto! Paris: François Ruy-Vidal et Harlin Quist, 1971.

Nathalie Granger, followed by *La femme du Gange.* Paris: Gallimard, 1973.

India Song. Paris: Gallimard, 1973. Translated by Barbara Bray (New York: Grove Press, 1977).

Le Camion, followed by *Entretien avec Michelle Port.* Paris: Minuit, 1977.

Le Navire Night; Césarée; Les Mains négatives; Aurélia Steiner. Paris: Mercure de France, 1979.

Véra Baxter ou Les Plages de l'Atlantique. Paris: Albatros, 1980.

L'Homme assis dans le couloir. Paris: Minuit, 1980. Translated by Barbara Bray under the title *The Man Sitting in the Corridor* (New York: Blue Moon, 1991).

Agatha. Paris: Minuit, 1981.

L'Homme atlantique. Paris: Minuit, 1982. *The Atlantic Man.* In *Two by Duras.* Trans. Albert Manguel. Toronto: Coach House, 1993.

Savannah Bay. Paris: Minuit, 1982. 2nd ed. augmented, Minuit, 1983.

La Maladie de la mort. Paris: Minuit, 1982. Translated by Barbara Bray under the title *The Malady of Death* (New York: Grove, 1986).

L'Amant. Paris: Minuit, 1984. Translated by Barbara Bray under the title *The Lover* (New York: Pantheon, 1985).

La Douleur. Paris: P.O.L., 1985. Translated by Barbara Bray under the title *The War: A Memoir* (New York: Pantheon, 1986).

Les Yeux bleus cheveux noirs. Paris: Gallimard, 1986. Translated by Barbara Bray under the title *Blue Eyes, Black Hair* (New York: Pantheon, 1987).

Emily L. Paris: Minuit, 1987. Translated by Barbara Bray (New York: Pantheon, 1989).

La Pluie d'été. Paris: P.O.L., 1990. Translated by Barbara Bray under the title *Summer Rain* (New York: Scribner's, 1992).

L'Amant de la Chine du nord. Paris: Gallimard, 1991. Translated by Leigh Hafrey under the title *The North China Lover* (New York: New Press, 1992).

Plays

Les Viaducs de la Seine-et-Oise. Paris: Gallimard, 1959. Translated by Barbara Bray and Sonia Orwell under the title *The Viaducts of Seine and Oise,* in *Three Plays* (London: Calder and Boyars, 1967).

Théâtre I: Les Eaux et forêts; Le Square; La Musica. Paris: Gallimard, 1965.

L'Amante anglaise. Cahiers du Théâtre national populaire, 1968.

Théâtre II: Suzanna Andler; Des Journées entières dans les arbres; Yes, peut-être; Le Shaga; Un Homme est venu me voir. Translated by Barbara Bray and Sonia Orwell, Paris: Gallimard, 1968. *Three Plays: The Square; Days in the Trees; The Viaducts of Seine and Oise* (London: Calder and Boyars, 1967).

Susanna Andler; La Musica; L'Amante anglaise. Translated by Barbara Bray. London: Calder, 1975.

La Musica deuxième. Paris: Gallimard, 1985.

La Mouette de Tchékhov. Paris: Gallimard, 1985.

Savannah Bay. Paris: Minuit, 1983. Augmented ed., 1983. Translated by Howard Limolli, in *Agatha and Savannah Bay* (Sausalito, Calif.: Post-Apollo Press, 1992).

L'Eden cinéma. Paris: Mercure de France, 1977. Translated by Barbara Bray under the title *The Eden Cinema,* in *L'Eden Cinéma.* (Paris: Actes Sud-Papiers, 1988).

Agatha. Paris: Minuit, 1981. Translated by Howard Limolli, in *Agatha and Savannah Bay* (Sausalito, Calif.: Post-Apollo Press, 1992).

Théâtre III: La Bête dans la jungle. Based on Henry James. Adaptation by James Lord and Marguerite Duras. *Les Papiers d'Aspern.* Based on Henry James. Adaptation by Marguerite Duras and Robert Antelme. *La Danse de mort.* Based on August Strindberg. Adaptation by Marguerite Duras. Paris: Gallimard, 1984.

Screenplays

Hiroshima, Mon Amour. Paris: Gallimard, 1960. Translated by Richard Seaver (New York: Grove Press, 1961).

Une Aussi Longue Absence. In collaboration with Gérard Jarlot. Paris: Gallimard, 1961. Translated by Barbara Wright, in *Hiroshima, Mon Amour and Une Aussi Longue Absence.* (London: Calder & Boyars, 1966).

India Song. Paris: Gallimard, 1973. Translated by Barbara Bray (New York: Grove Press, 1976).
Nathalie Granger [and] *La Femme du Gange.* Paris: Gallimard, 1973.
Le Camion [and] *Entretien avec Michelle Porte.* Paris: Minuit, 1977.
Le Navire-Night et autres textes. Paris: Mercure de France, 1979.
Vera Baxter ou les plages de l'Atlantique. Paris: Albatros, 1980.

Films

La Musica, 1966.
Détruire dit-elle, 1969.
Jaune le soleil, 1971.
Nathalie Granger, 1972.
La Femme du Gange, 1973.
India Song, 1974.
Baxter, Vera Baxter, 1976.
Son Nom de Venise dans Calcutta désert, 1976.
Des Journées entières dans les arbres, 1976.
Le Camion, 1977.
Le Navire-Night, 1979.
Césarée, 1979.
Les Mains négatives, 1979.
Aurélia Steiner, dit Aurélia Melbourne, 1979.
Aurélia Steiner, dit Aurélia Vancouver, 1979.
Agatha ou les lectures illimitées, 1981.
Dialogo di Roma, 1982. 1982.
L'Homme atlantique, 1982.
Les Enfants. With Jean Mascolo and Jean-Marc Turine, 1985.
L'Eden Cinéma, version scénique. Actes Sud-Papiers, 1988.
L'Homme assis dans le couloir. Paris: Minuit, 1980. *The Man Sitting in the Corridor.* Trans by Barbara Bray. New York: Blue Moon, 1991.

Interviews in Books

Brèves rencontres. Denise Bourdet. Paris: Grasset, 1963.
Quinze écrivains. Madeleine Chapsal. Paris: Huillard, 1963.
Vu et entendu. Pierre Dumayet. Paris: Stock, 1964.
Les Voies de l'écriture. Hubert Nyssen. Paris: Mercure de France, 1969.
La Création étouffée. Jeanne Socquet. Paris: Pierre Horay, 1973.
Les Parleuses. Marguerite Duras and Xavière Gauthier. Paris: Minuit, 1974. Translated and with an afterword by Katharine A. Jenson under the title *Woman to Woman* (University of Nebraska Press, 1987).
Les Lieux de Marguerite Duras. Michelle Porte. Paris: Minuit, 1977. Translated by Edith Cohen under the title *The Places of Marguerite Duras. Enclitic* 7.1 (1984): 54–61, and 7.2 (1984): 55–62.
Marguerite Duras à Montréal. Suzanne Lamy and André Roy, eds. Quebec: Spirale, 1981.
Eloge de l'insomnie. Michele Manceaux. Paris: Hachette, 1985.

Journalism

L'Eté 80. Paris: Minuit, 1980.
Outside: Papiers d'un jour. Paris: Albin Michel, 1981. Reprint, Paris: P.O.L., 1984. Translated by Arthur Goldhammer under the title *Outside: Selected Writings* (Boston: Beacon, 1986).
Le Monde extérieur: Outside 2. Paris: P.O.L., 1993.

Essays/Memoirs

"Les Yeux verts." *Cahiers du cinéma* (Paris), 312–13 (June 1980). Translated by Carol Barko under the title *Green Eyes* (New York: Columbia University Press, 1990).
La Pute de la côte normande. Paris: Minuit, 1986. *The Slut of the Normandy Coast.* Translated by Alberto Manguel in *Two by Duras* (Toronto: Coach House, 1993).
La Vie matérielle. Paris: P.O.L., 1987. Translated by Barbara Bray under the title *Practicalities: Marguerite Duras speaks to Jérôme Beaujour* (New York: Grove Widenfeld, 1990).
Yann André Steiner. Paris: P.O.L., 1992. Translated by Barbara Bray under the title *Yann André Steiner* (New York: Scribner's 1993).
Ecrire. Paris: Gallimard, 1993.
C'est tout. Paris: P.O.L., 1995.
La Mer écrite. Photos d'Hélène Bamberger Turin: Marcal, 1996.

Cassette

La Jeune fille et l'enfant. Adapted from *L'Eté 80* by Yann Andréa, read by Marguerite Duras. Paris: Des Femmes, 1981.

SECONDARY SOURCES

Alleins, Madeleine. "Un langage qui recuse la quiétude du savoir," in *Moderato cantabile.* Paris: Minuit, 10/18, 1958, 159ff.
———. *Marguerite Duras Médium du réel.* Lausanne, Switzerland: L'Age d'Homme, 1984.
Ames, Sanford. *Essays on Marguerite Duras.* New York: Peter Lang, 1988.
Andréa, Yann, *M.D.* Paris: Minuit, 1983.
Barthes, Roland. *Le Degré Zéro de l'Ecriture.* Paris: Seuil, 1953.
Blanchot, Maurice. "*Détruire.*" In *Marguerite Duras.* Paris: Albatros, Ca Cinéma series, 1979, 139 ff.
Blot-Labarrère, Christiane. *Marguerite Duras.* Paris: Seuil, 1992.
Cahiers Renaut-Barrault, 89 (1975).
Cismaru, Alfred. *Marguerite Duras.* New York: Twayne, 1972.
Cohen, Susan D. *Women and Discourse in the Fiction of Marguerite Duras.* Amherst: University of Massachusetts Press, 1993.
Coward, David. *Moderato Cantabile.* London: Grant and Cutler, 1981.
Cranston, Mechthild. *In Language and in Love Marguerite Duras: The Unspeakable.* Potomac, Md.: Scripta Humanistica, 1992.

Eisinger, Erica, M. "Crime and Detection in the Novels of Marguerite Duras. *Contemporary Literature* 15, 4 (Autumn 1974): 503–20.

Evans, Martha Noel. *Masks of Tradition.* Ithaca, N.Y.: Cornell University Press, 1987.

Fernandes, Marie-Pierre. *Travailler avec Duras.* Paris: Gallimard, 1986.

Gallop, Jane. *The Daughter's Seduction.* Ithaca, N.Y.: Cornell University Press, 1982.

Glassman, Deborah N. *Marguerite Duras: Fascinating Vision and Narrative Cure.* Rutherford, N.J.: Fairleigh Dickinson University Press, 1991.

Guers-Villate, Yvonne. *Continuité discontinuité de l'oeuvre durasassienne.* Brussels: Editions de l'Université de Bruxelles, 1985.

Hill, Leslie. *Marguerite Duras: Apocalyptic Desires.* London: Routledge, 1993.

Hofmann, Carol. *Forgetting and Marguerite Duras.* Niwor, Colo.: University of Colorado Press, 1991.

Husserl-Kapit, Susan. "An Interview with Marguerite Duras." *Signs* 1 (Winter 1975):428.

Irigaray, Luce. *Ce Sexe qui n'en est pas Un.* Paris: Minuit, 1977.

Jardine, Alice. *Gynesis: Configurations of Woman and Modernity.* Ithaca, N.Y.: Cornell University Press, 1985.

Kaivola, Karen. *All Contraries Confounded: The Lyrical Fiction of Virginia Woolf, Djuna Barnes, and Marguerite Duras.* Iowa City: University of Iowa Press, 1991.

Knapp, Bettina L. "Marguerite Duras." In *Off-Stage Voices.* Troy, N.Y.: Whitston Publishing Co., 1975, 423–34.

Kneller, John W. "Elective Empathies and Musical Affinities." *Yale French Studies* 27 (1961): 114–20.

Lacan, Jacques. *Ecrits: A Selection.* Trans. Alan Sheridan. New York: Norton, 1977.

Magazine littéraire 158 (March 1980):8–21.

Marguerite Duras by Marguerite Duras. Trans. Edith Cohen and Peter Connor. San Francisco: City Lights Books, 1987.

Marini, Marcelle. *Territoires du féminin avec Marguerite Duras.* Paris: Minuit, 1977.

Mistler, Jean. "Un essai non une oeuvre achevée." In *Moderato cantabile.* Paris: Minuit, 10/18, 162.

Murphy, Carol J. *Alienation and Absence in the Novels of Marguerite Duras.* Lexington, Ky.: French Forum, 1982.

Noguez, Dominique. "La Gloire des mots." *L'Arc* 98. Paris: Editions Le Jas, 1985, 24–40.

———. "Les India Song de Marguerite Duras." *Cahiers du 20e siècle 9: cinéma et littérature.* Paris: Klincksieck, 1978.

Papin, Liliane. *L'Autre scène. Le Théâtre de Marguerite Duras.* Saratoga, Calif.: Anma Libri and Co., 1988.

Picon, Gaetan. "Les Romans de Marguerite Duras." *Mercure de France* 333 (1958): 309–14.

———. "*Moderato cantabile* dans l'oeuvre de Marguerite Duras." In Duras, *Moderato cantabile.* Paris: Minuit 10/18, 169 ff.

Pautrot, Jean-Louis. *La Musique oubliée.* Geneva: Droz, 1994.

Poulet, Robert. "La Règle du jeu transgressée." In Duras, *Moderato cantabile.* Paris: 10/18, 1962, 153–156.

Renouard, Madeleine, and Ninette Bailey, eds. *La Chouette* 6 (September 1981; special issue on Duras). French Department, Birbeck College, University of London.

Ricouart, Janine. *Ecriture féminine et violence.* Birmingham, Ala.: Summa Publications, 1991.

Rose, Jacqueline. *Feminine Sexuality.* New York: W. W. Norton, 1982.

Rykner, Arnaud. *Théâtres du Nouveau Roman.* Paris: José Corti, 1988.

Scarry, Elaine. *The Body in Pain.* Oxford, England: Oxford University Press, 1985.

Schneider, Ursula W. *Ars Amandi: The Erotic Extremes in Thomas Mann and Marguerite Duras.* New York: Peter Lang, 1995.

Schuster, Marilyn E. *Marguerite Duras Revisited.* New York: Twayne Publishers, 1993.

Selous, Trista. *The Other Woman: Feminism and Femininity in the Work of Marguerite Duras.* New Haven, Conn.: Yale University Press, 1988.

Seylaz, Jean-Luc. *Les romans de Marguerite Duras. Essai sur une thématique de la durée.* Paris: Archives des Lettres modernes, no. 47, 1963.

Skoller, Eleanor Honig. *The In-Between of Writing.* Ann Arbor: University of Michigan Press, 1993.

Tison-Braun, Micheline. *Marguerite Duras.* Amsterdam: Rodopi, 1985.

Todorov, Tzvetan. *Symbolisme et Interpretation.* Paris: Seuil, 1978.

Vircondelet, Alain. *Duras: A Biography.* Trans. Thomas Buckley. Normal, Ill.: Dalkey Archive Press, 1994.

Willis, Sharon. *Marguerite Duras: Writing on the Body.* Chicago: University of Illinois Press, 1987.

Index

◆

The Volume Editor

Bettina L. Knapp is professor of French and comparative literature at Hunter College and the Graduate Center of the City University of New York. She has received a Presidential Award from Hunter in the area of scholarship/creative activity, as well as a Guggenheim Fellowship and a grant from the American Philosophical Society. She is the author of *Antonin Artaud: Man of Vision; Theater, and Alchemy; Louis Jouvet: Man of the Theatre; Jean Racine: Mythos and Renewal in Modern Theatre; Off-Stage Voices; French Theatre 1918–1939; The Reign of the Theatrical Director; Archetype, Dance, and the Writer; That Was Yvette; Aristide Bruand; Women in Twentieth-Century Literature; Anaïs Nin; Emily Dickinson; The Brontës,* and *Women In Myth.* She is also the author of *Jean Genet, Fernand Crommelynck, Georges Duhamel, Jean Cocteau, Maurice Maeterlinck, Jean Genet, Sacha Guitry,* and *French Theater Since 1968* in Twayne's World Authors series.

The General Editor

Robert Lecker is professor of English at McGill University in Montreal. He received his Ph.D. from York University. Professor Lecker is the author of numerous critical studies, including *On the Line* (1982), *Robert Kroetch* (1986), *An Other I* (1988), and *Making It Real: The Canonization of English-Canadian Literature* (1995). He is the editor of the critical journal *Essays on Canadian Writing* and of many collections of critical essays, most recently *Canadian Canons: Essays in Literary Value* (1991). He is the founding and general editor of Twayne's Masterwork Studies and the editor of the Twayne World Authors Series on Canadian writers. He is also the general editor of G. K. Hall's Critical Essays on World Literature Series.